THE 1890s

Ken Stewart is Associate Professor of Literature and Head of the Department of Humanities at the University of Western Sydney, Macarthur. He has published widely on nineteenth and twentieth century Australian literature, and was for ten years co-editor with Julian Croft of *Notes and Furphies*.

UQP STUDIES IN AUSTRALIAN LITERATURE

General Editor: Anthony J. Hassall
                      James Cook University of North Queensland

Advisory Editors: Bruce Bennett
                      Australian Defence Force Academy

                      Jennifer Strauss
                      Monash University

Also in this series:

Adam Shoemaker, *Black Words, White Page: Aboriginal Literature 1929-1988*

J.J. Healy, *Literature and the Aborigine in Australia*

David Brooks and Brenda Walker (eds), *Poetry and Gender: Statements and Essays in Australian Women's Poetry and Poetics*

Anthony J. Hassall, *Strange Country: A Study of Randolph Stow*

Cliff Hanna, *The Folly of Spring: A Study of John Shaw Neilson's Poetry*

Philip Neilsen, *Imagined Lives: A Study of David Malouf*

Livio Dobrez, *Parnassus Mad Ward: Michael Dransfield and the New Australian Poetry*

Shirley Walker, *Flame and Shadow: A Study of Judith Wright's Poetry*

Julian Croft, *The Life and Opinions of Tom Collins: A Study of the Works of Joseph Furphy*

Carole Ferrier (ed.), *Gender, Politics and Fiction: Twentieth Century Australian Women's Novels*

Elaine Barry, *Fabricating the Self: The Fictions of Jessica Anderson*

Jennifer Strauss, *Boundary Conditions: The Poetry of Gwen Harwood*

Martin Duwell and Laurie Hergenhan (eds), *The* ALS *Guide to Australian Writers: A Bibliography 1963-1990*

Laurie Hergenhan, *Unnatural Lives: Studies in Australian Convict Fiction*

Ken Gelder, *Atomic Fiction: The Novels of David Ireland*

Paul Salzman, *Helplessly Tangled in Female Arms and Legs: Elizabeth Jolley's Fictions*

Anthony J. Hassall, *Dancing on Hot Macadam: Peter Carey's Fictions*

Michael Ackland, *That Shining Band: A Study of Australian Colonial Verse Tradition*

Ken Stewart, ed. *The 1890s: Australian Literature and Literary Culture*

In preparation:

Philip Mead (ed.), *Kenneth Slessor: Critical Essays*

David Brooks (ed.), *A.D. Hope: Critical Essays*

Fiona Giles, *Too Far Away: Nineteenth Century Women Writers*

Annette Stewart, *Barbara Hanrahan*

Catherine Pratt, *Henry Handel Richardson*

Bruce Bennett, *Australian Short Fiction*

Dennis Haskell, *Bruce Dawe*

Margaret Harris (ed.), *Christina Stead*

THE
1890s

AUSTRALIAN LITERATURE AND
LITERARY CULTURE

EDITED BY
KEN STEWART

University of Queensland Press

First published 1996 by University of Queensland Press
Box 42, St Lucia, Queensland 4067 Australia

The typeset text for this book was supplied by
the editor in camera-ready form
Printed in Australia by McPherson's Printing Group

Distributed in the USA and Canada by
International Specialized Book Services, Inc.,
5804 N.E. Hassalo Street, Portland, Oregon 97213–3640

Cataloguing in Publication Data
National Library of Australia

The 1890s : Australian literature and literary culture.

  Bibliography.

  1. Australian literature — 19th century — History and
criticism. 2. Literature and society — Australia — History.
3. Australian literature — 19th century — Social aspects.
I. Stewart, Ken, 1943–   . (Series : Studies in Australian
literature (St. Lucia, Qld.)).

A820.2

ISBN 0 7022 2867 2

To

Barry Andrews
(1943 - 1987)

Acknowledgments

For their help in the preparation, typing and programming of this book I am especially grateful to Sally Nicol, Julian Croft and Michael Sharkey. For their assistance and advice in various ways I am indebted to Frances de Groen, Rosanne Fitzgibbons, Rosalind Gibbons, Tony Hassall, Peter Kirkpatrick, Brian Matthews, James Packer and Annette Stewart.

Contents

Editor's Note

In this book "the 1890s" may mean, according to context, either the specific decade, or the general complex of trends and characteristics associated with the period 1885 to 1905 (approximately). The chapters have been commissioned, co-ordinated and edited to represent current debate and contests concerning place (especially city and country), gender, mythology, and national identity, but also to break away from this controlling "centre" to explore or debate other issues and to illustrate the diversity of the period. My original intention was to include a chapter on Aboriginality. Regrettably the prospective contributors (only a few people have properly researched this subject concerning the 1890s) were unable to provide chapters at present. Perhaps, in any case, a specific chapter on Aboriginality is not appropriate in a book focussing on white culture: in Australia the 1890s is probably less, or more unfortunately, significant for Aboriginal people than for others.

Ken Stewart

Notes on Contributors

PATRICIA BARTON worked in the Department of English, Australian Defence Force Academy, Canberra, for several years. She has published a scholarly edition of Ada Cambridge's *Unspoken Thoughts*.

JULIAN CROFT is Professor of English at the University of New England, Armidale, NSW. He has published *The Life and Opinions of Tom Collins* and numerous other critical writings, and a novel and several collections of verse.

ROBERT DINGLEY is a Senior Lecturer in English at the University of New England, Armidale, NSW. He has published criticism on English literature of the Romantic and Victorian periods and on nineteenth century Australian literature.

JOHN DOCKER is a research scholar at the Australian National University, Canberra. His books include *In A Critical Condition, The Nervous Nineties* and *Postmodernism and Popular Culture*.

JOY HOOTON has recently retired from the English Department, Australian Defence Force Academy, Canberra, where she was Associate Professor. Her publications include *Stories of Herself When Young* and, with Barry Andrews and W. H. Wilde, *The Oxford Companion to Australian Literature*.

MARK HORGAN lives in Armidale, NSW, and has written a thesis on Lawson and Paterson for the Department of English, University of New England.

RICK HOSKING is a Senior Lecturer in the Department of English and Australian Studies, The Flinders University of South Australia. He has written short stories, and essays on Australian literature; and has recently completed a novel to be published in 1996.

CHRISTOPHER LEE has published on nineteenth century Australian literature, and is a Lecturer in English at the University of Southern Queensland.

VERONICA KELLY is a Senior Lecturer in the English Department, University of Queensland. She has published a study of playwright Louie Nowra and other writings on Australian drama and theatre, co-edits *Australian Drama Studies,* and is currently Queensland theatre critic for the *Australian.*

NEVILLE MEANEY is Associate Professor of History at the University of Sydney. He has published widely in Australian and American history, and is author of *The Search for Security in the Pacific* and *Under New Heavens.*

TERESA PAGLIARO is a Melbourne-based researcher who has published on nineteenth century topics and has successfully completed a doctoral thesis on A. W. Jose.

PETER PIERCE has recently been appointed to the Chair of Australian Literature, James Cook University of Northern Queensland. His latest book is *Australian Melodramas: Thomas Keneally's Fictions.*

GEOFFREY SERLE lectured in History at Melbourne University and Monash University, and was from 1975-88 General Editor of *The Australian Dictionary of Biography.* His books include *The Golden Age, The Rush to be Rich, From Deserts The Prophets Come* and *John Monash.* He lives in Melbourne.

MICHAEL SHARKEY is a Senior Lecturer in English at the University of New England, Armidale, NSW. He has published widely on Australian literature, reviews for the *Australian* and other newspapers and journals, and has brought out several volumes of poetry.

KEN STEWART is Associate Professor of Literature and Head of the Department of Humanities at the University of Western Sydney Macarthur. He has published widely on nineteenth and twentieth century Australian literature, and was for ten years co-editor with Julian Croft of *Notes and Furphies*.

HELEN THOMSON is a Senior Lecturer in the Department of English, Monash University, Melbourne. She has edited and published several volumes of the fiction and other writings of Catherine Helen Spence.

Introduction

Ken Stewart

1

The Language of "Youth"

In the late nineteenth century, as today, every white person knew that Australia was a young country. Oscar Wilde once remarked, with quite as much historical acumen as wit, that the youth of America is its oldest tradition. Australia seemed conspicuously more youthful even than America, since white settlement was more recent, and the "mother country" could retain a "parental" role. But its youth was not to be measured exclusively in years, and did not indicate merely the "short" period between white settlement and the present. Australia was young as a person is young: the anthropomorphic metaphor established associations of human vitality, immaturity and of an awaited future, and at the same time erased the indigenous peoples.

The notion of the young country, even today, is more a matter of language than of fact. Within most national discourses, youth is encoded: the period from 1788 to 1888, or even to 1988, is to be accepted as short because the code and metaphor say so. Australia, youth; Britain and Europe, age: continually "Australia" signifies within this binary. The establishment of numerous other nations since the "birthdates" of 1788 and 1901 have not undermined the common acceptance of Australia's youth as a fact. The trope has been reified into a truth.

In the 1890s Australia could be represented as a beautiful and athletic young woman, her torch lighting the future; or a young bushman or axeman, an allegorical emblem of industry or pioneering; or a baby blowing bubbles, naive, lovable, immature; or a little boy, often from Manly. The metaphor might be simultaneously a metonymy: the young person *is* an Australian; Australians *are* "young and free", as "Advance Australia Fair" decreed. You might easily feel that Australians were not actually, and certainly not typically, old; and that a young country had "more" future, and more opportunity with a longer life to come, than an "old" country.

Youth transcended place, and encompassed both genders. Whether they are located in the city, the bush, or some imaginary setting, many figures in late nineteenth-century literature seem "truly" Australian precisely because they are young. Males are typically practical, and females "bookish"; but although women writers, especially, were now appropriating some formerly "masculine"characteristics for their bookish heroines, particularly Ada Cambridge with Sue Delavel in *A Marked Man,* and "Tasma", Rosa Praed, Catherine Martin and Miles Franklin, youth remained the Australian *sine qua non.* The athletic, horse-riding, book-loving and brilliant young woman is the literary ancestor of David Ireland's modernised Alethea: she represents truth, Australia, and the Woman of the Future. Ethel Castella popularised the figure in "The Australian Girl":

> Her frank, clear eyes bespeak a mind
> Old world traditions fail to bind
>   She is not shy
> Or bold, but simply self-possessed;
> Her independence adds a zest
> Unto her speech, her piquant jest
>   Her quaint reply.
>
> O'er classic volumes she will pore
> With joy; and true scholastic lore
>   Will often gain
> In sports she bears away the bell,
> Nor, under music's siren spell,
> To dance divinely, flirt as well,
> Does she disdain

The familiarity of the young Australian was reinforced in the late nineteenth century by actual historical circumstances. The children of older white native Australians, and of the immigrants of the 1850s and 1860s, were born in Australia, and now outnumbered their old or overseas-born parents; yet the immigrants of the 1880s and 1890s were themselves predominantly fairly young — under forty-five — and *their* children were noticeably younger. Since the population increase was exponential, virtually doubling decade by decade after 1850 until 1900, one can understand why readers found no surprise with a literature which seemed to confirm that there were fewer old people in Australia than elsewhere. Although the effects remained of an earlier gender imbalance which had helped to "masculinise" Australian society, the external visibility of youth was increasing daily. The use of the vernacular and the Australian accent by young people reinforced the identification of Australia with youth, especially in popular literature and theatre.

Literary critics frequently refer to a "self conscious" nationalism in the language of literature in the 1890s. This term is misleading when it suggests that vernacular mannerism and certain Australian linguistic codes were not really normative or "unconscious". When Australians, or for that matter Europeans, speak of the young country, they may not necessarily intend to promote the *nationalistic* awareness that nevertheless creates a particular sense of Australian identity. Probably, some critics have simply preferred a "correct", "standard" or "literary" English to the normative Australian speech they describe as "self conscious". The associations of youth in relation to Australia may create ambiguity, especially since responses vary from one reader to another. Is James Cuthbertson's poem "The Australian Sunrise", for example, simply a lyric about dawn in the bush, or is it as well a celebration of new nationhood? Is the death of the child Mary O'Halloran in Joseph Furphy's *Such Is Life* an exclusively personal disaster, or is it an "Australian" tragedy, a "nationalistic" statement concerning young Australia? Some writers, notably Henry Lawson in "The Union Buries Its Dead" and "The Drover's Wife", assume the reader's familiarity with an official national rhetoric in order to deconstruct it.

"The young country" was a potent political and ideological tool, available to socialists, radicals, self-help conservatives, monarchists, imperialists, republicans, feminists and "masculinists" alike. The trope itself was a bright varnish which advertised Australian identity, but not explicitly or excessively in terms of ethnic, religious, cultural and political legacies. You could supply your own "true Australian", as long as he or she were young.

Radical commentators sometimes overlook the extent to which "youth" was employed by conservatives. "Advance Australia Fair", which was sung by a mass choir at the inauguration of the Commonwealth, concisely celebrates Australia's "sons" (the country was desegregated by new words when the song became the national anthem in the 1970s), a capitalist ethic, work, wealth, geographical isolationism and Empire; and simultaneously erases Aborigines. Rolf Boldrewood's *A Sydney Side Saxon* (1891) tells the story of a young ploughboy from Kent who becomes an Australian cattle baron, and even *Robbery Under Arms* attempts to show how young Dick Marston, the true Australian, can be reclaimed and enriched by hard work and a good wife. Steele Rudd's very popular comic realism provided an antidote to Boldrewood's parable romance, since Dad and his family are battlers, but the dominant discourse remains "self help" and patriarchal capitalism. Dad, the elderly immigrant father-figure, may be a bully towards his more sympathetic, potentially wayward naive Australian children, but his family must properly remain virtually a small company under his control ("their hands but my head") if they are to survive.

Although feminists and women's suffragists were pioneers in a loose international movement, and were publicised in journals in Europe and America, most found no inconsistency in employing the nationalistic rhetoric of youth. Some such overtones were inevitable, since the quest for suffrage and political representation had obvious federal and national implications. The title of Louisa Lawson's magazine the *Dawn* harbingered a new day not only for women but also for Australians and Australian families within a new nation state.

At a glance the literature of the 1890s may appear incompatible with its contemporary political history, a paradox which has bedevilled much commentary. How can the apparently optimistic code of the young country, and the prevalence of a sunny nationalism in much writing, be reconciled with the apathy and disillusion widely shown towards Federation and the drafting of the Constitution, and the miseries of drought and economic recession? A thorough answer would require a more theoretical discussion of nationalism than is possible here. Several factors are important. The code of youth was already in place and virtually "official" but it accommodated "the mother country". It decreed a way of writing and talking which affirmed that Australia was a good idea rather than a necessary political entity, a state. One can imagine, and find, equivalents to the conservative "if it's not broken, don't fix it" argument employed today by opponents of a republic. An accepted way of talking, moreover, is not necessarily a reflection of current conditions: a sunny Australia in the theatre or a book would cheer you up. The very diversity of possible national identities was itself a matter for the "fathers" of the Constitution to consider; and the dominant code of the young country could confirm that "Australia" in a sense already existed. Many of the national mythologies were artificial and "new", but even those that were "transmitted" from the past were being newly discovered by immigrants, and did not exert an urgent or overwhelmingly binding pressure, of the kind which race, religion or politics is traditionally said to exert in the formation of nation states. The same rights that were already extended were to be conferred again, perhaps in a slightly different form, by a constitution. The Empire was an emotional necessity and a source of national security and political stability which, for most, transcended nationality and would not be removed, merely redefined, by Federation. The Utopian and radical writers who sought a unified or single socialist state did not represent the populace as a whole; and responses, in life and literature, to landscape and an Australian local culture, spirit and type did not *need* Federation or a new single state. In all this, it is possible to respond to a combination of new awarenesses reflected in the texts of the 1890s, which individuate it from earlier decades, without having to assume "a common centre"[1] or the endorsement of a monolithic thesis.

The Young Country provided an important, perhaps dominant code, which was almost universally employed; but it was not the only code. Its power in the 1890s created a context for the *inevitable* articulation of disappointment, one for use of an alternative "Australian" code of stoicism, iconoclasm and scepticism. You do not feel young and free in a depression, a drought, or a strike; some writers felt, in the 1890s and later, robbed. Looking backwards in 1922, rather than *Dawnwards* in the 1890s, Bernard O'Dowd could declare to the Melbourne Institute of Arts and Literature:

> O that we who love our country (and incidentally don't want any other!) could inspire into the young folk coming along some of the enthusiasm of the eighties and nineties ... which made of Australia a passion and a dream, an Eldorado more glorious than even Raleigh conceived of, a Utopia Thomas More had not dared to dream of, a very New Jerusalem of freemen and mates and ideal social ways descended on the earth![2]

2

The Quickening

Whatever may be said about the significance and quality of the literature of the 1890s, in terms of sheer quantity the decade was by far the most productive of the nineteenth century. This is reflected in the wider range of fiction available, and in the sales of "literary balladists" like A. B. Paterson (on a national per capita basis almost certainly the most popular poet in the world). Before 1890, 498 titles of Australian fiction had been published in book form. Fiction made up 47% of the aggregate of verse and fiction titles up to and including 1889.[3] (In the 1880s, when many of the tastes and trends which flowered in the 1890s were seeded, fiction still constituted only 49% of the aggregate for that decade). In the 1880s 195 fiction titles were published; in the 1890s the figure was 539. The number of verse titles remained fairly static: 201 in the 1880s, 227 in the 1890s (a decline, on a per capita assessment). Fiction in the 1890s constituted 70% of the fiction/verse aggregate of book titles, and had become easily the dominant genre. It is true that in the 1900s (1900-1909), 72 more titles of fiction, and 87 more titles of verse, were published than in the 1890s; and also that much fiction in the 1880s had been published in periodicals and newspapers, a high proportion of which was never brought out in books. Nevertheless, the accelerations in publishing, and the reorientations of preference, established trends in the 1890s that were not to be reversed.

As in previous decades, most fiction was published by overseas firms, for distribution in Britain as well as Australia, and this dual market may have affected styles and choice of subject matter, probably favouring the "Anglo-Australian" writing, and disadvantaging the vernacular. Against this, it should be said that much popular fiction was first serialised in Australian periodicals. Despite the increasing popularity of vernacular bush realism published in the *Bulletin*, and by the new Australian company Angus and Robertson, romance remained in the 1890s the most widely published fictional genre. The attention given to the *Bulletin* by later and contemporary commentators rightly emphasizes a new "school", but it has deflected recognition of the *increasing* influence of overseas publishers and of the popularity of romance. Although the *Bulletin* was an alternative, not an exclusive hegemonic centre, its rise does reflect the decline in the 1890s, owing to the Depression, of Melbourne as a colonial literary centre. Tables printed at the end of this chapter indicate the number and the place of publication of titles listed in E. Morris Miller and F. J. Macartney's bibliography *Australian Literature* in each decade of the nineteenth century, and the ratio of fiction to poetry in each decade.

Popular romance articulated a range of dreams, fears, hopes, needs and fantasies: there were adventures in imaginary Lemuria, or on the high Pacific seas; there were pilgrimages to prosperity, status and love; there were Asian invaders to counter and repel; there were male and female sexual fantasies, of both writer and reader, to express or to gratify in a dreamworld of fiction. Many romances reflected typical concerns in British and European fiction, but the changing colonial situation was influential: the invasion novel discussed in this book by Neville Meaney takes a different form in Australian circumstances; the self-help romance permits the hero to aspire to quasi-aristocratic wealth and status; the "domestic" romance begins to subvert the genre, as Susan Sheridan has pointed out, in the interests of the colonial woman; utopian and futuristic fiction vaguely reflects dreams and hopes for new and clean beginnings.

The celebrated "rise of the short story" in the late 1880s and the 1890s is a furphy. The *Bulletin* dropped serials and favoured the short story, and Lawson instituted an original and proletarian voice and innovative forms. However, 140 collections had been published before 1894, when Henry Lawson's first collection appeared.[4] They permit appreciation of Lawson's *transformations* as well as his innovations.[5]

A decline in the popular acceptability of poetry (other than ballads) — or at least a change in editorial practice — is reflected in the reduced space verse received in weeklies such as the *Sydney Mail,* and in the increased proportion of fiction in the *Bulletin.* Despite the successes of Paterson and Lawson, in many books and periodicals it is hard to find a horse or a gumtree: as in previous decades, love, death, religion and ethical matters are common themes. This latter verse provides no evidence to confirm G. A. Wilkes's observation that "literature inspired by national sentiment or the zeal of the reformer is artistically the most insecure of all";[6] the less nationalistic verse runs a still greater risk of being hackneyed and derivative. Some of the more interesting nationalistic verse is a self-reflexive and metonymic exploration of ideas. O'Dowd, for example, uses landscape to define ideals rather than to represent "reality", linking the local to the Platonic.

The increase in literary production in the late 1880s and 1890s reflected a new viability, economic and cultural, in Australian literary operations. A. G. Stephens, the literary editor of the *Bulletin* from 1894 to 1906, was delighted:

> What a change since Gordon's day! ... His world was Melbourne, with an occasional extension to the Wimmera bush. And outside Melbourne — or, on a liberal estimate, Victoria, Gordon at his death was practically unheard of. A few sportsmen, a few *literati,* made the circle of his admirers: his name is purely posthumous. The quickening of the Australian literary sense in the past ten years is wonderful to look back upon.
>
> *Bulletin,* 29 August, 1895.

Stephens' faith in the "quickening" was both fallacious and productive. In certain moods he mentally translated the acceleration and changes of direction into a *zeitgeist,* infusing and confusing his multi-faceted hopes and predilections with the new circumstances, in "the young country"; but his and the *Bulletin*'s verbal flair and show of dogmatic enthusiasm added to the acceleration of literary production and the awareness of national identity, if not to a "quickening of the Australian literary sense". Promotiong the "sunny" present and patronising the colonial past, he could write of "the old days" of the Melbourne *literati,* of David Blair, Kendall and others, as if contemporary equavalents like James Smith, John Sandes, Douglas Sladen and Rolf Boldrewood were dead and buried. But his "sunny" optimism, masculinist bush nationalism, anti-academicism, anti-Englishness, and hare-brained eugenics co-existed with an internationalism that valued and promoted contemporary and "classical" American, European and British writing (especially Shakespeare), acknowledged the "darker" forces (represented by Baynton and Lawson, whose texts he at times editorially mutilated), and put Australian literary "achievement" into a sobering perspective. Stephens was as much a traditional cultural missionary as the predecessors he ridiculed.

3

Cross Currents and Cross Purposes

The "1890s debate" is not a simple dialogue directed by unchanging assumptions and goals, or fixed questions and answers. It is usually perceived today as a dynamic of interactions amongst contending discourses, which include radical nationalism,[7] new criticism,[8] moral and meta-physical Leavisism,[9] a "new" radicalism of the 1970s,[10] urban historicism,[11] post-1960s feminism,[12] and postmodernism. Any list is bound to be misleading if it fails to stress the potential for individual difference within each "school", or if it suggests either that the schools are invariably incompatible with one another, or that each can be easily represented by just one or two exemplars. The nationalist A. A. Phillips, for example, often employs the methodology of new criticism, and like other radical nationalists pursues arguments which do not necessarily endorse the celebrated central thesis of Russel Ward in *The Australian Legend*. Many commentators accepting the conventionally evaluative and formalist modes of New Criticism, and aware that Furphy, Richardson, Brennan and Lawson were writing in the 1890s, implicitly disagree with G. A. Wilkes on Wilkes's own terms when he argues, using a loaded adjective, that the "literary" significance of the decade has been overestimated. Most feminist literary critics have not employed the strategies of deconstruction and the hypotheses of Lacanian analysis which underlie Kay Schaffer's influential *Women and the Bush* (1988), and some have opposed them.

Perhaps the most widely misrepresented of commentators is Vance Palmer, whose nowadays unduly notorious study *The Legend of the Nineties* (1954) is often simplistically accepted as a natural target by detractors whose revisions he frequently anticipates. Palmer demonstrates the disparity between the dreams of poets, radicals and nationalists and the anxieties of the populace. There is a tension throughout his book between his obvious "radical nationalist" sympathies with the legend-makers, and his own cultural priorities, literary preferences and honest historical observations.

Palmer sees "the Australian people" as democratic isolationists whose dream is to build up "something like an earthly paradise for the common man": but he adds immediately, "or perhaps the uncommon man of the future!" (p.10). His phrase "the Australian people" turns out to be ambivalent shorthand, since the book demonstrates popular fears, disillusion and apathy, insisting that "it would be too much to pretend that this dream affected the whole country" (p.18), and that the dream "cannot be limited to a particular decade" (p.13). In fact, Palmer concludes, only the "most conscious spirits", mainly writers and political radicals, were affected by the dream.

Democratic isolationism and the defence of local opportunity, Palmer continues, led to an almost paranoiac concern with the activities of foreign power, and aroused "fantastic fears" that the Russian, German and French activities in the Pacific, and "the hoardes of Asia", might jeopardise Australian security. In politics, the unions, motivated by self-interest and spurred by radical social theory, were influenced by the radical dream, but they overestimated their own impregnability, failing to appreciate the financial, social and organisational power of employers, who could enlist governments and the agencies of law on their side. As the conflict between labour and capital intensified, unemployment brought division, disillusion, anxiety and suffering. The long wait for Federation saw a decline in the popular influence of radical thought and Utopian vision, together with increasing scepticism, apathy concerning the constitution and "nationalistic" policies, and self-interested interstate conflict.

Concerning literature and the arts Palmer acknowledges that the dream was in fact both "a limitation and a spur toward creative effort" (p.10), and that "in our search for a literary tradition we have made too much of a narrow period" (p.14). The cultural ethos of the period, he finds, led to an emphasis on "the social being" at the expense of "the interior life of the individual" (p.170). He does not celebrate Henry Lawson's early radical phase, but praises his sensitivity and empathy with suffering and poverty in a harsh environment: "the emphasis was nearly always on defeat and disillusionment, and heroism lay in accepting these with a humorous resignation" (pp.10-11).

Palmer describes the Chinese immigrants as law-abiding and peaceful people whose presence threatened hopes of white democracy, and who were not included in their "general conception of the brotherhood of man" (p.16). For similar reasons, he argues, the Aborigine was taken as "a comic or hostile figure", to be excluded from the coming commonwealth (p.17). Even concerning female culture some prompt (perhaps it is Nettie) arouses in him a few prescient glimmers of issues later taken up by feminists: in a resounding understatement, he observes that the distinctive manner of emerging Australian writing was "perhaps a little inclined to over-emphasize purely masculine qualities" (p.128). J. F. Archibald is censured for his "distrust of feminine influence in the arts" (p.92), and Henry Lawson for never providing "an understanding glimpse of his mother" (p.113). It is as if there are two Vance Palmers, the official Radical Nationalist, and the individual "other". Although Palmer does not take the step of transforming his reservations into fully fledged critique, his perceptions concerning racism, cultural isolation, masculinism, disillusion with radical and national politics, and the rampant "bourgeois individualism" of the 1890s, provided signposts towards the 1970s revisions.

One of the most influential and disciplined challenges to perceptions of "the bush" and a proletarian ethos as the source of values and attitudes which formed Ward's "Australian legend" is only in part anticipated by Palmer. Graeme Davison, writing in 1978, suggests that:

> The 1890s have been rightly interpreted, by Russel Ward, Vance Palmer and others, as the watershed in the creation of an "Australian legend". But the "apotheosis", as Ward calls it, was not the transmission to the city of values nurtured on the bush frontier, so much as the projection onto the outback of values revered by an alienated urban intelligentsia. How far itinerant bush workers absorbed these values, or shared them already, remains very much an open question.[13]

For Davison's less moderate followers, however, the question is closed. Leigh Astbury, Kay Schaffer and Marilyn Lake take for granted the projection of urban radical values on to a rural populace.

The problem with Davison's thesis is inherent in the categories he sets up: "bush workers" are placed in an unworkably rigid opposition to "an alienated urban intelligentsia". He does not explore whether a *rural* "intelligentsia" (Davison uses the term simply to signify educated, well-read people who engage with intellectual issues) may have been as susceptible to European and American ideas as were city journalists, while at the same time being conditioned by rural and provincial experience, needs and circumstances. He focuses exclusively on the alleged influence of a few *Bulletin* journalists, living in Sydney boarding houses at a specific time (the late 1880s).

Davison fails to consider that by the 1880s country dwellers had access if they chose to many of the same literary and intellectual influences as city dwellers, through school education, private libraries, mechanics institutes, the country press (which in the 1890s published much original verse and numerous Australian novels), the dispatch to the country of literary weeklies and periodicals, the provision of books by employers, shared purchases of books and magazines, literary and political clubs and societies, and the immigration to the country of educated and "literary" persons. A rural "intelligentsia" was experienced and depicted by Furphy, Cambridge, Praed, Boldrewood, Catherine Martin, and even at times Henry Lawson: it was not a close-knit or ideal community or group, and most of its isolated members never met; but its dispersed presence and influence challenge the unworkably rigid opposition between "bush/workers" and "city/ intelligentsia" which continues to provide the frame for most discussion of the 1890s.

A higher proportion of authors and editors lived, or travelled widely and for long periods, in rural areas than Davison concedes: they include Furphy, Bayldon, the young Mary Cameron, Will Ogilvie, and for most of his life John Farrell. A rural literary culture was sufficiently well established to create and transmit its own diverse self-images; it also received and assimilated ideas from the city and overseas. The overwhelming majority of recognised urban editors, journalists, poets and fiction writers in the 1880s and 1890s had either grown up in rural areas or spent crucial periods of their early careers there.

The Ward and Davison theses need to be fused and re-fashioned into a less ambitious proposition. In a *fin-de-siecle* period of increasingly interactive communication, inevitably "something" was transmitted from the rural proletariat. Whether these were "values", and a fixed construction of an exclusive, everlasting Australian "type" or "legend", is open to question: the convict, bush and later "literary" ballads, the *sine qua non* of Ward's evidence, do not (as it turns out) consistently affirm egalitarian values, or privilege a single national type.[14] Perhaps the complex and transmuted legacy of the proletariat, urban or rural, may best be identified as semiotic, consisting of vernacular idiom, signals, rituals, ways of talking which, though inherited, are transformed, and adapt their significance within the new environments in which they come to be used.

Australian feminism in the late nineteenth century, like other reformist and radical movements, was a local and sometimes "nationalistic" engagement in an international ideological dialogue and political movement. Feminism, though dynamic, was not new, and was nurtured or reinforced by earlier ideas, notably mid-century American transcendentalism. The collective momentum of the movement, however, was in the 1890s much stronger, and some popular manifestations (the suffrage and political representation campaign, the New Woman, educational and career opportunities, and feminist emphases in magazines and women's columns) had forcibly entered public consciousness. Although Australian feminism was influenced by international developments, the movement in the colonies was pioneering and participatory rather than derivative, and was in some respects more advanced than in other countries: American feminists in particular looked to Australian and New Zealand political achievements as innovatory models.

Since the 1970s feminists have explored or revised the culture and historiography of the 1890s from many perspectives, examining the nature of colonial feminism and masculinism, the depiction of colonial women, the recognition of neglected or undervalued writing, the cultural circumstances conditioning women writers, the depictions of women by male writers, the creation of masculine and feminine myths and the cultural subsumation of the latter, and the applicability of twentieth-century psychoanalytical, linguistic and cultural theory to the texts of the 1890s and its literary historiography. Critics today argue that both the contemporary and twentieth-century denigration of women's writing of the 1890s was "the necessary condition of the elevation of the Bush legend to the status of national myth"[15]; they stress in particular the enabling and subversive potential of 1890s romance written by women.

In a controversial article often accepted as a milestone, Marilyn Lake[16] defines 1890s "masculinism" as a *political* position and strategy, diametrically opposed to contemporary feminism, and adopted to gratify the interests and wants of men. Until 1920 when it was modified and feminised by new legislation and social pressure, this strategy used the bush legend to legitimate, socially and in law, the unfettered, freedom-seeking male (whether married or single, urban or rural); and it disenabled women by mocking men's domestic responsibilities. The thesis has been opposed by John Docker[17] who, identifying Lake as the chief proponent of "the Feminist Legend of the Nineties", argues that, like the Radical Nationalists and the New Critic/Leavisites before her, Lake is single-mindedly "historicist", and therefore astray, in her search for "essences and unities" and "a common centre to a culture".[18] Docker is also sceptical of Lake's Foucauldian claims for a specific period. He prefers a postmodernist, anti-historicist approach which sees both the *Bulletin* and the 1890s in general as an open, "multifaceted and multi-stranded" interactive text.

Docker's *The Nervous Nineties*[19] is rather like the Sydney or Melbourne not-so-Royal not-so-Agricultural Show. He finds that the most celebrated ring event, the great Australian legend contest, is held at an illusory centre, not necessarily more significant and interesting than the "side"-shows where much of the 1890s took place: the halls of Debate, the Utopian contests, the Lemurian river caves, Furphy the great Menippean, the circling up-and-down Lawson Ferris wheel, the Gothic ghost rides of Rosa Praed. The advantage of Docker's approach, whether we accept or reject his postmodernistic de-centreing mission, is that it permits a broader guide, and a lively map, which assists readers to choose their own Show.

4

Reading the 1890s Today

Henry Lawson and Barbara Baynton

Some of Docker's signposts will be followed in later chapters. The questions I want to open up here are (1): to what extent, in a changing environment, were the writings of males feminised — positively affected, obviously or indirectly, by late nineteenth century feminism?; (2) was writing by women affected by forces opposing feminism? and (3) will a 1990s feminised close-reading assist our response to the more familiar writers of the 1990s? We can only begin to open the gate, but to keep it closed is to leave writers like Henry Lawson to the nationalists and non-feminist New Critics. Feminist post-structuralists, particularly Kay Schaffer in *Women and the Bush* (1988), have examined writers like Lawson primarily as cultural products, to show how their works have been enlisted by masculinist nationalists. Historicists such as Marilyn Lake have necessarily selected their authors and illustrative texts to support a thesis: for Lake's purpose Randolph Bedford is more relevant than Rudd or Furphy. Although both feminist approaches are opposed to masculine nationalism, their readings preserve and deal with masculine nationalist emphases.

Lawson, Furphy and Rudd could not have written in the 1870s as they did in the 1890s. Feminism had begun to enter the home, as well as magazines, newspapers, coteries and parliaments. Both male and female response was complex, and variable, and inescapable. Lawson felt the repercussions as closely as he knew his mother, and Mary Cameron/Gilmore and her mother: intimately, confusedly, angrily, compassionately, guiltily. Furphy, more explicitly than Lawson, invoked the public controversy in his fiction: in the treatise of Rory O'Halloran, for example, or the case studies in *Rigby's Romance* and *The Buln Buln and the Brolga*. His biography[20] details a psychic battle between the demands of domestic duty and responsibility which he sanctioned, and the prospect of an escape which he scorned, proudly informing A. G. Stephens that he had "never ... been on the razzle-dazzle, nor ... addicted to Flossie", and that Lawson should study Epictetus.

These writers were not feminist; they were the first Australian males to represent experience of gender relations under new late-Victorian, late-colonial conditions and terms. Their changing social and domestic experience, together with new narrative conventions and strategies, germinates a less melodramatic, closer up, more intimate depiction of gender conflict than in most earlier Australian fiction by males. In the latter the paterfamilias may be more detached. The later writers' social class, reading and rural experience also condition their inescapable awareness of indispensable unpaid female labour, and of female distress. To say that their feminised writing undermines or challenges the projections of masculinist nationalism is not to argue of course that their writing is consistently feminised; but to infer, as some critics do, that women are as absent from these texts as they are from the Australian legend, is to mistake the legend for the writing.

The new feminism both aggravated and reframed male suspicion and aggression. The male writers are extensively capable of endorsing, reflecting, or depicting insecurity, misogyny, domestic irresponsibility, contempt for the feminine, and male fantasy; and such writing reflects an increasing masculine uncertainty or ambivalence concerning the ideals of masculinity. Compare Maurice Frere and Sylvia with Joe and Mary Wilson: the new male's threatened *awareness* (not necessarily endorsement) of responsibility accounts for aggression, insecurity or guilt. I suspect that feminism also underlies the escapist fantasies of writers like Randolph Bedford. In Lawson, Rudd and Furphy, an implicit cautionary *fear* of excessive drinking recurs, along with some disturbing black comedy to document its effects. In *On Our Selection* there is a continuing empathy for Mother and Sarah as subordinates; and a new delight in the falls and gaffes of the patriarchal Dad, or in the liberating Carnival of the holidays in the city, where he appears foolish.

Lawson, Rudd and Furphy frequently endorse woman as victim, or undermine stereotyped masculine ideals by creating anti-heroes, like Tom Collins, or the drinkers in "That Pretty Girl in the Army", or Steelman. The "insider" male narrator may be used to point up the insensitivity or folly of the male group (frequently in Lawson), or of individuals within it (as in many of Rudd's stories), or in Furphy's case the insensitivity of the male narrator himself in comparison with females (particularly Mollie Cooper). If male solidarity is endorsed (and amongst Furphy's bullock drivers and Lawson's unionists it is not always), its price, and the ethical dilemma it creates, are frequently underlined.

Lawson's other bush, the one left out of the idealising masculinist arguments and feminist rebuttals, is inhabited by thugs, con-men, boozers, louts, numbskulls, liars and schoolboyish bushmen; the rhetoric, not the reader's "interpretation", says so. From Middleton's Rouseabout, who like the alcoholic Middleton "hasn't any opinions, hasn't any ideas" to Barcoo Rot and One-Eyed Bogan, male figures of this kind illustrate the author's dictum that "the poetical bushman does not exist; the majority of men out back now [1893] are from the city. The real native out-back bushman is narrow-minded, densely ignorant, invulnerably thick-headed. How could he be otherwise?"[21] And if among Lawson's female characters there is a romanticised or guilty surplus of God's police, there is also a fair sprinkling of moral police*men*: both types effectively endorse Louisa Lawson's attacks on escapist and feckless young men and husbands.

Lawson claimed that he originally intended Joe Wilson to be "a strong character"; "it seems to me that the man's natural sentimental selfishness, good-nature, softness or weakness — call it what you like — developed as I wrote on."[22] The transition and the ambiguity show a tension in Lawson and in the Joe Wilson stories between the "official", socially endorsed male self, and the "soft" or "good natured" self; he also recognised this when he wrote that he himself "should have been born a girl". The Joe Wilson stories are especially valuable for their unsentimental exploration of Joe's failure to live up to socially required ideals of masculinity; and for their balancing of the claims of society against the needs of the male individual. This ambivalence makes Lawson important for the 1990s: his writing interrogates the social construction of gender.

The feminised Lawson is most obvious in "Telling Mrs. Baker", a story which illustrates perfectly the moral dilemma of mateship, and the domestic irresponsibility pointed to in Lake's thesis. Bob Baker, a drinking, womanising, selfish, on-the-move waster, has died in the horrors. Jack and Andy have to tell his wife that he died working, of fever and dysentery; and that his last words were of his wife and children. It is a lie, but to save Mrs. Baker from disillusion and pain, the truth can not be told; besides Bob himself was a mate, and you protect a mate and his memory at all costs. That is the official text; it is accompanied by an ironical counter-text, which the masculinist nationalists fail to acknowledge.

The game of telling begins with the ironical title; Mrs. Baker is never really told, she is merely lied to. She remains the woman in the dark, in a situation controlled by men. The bushman's "truth" is falsehood; but the unease felt by the insider bushman narrator is protracted for the reader in the long, comically nerve-racking account of the death of the "noble" bushman. This drawn out and embarrassing fabrication keeps the theme of male deception central, and at the same time uncomfortably makes the point that, once begun, it must be never-ending. But the narrator Jack is suspicious of the official duplicity policy. He debates the issue. He deconstructs "the good bloke": to be "a jolly, open-handed, popular man ... means that he'd been a selfish man as far as his wife and children were concerned." Baker's "generosity" was "born of vanity or moral cowardice". Andy "wins" the debate, but Jack's and the reader's qualms continue: sprinklings of irony keep us edgy. (Looking through Bob Baker's papers, Andy comments "I'm just going to see that there's nothing here that will make liars of us.") Miss Standish, an educated city woman who makes up stories for the *Bulletin*, co-operates in the lie. This New Woman is an alternative female type, clearly preferred to the woman as victim in the bush: but the comic valour of the lying process is itself an ironical indictment of the bush ethic. The story ends with the romantic convention that the "decent" mates are rewarded with a kiss by the "ideal" girl. When she exclaims with exaggerated effusiveness, and four exclamation marks, "I want to thank you for her sake ... You are good men! I like the Bushmen! They are grand men — they are noble! ... And you, too!", the ironical undertones tingle with a warning against the sentimentality of the romance we are being permitted.

A paradox of the feminist revision is the canonisation of Barbara Baynton. As Thea Astley insists, her powerful stories denude the "Teeth Father",[23] expose male brutality, and undo the mateship legend; and Baynton herself was an astonishingly tenacious woman. We understand the paradox of Baynton as feminist icon when we discover that she campaigned against women's suffrage, quarrelled with feminists, worshipped the Bush Anzac, rejected the New Woman, and became, according to most accounts, an overbearing, quasi-aristocratic snob.[24] I feel a nagging dissatisfaction with the values and ideological effect of her fiction as well, and I do not agree with Astley's familiar claim that her stories "undoubtedly *equate* [my emphasis] maleness with brutality and savagery".[25]

Baynton was in many respects a female Australian equivalent to Stephen Crane. A. G. Stephens published her first story in the *Bulletin* in December 1896; Crane's *Maggie: A Girl of the Streets*, the first significant American naturalistic novel, had appeared in 1893, and his most celebrated work, *The Red Badge of Courage*, in 1895. His writing was known in literary circles in Sydney, and was discussed several times in the *Bulletin*.

American naturalism differed from the European variety through its more definite and uncluttered focus on heredity and environment, "nature red in tooth and claw", though Crane found in city life the jungle that Baynton makes of the Bush. In American naturalistic fiction, the human animal is driven by appetite (sex, thirst, hunger), aggression, fear and the instinct to survive, in a universe in which nature and humanity are one. National myths and dreams are undone; reason, classicism, and romanticism are devalued. Until Dreiser and Cather, American naturalism, like Baynton's, tended to focus with humourless directness on "lower-class" life by adopting narrative strategies of selective impressionism and fragmentation taken over from painting. These were preferred to the more cumulatively detailed surface documentation of European and English naturalism. Crane would also employ the imagery of the Christian religion with cold irony, or demythologising impersonality, as in the celebrated phrase from *The Red Badge of Courage* "The red sun was pasted in the sky like a wafer", a usage paralleled, though more pointed, in Baynton's title "The Chosen Vessel", and in her quasi-Madonna imagery, and use of Biblical names like Mary and Peter. Crane, like Baynton, gives nature human attributes, not to commit the "pathetic fallacy", but to enforce the doctrine that humanity and nature are the same thing.

A problem for Crane was that his readers felt a sympathy for characters like Maggie which made his deterministic pessimism seem reformist; he added to the ambiguity by occasionally imposing on his naturalism a tweak and a nudge which furthered the sympathy. I think that kind of ambiguity is also present in *Bush Studies*. There is a tension between the irresistible signals of a quasi-Darwinist, determinist naturalism and a sympathy for the victims. (They are usually women, but the inclusion of a male victim in "Scrammy 'And" may help to confirm the impression that the author is more interested in biological nature than in gender and "women".)

Baynton liberally added terror. The term "Gothic" is continually misapplied to her fiction, since her implicit anti-Gothicism (like her anti-religious quality) rejects the non-natural trappings of eeriness, along with mystery, the supernatural, and the Gothic fright for fright's sake. You always know the cause of fear in Baynton; whether human, canine, or vegetable, its origin is in nature.

I think Crane and American naturalism provide the code Baynton intended for reading *Bush Studies*. There is a rhetoric of doctrinal acceptance in her writing: "Down, down the woman drew her prey";[26] "As a wounded tigress might hold and look, she held and looked";[27] "even babes soon know on whom to impose",[28] and so on, as if "nature" is to be seen at work, unadorned by "civilising" detail. In "The Chosen Vessel", the woman may seem in a sense "complicit" with the rapist (as Kay Schaffer observes without invoking Crane); Baynton originally wrote that "the dog also was guilty",[29] because it too is part of nature, metaphorically humanised. Some readers want to respond hopefully to the recurring indications and images of pregnancy, birth, the child, the biological cycle, but Baynton does not ask us to; in her fictional world, it appears, you might be better off painlessly dead. In "A Dreamer", the death of the old mother coincides with the death of the new mother as child, and with the growth of the new child in the womb — towards pain, fear and death. The entire cycle is fictionally unified and enveloped in the associations of the frightening in nature.

The problem for feminism, inherent in such writing, is not only that nature, rather than men, is "guilty"; the survival doctrine also signals a pessimistic and reactionary conservatism within society, disabling to ethically based feminist ideology, particularly a feminism which values woman as potentially more than the victim or the object of protection. At first these stories may appear to support in an extreme way Lake's thesis about domestic responsibility and self-interested masculinism, but the determinist signals cancel this out.

Woman in Baynton is scarcely a desirable paradigm. Squeaker's mate, for example, assumes the pipe, clothing and responsibilities of the conventional man, but scarcely the individuality or metaphysical "self" of a person. The men, apart from Squeaker, are shown as fair, practical, considerate, hardworking, and strong; the "mate" (an ironical pun conjoining masculine friendship and the heterosexual biological relationship) is perceived as virtually one of the men, and like them is "barren". In this context, and especially if we remember Baynton's anti-suffragist opinions, Squeaker's mate may appear to deserve the property rights unfairly held by Squeaker, not because she is a person or a woman, but because she is a female man. *Her* man, so his name implies, is a "mouse" — he is not like the other decent blokes. The proper men have nothing to do with the tree crushing the woman: it falls because nature caused it to fall, it was worm-eaten; to read the tree as a phallic symbol is incompatible with what is to follow. The other women, the wives, more suspicious and predatory than the men, disown Squeaker's mate, "challenge her right to womanly garments". Because it is "in the ordering of things", is decreed by nature, "that by degrees most husbands accept their wives' view of other women",[30] the men are persuaded against their more kindly initial judgement to leave the paralysed woman unattended, except by the repulsive Squeaker — to whom the women give "many a feed, agreeing that it must be miserable for him."

Rhetorically, then, the text seems to confirm the judgement of the *kindly* men that Squeaker is a "nole woman": that apparently is what Baynton wants us to believe. Like the other women, he abandons the injured mate, and also deprives her of tobacco: "several of the men who sometimes in passing took a look in would have made up her loss had they known".[31] Squeaker's second mate is younger, pregnant, and in need of protection. To the reader it may appear that, like the original mate, she has come to the wrong man; but both women are ill-favoured by nature, so apparently Squeaker will do. The new mate is hostile to the original mate, out of biological self-interest, rivalry and fear: they fight over water, a traditional female symbol, and the most elemental need of the human animal.

The woman in "A Dreamer", "The Chosen Vessel" and "Billy Skywonkie" comes from the city to the barbarous bush; in "Billy Skywonkie" she escapes back to the city. Is this City seen as civilisation, hope, refuge? The textual opposition invites that reading (though it fails to reconcile it with American naturalistic doctrine); and certainly Baynton herself came to prefer cities. Who would not, married into wealth, rank and comfort, dividing time between London and Melbourne? But Baynton was less delighted by the faces in the Sydney streets before her second marriage, when her non-Christian duty was "to sell Bibles from door to door in order to secure a living for herself and young family".[32] The time has come to deconstruct Baynton's unreal fictional city: it signifies and is privileged in opposition to the "barbaric" rural working-class country; it is the site of comfortable governessing, marriage, protection and wealth. Beautiful antiques and mansions might occupy it, but no lower-class "animals".

Crane may be a compass for reading *Bush Studies*, but I suspect that Marx is a key.

*   *   *   *   *

In this book "the 1890s" means, according to context, either the specific decade, or the "movement" or complex of strands which was discernible in that decade and can be contained very approximately by the years 1885 and 1905. The contributors have not been tied to a specific "theory" or methodology; indeed they have been selected to represent an interrelated diversity of critical approaches and emphases.

The book makes no attempt to shy away from the "Australian legend" debate, and from associated questions of national identity, gender, and the city and the country; but it does supplement these issues with explorations of neglected areas of the nineties, and of matters that may be well known but have become inaccessible. What was happening in Melbourne, while the *Bulletin* and other celebrated 1890s initiatives flourished in Sydney? What is the evidence and significance of an Australian popular culture of 1890s racism and the "yellow peril"? What is the significance of the Boer War and of invasion-scare novels, and how pertinent is "the bush legend" to *these* matters? What were the literary myths and cultural preoccupations that created alternatives (for women and children for example) to the "legend"? The specific discussions of John Docker and Veronica Kelly also introduce elements of postmodernist theory and of recent cultural studies. The Lawson-Paterson verse debate in the *Bulletin* is well known, but nowadays inaccessible: an examination of its context, stages and content may be informative, and may also rebut some misconceptions of it. An analysis of Arthur Jose's editing of Lawson, and of his other cultural activities, foregrounds an important shaping influence on the writing and production of Lawson's texts, and supplements our awareness of the more frequently emphasized editorial and cultural influence of figures such as A. G. Stephens and later David McKee Wright. Close readings of texts that have attracted attention in the 1980s and 1990s are represented, along with new readings of familiar writers. In her chapter on Norman Lindsay, Joy Hooton examines the formative influence of the 1890s on one writer, in ways which look beyond his own assertions, and later constructions of him.

This collection of essays seeks neither to be "comprehensive" nor to define a "spirit of the age". It aims to reflect the 1890s of the 1990s, and perhaps to create a kind of "centennial" 1890s, showing a slice of the diverse interests, assumptions and values of critics and readers today.

The book is dedicated to the memory of Barry Andrews, my close and exuberant friend from 1960, when we started University together, until his death in 1987. Nearly all the contributors were Barry's good friends and colleagues; his favourite literary subject was — the 1890s.

TABLE ONE

NUMBER OF TITLES OF VERSE AND OF FICTION PUBLISHED IN EACH DECADE OF THE NINETEENTH CENTURY

(BASED ON A COUNT OF TITLES LISTED IN E. MORRIS MILLER AND F.J. MACARTNEY'S
AUSTRALIAN LITERATURE: A BIBLIOGRAPHY, SYDNEY: ANGUS & ROBERTSON, 1950)

	Before 1840	1840-9	1850-9	1860-9	1870-9	1880-9	1890-9	1900-9
Verse	14	31	58	109	146	201	227	314
Fiction	4	20	43	80	156	195	539	611
Mixed	-	2	4	5	23	33	12	23
TOTAL	18	53	105	194	325	429	778	948

TABLE TWO

PLACE OF PUBLICATION OF NINETEENTH CENTURY TITLES OF FICTION
(BASED ON A COUNT OF TITLES LISTED IN MILLER AND MACARTNEY).

	Before 1840	1840-9	1850-9	1860-9	1870-9	1880-9	1890-9	1900-9
Overseas	1	17	32	49	76	109	378	430
Melbourne	-	-	4	11	46	44	63	61
Sydney	1	4	3	10	14	19	59	88
Adelaide	-	-	1	2	9	8	5	4
Brisbane	-	-	-	-	1	1	3	7
Hobart	2	-	1	1	4	5	4	3
Perth	-	-	-	-	-	-	-	2
Other	-	-	1	5	-	6	15	9
Unknown	-	-	1	-	-	-	1	4
Melb/Lond	-	-	-	1	1	2	5	1
Syd/Lond	-	-	-	1	5	-	2	-
Syd/Melb	-	-	-	-	-	1	4	1
Syd/Adel	-	-	-	-	-	-	-	1
Lond/Adel	-	-	-	-	-	-	-	-

TABLE THREE

PLACE OF PUBLICATION OF NINETEENTH CENTURY TITLES OF VERSE
(BASED ON A COUNT OF TITLES LISTED IN MILLER AND MACARTNEY)

	Before 1840	1840-9	1850-9	1860-9	1870-9	1880-9	1890-9	1900-9
Overseas	2	4	5	13	13	24	34	49
Melbourne	-	3	19	33	46	53	54	99
Sydney	8	13	10	19	33	50	51	83
Adelaide	-	-	10	8	15	19	30	27
Brisbane	-	-	-	1	4	10	4	9
Hobart	4	10	2	12	4	6	4	9
Perth	-	-	-	-	2	1	1	4
Other	-	-	10	20	26	34	38	34
Unknown	-	1	1	-	-	1	-	-
Syd/Lond	2	1	1	-	-	-	-	-
Hobart/Lond	-	-	1	-	-	-	-	-
Melb/Edinb	-	-	-	-	-	-	-	-
Bris /Lond	-	-	-	-	1	-	-	-
Melb /Lond	-	-	-	-	2	-	6	-
Adel/Melb	-	-	-	-	-	2	-	-
Melb/Syd	-	-	-	-	-	1	-	-

TABLE FOUR

PLACE OF PUBLICATION OF NINETEENTH CENTURY ANTHOLOGIES CONTAINING BOTH VERSE AND FICTION
(BASED ON A COUNT OF TITLES LISTED IN MILLER AND MACARTNEY)

	Before 1840	1840-9	1850-9	1860-9	1870-9	1880-9	1890-9	1900-9
Overseas	-	-	-	1	1	3	-	1
Melbourne	-	-	1	1	7	21	6	5
Sydney	-	-	1	-	6	3	2	5
Adelaide	-	-	-	-	2	3	2	1
Brisbane	-	1	-	-	-	1	-	1
Hobart	-	-	-	2	1	1	-	1
Perth	-	-	-	-	-	-	-	1
Other	-	1	1	-	5	2	2	2
Lond/Syd	-	-	-	-	-	-	-	-
Syd/Melb	-	-	-	-	1	-	-	5
Melb/Lond	-	-	-	-	-	-	-	1

TABLE FIVE

FIGURES SHOWING AGGREGATES OF VERSE AND FICTION TITLES PUBLISHED IN MELBOURNE, SYDNEY AND OVERSEAS RESPECTIVELY
(BASED ON A COUNT OF TITLES LISTED IN MILLER AND MACARTNEY)

	Before 1840	1840-9	1850-9	1860-9	1870-9	1880-9	1890-9	1900-9
Melbourne	-	3	24	45	99	118	123	165
Sydney	9	17	14	29	53	72	112	176
Overseas	3	21	37	63	90	136	417	480
Lond/Melb	-	-	-	1	3	3	11	2
Lond/Syd	-	2	-	2	5	-	2	-
Edin/Melb	-	-	-	1	-	-	-	-
Syd/Melb	-	-	-	-	1	1	4	5

Additional Notes:

1. These tables do not fully reflect the increasing ascendancy of Sydney over Melbourne as a venue for publication in the 1890s, since they do not indicate the sales and popularity of particular titles.
2. The aggregate of all titles published until and including 1909 was 2850, of which 2155 were published between 1880 and 1909 (inclusive).

Victorian Writers in the Nineties

Geoffrey Serle

"Back in the nineteenth century", A. G. Stephens (AGS) once remarked, "when Melbourne led Australian letters ... "[1] Well, that can hardly be claimed for the 1890s — Lawson, Paterson, Archibald, Stephens and the *Bulletin* dominate, then and now. However, an area-study based on Victoria may throw a little light on the legend of the nineties and on the *Bulletin* school.

We know something of the richness of the cultural and intellectual life in boom Melbourne at the close of the eighties. There were literary societies galore — the highly fashionable Shakespeare Society (claimed to be the largest in the world), the Burns Society, an Ibsen Society, groups devoted to Chaucer, Milton, Lamb, Browning (and later Robert Louis Stevenson).[2] Kipling and Conan Doyle were all the rage. The daily and weekly metropolitan and provincial newspapers were of astonishing quality by world standards. Ada Cambridge remarked on "how high and dignified is the moral and intellectual as well as (comparatively speaking) the literary standard of our representative journalism"; the *Argus* stood out but Cambridge could also praise "the literary beauty and philosophical significance" of some of the *Age*'s Saturday leaders.[3] For hard-reading men and women there was the great Public Library, first-rate bookshops (nearly three times as many as in Sydney) such as Robertson's, Cole's and Mullen's — and Mullen's lending library: "Half the respectable families in Melbourne belong to Mullen's."[4] The University of Melbourne, having recruited some brilliant young Britishers (Lyle, Masson, Baldwin Spencer, Tucker),[5] was reaching for a new level of quality. Though most of the educated migrants lived for the journals from Home, there was a developing local sense: the Historical Society of Australasia, a branch of the Royal Geographical Society, produced primitive pioneer historical works by Rusden, Blair, Labilliere, Shillinglaw, Sutherland and others. And consider, not least, the quality of the quarterly *Melbourne Review* (1876-85)[6] and the monthly *Victorian Review* (1879-86), both of which had had to succumb to the competition of the great English journals, mainly because the latter were cheaper. The colonial evangelists, nobly but too optimistically, had seen reading of the great books as a pathway to superior moral enlightenment. But these migrant teachers, attempting to instil a great tradition, perhaps primarily encouraged a sense of exile among their charges. There was also the wowser, high-moral-tone aspect of the age: the Library trustees allegedly banned a Kipling work because of a reference to Anglo-Indian society "playing tennis with the Seventh Commandment", and a leading Melbourne editor was believed to routinely excise "darling" from stories.[7]

Dramatic developments were occurring in Melbourne in art and music (associated especially with the Centennial Exhibition). Creative literature, however, seemed to be stagnating: seemingly it was a spectator literary culture. Marcus Clarke and Adam Lindsay Gordon, who had won wide recognition, had died. Who *were* the poets and novelists of any quality of the eighties (other than Ada Cambridge)?

We had better clear some ground. Many short-term migrant writers came and went. The prolific visiting Englishmen E. W. Hornung, Hume Nisbet, Morley Roberts and Douglas Sladen had all left for Home by 1890. So had Fergus Hume from New Zealand. Francis Adams, long out of Victoria, departed in 1890, and Nat Gould, an occasional visitor, eventually in 1895. "Tasma" (Jessie Couvreur) had also left finally in 1884, but in 1889 was to publish the important novel *Uncle Piper of Piper's Hill*, set in Melbourne, and other novels later. Young Victorians who had also sailed for Europe included Patchett Martin (in disgrace, after being cited as a co-respondent), J. F. Hogan, Ethel ("Henry Handel") Richardson and W. J. Turner.

The literary establishment of the nineties, such as it was, still consisted of the septuagenarians David Blair (1820-99), Dr. James Edward Neild (1824-1906), James Smith (1820-1910), and Henry Gyles Turner (1831-1920), who had all arrived in Victoria as adults in the early 1850s.[8]

Blair, sometime Presbyterian minister, radical democrat and politician, and above all a phenomenally prolific journalist over forty years — he is believed to have written thousands of leaders as well as articles, criticism and reviews — was a spent force by the nineties. His two chief publications had been the slapdash *History of Australasia* (1878) and the *Cyclopedia of Australasia* (1881). In unhappy old age he was consumed by jealousies: Charles Pearson was a "wooden-headed pedant", and James Smith was "a thorough quack in literature" who, like W. H. Fitchett, stole everything.[9]

Neild was a forensic pathologist, university lecturer and wide-ranging journalist whose chief interests were the theatre, music, literature and art. Throughout his Victorian career he campaigned against "colonophobia" — prejudice against colonial products — and was a good patron to writers and other artists in need. But, as Harold Love establishes, his great claim to fame is as a theatre critic (for the *Australasian* from 1865 to 1890).[10]

James Smith was an even more productive journalist than Blair, ranging over literature, art and drama. He edited *Punch* for a few years from 1859 and the *Australasian* in the seventies, wrote constantly for the *Argus* (which in the eighties paid him an annual retainer of Five Hundred Pounds) and the *Victorian Review*, and was a trustee of the Library, Gallery and Museums for thirty years. He claimed to have averaged over one thousand Pounds a year from his writings between 1854 and 1888.[11] However, he lost everything in the depression, and throughout his eighties was writing for the *Age* and compiling the three-volume *Cyclopedia of Victoria* (1903-

05). Smith's conversion to spiritualism had strained his close friendship with Turner and others. His reputation has suffered from his notorious condemnation of the 1889 "Impressions" exhibition, but he had encouraged Buvelot and the young Tom Roberts, and he reviewed *Such Is Life* enthusiastically (when eighty-three) and wrote warmly to Furphy about it.[12]

Henry Gyles Turner was a paradoxical figure: an extreme Spencerean individualist and a conservative banker who established the Commercial Bank of Australia on a sound footing, and who then had to survive its near ruin in the nineties and reconstruct it before retiring at seventy; a libertarian in theology and a Unitarian preacher; and a radical with regard to Imperialism, the Aborigines and White Australia. A sportsman and bushwalker, a Yorick and Eclectic, he was the chief sponsor and later editor of the *Melbourne Review*. In fact he wrote his major works in the later nineties — *The Development of Australian Literature* (with Alexander Sutherland) and his history of Victoria (1904). Most of his writings suffer from cautious conventionality and do not truly reflect the genial, witty, respected, and in various ways unconventional, Turner.[13]

There were others getting on in years such as the surviving stalwarts of the Yorick Club from its great days about 1870. George Gordon McCrae (1833-1927), poet, artist, bushman and convivial man of letters, produced no volume between 1883 and his final collection of verse in 1915 and his novel *John Rous* in 1918. Dr. Patrick Moloney (1843-1904), physician, poet, translator of Horace and frequent contributor to *Punch* and the *Australasian*, was to leave Victoria in 1898. J. J. Shillinglaw (1831-1905), public servant, journalist and historian, is the third of the convivial friends who behaved as eccentrically as literary men are supposed to. McCrae, at least, was closely associated with Dr. Stephen (1850-96) and Kathleen (1853-1926) Mannington Caffyn, migrants in Melbourne from 1883, aesthetes, medical and social radicals, and both talented novelists. At their Brighton salon the boy Hugh McCrae "for the first time ... saw the coast-line of Bohemia,

twinkling and dangerously beautiful"; Mrs. Caffyn was
posing for Charles Conder.[14] George Gordon McCrae
described Caffyn as "the best talker I have heard" and
AGS named him as of the *Bulletin* contributors perhaps
"the one who rose highest as an artistic story-teller".[15] But
the Mannington Caffyns too are marginal to our purpose for,
lamentably, they returned to England in 1892. Both may
have written (or part-written) their first novels in
Melbourne. Stephen's *Miss Milne and I*, set in London and
Sydney, ran through four impressions in 1894. Kathleen's
avant-garde *The Yellow Aster* (1894) was received
sensationally in London and she continued to write
prolifically and successfully, sometimes as "Iota".[16]

Another veteran, "Rolf Boldrewood" (1826-1915), after
thirty-five years away from Victoria, about 1895 retired to
Melbourne where he wrote his last novels. Similarly, the
historian George Rusden (1819-1903) after ten years in
England returned to Melbourne to continue his study of
Shakespeare.

The generation gap between all these migrants and the
new native-born writers of the nineties, whom I list below,
was huge.

For convenience (and to avoid reproaches) I have
excluded two important writers from this list although
both have claims as Victorians. William Astley ("Price
Warung", 1855-1911), a small-child migrant from England,
had a good education in Melbourne, and between 1875 and
1891 worked as a journalist at Richmond, Echuca,
Casterton, Warrnambool and Nhill, as well as in New
South Wales and Tasmania. His 1890-91 associations are
important, and four of his five books were to be published
in Melbourne. But he settled in Sydney, published his
convict stories in the *Bulletin* and, as a high-quality
journalist and Federationist also, must be allowed to have
been primarily a Sydney writer. Victor Daley (1858-1905)
also spent about half his colonial years in Melbourne but
left few traces there (he was carousing with Ted Dyson in
1889). I have included Fitchett, G. E. Morrison and
Alexander Sutherland, primarily non-fiction writers, who
had wide international impact as none of the others on the

list did. Charles Henry Pearson (1830-94), historian, first headmaster of Presbyterian Ladies' College and radical minister of education, whose *National Life and Character* (1893) was of world significance, might be added. Then there was Baldwin Spencer (1860-1929, *Native Tribes of Central Australia*, with F. J. Gillen, 1899). (This may serve to remind Aust Lit practitioners, whose narrowness in this regard is damnable, that apart from the intellectual contributions of historians, biographers and other non-fiction writers it is possible that some of them can write.)

Furphy, Cambridge, O'Dowd, Neilson and McCrae stand out on the list as major writers. I am not, however, primarily concerned to make literary judgments, rather to consider those who were regarded at the time as important.

W. H. FITCHETT (1841-1928), a child-migrant, was a very prominent Methodist minister, principal of Methodist Ladies' College and a vivid journalist. He was editor from 1892 to 1903 of the Australasian edition of *Review of Reviews*, but made his fame throughout the British Empire with his weekly articles by "Vedette" in the *Argus* from 1896. *Deeds that Won the Empire* (1897) sold in hundreds of thousands and is even said to have been an important influence on Winston Churchill's style. Further volumes commemorating imperial valour, a biography of Wesley and several poor novels followed.

Joseph FURPHY (1843-1912), born at Yering, had little schooling and was mainly educated by his mother. He worked on the diggings and farmed for several years, in 1873-83 was a bullock-driving carrier in the Riverina, then worked as a mechanic in his brother's foundry at Shepparton. As a youth he had written some verse. Soaked now in radical ideas germinating in the outback, but a great original — ironist, satirist, humorist — he was a complete *Bulletin* man though much more inclined to socialism: he referred to "the hideous depression brought on by the unbridled greed of vile men in high places ... so-called Christians who could not see prosperity in the country without looting it". But he probably acquired much of his knowledge of Shakespeare and of general literature from the Melbourne press. Between 1889 and 1900 the *Bulletin* published about thirty items — verse, pars, criticism — at first by "Warrigal Jack", later by "Tom Collins". He probably began *Such Is Life* in the late eighties. By 1896 he had finished but, sadly with regard to its possible impact, seven years followed before publication — writing it out, typing it, adding new sections, cutting others which became *Rigby's Romance* and *The Buln-buln and the Brolga*. He said his second-greatest surprise was the note from J. F. Archibald about his first contribution; his greatest was AGS telling him "S'Life" would become a classic. He was in no sense a professional writer; money was no objective.[17]

Ada CAMBRIDGE (1844-1926), an important novelist and poet of the eighties and nineties, migrated from England in 1870 after marrying the Rev. G. F. Cross and spent about twenty years in country parishes before moving to Williamstown. She had contributed to English journals in her youth and continued to write steadily, despite childbearing and illnesses, almost all her life. From 1872 she contributed regularly to the *Australasian* and occasionally to the *Age, Sydney Mail, Centennial Magazine* and other outlets. Of more than twenty novels, *The Three Miss Kings* (1891, *Australasian* serial 1883) and *A Marked Man* (1890, *Age* serial 1888-89) are among her best; several were not published in book form. Their quality varied considerably — a few were written quickly for the popular market — but most were serious novels in a period when few others were writtten. And although most were romances, they insistently questioned "romantic love as the basis for marital choice" and were wise and witty commentaries on colonial life. Her anonymous volume of poetry, *Unspoken Thoughts* (1887), in its concern with religious doubt, women's rights and social justice, and in its awareness of current intellectual debates, reached far above almost any other Australian poetry of the period. Her autobiography *Thirty Years in Australia* (1903) was an important commentary on her times.[18]

Alexander SUTHERLAND (1852-1902) was born in Glasgow, migrated with his family to Sydney in 1864 and moved to Melbourne in 1870. This extraordinary allrounder was headmaster of Carlton College 1877-92, co-editor of the *Melbourne Review*, historian, biographer, critic, poet, novelist, artist, musician, and eventually University registrar and lecturer in English. His *Thirty Short Poems* was published in 1890 and *The Origin and Growth of the Moral Instinct*, acclaimed by Morris Ginsberg as a pioneer work in sociology, in 1898. Sutherland tended to align himself with the elder generation, especially Turner.

Mary GAUNT (1861-1942), daughter of a famous magistrate, was born at Chiltern and educated at Grenville College, Ballarat. One of the first female students at the University, she abandoned her arts course after one year. Professor E. E. Morris, editor of *Cassell's Picturesque Australasia*, encouraged her to write and accepted her entry on "Gold". Determined to be financially independent, in the late eighties she was published in the *Age, Argus, Australasian, Bulletin* and *Sydney Mail*. In 1888 she made Fifty Pounds from her writings. Her novel, *Kirkham's Find* (1897) set on the goldfields, was republished in 1988. In 1894 she married Dr. H. L. Miller of Warrnambool and before his death in 1900 published a collection of short stories, two more novels and a serial in the *Argus*. In 1901 she left for London and pursued a fairly successful career as novelist and travel writer.[19]

G. E. ("Chinese") MORRISON (1862-1920), born in Geelong, transcontinental pedestrian, investigator of blackbirding, explorer of New Guinea and medical graduate of Edinburgh University, returned to Victoria in 1890 and worked at Ballarat Hospital. Having then walked across China to Burma, his *An Australian in China* (1895) won him fame and the post of *Times* correspondent. He returned only once to Australia, twenty-two years later.

J. B. O'HARA (1862-1927), born in Bendigo, battled his way out of a distressing family background to academic success at the University and, as sole proprietor from 1894 to 1917 of the co-educational South Melbourne College, achieved phenomenal examination results. His ambition, however, was to be a poet and although his *Songs of the South* (1891, 1895) won encouraging English reviews and extreme enthusiasm in the journal *Austral Light*, in the long run "bland, meditative" and "smooth melodiousness"

were typical critical conclusions. He published nine
volumes of verse.[20]

Sydney JEPHCOTT (1864-1951), born in the Upper
Murray district, educated himself by wide reading,
throughout his life was a cattlefarmer, and had an
extraordinary range of literary friendships. Kendall
inspired him to write verse, Francis Adams saw *The Secrets
of the South* (1892) through the press; Jephcott made an
unpublished selection of Adams's poetry. He was a highly
original character: his correspondence displays
considerable intellectual range and vigour.

Edward DYSON (1865-1931), born at Morrison near
Ballarat, left state school at twelve to work in goldmines.
The family moved to Melbourne in 1883, Ted worked in
factories and was the economic mainstay of a large family
including his younger brothers Ambrose and Will. From the
mid-eighties he began contributing stories and verse to the
press, often as "Silas Snell". Archibald noticed his mining
stories: "A Golden Shanty", written when eighteen,
headed the *Bulletin*'s 1889 Christmas anthology, and from
1888 many of the verses appeared which were eventually
published as *Rhymes from the Mines* (1896). Dyson founded
the weekly *Bull-Ant (Ant)*, 1890-92, which he largely
wrote himself and which reflected his radical politics: he
revered George Higinbotham and supported the strikers in
1890. Facile and versatile, he freelanced so successfully for
Punch especially, as well as the *Bulletin,* that by the later
nineties he was earning over Six Hundred Pounds a year.
The stories *Below and on Top* were published in 1898.
Novels and other collections of stories followed, notably *In
the Roaring Fifties* (1906) and *Fact'ry 'Ands* (1906). "The
most professional Australian writer of his generation",
probably the only freelance to make a good living, his
literary achievement did not match his talent. "Quantity
pays better than quality," he said.[21]

William GAY (1865-97), born in Scotland, studied
briefly at Glasgow University but for his health's sake
migrated to New Zealand in 1885. Arriving in Melbourne in
1888, he taught and tutored, and contributed much verse,
criticism and a serial to the *Australian Herald,* and wrote

for *Cassell's Picturesque Australasia*. Stricken with tuberculosis, he settled in Bendigo in 1893 and was largely confined to bed. With strong interests in philosophy and science, he was a talented intellectual; his powerful critique of Whitman was published in two booklets in 1893 and 1895. He wrote some good sonnets and the long "Christ on Olympus"; one sonnet on Federation, a cause he warmly supported, was famous.

Marion Miller KNOWLES (1865-1949) was a prolific, and in her earlier years popular, writer of verse, short stories and novels of which eight were published in book form. Born and brought up at Woods Point, in 1878 she became a pupil-teacher with the Education Department. For several years she was a relief teacher in various parts of the colony and claimed to have "learned much in those suffering days of human nature". From 1893 until her marriage in 1901 she taught at Box Hill. She first contributed verse and stories to the *Australasian* in the mid to late eighties under the name "John Desmond", and in the nineties was frequently published, as Marion Miller, in the *Australasian* and *Austral Light* which lauded her as "the first Australian Catholic poetess". Her first novel, *Barbara Halliday*, was published in 1896 and *Songs from the Hills* in 1898; both ran to four editions. The content of her simple verse was largely the Bush, children, love and death. Her fiction was largely sentimental romance based on country life, with some aptitude for characterisation and a leading devotional strain. She eventually worked for the *Advocate* which published several of her serials, as did the *Irish Catholic* (Dublin).[22]

Bernard O'DOWD (1866-1953), born at Beaufort, was educated at several state schools and, having won a rare state scholarship, at Grenville College, Ballarat. Fortunate in his teachers, and the best-educated of all on this list, O'Dowd profited from much which Ballarat could offer — debating, libraries, involvement in public affairs, publication of his verse in the *Courier*. In 1886 he moved to Melbourne, having been appointed to the Crown Solicitor's Office; next year he became assistant to the Supreme Court librarian, was soon editing and ghosting law books, and eventually became parliamentary draughtsman. He graduated BA (1891) and LLB (1895). Of encyclopedic mind, O'Dowd had long abandoned Catholicism for secularism, and investigated or belonged to any and every intellectual movement. He contributed general journalism and poems to the *Bulletin* as a public servant writing under pseudonyms. Increasingly radical, he was a founder, major editor and writer for the socialist *Tocsin* in 1897 and later prominent in the Victorian Socialist Party. His famous sonnet "Australia" was published as a *Bulletin* prizewinner on 12 May 1900. Closely associated now with AGS, his first volume, *Dawnward?*, was published by the *Bulletin* in 1903. In the long run O'Dowd was more important as an intellectual than as a poet.

Grace Jennings CARMICHAEL (1867-1904) was born at Ballarat and moved to a station near Orbost when about thirteen. She began writing about the Bush, sometimes storing her manuscripts in a hollow log in a remote clearing. Her mother and stepfather disapproved of her writing but her tutor persuaded them to tolerate it. When fifteen she contributed a story to the *Bairnsdale Advertiser*: "the success determined all my future career". A poem was accepted by the *Weekly Times*, another in November 1885 by the *Australasian* where she subsequently consistently published and in the *Argus*. She moved to Melbourne in 1886, contributed to the *Centennial Magazine* in 1890, trained as a nurse, publishing *Hospital Children* in 1891, worked in Melbourne and near Geelong, and belonged to the Austral Salon. In 1895, with the help of her friend Lady (Janet) Clarke, her *Poems* were published in Melbourne and London. That year Jennings Carmichael also lectured on "The Spirit of the Bush", refuting the notion of "weird melancholy". She married, moved to South Australia, then England where she died in poverty in 1904.[23]

Randolph BEDFORD (1868-1941), born in Sydney, after some years knocking about settled in Melbourne for nearly all the period 1888-1900. He worked for the *Age* and suburban newspapers, in 1892 edited the *Toora and Welshpool Pioneer*, then freelanced. An anti-imperialist, a devotee of the *Bulletin*, he contributed to it and *Bull Ant*.

In 1897 F. W. Haddon seized on some of his long stories for the *Argus*. In 1897 Bedford founded the monthly *Clarion*. At the end of the nineties he was writing his autobiographical novel, *True Eyes and the Whirlwind* (1903). Both writer and man of action, he was a brilliant journalist and raconteur, but essentially a popular writer, vigorous but careless.

Mary FULLERTON (1868-1946) was born at Glenmaggie, Gippsland, and attended the local state school; she recalled that her mother was "the first in impressing by heredity, and by precept in me a delight in poety and in literature generally". By eleven she had read *Paradise Lost* three times and was steeped in Shelley, Byron and the Bible. She also came to be steeped in the *Bulletin* and Lawson's early verse. In the early nineties, "hungry for mental contacts", she moved to Melbourne. Little is known of her there until the late nineties when she was active in the women's movement and later in the Political Labor Council. The one early publication I have traced is an interview with Mary Gaunt, signed M.E.F., in the *Sydney Mail* (20 February 1898), which indicates practice of shorthand. She published in the *Australasian* and *Leader* sketches eventually included in her *Bark House Days* (1921), and produced her first volume of verse in 1908. In 1922 she left permanently for England and became a close friend of Miles Franklin.[24]

John Shaw NEILSON (1872-1942), born at Penola SA, became a major lyric poet of great delicacy. Almost entirely lacking in formal education, he worked as a rural labourer — fencing, shearing, harvesting, roadmaking, scrub-clearing — for most of his life. He was trying to write verse from about fourteen and had eight lines of rhyme published in the *Leader* in 1890. In 1893 he and his father won the junior and senior prizes in the Australian Natives' Association poetry competitions. In 1893 and 1894 the *Australasian* published two poems and the *Nhill and Tatiara Mail* about a dozen. The *Bulletin* had one poem in 1895 and another in 1896 when his eventually vital association with Stephens, A.G. was formed. However, he wrote or published almost nothing in the following five years.[25]

Hugh McCRAE (1876-1958) was born in Hawthorn, educated at Hawthorn Grammar School, as the son of George Gordon and grandson of Georgiana was the only one on this list to have a strong literary background, and eventually became a major poet. In the mid-nineties he was articled to an architect and began contributing poems to the *Bulletin*, the *Champion* and *Free Lance* (which also published his stories). In 1896 or 1897 he met the younger Norman Lindsay ("either altogether a devil or altogether a god") who gave him a forced education in the classics. "Books brought us together." In 1901, encouraged by AGS, McCrae followed Lindsay to Sydney.[26]

This choice of 17 significant writers of the nineties is necessarily arbitrary at the margin. In 1890 all were under 50 years old, 15 were under 30, 9 were 25 or less. 13 were Australian born, 2 British adult migrants, 2 British child-migrants. All are in the *Australian Dictionary of Biography*. Of the 13 native born, 12 were born in rural/provincial areas (6 in the gold-towns), only 1 in Melbourne. These remarkable facts require some pondering. Of the 13 educated in Victoria, only 2 were so in Melbourne, 3 became university graduates, and perhaps 4 more remained at school beyond 14. All 17 were children of migrants: 6 English, 5 Scottish, 4 Irish, 2 mixed British.

Consider now what the next generation, all 30 or less, were doing about 1899.

Marie McKeown PITT (1869-1948), born at Boggy Creek, north-east Gippsland, was schooled on and off at Wy Yung until twelve, worked throughout her childhood and later on the family farm at Doherty's Corner, near Bruthen, had her first verses published in the *Bairnsdale Advertiser* in the 1880s, married in 1893, moved to Tasmania and was to return to Victoria in 1903.

Jeannie Taylor GUNN(1870-1961) was teaching in the nineties, married Aeneas Gunn in 1901 and departed for the Northern Territory.

Walter MURDOCH (1874-1970), a child-migrant, after graduating with first-class honours in logic and philosophy at the University was conducting his own school, Camberwell College. In 1899-1900 he had three stories in the *Argus* (by "W. L. Forbes") and on 6 May 1899, in his first substantial article, wrote derisively about current Australian poets.

Percival SERLE (1871-1951) was writing criticism for the Kew newspaper and *Tatler* and an athletics column for the *Sportsman*, mocked young Murdoch for his cocksure views, and was suffering rude comments on his own verse in the *Bulletin*'s "Answers to Correspondents".

Mary Grant BRUCE (1878-1958) arrived in Melbourne from Sale in 1898. She had won the Shakespeare Society's prize three years running and, warmly encouraged by J. E. Neild, had just had her first story published in the *Leader* which gave her charge of its children's page.

Winifred JAMES (1876-1941), daughter of a Wesleyan minister, was born in Melbourne and educated privately. She was about to move to Adelaide and run a teashop before returning in 1903 and contributing her first stories to the *Australasian*. She was to move to London in 1905.

Louis ESSON (1878-1941), born in Edinburgh, another child-migrant, brought up by the Paterson family in art and literary circles, had begun an arts degree at the University but did not complete it.

Norman LINDSAY (1879-1969) followed his brother Lionel from Creswick to Melbourne in 1896 and made a precarious living from cartoons and illustrations for minor newspapers. While leading a rackety Bohemian life, he was reading widely and had already fallen under the spell of Nietzsche.

Frank WILMOT ("Furnley Maurice", 1881-1942) had left state school at thirteen, was working at Cole's Book Arcade and already writing verse. When eleven he had sent a poem to the *Bulletin*: Archibald sent an encouraging note. In 1897 he was published in *Tocsin* ("A 16-year old Democrat sends the following") and in the *World*, in 1898 had eight poems and a story in *Tocsin*, then in 1899 poems in the *Australasian, Sun, Outpost* and *Arena*.

Katharine Susannah PRICHARD (1883-1969) was still at South Melbourne College; she called J. B. O'Hara "a wonderful schoolmaster" who encouraged her scribbling.[27]

Bernard CRONIN (1884-1968), a child-migrant, was soon to graduate from Dookie Agricultural College.

Nettie Higgins PALMER (1885-1964) was a most promising student at Presbyterian Ladies' College.

Frederick MACARTNEY (1887-1980) had just left state school at twelve.

Martin BOYD, Frank Dalby DAVISON and **Leonard MANN** were little more than toddlers.

Of these 17, 12 were Victorian born (7 Melbourne, 5 country, 3 gold-towns), 5 child-migrants (including 2 from Victorian families), none adult migrants. All are or will be in the ADB. 12 out of 17 were brought up and educated in Melbourne; about 10 were schooled beyond 14; 3 became university graduates. In contrast to the earlier list of writers of the nineties, this displays a marked swing to the city. 10 of the 17 had British, Irish or British/Irish parentage, 3 had one migrant and one native-born parent, and probably 4 had Australasian-born parents.

Remarkably, of the 34 on the two lists 32 were Australian born or child-migrants (25 Australian born, 7 child-migrants ranging from babies to a 12-year-old): Cambridge and Gay were the exceptions. These figures relate to my bold, half-tongue-in-cheek observation years ago in *From Deserts the Prophets Come* that after Clarke and Buvelot "there is hardly one major Australian creative artist ... who is not a native Australian".[28] (I should now hastily rule out the post-1950 period.)

One extraordinary regional feature is seen in the isolated Gippsland girls, born in the 1860s, writing nature verse in celebration of the Bush: Mary Fullerton of Glenmaggie; Marie McKeown of Doherty's Corner; Nellie Clerk of Mirboo North; Jennings Carmichael of Orbost. Marion Miller of Woods Point might also be included over the strict geographical border. The sisters Mable Temple (1871-92) and Hilda Temple Kerr (1874-1956) of the Orbost area were a few years younger. Allan McLean (1840-1911) of Maffra, later premier of Victoria, had published *Rural*

Poems in 1888. Mary Grant Bruce of Sale was soon to become the most famous of them all. George Dunderdale's (1822-1903) *The Book of the Bush* (1898) is the other notable local work of the period.

Patrick Morgan, whose *The Literature of Gippsland* (Churchill, 1983, 1986) is an important contribution to the history of the region, defines "a poetry of ferny glades, sparkling mountain streams, majestic trees, far purple ranges, sunshine and stillness",[29] in the Harpur-Kendall tradition which lasted long. Nearly all these women left Gippsland for a wider world; Fullerton and Pitt, at least, became social rebels. We may wonder over what mix of parents and family, teachers, local editors, and of environmental influences, inspired and developed them.

In 1890 Nhill, in the west Wimmera, was a farming town hardly ten years old, with a population of barely one thousand in a shire of perhaps four thousand people. But it was glad confident morning; the town already had its mechanics' institute and free library. In 1889 Frank Shann, Anglican clergyman, teacher and journalist, father of Edward the future historian and Frank the headmaster, had arrived to edit the *Nhill and Tatiara Mail* and was soon producing a four-page literary supplement! Next year, on his motion, the Nhill Literary and Debating Society was formed, presided over by E. J. Stephens, the cultivated proprietor of the town's second newspaper and of an extensive provincial chain. By 1893 Nhill had a school of art (which Percy Leason later attended), affiliated with the Horsham Working Men's College. In 1890 William Astley, an old friend of Shann from 1878 at Echuca and later in Tasmania, arrived to work on the other paper. He played for the local cricket team (Barry Andrews would have been delighted to know) and at Nhill probably wrote some of his convict stories. He left for Sydney early in 1891. John and John Shaw Neilson were working in the Nhill area and lived in the town 1893-95. They heard Shann speak at the Literary Society, but are not known to have spoken at meetings. Shaw Neilson gave recitations, including "The Skylark" and Whittier poems, at local ANA gatherings. Shann published his poems and Neilson never forgot his comment on fondly remembered lines: "They are ringing in my head yet". Neilson was already writing limericks with local references.[30]

Other striking examples of such regional/rural interest might be discovered, though it seems unlikely. Geelong, Ballarat and Bendigo seem to have contributed little.

Some thirty years ago Chris Wallace-Crabbe referred to Australian writers' historical "utter independence of one another ... no significant imaginative connection ... discontinuity ... the writers turn away to see what they can pick up from the great library which is Europe".[31] (But the Gippsland poets and Jephcott knew their Kendall and possibly Harpur.)

In the nineties there was no society or club in Melbourne which effectively brought writers together. The Yorick Club, founded in 1868 by F. W. Haddon (*Argus* editor 1867-98) with David Watterston (later editor of the *Australasian*) as a prominent member, aimed to bring together "literary, artistic, scientific and professional men". G. G. McCrae, Clarke, Neild, Moloney, Shillinglaw and the Rusden brothers gave it tone, but by the nineties the survivors were aged and, though Kipling and Mark Twain were greeted in great style, the club had lost its impetus. The Bohemians, founded in 1875 largely for the cricketing purposes of "old University and public school men", also went in for music and amateur theatricals — Turner wrote for their entertainments — but otherwise it had no literary relevance; lawyers — and cards, racing and billiards — came to predominate. The Savage Club, founded in 1894, was more promising — Bedford and George Darrell were early members — but "the field in Melbourne [was] too limited to confine prospective nominees to the ranks of professional writers, musicians, artists, and actors as enforced by its adopted parents in London". Twenty years later, however, it had many writer members whose fellowship may then have been of some significance.[32]

A belated Whitman movement in Melbourne about 1890 was a minor coagulant force. Thomas Bury ("Tom Touchstone" of the Ballarat *Courier*) was well read in American writing, and Walt Whitman's poetry and philosophy were his chief enthusiasm. Francis Adams was another spreading the word. Bury introduced the young O'Dowd to Whitman's writings: his conversion was such that in his early Melbourne years he constantly carried and quoted from a copy of *Leaves of Grass* (Oscar Wilde had done much the same a dozen years earlier), wore blades of grass in his buttonhole, and envisaged his future role as a preacher-poet. In 1890 O'Dowd struck up a correspondence with the "sublime old bard of Democracy", addressing him as Master, telling him that he had named his first-born son after him, and of the enthusiasm of the Australeum, a small weekly literary club he had formed. He spread the gospel at his numerous classes and lectures to the Australasian Secularist Association, the Australian Natives' Association, the Collins Street Literary Society, workingmen's clubs and others, and at length persuaded the Public Library to purchase *Leaves of Grass*. Another propagator of Whitmanism and American radical thought was the Rev. Dr. Charles Strong in his *Australian Herald*, partly influenced by the devotion of his contributor William Gay who, as we have noted, wrote critical studies of Whitman and also an obituary sonnet. Though not associated with local devotees, Furphy too was considerably influenced by the American Transcendentalists.[33]

In 1889, largely on Neild's suggestion, the Royal Society of Victoria formed a literature and art section which proceeded to meet monthly for some years at least. The chief limitation was that those who attended were interested in, rather than practitioners of, the arts.[34] We should also mention the numerous local and church literary and debating societies of the period.

The active suffragist movement from the eighties, and the growing number of women journalists (notably Lucy Gullett, Alice Henry who for twenty years wrote for the *Argus* and *Australasian* before going overseas in 1905, and Florence Blair (David's daughter, later Mrs. Baverstock) were mildly reflected in the formation of women's cultural associations, whose longevity is significant. In 1890 Miss Hirst Browne, a journalist, moved to establish a small club for active practitioners of the arts. After five months the Austral Salon put on the most brilliant ball for years (according to *Punch*) at the Town Hall, "representing the elite of Melbourne society"; the Governor's lady was president, Lady Clarke and Lady Davies vice-presidents. The Salon took rooms in Collins Street and met fortnightly for literary, musical and dramatic presentations, often to crowded audiences. Florence Blair, her sister Lily (later Mrs. Percy Hunter), the journalist Agnes Murphy and Jennings Carmichael were among the literary speakers. We know little more: the Salon's early records were destroyed by fire, but it still exists. In 1890 also the famous Congregational minister Dr. Llewellyn Bevan founded the Daughters of the Court "to check ill-natured and useless gossip, and to encourage a spirit of helpfulness in the daily work of life"; it soon had intercolonial and overseas chapters and courts, despite or because of its temporary medieval flummery. Bevan's zeal for female emancipation was reflected in its journal the *Court* (1894-97). In 1898 "the literary coterie known as the Friends in Council" was formed and continued to meet monthly for book discussions for at least half a century. The Women Writers' Club (confined to those published), eventually absorbed into the Lyceum Club, was founded in 1900 or 1901; Ada Cambridge was first president, Stella Allan ("Vesta") succeeded her, and Mary Gaunt and Jeannie Gunn were members. But in Melbourne in the nineties no woman of the stature of Louisa Lawson or Rose Scott in Sydney emerged to lead either the general or literary cause before about 1900 when Vida Goldstein became prominent.[35]

The Lindsay brothers' room in Collins Street in the late nineties was a lively centre for writers, artists and their hangers-on. For a year or so some of them met regularly at Fasoli's[36] restaurant as the Ishmael Club. Bedford and Ted Dyson (slightly surprisingly for grown men) took the lead in puerile scatological and blasphemous rituals combined with facetious speechifying. "Let us be iconoclasts ... it remains for us to love wine, women and art ... and live for the moment" was one of their toasts. Melbourne in the nineties developed its own pale version of Bohemia, based on Murger's *La Vie de Boheme*, the popularity of the opera *La Boheme* and du Maurier's *Trilby*, a rebellious flouting of prevailing conventions in which of course respectable women had no part, a sort of cult of the artist. As Sarah Stephen has remarked, Murger's tale had "themes of good fellowship, a commitment of values in art, and to the philosophy of 'light hearts and empty pockets'" which "provided them with ways of describing their lives and defining their identity as artists. The reader was instructed in the codes and manners of Bohemia ... meals were cadged, love affairs came and went, landlords were mocked and cheated and scarce money was spent with recklessness". Memories of Clarke and Gordon possibly provided some local inspiration. The Victorian Artists' Society's smokenights and the art students' Prehistoric Order of Cannibals had some Bohemian inspiration. No doubt too there were many personal affectations: the *Bulletin*'s Melbourne correspondent cruelly disposed of J. Howlett Ross: he "fancies himself as a poet ... pervades Melbourne in long poetic hair and a big slouched hat. He thinks he looks like Tennyson." The dining clubs for intellectual converse such as the still surviving Beef Steaks (founded 1886) and the Boobooks (1902, O'Dowd was a member) can hardly be described as more than fringe Bohemia. But what did Furphy, O'Dowd, Neilson and nearly all the writers of the nineties on our list, including all the women, have to do with Bohemia?[37]

1899 saw the foundation of the Australian Literature Society, but its second official meeting was delayed until 17 October 1900 when Rolf Boldrewood was president and H. J. C. Lingham, poet, actor and musician, was secretary. The society's objectives then were "the study of Australian Literature" and "the encouragement of Australian authors"; a committee was appointed to read, criticise and aid publication of works submitted, as the Society of Authors did in London. Subsequent changes of office-bearers and committee indicate dissension. In the early 1900s however, it seems to have been comparatively stable: O'Dowd, Mary Fullerton, O'Hara and Howlett Ross were leading members. But from 1904-05 the Literature Society of Melbourne, inspired by Walter Murdoch and Professor T. G. Tucker, briefly predominated.[38]

The *Bulletin* was the chief lifeline and indeed was the best literary club Melbourne had (not that the contributors ever seem to have arranged to meet as a group). It was, after all, a national paper. Moreover, as one writer remarked, it "treated its contributors like men; not like cattle";[39] it paid promptly and properly. At least ten important Victorian writers were contributing: G. G. McCrae (from the eighties), Hugh McCrae (from 1896); Dyson (his first offerings were in 1885); Mary Gaunt (1888 or 1889); Jephcott (1889); Bedford (1889 or 1890); Furphy (1889); O'Hara (early nineties); O'Dowd (1894); Shaw Neilson (1895). Mary Fullerton was excited by the journal from its first issue and, probably in the late nineties, met and was encouraged by Archibald. Florence Blair as "Cleo" (succeeding Ina Wildman) was writing the *Bulletin*'s women's column from 1896 to 1898. Of about 1450 stories in the *Bulletin* in the nineties, Astley contributed most, Dyson ran second, and New South Welshmen filled the next six places.[40] In a review in 1895 AGS mentioned six outstanding contributors of whom none was Victorian.[41] What Victorian writer of the nineties (Bedford and Astley apart) ever met or corresponded with Lawson, Paterson or Brennan? A few, however, including Furphy, O'Dowd and Neilson corresponded with AGS. Graeme Davison in his fine article, "Sydney and the Bush", argued that the *Bulletin*'s creative writers should primarily be seen as an "emerging urban intelligentsia" creating images of the Bush, but he rather overstated his case. Most of these Victorian contributors were not only from and educated in the Bush, but worked there or had worked there for long periods. And in claiming that Banjo Paterson was "the one important figure with even fair 'bush' credentials", he overlooked Furphy and Neilson.[42]

Nothing like a literary coterie in a club or around a Melbourne newspaper or periodical can be discerned. Who knew whom, who discussed the craft with a fellow writer or showed each other their drafts? The evidence is thin. The Ishmael Club, centreing on Bedford, Dyson (they saw each other constantly) and the Lindsays, has some minor importance. Bedford, as editor then of the *Clarion*, possibly had a wider acquaintance with writers than anyone else. Dyson seems not to have had many close associations with other journalists. As a hard-up family man in precarious health, O'Dowd was not attracted to Bohemianism. But in his lecturing and tutoring capacity he moved freely among diverse cultural groups, knew Sutherland, Strong and others, and already had a greater general intellectual influence than any other writer. One great friend of his from 1889 was Jephcott; they often discussed the writing of poetry, Jephcott addressed him by letter as "Dear Old Man".[43] Jephcott also knew Francis Adams well, Boldrewood and several writers based in Sydney including T. C. Heney. Gay's visitors to his Bendigo bedside included Alfred Deakin, O'Hara, Sutherland and Professor Morris. Ada Cambridge's literary admirers included Turner, Neild, Smith and Deakin: she was a friend of Jennings Carmichael, and later knew Boldrewood and those associated in the Women Writers' Club. Turner, G. G. McCrae and Sutherland were closely associated. Furphy visited Melbourne roughly annually to attend Churches of Christ conferences and to read in the Public Library. But seemingly he met no writer until in 1901, after an introduction from AGS, he called on Dyson: "I have met few men who stand so high in my esteem". He may never have met O'Dowd of whom he wrote: "He is an ideal democrat — able and scholarly, strong and sympathetic, temperate and uncompromising, absolutely without fear and without reproach".[44] Other friendships and associations may be discovered, but overall it is clear that fairly few contacts were made.

In 1898 Gyles Turner and Sutherland published their *Development of Australian Literature*. This careful and sensible "attempt to define the growth and present position of Australian Literature" set a canon on which there was probably wide agreement. In A. D. Hope's opinion, their "standards were academic and comparatively severe". And they bluntly raised one aspect of the nineties: "less frequently do we ask what other people have to say about

Australian literature; we are growing more and more concerned to know what it is that Australian literature has to say to ourselves".[45] Gordon, Clarke and Kendall were the only writers treated at length. For the rest, in Turner's "General Sketch" Ada Cambridge has 8 pages, Boldrewood 6, G. G. McCrae and Praed 4, "Tasma" 3, and Harpur, Michael, Heney, Essex Evans, Brunton Stephens, Paterson, Dyson, O'Hara, Gay, Carmichael, Gaunt and Ethel Turner a page or so; many more were mentioned. There is a worthy emphasis on contemporary writers. But Lawson is treated only as a poet and the *Bulletin* mentioned only in passing as a "nursing mother". In a lecture in 1904 Turner deplored the *Bulletin* school as "sordid", however skilled. Lawson, A. H. Davis and Miles Franklin stressed "ugliness" and the "seamy side" of Australian life: "There may be money in it, or there may be notoriety, but there is neither credit nor fame to be earned by devoting considerable literary ability to catering for the amusement of a class of readers that gloats on the kind of life presented in Rabelais, Balzac or Eugene Sue."[46] AGS attacked Turner and Sutherland's book for "critical slovenliness" and, understandably, for neglect of *Bulletin* writers. Ken Stewart places this in a context of Archibald's and Stephens': "attempt to wrest cultural hegemony from a literary establishment based mainly in Melbourne", in line with their "strong and satirical rejection of intellectual decadence and ostentation".[47]

After reading *While the Billy Boils* the rising statesman Alfred Deakin noted on 7 November 1896: "An indigenous literature is at last beginning ... in all the elements of true power, veracity and grim emotion Lawson is superior [to Paterson] ... He speaks for the workman, the tramp, the shearer — the true bushman — the inner Australian beyond civic or imported influences — the most Australian Australia ... There is a greater wealth of insight, of truth of detail and truth of spirit in this volume ... than in the whole of the alleged Australian literature which has preceded it ... He is a true Australian through and through."[48] So someone in Melbourne recognised what was going on.

While Deakin could not be a financial patron, he was a constructive critic and a true friend who would often afford much time and effort to aid writers. Remember he was the most admired public man of the day, still in his thirties. Stephen Mannington Caffyn, called home urgently to London in 1892, wrote to him: "I have the most vivid memory of the happy and helpful evenings I spent with you, had it been my priviledge [sic] to have met you earlier in my colonial career I can but think that my life would have been moulded on a better basis." Deakin wrote at length to Sutherland about his volume of poems and again in 1898 about *Origin and Growth of the Moral Instinct*. Lacking local readers, Sutherland was greatly moved by Deakin's "extreme warm-heartedness". In 1894 Jephcott sent Deakin a copy of *Secrets of the South*, and received a long, friendly, critical reply. An extended correspondence followed: Deakin sent a copy of Matthew Arnold's poems, Jephcott sent his photograph, Deakin took Jephcott home when he visited Melbourne and arranged for him to lecture in the cause of Federation. (Years later Jephcott developed an ambition for a political career as a Deakinite and offered to take Alfred on an extended riding-tour of the Monaro, among other things to view Bombala and Dalgety as possible capital-sites — not quite Deakin's thing!) In the last two years of Gay's life Deakin corresponded warmly and, as best he could, helped him to gain publicity for the writings by which Gay was bravely attempting to support himself.[49] Deakin chaired Jennings Carmichael's 1895 lecture on "The Spirit of the Bush", and was later president of the Australian Literature Society. He encouraged Katharine Prichard, a family friend, in her writing ambitions. In 1905 he put up a fiery defence of Australian writers at a meeting of the Trinity College Dialectic Society. "Ada Cambridge's work would compare with much of the best in England and America". "Our bushmen, with their swags, may at first look strange, or even uncouth, as they climb towards the lofty Olympians, but we have every faith that at last, and by their own paths, they will arrive".[50] Lord, send us another Deakin or Whitlam!

The daily newspapers were of minor literary importance. They usually ran an imported serial (unpredictably an occasional Australian one) on Saturday; book-reviews were almost unknown. The weeklies, the *Australasian, Leader* and *Weekly Times* (subsidiaries of the *Argus, Age* and *Herald*), like the *Sydney Mail* and *Town and Country Journal*, were another matter. They catered mainly for rural residents, many of whom did not take a daily paper; indeed, one of the weeklies was often their only reading. In 1889 the eminent philosopher Josiah Royce, Deakin's friend, had remarked that "None of our [American] weeklies can rival these in encyclopaedic character, in well-edited, many sided variety of appeal, joined ... with excellence of workmanship".[51] They were the most important and best paying local outlets for writers (other than the *Bulletin*).

Over the years Boldrewood had several and Ada Cambridge nine novels serialised in the *Australasian*, some of which, like "Dinah", were never published as books. (In her autobiography, however, Cambridge singled out the *Leader* for special praise.)[52] In the mid-nineties the *Australasian's* serials were usually English, but most of their short stories were Australian; Ethel Turner and J. A. Barry of New South Wales contributed often and Carmichael occasionally, but Carmichael and Marion Miller were by far the most frequently accepted poets — Essex Evans of Queensland, Sutherland and John Shaw Neilson appeared occasionally. The editor from 1885 to 1903 was David Watterston. Carmichael, Knowles, Alice Henry and Mary Gaunt all acknowledged his kind guidance (though Gaunt recalled that "he always managed to keep me in a chastened condition"). According to Knowles, "Not content with merely accepting or declining submitted M.S.S. in verse or prose, he invariably wrote a few lines to the author, pointing out weaknesses or defects that could be remedied by the exercise of patient 'polishing'".[53] Conventionally decorous and middlebrow or worse in his tastes, Watterston catered for a different public from the *Bulletin's*.

Throughout the nineties Melbourne lacked any leading periodical which might provide a critical literary forum and focus for serious writers. The depression, far more acute than in the other colonies, wiped out most of any potential market. (Moreover, Melbourne, until well into the twentieth century, could not provide any equivalent to the *Bookfellow, Lone Hand* or *Triad*, let alone the *Bulletin* — one aspect of Sydney's dominance as literary centre.) Turner's hopes of reviving the *Melbourne Review* came to nothing. No quarterly had survived and no newcomer managed more than one or two issues.

What monthlies there were varied greatly in approach and usually had a short life; hardly any were primarily literary in emphasis.

Centennial Magazine (1888-90, one shilling, a joint Sydney-Melbourne venture, presumably paid contributors) died in September 1890, allegedly from poor business management and lax editing. This journal was wide ranging, attempted to combine the intellectual and the popular, serialised Boldrewood especially, and included much interesting matter. Victorian contributors included Blair, G. G. McCrae, James Smith, Baldwin Spencer, Sutherland; and the artists Conder, Roberts and Streeton.

Australasian Critic (October 1890-September 1891, sixpence, presumably non-paying, little fiction or verse) was a product of the recently arrived professors, Spencer and Tucker. Its main sections were "Literature" (controlled by Professor E. E. Morris), "Science" (a strong emphasis) and "Music, Art and Drama". H. M. Green praises it highly: short articles, "extraordinarily modern-looking review ... serious without being solemn ... academicism at somewhere near its best ... almost too good to be true".[54] But Morris was not much in sympathy with current literary trends.[55]

Austral Light (1892-1920, formerly *Catholic Magazine*, sixpence, editor uncertain but Benjamin Hoare prominent, presumably non-paying) is a hitherto unrecognised important journal of the nineties at least, a Church-sponsored cultural journal including stories and verse by Knowles, O'Hara, Dunderdale and Howlett Ross. It reviewed Lawson and Paterson enthusiastically and contained much on Gordon and Kendall.

Australian Journal (1865-1962, sixpence, publisher A. H. Massina & Co., edited by William Mitchell 1878-1909) had declined to little more than light reading by the nineties and, although it occasionally included local serials and stories, was largely written by staff-members.[56]

Review of Reviews for Australasia (1892-1934, 1914-31 *Stead's Review of Reviews*, sixpence-ninepence, paid contributors) was essentially W. T. Stead's English paper with a local supplement edited by Fitchett 1892-1903. The first number sold 15,000 copies. There was little fiction or verse but many reviews. Green brushes it off, perhaps unjustly: "brightly written and contained nothing that might trouble the reader to think".[57]

Clarion (January 1897-1909, shilling-sixpence, owned and edited by Bedford, offered "liberal rates of payment"), a *Bulletin*-type publication, included a large component of stories and verse by Dyson, Neilson, McCrae and others. It seems to have made little contemporary or historical impact, but needs investigation.[58]

Book Lover: a Literary Review (1899-1921, owned, edited and largely written by H. H. Champion, penny-twopence, initially mainly news and information about books and authors though it included some verse) eventually developed to resemble the *Bookfellow* but lacked its quality. (From the late nineties the Book Lovers' Library and bookshop, conducted by Champion's wife Elsie, became a great Melbourne institution.)[59]

An annual, the *Antipodean*, published in Melbourne by George Robertson, but edited from afar by Essex Evans, Paterson and J. T. Ryan, appeared in 1892, 1894 and 1897. They were good popular medleys to which Dyson, O'Hara, Carmichael and Lillian Blair contributed.

Two dozen or more weekly papers started out in high hopes during the nineties. Nearly all collapsed after a few weeks — so many ambitious editors and publishers unheard of by posterity. Two are worth some notice.

Bull-Ant (March 1890-March 1891, *Ant* April 1891-June 1892, owned by Dyson, Tom Durkin and J. H. and C. Smith

with Dyson as editor, penny-threepence) set out as a
version of the *Bulletin* but was not as funny, on the whole a
pale copy. It had many small pars, aimed to attract
readers' contributions, had a humorous football column and
striking cartoons by Durkin. Its politics were close to the
Bulletin's but explicitly pro-Labor. Dyson wrote much of it.
The first issue sold 9,700 copies and it continued to do well
until it lost one hundred Pounds in a libel action brought by
a policeman. It included stories and verse and produced a
Christmas issue of stories. What did they pay? But for the
terrible times, they would probably have established a
lasting, successful journal.

Tatler: Art, Literature, Music and the Drama (August
1897 — September 1898, twopence-threepence, published by
Robertson, edited by E. A. Vidler) contained verse and
literary criticism but was stronger on art, overall dull.

Bohemia, The Bohemian (1890-92) was no more than a
frolic by conservative young *Argus* journalists. *Free Lance*
(1896) was promising but lasted only six months, and the
Lindsay brothers' *Rambler* eleven weeks in 1899. *Punch*
(1855-1925) and *Table Talk* (1885-1939) had considerable
merits but little interest in literature. However, the chatty
Table Talk perhaps conveyed more of a sense of the
community of artists as a whole than any other paper.

An extraordinary variety of journals had some
subsidiary literary content, sometimes including stories and
verse: *Advance Australia* (1897-1920), the ANA's journal
edited in 1897-99 by Fred Davison; the Catholic *Advocate*;
Australian Cycling News (1883-1901, 1900-01 as the
promising journal *Outpost*); the Henry Georgeist *Beacon*
(1893-1900); *The Champion* (1895-97, edited by H. H.
Champion); the Spiritualist *Harbinger of Light* (1870-
1956); the extraordinary one-man (H. Palmer) irregular,
sceptical *Imperial Review* (1879-1915, 58 issues); the Labor
Tocsin (1897-1906); and the *Australian Herald* (Australian
Church). There is research to be done here. How many of
these could pay anything? And whereas Melbourne had
two women's journals in the eighties (preceding *Dawn*), in
the nineties there were none.

When the *Ant* died, the *Bulletin* remarked that it was a good little paper which "died of cheap imported literature";[60] moulds were often imported from London. Dyson constantly railed against the imported penny English papers and pleaded for protection; a halfpenny tax imposed in May 1892 on all imported newspapers was too late to save the *Ant*. According to the *Bulletin*, "There is no 'space' for Australian writers in the journals. Stolen clippings fill the columns, or when the literary matter is not filched, unpaid for, it is bought at second hand, or on starving terms from literary sweaters in England."[61] Australian editors habitually lifted and rewrote each other's copy. Victorian postal rates on periodicals and newspapers were substantial, while New South Wales allowed free postage and rates from London were low. *Table Talk* in 1889 had unavailingly campaigned for free postage, claiming (probably correctly) that the *Centennial Magazine* was originally intended to be published in Melbourne, and that (unbelievably) "The *Bulletin* would also have been published in Melbourne, where nearly all the contributors reside"! In 1892 *Table Talk* claimed that the popular market was flooded by about forty British and American penny weeklies, as well as pictorial comics, imported in bulk, against which local publishers and printers could not compete.[62] After a short-lived Reporters' Association in 1889-90, the Australasian Institute of Journalists, founded in 1892, was also soon crushed. The Caxton Fund, established twenty years earlier, had been dormant but from 1893 "administered small grants efficiently" to writers in distress.[63]

If ever there was a sweated trade it was journalism and writing in general.

George Robertson (1825-98) of Melbourne, the chief Australian publisher, had produced the major works of Clarke, Gordon and Kendall.[64] In his old age, in semi-retirement in the depressed nineties, his publishing programme contracted. Nevertheless, the firm produced about thirty works of fiction, including four of Astley's five books, Dyson's *Below and on Top*, Montgomery's two books, novels by the Quinn brothers, Mouat's *Rise of the*

Australian Wool Kings, and in poetry one of Essex Evans'
more important volumes. Robertson's output far outstripped
that of Melville, Mullen (& Slade). Edgerton & Moore, E.
A. Petherick and E. W. Cole produced occasional volumes.
Melbourne was still publishing more titles than Sydney in
the nineties. Of those then producing books, Astley, Dyson,
Gay and the prolific Knowles then and later invariably
published in Melbourne or elsewhere in Australia.

But London dominated, publishing in the nineties about
three-quarters of Australian fiction (although only a small
proportion of Australian verse). Boldrewood in the nineties
published there 12 books with Macmillan; Ada Cambridge,
who used an agent, 9 (mainly with Heinemann and Ward
Lock — overall she used 9 London publishers!) of which 3
had Melbourne editions; Mary Gaunt 4 (1 with a Melbourne
edition). The Caffyns, Catherine Martin, Simpson
Newland and Ethel Turner also published there
exclusively for their fiction, George Dunderdale also for
his two important books, and the lightweight Campbell
McKellar (5 books). It was asserted that nine-tenths of the
copies of Donald Macdonald's *Gum Boughs and Wattle
Bloom*, published in England, sold there.[65] After the first
Melbourne edition of *Deeds that Won the Empire*, Fitchett
of course published in London. Of the few poets who
published volumes, O'Hara (3 books, 1 London, 1
Melbourne, 1 both), Jephcott and Carmichael also used
London. English books were cheaper than the colonial
product; on the other hand the plaint was often heard that
copies only trickled out to Australia with little or no
publicity or impact. The potential advantages were huge:
Boldrewood's reputation in Australia was made after the
great success of *Robbery under Arms* in England — similarly
with Cambridge after the success of *A Marked Man*. In 1901
Gyles Turner placed his two-volume *History of the Colony
of Victoria* (1904) with Longmans Green, but only one
thousand copies were printed and they sold poorly.[66]

Francis Adams remarked that in Australia "literary
society is the synonym for the company of journalists".[67]
(That the Victorian census classification of authors,
editors, writers and reporters between 1881 and 1891

quadrupled to 359 may be seen primarily as a growth of journalists.)[68] But Adams is largely misleading in that hardly any of the writers of the period were primarily journalists. Many of them became journalists only in the sense that, whether or not they were part-time amateur writers or freelances hoping to become professional writers, the press was far and away their best market. The freelance Dyson, by mixing popular journalism with popular stories and verse, became the only successful professional writer in the full sense. Ada Cambridge was almost so, mixing serious novels (and poetry) with others more overtly written for the market. She must often have earned about two hundred Pounds a year, sometimes more, chiefly from serials, as a supplement to her husband's meagre income as a clergyman. *The Age* paid her One Hundred and Ninety Seven Pounds for "A Black Sheep" (*A Marked Man*).[69] Next comes a group of essentially amateur, spare-time serious writers, not writing primarily for money or aiming to become professional but no doubt welcoming occasional extra income: Furphy, and the poets Carmichael, Jephcott, McCrae, Neilson, O'Dowd and O'Hara — although there is doubt about how often the newspapers ever paid for poems, which may be another point in the *Bulletin*'s favour. Marion Miller Knowles stands apart as a full-time teacher who made a modest income from her writings. Bedford was essentially a full-time journalist who by the way placed stories; Morrison became a famous journalist because of the famous book he wrote; Fitchett was a part-time journalist who made a killing from his books of journalism. Gaunt, more successsfully than Fullerton, aimed at becoming a professional writer via journalism. Sutherland and Gay, essentially serious writers, are broadly unclassifiable. Sutherland, the retired teacher, in the depression had to take up the higher journalism; Gay, on his deathbed, bravely continued to seek income from his writings of small market-appeal to reduce the demand on his friends.

Of all these writers only Furphy and possibly Cambridge were in a position to attempt a serious novel with little regard to financial betterment. (By the way, what *is* the best novel published in the nineties? One by Cambridge, none by Boldrewood, *An Australian Girl, Seven Little Australians, Paving the Way*? Perhaps *Notes & Furphies* might conduct a poll.) Novelists (other than Furphy) wrote for the serial market. Writing for immediate publication as a book was a forlorn hope economically, but if published as a book after publication as a serial so much the better. But who, anywhere in Australia in the nineties, other than Furphy and Cambridge, was capable of writing a first-rate novel?

Arthur Jose's well-known remarks in *The Romantic Nineties* need not be taken seriously. "I am convinced that the Melbourne of the Nineties was not romantic. Its literary circles were obsessed with respectability, the respectability which they believed fervently to be of the ruling English type, for which Ada Cambridge wrote her polite and soothing novels [!] ... The Melbourne of the Nineties — and of the next decade also — scoffed at our [Sydney] realism as 'Kipling and water', and stressed form and phraseology, and 'the maintenance of an artistic outlook'".[70] The trouble with Jose was that he saw too much of his friend E. E. Morris (whom he describes anonymously on p.39) and his associates; he could not have met Dyson, O'Dowd or the McCraes. (But we know so little — how did Dyson and O'Dowd regard Lawson and Paterson?) However, the prejudices of Turner and Sutherland provide a little basis for Jose's impression. His further remarks on the Melbourne refugees in Sydney carry little weight. Certainly the artists Roberts, Streeton and, later, the Lindsays transferred (for good reasons), but no important writer except Astley (recognising his market) and Hugh McCrae later. (And only Carmichael and Gaunt moved to England in this period.)

In terms of the quality of the literary contribution by Victorians in the nineties, Cantrell was probably not far astray in allowing them not much more than one-tenth of the space in his anthology.[71] AGS allowed them roughly the same in the *Bulletin Story Book* (1901). None of the Victorians was a bestseller remotely rivalling Lawson, Paterson, Ethel Turner or "Steele Rudd", except perhaps

Dyson. In intellectual content or profundity, however, Furphy and O'Dowd were rivalled or outstripped only by Brennan.

I have to conclude by admitting that the works of the Victorian writers of the nineties provide relatively little indication of national trends in literary development or signposts to the future. No writer remotely rivalled the heroic professional leadership of Tom Roberts in art and Marshall-Hall in music. The painters especially were tackling the "national" problem much more effectively and it was they who provided much of the glamour of the legendary nineties. Apart from the Caffyns, the young Lindsays and the McCraes, writers seem to have associated little with painters. And there was little literary reflection yet of the "Melbourne ethos", deriving especially from George Higinbotham through Deakin, H. B. Higgins and Charles Strong, which O'Dowd, the Palmers and Louis Esson were to develop in terms of literary nationalism. Nor had the Victorian writers of the nineties, despite an evident growth in numbers and despite the space afforded them by the *Australasian* and other journals (as well as the *Bulletin*), made any marked impact on the serious reading public or done much to create a supportive local audience. One important observation possibly to be made is the high importance of mechanics' institute libraries in the development of Furphy, Neilson, O'Dowd and others.

Nor does the evidence from Victorian writing add much illuminating to the legend of the nineties or to the nature of the *Bulletin* school. The left-wing, utopian-type writers like Furphy and O'Dowd had yet to make their full impact. The many Victorian contributors to the *Bulletin* (mainly poets) exemplified its breadth rather than its leading characteristics. They contributed relatively few yarns or rural stories; and who, other than Dyson, wrote ballads? Which of them can be said to have contributed to linking high culture with the folk or working class? Who among them notably celebrated the past (other than Dyson) and who conducted much in the way of investigation of the present? Until Mary Grant Bruce, who competed in children's literature with Ethel Turner, Louise Mack and Ethel Pedley? Who, other than Dyson and O'Dowd ambivalently, contributed to the tense assessments of the virtues and vices of city and country life? Overall, however, many of the Victorian writers contributed to the creation of national Federationist sentiment.

Qualitatively and quantitatively, the growth of writing in Victoria in the next thirty years was to be painfully slow.

Vision Splendid or Sandy Blight? The Paterson-Lawson Debate

Mark Horgan and Michael Sharkey

Two years before his death, A. B. 'Banjo' Paterson published an account of a literary debate with Henry Lawson which ran for some three months in 1892.[1] From Lawson's angle, the debate concerned literary realism in portraying city and bush experience. For Paterson, the debate concerned a defence of bush values against what he interpreted as Lawson's attack on the sterling characters who put their mark on a landscape which held, at times, undoubted attractions for the pioneer.

The debate was not a simple matter of presenting opposing stereotypes. Each participant saw the bush as an important source of artistic inspiration, and each had sufficient experience of city and bush life to avoid the simplicities. Paterson's view served to consolidate the romancing of the bush experience, and Lawson's point that portraying life with all its difficulties was no treason to nation or art seems to have been largely lost upon Paterson and a host of writers and readers of the *Bulletin* who joined the fracas. For many, the debate was amusing; for J. F. Archibald, editor of the paper, it was no doubt profitable; but the goose which laid the golden egg was preserved by his pacing of contributions, and by the control which he and his sub-editor A. G. Stephens exercised over the progress of the argument in the years following.

In Paterson's response to Lawson's descriptions of country life there is a good deal of genial mockery by the countryman of the effete city-dweller. Both participants were resident in Sydney for the course of the exchange, though they incidentally represented different castes of society, and their literary dealings with each other made capital of class antagonisms.

By 1892 the *Bulletin* was a paper distinguished by its trenchant editorial espousal of white republicanism, naval and military self-reliance, organised labour, anti-imperialism and protectionist federalism. Through the late 1880s, the paper had responded to the great strikes and depression of the era with denunciations of social ills; it had weathered editorial and financial crises of its own, and William MacLeod's managerial skills, as much as Archibald's literary acumen, were essential elements of its survival and success. Sylvia Lawson has suggested that "the paper's major sixteen years was an acutely contradictory projection, at once provoked by capitalism, empowered and circumscribed by it".[2] The paper's dynamic capacities from 1892 were enhanced by its ability to engage its readers in its activities: on 5 March 1892, Archibald directly invited readers to contribute material. Claiming "Every man can write at least one book", Archibald offered payment for short stories, or ballads "especially on bush, mining, sporting, social, or dramatic themes". Archibald's most memorable advice to intending authors was to "boil it down". The paper which had effectively taken the city to the bush was seeking to enfranchise all its subscribers, and thus astutely prosecute its own ends.

Lawson and Paterson were not unknown names when their debate commenced; nor were they particularly bright stars at the time. The *Bulletin*'s strength lay in its eloquent defiance of oppressions at every level in political and business administration, besides its growing literary excellences. In its social campaigns it could at times count such worthies as Henry Parkes, Cardinal Moran, Rabbi Davis and William Bede Dalley among its unlikely allies. Among its black-and-white artists, Phil May and Livingston Hopkins ("Hop") were star assets. Their work ranged over a host of local and largely metropolitan issues. Victor Daley, John Farrell, Edward Dyson, Louise Mack, Dowell O'Reilly and Ethel Turner were regular contributors by the time Lawson first appeared in the paper in October 1887 ("A Song of the Republic"). Lawson's first story, "His Father's Mate", appeared in the paper in December 1888. Paterson's first verse was published in the paper in 1885 ("El Mahdi to the Australian Troops"); his prose in 1889. Ed Dyson's realistic prose sketches and tales generated sufficient following for the *Bulletin* to name its first book publication — an anthology of *Bulletin* stories and verse — *The Golden Shanty* in 1890, after one of Dyson's most successful yarns. At a later stage in the Lawson-Paterson debate, Dyson held out for a reconciliation on the grounds that both parties were simultaneously right and wrong.

There had been many picturesque descriptions of life in the bush, and of the allure of a life on the land, in Australian verse before Lawson and Paterson took each other to task. For early colonial poets, the bush might serve as an anodyne against the woes of the city: it might represent a chance to make a fresh start; or it might prove a place of heartbreaking exile and sudden death. Pioneering virtues — struggle, enterprise, healthy virility and so on — surfaced in Australian verse from Charles Tompson's time, though *Bulletin* versifiers rang the changes on the theme of country pleasures in ways that departed at times from conventional usage. John Farrell's Australian landscape is no potential Eden, nor a theatre of regular horrors, but a droll sort of Cockayne where the tall story is of a piece with macabre "natural"' features. By 1892, the vein of bleak humour in much of the *Bulletin*'s black-and-white work, and in its complement of topical verse and prose might be expected to indicate a stronger leaning toward realism than to the nostalgias for a golden age. The "bush", and "real" Australia, as location for beauty and the virtues, was among other things a useful construct for a largely urbanised population which was unable by the 1890s to entirely ignore the signs of weakness and woe within its immediate surroundings. Despite the palliatives — Bernhardt at the theatre, the vaudeville, sports and picnics, or the Paris end of Collins Street and the Botanical Gardens, escape might be imagined through a larger vista — the painted backdrop to a bushranger melodrama, or the "vision splendid of the sunlit plains extended" in Paterson's "Clancy of the Overflow".

According to Paterson's recollection,

> One day he [Lawson] suggested that we should write against each other ... "We ought to do pretty well out of it", he said. "We ought to be able to get in three or four sets of verses each before they stop us". This suited me all right for we were working on space and the pay was very small in fact I remember getting thirteen and sixpence for writing "Clancy of the Overflow"[3]

Lawson opened proceedings with the poem "Borderland" (later titled "Up the Country") on 9 July 1892:

> I am back from up the country — very sorry that I went —
> Seeking for the Southern poets' land whereon to pitch my tent;
> I have lost a lot of idols, which were broken on the track —
> Burnt a lot of fancy verses, and I'm glad that I am back.
> Further out may be the pleasant scenes of which our poets boast,
> But I think the country's rather more inviting round the coast —
> Anyway, I'll stay at present at a boarding-house in town
> Drinking beer and lemon-squashes, taking baths and cooling down.
>
> Sunny plains! Great Scot! — those burning wastes of barren soil and sand
> With their everlasting fences stretching out across the land!
> Desolation where the crow is! Desert! where the eagle flies,
> Paddocks where the luny bullock starts and stares with redden'd eyes;
> Where, — in clouds of dust enveloped, roasted bullock-drivers creep
> Slowly past the sun-dried shepherd dragged behind his crawling sheep.
> Stunted "peak" of granite gleaming, glaring! like a molten mass
> Turned, from some infernal furnace, on a plain devoid of grass.
>
> Miles and miles of thirsty gutters — strings of muddy waterholes
> In the place of "shining rivers" (walled by cliffs and forest boles).
> "Range!" of ridges, gullies, ridges, barren! where the madden'd flies
> Fiercer than the plagues of Egypt — swarm about your blighted eyes!
> Bush! where there is no horizon! where the buried bushman sees
> Nothing. Nothing! but the madding sameness of the stunted trees!
> Lonely hut where drought's eternal — suffocating atmosphere —

Where the God forgotten hatter dreams of city-life and beer.

Treacherous tracks that trap the stranger, endless roads that
    gleam and glare,
Dark and evil-looking gullies — hiding secrets here and there!
Dull, dumb flats and stony "rises" where the bullocks sweat and
    bake,
And the sinister "gohanna", and the lizard, and the snake.
Land of day and night — no morning freshness, and no
    afternoon,
For the great, white sun in rising brings with him the heat of
    noon.
Dismal country for the exile, when the shades begin to fall
From the sad, heart-breaking sunset, to the new-chum, worst of
    all.

Dreary land in rainy weather, with the endless clouds that drift
O'er the bushman like a blanket that the Lord will never lift —
Dismal land when it is raining — growl of floods and oh! the
    "woosh"
Of the rain and wind together on the dark bed of the bush —
Ghastly fires in lonely humpies where the granite rocks are pil'd
In the rain-swept wildernesses that are wildest of the wild.

Land where gaunt and haggard women live alone and work like
    men,
Till their husbands, gone a-droving, will return to them again —
Homes of men! if homes had ever such a God-forgotten place,
Where the wild selector's children fly before a stranger's face.
Home of tragedy applauded by the dingoes' dismal yell,
Heaven of the shanty-keeper — fitting fiend for such a hell —
And the wallaroos and wombats, and, of course, the "curlew's
    call" —
And the lone sundowner tramping over onward thro' it all!

I am back from up the country — up the country where I went
Seeking for the Southern poets' land whereon to pitch my tent'
I have left a lot of broken idols out along the track,
Burnt a lot of fancy verses — and I'm glad that I am back —
I believe the Southern poet's dream will not be realised
Till the plains are irrigated and the land is humanised.
I intend to stay at present — as I said before — in town
Drinking beer and lemon-squashes — taking baths and cooling
    down.

The poem drew on Lawson's memories of childhood at
Pipeclay near Mudgee, and Gulgong and his family's poor
life there. Lawson had also worked at Albany in Western
Australia (on the *Albany Observer* newspaper) in 1890, and
in Brisbane (for The *Boomerang* until the paper retrenched
him and others) in 1891. Lawson's country experience was
not negligible; it provided him with a digest of up-country

and provincial disappointments. His landscape is at odds with picturesque conventions, because he tells us he has found it so. Tracks are treacherous, the vista is monotonous, and the human and beastly inhabitants crazed and suffering through all seasons.

Lawson had not in fact made a lengthy inland journey. His travel was by coastal steamer or train (though his return from Brisbane to Sydney involved pedestrian travel) through the coastal fringe. For all the poem's exaggeration of seasonal extremes and dismal working conditions, Lawson had observed a great deal. His father's disillusionment with prospecting in worked-over diggings, his mother's dissatisfactions, his own abruptly-terminated positions with recent employers, and subsequent treks in search of work gave point to Paterson's remark that Lawson did his prospecting on foot. Paterson's viewpoint was rather that from the back of a horse, with the implied allegiance to caste which went with horse-ownership.

In the same issue of the *Bulletin*, Lawson published a parody, "Rise Ye! Rise Ye!", cast in the unaspirated vernacular of the populist orator — or demagogic bard. There is much about each poem to suggest that Lawson could be tongue-in-cheek about his own "principles". His principles were made memorable, however, by his facetious expression of them in the tilt at "Southern poets" and in the mock-heroic call for revolution.

In response to Lawson's catalogue of rural hardships, Paterson's "In Defence of the Bush", published on 23 July 1892, set the tone for future transactions. Lawson is directly addressed, and Paterson proceeded to enthuse again over the vision splendid:

ON READING HENRY LAWSON'S *"Borderland"*

So you're back from up the country, Mister Lawson, where you
   went,
And you're cursing all the business in a bitter discontent;
Well, we grieve to disappoint you, and it makes us sad to hear
That it wasn't cool and shady — and there wasn't plenty beer,
And the loony bullock snorted when you first came into view;
Well, you know, it's not so often that he sees a swell like you;
And the roads were hot and dusty, and the plains were burnt
   and brown,

And no doubt you're better suited drinking lemon-squash in town.

Yet, perchance, if you should journey down the very track you went
In a month or two at furthest you would wonder what it meant,
Where the sunbaked earth was gasping like a creature in its pain
You would find the grasses waving like a field of summer grain,
And the miles of thirsty gutters blocked with sand and choked with mud,
You would find them mighty rivers with a turbid, sweeping flood;
For the rain and drought and sunshine make no changes in the street,
In the sullen line of buildings and the ceaseless tramp of feet;
But the bush hath moods and changes, as the seasons rise and fall,
And the men who know the bush-land — they are loyal through it all.
. . . .
But you found the bush was dismal and a land of no delight,
Did you chance to hear a chorus in the shearers' huts at night?
Did they "rise up, William Riley," by the campfire's cheery blaze?
Did they rise him as we rose him in the good old droving days?
And the women of the homesteads and the men you chanced to meet —
Were their faces sour and saddened like your "faces in the street,"
And the "shy selector children" — were they better now or worse
Thank the city urchins mentioned who would greet you with a curse?
Is not such a life much better than the squalid street and square
Where the fallen women flaunt it in the fierce electric glare,
Where the sempstress plies her sewing till her eyes are sore and red
In a filthy, dirty attic toiling on for daily bread?
Did you hear no sweeter voices in the music of the bush
Than the roar of trams and 'busses and the war-whoop of "the push;"
Did the magpies rouse your slumbers with their carol sweet and strange?
Did you hear the silver chiming of the bell-birds on the range?
But, perchance, the wild birds' music by our senses was despised,
For you say you'll stay in townships till the bush is civilised.
Would you make it a tea-garden and on Sundays have a band
Where the "blokes" might take their "donahs" with a "public" close at hand?
You had better stick to Sydney and make merry with "the push,"
For the bush will never suit you, and you'll never suit the bush.

For Paterson, the bush offers variety and challenge; it is the school for masculine virtues not found in the city. His depiction of the miseries of city life — the lot of the urban proletariat (Lawson's "faces in the street", including young 'Arvie Aspinall of the prose sketches) — is almost gratuitous, a counter to Lawson's panorama of the rural workforce. Paterson does not advance any argument about appropriate language to describe the bush; he marks time. Lawson's own portrayals of city life had never tended to constitute a brochure of pleasures, but concentrated on the stultifying effects of industrial conditions. The Arvie Aspinall series of stories commenced in 1892 lent some support to Paterson's view that the city was for many a prison; but Lawson's procedure in the Arvie Aspinall stories might more pointedly have been criticised by Paterson for its bathetic elements. Lawson could also overdo the "atmosphere" when it suited his purpose.

Lawson and Paterson shared some redundant views of the city life, perhaps unsurprisingly in view of their work experiences and aspirations. Paterson's background was pastoral, and it provided him with "copy" for stories and verse. His parents had managed properties: their own station "Buckinbah" was sold during the economic bust of the late 1880s, and Paterson, who had been despatched to school at Sydney Grammar, commenced work in a solicitor's office, at an age when Lawson was to take to painting railway carriages for his living. Paterson mentally fled the city where he worked through his characterisations of up-country life (notably in the southern mountains of New South Wales). His interest in country matters was linked to the fortunes of his family — for which he took responsibility after the death of his father in 1889. In his 1889 pamphlet *Australia for the Australians*, Paterson advocated reform of land tenure and the tariff, and the commencement of irrigation works.[4] Conservative in bent, Paterson sought non-doctrinaire practical programmes to protect unlanded labourers and facilitate trade between the Colonies. Thus rural themes — in verse and prose tales, and in the polemic against Lawson — centred on a civilised life of self-containment and adventure which appeared impossible in the city environment. Where Lawson had early in his literary career projected a revolutionary resolution to grievances, Paterson held to a sense of duty to work within the structures of society — so much so that he cited care of his family and his polo horses in extenuation of postponement of his wedding.

The city was an ambivalent convenience for Lawson; it remained for him largely a cobblestoned bush. He did not avail himself of the diversions of the push, tea-gardens and other delights which Paterson suggested. In his next sally, "In Answer to Banjo and Otherwise" (6 August 1892), Lawson returned to his *raison d'etre* — the stripping away of blinkers on perception of conditions anywhere. Sentiment was a luxury, and while "drinking beer and lemon-squashes" might be preferable to contending with dismal country, Lawson was not deflected by Paterson into a defence of city ways; he kept to his first bugbear, "the over-written West":

> It was pleasant up the country, Mr. Banjo, where you went,
> For you sought the greener patches and you travelled like a
> gent.,
> And you curse the trams and 'busses and the turmoil and the
> "push,"
> Tho' you know the "squalid city" needn't keep you from the bush;
> But we lately heard you singing of the "plains where shade is
> not,
> And you mentioned it was dusty — "all is dry and all is hot."
> True, the bush "hath moods and changes," and the bush-man hath
> 'em, too —
> For he's not a poet's dummy —he's a man, the same as you;
> But his back is growing rounder — slaving for the "absentee" —
> And his toiling wife is thinner than a country wife should be,
> For we noticed that the faces of the folks we chanced to meet
> Should have made a greater contrast to the faces in the street;
> And, in short, we think the bushman's being driven to the wall,
> But it's doubtful if his spirit will be "*loyal* thro' it all."
> Tho' the bush has been romantic and it's nice to sing about,
> There's a lot of patriotism that the land could do without —
> Sort of BRITISH WORKMAN nonsense that shall perish in the
> scorn
> Of the drover who is driven and the shearer who is shorn —
> Of the struggling western farmers who have little time for rest,
> And are ruin'd on selections in the squatter-ridden west —
> Droving songs are very pretty, but they merit little thanks
> From the people of a country which is ridden by the Banks.
> And the "rise and fall of seasons" suits the rise and fall of rhyme,

But we know that western seasons do not run on "schedule
    time;"
For the drought will go on drying while there's anything to dry,
Then it rains until you'd fancy it would bleach the "sunny sky"
—

Then it pelters out of reason, for the downpour day and night
Nearly sweeps the population to the Great Australian Bight,
It is up in Northern Queensland that the "seasons" do their best,
But its doubtful if you ever saw a season in the west,
There are years without an autumn or a winter or a spring,
There are broiling Junes — and summers when it rains like
    anything.
In the bush my ears were opened to the singing of the bird,
But the "carol of the magpie" was a thing I never heard.
Once the beggar roused my slumbers in a shanty, it is true,
But I only heard him asking, "Who the blanky blank are you?"
And the bell-bird in the ranges — but his "silver chime" is harsh
When it's heard beside the solo of the curlew in the marsh.
Yes, I heard the shearers singing "William Riley" out of tune
(Saw 'em fighting round a shanty on a Sunday afternoon),
But the bushman isn't always "trapping brumbies in the night,"
Nor is he for ever riding when "the morn is fresh and bright,"
And he isn't always singing in the humpies on the run —
And the camp-fire's "cheery blazes" are a trifle overdone;
We have grumbled with the bushmen round the fire on rainy
    days,
When the smoke would blind a bullock and there wasn't any
    blaze,
Save the blazes of our language, for we cursed the fire in turn
Till the atmosphere was heated and the wood began to burn.
Then we had to wring our blueys which were rotting in the
    swags,
And we saw the sugar leaking thro' the bottoms of the bags,
And we couldn't raise a "chorus," for the toothache and the
    cramp,
While we spent the hours of darkness draining puddles round
    the camp.
Would you like to change with Clancy — go a-droving? tell us
    true,
For we rather think that Clancy would be glad to change with
    you,
And be something in the city; but 'twould give your muse a shock
To be losing time and money thro' the foot-rot in the flock,
And you wouldn't mind the beauties underneath the starry dome
If you had a wife and children and a lot of bills at home.
Did you ever guard the cattle when the night was inky-black,
And it rained, and icy water trickled gently down your back
Till your saddle-weary backbone fell a-aching to the roots
And you almost felt the croaking of the bull-frog in your boots
—

Sit and shiver in the saddle, curse the restless stock and cough
Till a squatter's irate dummy cantered up to warn you off?
Did you fight the drought and "pleuro" when the "seasons" were
    asleep —

Falling she-oaks all the morning for a flock of starving sheep;
Drinking mud instead of water — climbing trees and lopping
    boughs
For the broken-hearted bullocks and the dry and dusty cows?
Do you think the bush was better in the "good old droving days,"
When the squatter ruled supremely as the king of western ways,
When you got a slip of paper for the little you could earn,
But were forced to take provisions from the station in return —
When you couldn't keep a chicken at your humpy on the run,
For the squatter wouldn't let you — and your work was never
    done:
When you had to leave the missus in a lonely hut forlorn
While you "rose up Willy Riley," in the days ere you were born?
Ah we read about the drovers and the shearers and the like
Till we wonder why such happy and romantic fellows "strike."
Don't you fancy that the poets better give the bush a rest
Ere they raise a just rebellion in the over-written West?
Where the simple-minded bushman gets a meal and bed and rum
Just by riding round reporting phantom flocks that never come;
Where the scalper — never troubled by the "war-whoop of the
    push" —
Has a quiet little billet — breeding rabbits in the bush;
Where the labour-agitator — when the shearers rise in might
Makes his money sacrificing all his substance for the right;
Where the squatter makes his fortune, and the seasons "rise" and
    "fall,"
And the poor and honest bushman has to suffer for it all.
Where the drovers and the shearers and the bushmen and the
    rest
Never reach the Eldorado of the poets of the West.
And you think the bush is purer and that life is better there,
But it doesn't seem to pay you like the "squalid street and
    square,"
Pray inform us, "Mr. Banjo," where you read, in prose or verse,
Of the awful "city urchin" who would greet you with a curse.
There are golden hearts in gutters, tho' their owners lack the fat,
And we'll back a teamster's offspring to outswear a city brat;
Do you think we're never jolly where the trams and 'busses
    rage?
Did you hear the "gods" in chorus when "Ri-tooral" held the
    stage?
Did you catch a ring of sorrow in the city urchin's voice
When he yelled for "Billy Elton," when he thumped the floor for
    Royce?
Do the bushmen, down on pleasure, miss the everlasting stars
When they drink and flirt and so on in the glow of private bars?
What care you if fallen woman "flaunt?" God help 'em — let 'em
    flaunt,
And the seamstress seems to haunt you — to what purpose does
    she haunt?
You've a down on "trams and busses," or the "roar" of 'em, you
    said,
And the "filthy, dirty attic," where you never toiled for bread.

(And about that self-same attic, tell us, Banjo, where you've
  been?
For the struggling needlewoman mostly keeps her attic clean.)
But you'll find it very jolly with the cuff-and-collar push,
And the city seems to suit you, while you rave about the bush.
                                              HENRY LAWSON
      P.S. —
You'll admit that "up-the-country," more especially in drought,
Isn't quite the Eldorado that the poets rave about,
Yet at times we long to gallop where the reckless bushman rides
In the wake of startled brumbies that are flying for their hides;
Long to feel the saddle tremble once again between our knees
And to hear the stockwhips rattle just like rifles in the trees!
Long to feel the bridle-leather tugging strongly in the hand
And to feel once more a little like a "native of the land."
And the ring of bitter feeling in the jingling of our rhymes
Isn't suited to the country nor the spirit of the times.
Let us go together droving and returning, if we live,
Try to understand each other while we liquor up the "div."
                                                      H. L.

Lawson adheres to his point outlined in the opening verses
of "Borderland", concerning "broken idols" and "fancy
verses"; and Paterson's suggestion concerning seasonal
changes is tossed out of court. Paterson's selection of detail
— and his implied rejection of such images as Lawson
proposes to him — is crucial, since Lawson will continue to
hold that bush-poets evade the truth and offer romance in
place of the real thing. Lawson's "Answer" debunks the
golden age portrayed in Paterson's version of "greener
patches". As Paterson had made the debate personal with
references to Lawson's previous works and his fondness for
cool city oases, Lawson now tilts at Paterson's gentility and
his occupation, with the gibe "you know the 'squalid city'
needn't keep you from the bush".

Lawson shrewdly observes that the true bushman is not
a piece of literary furniture, but a working man with a
wife, and his loyalty may not be relied on if he
comprehends avenues of redress for his problems.
Patriotism associated with "the sort of BRITISH
WORKMAN nonsense" will not endure the long-term
political struggle of pastoral operatives. If the West has
formerly been romantic, it is now care-laden; droving songs
will not cheer Bank-ridden and squatter-ridden
mortgagees. In keeping with the exaggerations authorised
by a literary game, and at the same time associating a

multitude of literary misconceptions under one head, Lawson adds the seasonal and natural phenomena to the list of economic handicaps dogging the rural dweller. The shanty-keeper and the labour-organiser ("agitator" is the surprising epithet) might be expected to provide their peculiar brands of solace, but they join with the plagues of herd and flock, and the insufferable misrepresentation of the circumstances by romancing poets, to push the bushman's thoughts towards rebellion. The poets' Eldorado is a chimera. Although Lawson had once observed that urban relief might be obtained by shifting "some of the surplus suburbs of Sydney up country a few hundred miles",[5] such a utopian panacea could no longer be endorsed. Lawson had jettisoned his zeal for revolutionary propaganda after *The Republican* newspaper, which he nominally managed, went into a new phase in 1888; his political effusions were sporadic, and at times "duty" pieces only. An instance of the latter is the wooden incantation "Waiting for the Leader" published in the *Bulletin* on 24 December 1892. Loaded with archaisms and abstractions ("The millions scourged by Mammon's whips"; "They prate to us of lawful means"), the rhetoric is sustained for nine tedious stanzas, culminating in the proposal that revolution only *seems* to devastate, but in fact it purifies. Lawson's non-revolutionary vocabulary was effectively more memorable: dwelling upon tangibles and avoiding imponderables he replaced one set of commonplaces used to describe the bush with a more existential terminology which reflected the physical and conceptual effort of the pioneering Europeans.

In his Post-script to his Answer to Paterson, Lawson sought to abate his parting taunts by offering his rival a truce. Lawson allows that the bush, while not constituting an Eldorado, nevertheless offers the chance to feel "once more a little like a native of the land". Adverting, perhaps, to the initial proposal, Lawson suggests they may try to understand each other while they "liquor up the 'div'". Lawson's plain sympathies were for a bond of understanding between bush and city workers; each side's ignorance of the circumstances of the other prolonged the fruitless dichotomy.[6] Thus Lawson attempted to put

Paterson right concerning the "filthy dirty attic" in which Paterson claimed the seamstress of his verse lived: "the struggling needlewoman", Lawson observes, "mostly keeps her attic clean".

Paterson concluded his part in the debate with the poem "In Defence of the Bush (In Answer to Various Bards)". The poem was published on 1 October 1892, and by this stage several writers had joined the fray. Ed Dyson had inveighed (in "The Fact of the Matter", 30 July 1892) against bush-struck town-dwellers who speak out of ignorance; his poem is a remorseless recitation of commonplace bush vexations:

> I'm wonderin' why those fellers who go buildin' chipper ditties,
> 'Bout the rosy times out drovin', an' the dust an' death of cities,
> Don't sling the bloomin' office, strike some drover for a billet,
> And soak up all the glory that comes handy while they fill it.
>
> P'r'aps it's fun to travel cattle or to picnic with merinos,
> But the drover don't catch on, sir, not much high-class rapture he knows.
> As for sleepin' on the plains there in the shadder of the spear-grass,
> That's liked best by the Juggins with a spring-bed an' a pier-glass.
>
> An' the camp fire, an;' the freedom, and the blanky constellations,
> The 'possum-rug an' billy, an' the togs an' stale ole rations —
> It's strange they're only raved about by coves that dress up pretty,
> An' sport a wife, an' live on slap-up tucker in the city.
> I've tickled beef in my time clear from Burke to Riverina,
> An' shifted sheep all round the shop, but blow me if I've seen a
> Single blanky hand who didn't buck at pleasures of this kidney,
> And wouldn't trade his blisses for a flutter down in Sydney.
>
> Night-watches are delightful when the stars are really splendid
> To the chap who's fresh upon the job, but, you bet, his rapture's ended
> When the rain comes down in sluice-heads, or the cuttin' hailstones pelter,
> An' the sheep drift off before the wind, an' the horses strike for shelter.
>
> Don't take me for a howler, but I find it come annoying'
> To hear those fellers rave about the pleasures we're enjoyin',
> When p'r'aps we've nothin' better than some fluky water handy,
> An' they're right on all the lickers —rum, an' plenty beer an' brandy.
>
> The town is dusty, may be, but it isn't worth the curses

'Side the dust a feller swallers an' the blinded thirst he nurses
When he's on the hard macadam, where the jumbucks cannot
    browse, an'
The wind is in his whiskers, an' he follers twenty thousan'

This drovin' on the plain, too it's all O.K. when the weather
Isn't hot enough to curl the soles right off your upper leather,
Or so cold that when the mornin' wind comes hissin' through the
    grasses
You can cut your eyelids like a whip-lash as it passes.

Then there's bull-ants in the blankets, an' a lame horse, an'
    muskeeters,
An' a D. T. boss like Halligan, or one like Humpy Peters,
Who is mean about the tucker, an' can curse from start to
    sundown,
An' can fight like fifty devils, an' whose growler's never run
    down.

Yes, I wonder why the fellers what go buildin' chipper ditties
'Bout the rosy times out drovin' an' th' dust an' death of cities,
Don't sling the bloomin' office, strike ole Peters for a billet,
An' soak up all the glory that comes handy while they fill it.

If Paterson's heroic Clancy is possessed of extraordinary
courage and resilience, Dyson's Humpy Peters and
Halligan are also exceptional "types" of cussed denizens of
the bush. On 20 August 1892, a caricature of Paterson's
romantic portrayals was published by "H.H.C.C.":

THE OVERFLOW OF CLANCY
(On reading the Banjo's "Clancy of the Overflow.")

I've read "The Banjo's" letter, and I'm glad he's found a better
    Billet than he had upon the station where I met him years ago;
He was "slushy" then for Scotty, but the "bushland" sent him
    "dotty,"
    So he "rose up, William Riley," and departed down below.

He "rolled up" very gladly, for he had bush fever badly
    When he left "the smoke" to wander "where the wattle-blossoms
    wave,"
But a course of "stag and brownie" seems to make the bush-struck
    towny
    Kinder weaken on the wattle and the bushman's lonely grave.

Safe in town, he spins romances of the bush until one fancies
    That it's all top-boots and chorus, kegs of rum and "whips" of
    grass,
And the sheep off camp go stringing when the "boss-in-charge" is
    singing,
    Whilst we "blow the cool tobacco-smoke and watch the white
    wreaths pass."

Yet, I guess "The B." feels fitter in a b'iled shirt and "hard-hitter"
    Than he would "way down the Cooper" in a flannel smock and
        "moles,"
For the city cove has leisure to indulge in stocks of pleasure,
    But the drover's only pastime's cooking "What's this! on the
        coals."

And the pub, hath friends to meet him, and between the acts they
        treat him
    While he's swapping "fairy twisters" with the "girls behind
        their bars,"
And he sees a vista splendid when the ballet is extended
    And at night, he's in his glory with the comic-op'ra stars.
. . . .
I am sitting, very weary, on a log before a dreary
    Little fire that's feebly hissing 'neath a heavy fall of rain,
And the wind is cold and nipping, and I curse the ceaseless
        dripping
    As I slosh around for wood to start the embers up again.

And, in place of beauty's greeting, I can hear the dismal bleating
    Of a ewe that's sneaking out among the marshes for her lamb;
And for all the poet's skitin' that a new-chum takes delight in,
    The drover's share of pleasure isn't worth a tinker's d—n.

Does he sneer at bricks and mortar when he's squatting in the
        water
    After riding fourteen hours beneath a sullen, weeping sky?
Does he look aloft and thank it, as he spreads his sodden
        blanket?
    For the drover has no time to spare, he has no time to dry.

If "The Banjo's" game to fill it, he is welcome to my billet;
    He can "take a turn at droving" — wages three-and-six a day —
And his throat'll get more gritty than mine will in the city
    Where with Mister Lawson's squashes I can wash the dust
        away.

The author of this pleasantry, like Dyson, proposes that
romancers should gain real experience and write about it.
"H.H.C.C." takes no pride in having endured his billet, but
keeps his aim direct on Paterson's personal experience (sent
"dotty" by exposure to real bush conditions). There is no
attempt to build a bridge between city and bush toilers; the
debate brought few encouraging signs of reconciliation. On
27 August 1892, another nearly-anonymous writer, "K." of
Brisbane, joined the anti-Paterson ranks with "Banjo, of
the Overflow":

I had written him a letter, which I had for want of better
    Knowledge given to a partner by the name of "Greenhide Jack" —

He was shearing when I met him, and I thought perhaps I'd let him
  Know that I was "stiff," and, maybe, he would send a trifle back.

My request was not requited, for an answer came indited
  On a sheet of scented paper, in an ink of fancy blue;
And the envelope, I fancy, and an "Esquire" to the Clancy,
  And it simply read, "I'm busy; but I'll see what I can do!.
. . . .
To the vision land I can go, and I often think of "Banjo" —
  Of the boy I used to shepherd in the not so long ago,
He was not the bushman's kidney, and among the crowds of Sydney
  He'll be more at home than mooning on the dreary Overflow.

He has clients now to fee him, and has friends to come and see him,
  He can ride from morn to evening in the padded hansom cars,
And he sees the beauties blending where the throngs are never ending,
  And at night the wond'rous women in the ever-lasting bars.
. . . .
I am tired of reading prattle of the sweetly-lowing cattle
  Stringing out across the open with the bushmen riding free'
I am sick at heart of roving up and down the country droving,
  And of alternating damper with the salt-junk and the tea.

And from sleeping in the water on the droving trips I've caught a
  Lively dose of rheumatism in my back and in my knee,
And in spite of verse it's certain that the sky's a leaky curtain —
  It may suit the "Banjo" nicely, but it never suited me.

And the bush is very pretty when you view it from the city,
  But it loses all its beauty when you face it "on the pad;"
And the wildernesses haunt you, and the plains extended daunt you,
  Till at times you come to fancy that the life will drive you mad.

But I somehow often fancy that I'd rather not be Clancy,
  That I'd like to be the "Banjo" where the people come and go,
When instead of framing curses I'd be writing charming verses —
  Tho' I scarcely think he'd swap me, "Banjo, of the Overflow.

The debate was now taking the form of a simple parade of "evidence" on each side; the *ad hominem* arguments did nothing to develop any serious possibilities of extending realism into each camp. In "K."'s poem, those who idealize the outback are not simply urban aesthetes: their very masculinity is questionable.

A poem by Harry Morant ("The Breaker"), published at the same time as "K."'s satire, sought to make the landscape subsidiary to an over-riding metaphysical concern, though its archaic elegancies mitigated the attempt:

> The birds will soon their carols cease,
>   And crows are homeward hieing;
> The gloaming deepens, stars increase,
>   The weary day is dying —
> Its requiem, murmurous of peace,
>   The vesper winds are sighing.

(from "When the Light is as Darkness")

Stronger support came directly from John Le Gay Brereton, who had not yet met Lawson (they became friends from their first encounter in 1894). In "From Shadowland" (3 September 1892), Brereton applauded Lawson for being alive among so many "wretched poets" and "dull clowns" who could not tell "Sons of sin from sons of Song". The romantic view was again mocked by "M.T." on 3 September in "An Unorthodox Wail". The unorthodoxy related not to poetic form (like most of the exchange, the poem was a variant on the ballad-form), nor on the by-now familiar catalogue of outback horrors, but in the avowals of love for all the city's noise and habitual scenes. "M.T."'s poem legitimised the city's physical attributes, while denying the land its status as a fit subject for poetry:

> Oh! I want to go back to the city,
>   Away from this desolate place
> With its acres of "solitudes awesome"
>   And the horror if "infinite space."
> I am tired of "the wail of the plover,"
>   I am sick of "the magpie's sweet song"
> I loathe "the complaint of the curlew,"
> I've heard it too oft and too long.
>
> "Long tramps thro' the forests" are failures,
>   "Summer strolls by swift streams" apt to pall;
> I am weary of "fresh air and freedom,"
>   Since a surfeit I've had of them all.
> The sight of "a drover" is deadly,
>   The "crack of his whip" drives me mad,
> The low of wild cattle's depressing,
>   And "the bleat of the sheep" quite as bad.
>
> "Misty mountains may tow'r in the distance,"
>   And soulful ones rave of their height;
> *I* wonder how far they're from Sydney

If from them the city's in sight.
The "soil may be rich" and the cattle
 Exactly "the thing" in their breed;
I wish they were mine and I'd sell them
And make for that city with speed.

A telegraph-wire and a sparrow
 Furnish plenty of Nature for me,
And a walk to save 'bus-fare sufficeth
 To give me a relish for tea.
A sirloin on Sundays, or saddle
 Of mutton's enough of their kind
To prime me in "good points in cattle"
 And such, once I've left these behind.

I yearn for the roar of street traffic,
 For the howl of the newspaper-boy,
While the yell of the man with bananas
 Is a dream of delirious joy.
The bell-birds may chime for the poets,
 I pine for the shriek of a tram;
And "the rustle of leaves in the autumn"
 May be music — to me it's all sham.

Brickfield Hill or, say, William street (Upper)
 Are "mountain" enough to please me,
And for "soil" give me wood-blocks and pavements,
 "Rural streams" the green bay near the Quay.

For oh! there are hearts in the city!
 There are souls! there are welcoming eyes!
And I long for a sight of my fellows,
 For a word from the friends that I prize.

The poem marks some small advance in the debate. In acknowledging the sociable appeal of the city it is a kind of anticipation of Slessor's poem "William Street", though not unusual in celebrating the urban scene alone. The poem's value lies in its shifting the argument further towards that intellectualisation of landscape which would make its symbolism new, and put paid to the stock-in-trade imagery of the outback ballad as a power to command widespread readership. Deliberate death-blows would be aimed at the bush-ballad, and the horse-ballad in particular, during the years before the Great War when Arthur Adams and David McKee Wright encouraged more "social" and political satire, reflecting suburban themes and concerns.

Paterson found few enough voices directly taking his part in the verse exchanges. Ed Dyson contributed "*R E*

Those Bards" on 10 September 1892, which added little but endorsement of the view that one's attitude to the bush depends on the season when one observes it. He attempted to make a joke of the whole affair in order to reconcile the contenders:

> There's a story in the school-books of a pair of angry boys
> Who banged each other quite a deal and raised a lot of noise,
> And the reason of the ruction and a badly-broken head
> Was a point concerning colour — was a lobster black or red?
> The one said black, the other red; they started clawing hair,
> Till a bulging-browed philosopher by chance espied the pair.
> He went between the pugilists and said with manner mild:
> "A lobster's black when in the sea, but reddish when he's 'biled."
> *I* say the plains are splendid, and the plains are grand and green,
> Or yellow, dry and dreadful — it depends on when they're seen.
> And so the bards who bless the bush, or damn it in a song —
> They both are right, but each of them decidedly is wrong.

Paterson's cause was not well-served by allies like A. C. Fontaine, who contributed "The Men With Whom I Used to Shear" from Sydney's Lane Cove (17 September 1892). The poem celebrates the lost times, a version of the golden age:

> **The Men With Whom I Used to Shear**
>   *A Ballade of Lost Mates*:
>
> Yes! they are lost, why advertise!
> For some can't read, and some, I ween,
> May now have pens up in the skies;
> At least — if sheds up there are seen.
> Ah! some were straight and some were mean,
> And some are blacklegs now, I fear —
> Mad Harry, Smithy, Old Bill Deane,
> The men with whom I used to shear.
>
> Mick Ford could sing a rattling some,
> And always swore his yarns were true;
> He went to dig at Adelong,
> I don't know what he couldn't do,
> His brother made good tallies, too;
> From him I sometimes used to hear.
> But, Lord! they were a motley crew,
> The men with whom I used to shear.
>
> I often think of "Parson" Jack,
> For five whole years none heard him swear,
> They used to say he got the sack
> For drinking more than one man's share.
> Howbeit, we always found him square;
> But when he preached they used to jeer,
> A cent for hell they didn't care,

The men with whom I used to shear.

Where's Dick the Swell, I wonder, now?
    The fellows had a set on him.
When we cut out he had a row
    And very nearly killed Long Jim —
It made him feared at Cooranim
    In sixty-nine ('twas his last year);
They's filled his cup up to the brim,
    The men with whom I used to shear.

Where are they all? I'd like to know —
    In Sydney I can't find a mate,
I'll go out West beyond Dubbo,
    And find a shed before it's late,
Another day I shall not wait,
    I'll never make a cheque down here,
And I may meet by Mogong gate,
    The men with whom I used to shear.

Paterson's "In Defence of the Bush", which followed these effusions on 1 October, was no "ubi sunt", nor a convincing argument concerning literary realism. For the most part it recounted the attractions of the bush in nostalgic terms (from the position of a sojourner in the town):

Well, I've waited mighty patient while they all came rolling in,
Mister Lawson, Mister Dyson, and the others of their kin,
With their dreadful, dismal stories of the Overlander's camp,
How his fire is always smoky, and his boots are always damp;
And they paint it so terrific it would fill one's soul with gloom,
But you know they're fond of writing about "corpses" and "the tomb."
So, before they curse the bushland they should let their fancy range,
And take something for their livers, and be cheerful for a change.

Now, for instance, Mister Lawson — well, of course, we almost cried
At the sorrowful description how his "little 'Arvie" died.
And we wept in silent sorrow when "His Father's Mate" was slain;
Then he went and killed the father, and we had to weep again.
Ben Duggan and Jack Denver, too, he caused them to expire,
And he went and cooked the gander of Jack Dunn, of Nevertire;
And he spoke in terms prophetic of a revolution's beat,
When the world should hear the clamour of those people in the street;
But the shearer chaps who start it — why, he rounds on them in blame,
And he calls 'em "agitators" who are living on the game.
So, no doubt, the bush is wretched if you judge it by the groan
Of the sad and soulful poet with a graveyard of his own.

But I "over-write" the bushmen! Well, I own without a doubt
That I always see a hero in the "man from furthest out."
I could never contemplate him through an atmosphere of gloom,
And a bushman never struck me as a subject for "the tomb."
If it ain't all "golden sunshine" where the "wattle branches
    wave,"
Well; it ain't all damp and dismal, and it ain't all "lonely grave."
And, of course, there's no denying that the bushman's life is
    rough,
But a man can easy stand it if he's built of sterling stuff;
Tho' it's seldom that the drover gets a bed of eider-down,
Yet the man who's born a bushman, he gets mighty sick of town,
For he's jotting down the figures, and he's adding up the bills
While his heart is simply aching for a sight of Southern hills.
Then he hears a wool-team passing with a rumble and a lurch,
And although the work is pressing yet it brings him off his perch.
For it stirs him like a message from his station friends afar
And he needs to sniff the ranges in the scent of wool and tar;
And it takes him back in fancy, half in laughter, half in tears,
To a sound of other voices and a thought of other years,
When the woolshed rang with bustle from the dawning of the
    day,
And the shear-blades were a-clicking to the cry of "wool away!"
When his face was somewhat browner and his frame was firmer
    set,
And he feels his flabby muscles with a feeling of regret.
Then the wool-team slowly passes and his eyes go sadly back
To the dusty little table and the papers in the rack,
And his thoughts go to the terrace where his sickly children
    squall,
And he thinks there's something healthy in the bushlife after all.
But we'll go no more a-droving in the wind or in the sun,
For our fathers' hearts have failed us and the droving days are
    done.
There's a nasty dash of danger where the long-horned bullock
    wheels,
And we like to live in comfort and to get our reg'lar meals.
And to hang about the townships suits us better, you'll agree,
For a job at washing bottles is the job for such as we.
Let us herd into the cities, let us crush and crowd and push
Till we lose the love of roving and we learn to hate the bush;
And we'll turn our aspirations to a city life and beer,
And we'll sneak across to England — it's a nicer place than
    here;
For there's not much risk of hardship where all comforts are in
    store,
And the theatres are plenty and the pubs are more and more.
But that ends it, Mr. Lawson, and it's time to say good-bye,
We must agree to differ in all friendship, you and I;
And our personal opinions — well, they're scarcely worth a
    rush,
For there's some that like the city and there's some that like the
    bush;

And there's no one quite contented, as I've always heard it said,
Except one favoured person, and *he* turned out to be dead.
So we'll work our own salvation with the stoutest hearts we
  may,
And if fortune only favours we will take the road some day,
And go droving down the river 'neath the sunshine and the stars,
And then we'll come to Sydney and vermilionize the bars.

Paterson reiterated the attractions of town-life, even
while allowing that Lawson's realism concerning city
tragedies was striking. Lawson is not countered by
Paterson's humorous reductio that city-life brings bottle-
washing, beer-drinking, and escape to England where pubs
and theatres are more numerous. The proffered
reconciliation at the end is characteristic of Paterson's
horseback attitude, and the reference to the unalloyed
"sunshine and the stars" plunges the work back into the
realm of romantic nostalgia from which Lawson has
appealed to bush-balladists to make their escape.

Paterson did not answer Lawson in either of his poems,
and his optimistic promotion of outback life can be
considered as something of a *jeu d'esprit*. Lawson's high
spirits were evidenced in his tone during the exchange,
through the poems cited above, and in "The Grog-an'-
Grumble Steeplechase" (10 September 1892) which
facetiously displayed his sense that comedy and joy could
exist in the bush. Lawson was careful to make clear from
the outset that the events described occurred in a mythical
era:

'Twixt the coastline and the border lay the town of Grog-an-
  Grumble,
In the days before the bushman was a dull 'n' heartless drudge

By October 1892, Lawson was at Bourke, his travel assisted
by his Sydney publisher. Lawson believed that what he
saw on the outback expedition justified his stance; from
Hungerford over the Queensland border, he wrote to his
aunt Emma Brooks on 16 January 1893 that "it would take a
year to tell you all about my wanderings in the
wilderness", and referred to Hungerford as "this God-
Forgotten town".[7] Earlier, Lawson had observed of the
country en route to Bourke that he had been right and
Paterson wrong.[8]

Lawson's final verse contribution to the debate, "The Poets of the Tomb", was published on 1 October 1892, although it bore the date September and had been held over to complement Paterson's "In Defence of the Bush", with its reference "a bushman never struck me as a subject for 'the tomb'". In "The Poets of the Tomb", Lawson tilts in general at "bards that wish that they were dead" — Australian or English Decadents whose verse lamented "vanished hopes" and portrayed life as a gloomy affair. He included oblique digs at the bush school:

And yet as long as she-oaks sigh and wattle-blossoms bloom,
The world shall hear the drivel of the poets of the tomb.

Lawson observed that the graveyard poets "mostly wish their resting-place" were kept green; for himself, he was unconcerned whether wombats rooted in his grave or cows camped overhead. Lawson declared he would "live and fight" in the meantime. He did not seek to align himself with the dead, however glorious — nor with the living dead, as he perceived those who wore themselves out with self-absorption and who employed worn-out tropes. It is germane to note here that while the *Bulletin*'s first book publication had been humorous and realist in composition, Angus and Robertson's first verse publications (in 1888) had been H. Peder Steel's *A Crown of Wattle* and A. W. Jose's *Sun and Cloud on River and Sea:* picturesque and nostalgic verse of the sort which Lawson opposed.

In the 1890s Lawson's prose came to greater prominence than his verse. He could be expansive and judicious in his statements outside the constraints of ballad-form. The inherent structures of verse impelled arrangement of words for the sake of form, often at the expense of plain statement. The tendency for the form to deteriorate into "jingles" is amply demonstrated in the examples cited above. This is not to suggest that the ballad could not — or can not — contain startling effects, but that its strengths are not so much apparent when it is employed for discursive and polemical, rather than dramatic purposes. The earlier Georgian and Victorian ballads were addressed to hangings, violent deaths and thwarted

passions. Paterson's employment of ballad-form to narrate
heroic or sensational events comes closer to efficient
manipulation of the form than his insistent recitations of
the joys of outback life. The cadences of "The Man from
Snowy River" (1890), for instance, preserve many of the
rhythms of everyday speech, despite the closely-rhymed
scheme of the work. In Paterson's defences of the bush-
poet's procedure with regard to realism or romance, the
rhythm lends itself to jingling; the four-beat couplets of his
"In Defence of the Bush" set up a monotony of inflection
which cannot be escaped in reading or recitation. Lawson
and Paterson were on better rhetorical ground when they
conducted polemics in prose: the "special effects" could be
reserved to highlight points in their delivery. In
conducting the opening debate on the issue in verse, each
writer could amuse himself and his opponent by parodying
his own style or that of his rival. Others who joined the
debate, like P. Luftig ("The Song of the Bush'" 1 October
1892), could be said to be flogging a dead horse, by
remaining caught in archaic language and romantic
descriptiveness:

> List to the song by the camp-fire glare!
> The song of the bush hath a beauty rare.

The balladists continued to promote one side or the other of
the issue in simplistic ways through the remainder of the
nineties. Catalogues of gloom and care associated with the
bush came from Steele Grey ("Drought", 22 October 1892),
H. Fletcher ("In the Bush", 31 August 1895), J. P. ("The
Unknown Land", 14 September 1895), J. Drayman ("Where
Silence Reigns", 14 December 1895) and "Jim's Uncle" ("An
Outburst", 25 January 1896). A new cliché grew up to
replace the old from these efforts to portray the bush
realistically: the convention of the terrible bush. This had
some pedigree in novels of colonial experiences and
exploration, although sterling qualities and virtues might
have more usually contrived the happy resolution in such
works. By the time "Zef" published "A Vision of the
Gruesome" in the *Bulletin* (25 July 1896), the poet's

"dummy", the "typical" stockman or shearer, is made to declare:

> ... I've no existence save in dark imaginations
> Of the poets and the proseists in their stories and their rhymes.

The melancholy interpretation of the outback had become as hackneyed as the golden age connotations against which Lawson launched his attack. The ability to survive in such a daunting environment was joined to other elements of national pride in the 1890s. In order to cope with unromantic reality, roughness became part of the ideal — at once proto-Anzac and proto-Ocker: the ancestry of the hoon might include the city larrikin, Clancy of the Overflow and Middleton's Rouseabout.

In 1892 the *Bulletin* could recognise rural conditions for what they were, as the following "paragraph" makes clear:

Advt. from Victorian paper:

Christians. — Will any help weak Brother who was greatly blessed at Wesleyan Conference and earnestly desirous of new life, to situation; urgent, farm or otherwise.

The writer of this has tried a farm billet, and it is just the last thing in all this world that a weak brother should tackle. In fact, none but the most herculean variety of brother should attempt such a job. (27 August 1892)

By 1895 the hardship of rural life was lending itself to caricature. Steele Rudd's first sketch on selection life, "Starting the Selection", appeared in the *Bulletin* in that year, and the *Bulletin* publishing company brought out the illustrated volume *On Our Selection* four years later. Rudd drew on the experiences of his own family in the 1870s and 1880s to portray the rigours of pioneering life, though his realism in this initial volume, and more widely in later collections was undercut by farce — which came to predominate in *Dad in Politics and Other Stories* (1908). Barbara Baynton's *Bush Studies* represented an apotheosis of the "grim bush" commonplaces, with the additional revelation of sexual cruelty suffered by female characters. This refinement seldom characterised male writers' works, although George Chamier's New Zealand novel *A South-*

Sea Siren (1895) specifically stood the romantic view of colonial settlement on its head by taking the woman's story through its infernal circles. To be effective, realism required to be thorough-going in the face of conventional proprieties.

The Lawson-Paterson debate of 1892 was for all its facetiousness a watershed in literary consciousness. Lawson had offered a serious challenge to bush writers to maintain artistic integrity, and he pursued his aim in prose sketches like "In a Dry Season" (November 1892), "The Union Buries Its Dead" (*Truth*, 16 April 1893), "In a Wet Season" and "Hungerford" (16 December 1893). In his verse, Lawson continued to employ rhetorical short-cuts (in "The Southern Scout, or the Natives of the Land", published on 27 August 1892, for instance, "Freedom's marching orders" come to inhabitants of the "gardens where our mothers worked like men"). In his prose sketches and stories Lawson was inclined to leave out the wattle "because it wasn't there" in his characters' environments.

The sentiment which clogged bush poetry was a luxury to Lawson; whether relating to the physical landscape or the patriotism which overlooked injustice and oppression at home, such sentiment checked the development of self-understanding. Lawson's realism, like that of the Box Hill artists, could be interpreted by contemporaries who dwelt in nostalgia as a pernicious or misleading direction. A political element underlay the resistance to naturalism and realism in art: the choice of subject-material was sordid or morbid, its perpetrators jaded or disappointed. Replying to "Station Hand", a correspondent from Narromine in the *Bulletin* on 2 December 1893, A. G. Stephens suggested that Lawson's cynicism was "affected" and not to be taken too seriously. Archibald told a correspondent in October 1898 that the row between the parties was now "interminable" (15 October) — and so it has proved in other guises since. On 27 March 1897, Stephens called for town dwellers to show sympathy for the pioneers "who are fertilizing the desert with their lives". Lawson's prose "manifestoes" on "Some Popular Australian Mistakes" (18 November 1893, and a re-statement on 27 February 1897) attempted to clear the way for negotiation of some appropriate style. His efforts could not find a way around the allegiances of each party: Furphy's *Such is Life* (1903) was to explore the hieratic nature of bush society more thoroughly, and to seek to understand entrenched, even pig-headed attachments to inappropriate political principles among the pastoral proletariat. Lawson was to conclude of bush-romancers that they saw the bush as it should be, and not as it is (27 February 1893). Paterson's view, and that of his adherents, reinforced conservative patriotism as well as artistic principles: while hard work brought fertility and enjoyment, going against commonly-held (though class-bound) views marked an individual as eccentric or simple-minded.

Neither Lawson's nor Paterson's views could be taken as representative of those of their contemporaries. Lawson's politics were naive and his enthusiasms changeable; he did not have a thorough-going, first-hand knowledge of bush life, any more than he had such familiarity with urban society, though what he called instinct, and what was a result of reading, observation and conversation, confirmed his sense of the correctness of his literary approach. The image-builders were not likely to endorse his opinion: it offered too critical an insight into current nostalgias. Lawson did appear to draw more active sympathisers to his viewpoint within the columns of the *Bulletin*, though it is well to acknowledge that this journal was only one, if nonetheless a leader, among other taste-making and opinion-reinforcing organs.

Paterson's comic abilities are evident in the debate, and he developed his readership further in the nineties through the comic ballads collected in *The Man from Snowy River and Other Verses* (1895). By 1902, when a further collection appeared (*Rio Grande's Last Race and Other Verses*), Paterson's narrative and lyric reputation was well-established. The polarities represented in the 1892 debate continued to characterise Lawson and Paterson, and were part of the material of literary culture through the spectator participation they encouraged. The debate thus contributed to the sense of scepticism and utilitarianism which Stephens suggested characterised "the present hour" as Federation approached.[9] Stephens observed that religion held less sway over Australia every year; the people were effectively making their own legends, and nostalgia was to have its place in the romance of the nation. The debate helped to define what was worth loving about the nation: nationalism did not bring with it self-knowledge, but the issue of an appropriate style with which to describe the country and its inhabitants facilitated awareness of what was possible within the framework. In this sense, the debate was a model of the flexibility of form — whether a newspaper or the much-maligned ballad itself.

Looking for Mr Backbone: The Politics of Gender in the Work of Henry Lawson

Christopher Lee

In "The Politics of Respectability: Identifying the Masculinist Context", Marilyn Lake argues that what historians have labelled the "respectability" reform movements of the end of the last century were in fact "contests between men and women ... for the control of the national culture".[1] She maintains that the use of the concept "respectability" by historians to describe these reform movements has to date served as a blind to the gender-specific nature of this struggle. Instead, Lake identifies the main point of confrontation between these men and women, the masculinist nationalist bohemians and the feminist social reformers, as a debate over different ideologies of man (in a gender-specific sense).

Lake argues that the *Bulletin* was at the forefront of this battle because of its production of a concept of masculinity which identified manhood through the qualities of independence, individualism and freedom associated with a nomadic, vagrant, itinerant lifestyle. These qualities were then deployed through "a distinct set of male cultural practices"[2] such as drinking, smoking, and gambling, and then identified in the "lone hand" figure of the bushman, which it idealised and then apotheosised as the national identity. This model of man was separatist and misogynist and identified itself in opposition to the ideology of the domestic man which Lake traces back to the rise of Evangelicalism and the associated cult of domesticity in England.

This debate over different ideologies of man can be explicated of man and woman produced through the pages of the *Dawn* and the *Bulletin*. For in the 1880s and 1890s both the *Bulletin* and the *Dawn* are involved in the production of contradictory representations of man and woman. The *Bulletin*, as both Marilyn Lake and Sylvia Lawson have argued, is involved in the production of a concept of masculinity which takes its form from the independent, itinerant, bachelor bushman ultimately mythologised as the identity of the nation. This is justified by representing woman as either a vain, conniving, sometimes stupid spendthrift, bent on entrapment; or as a "bitter harridan", dedicated to the destruction of those of her husband's pleasures which the magazine associates with his manhood. The *Dawn*, however, is involved in the production of a concept of man which identifies masculinity with the values of home, hearth, wife, and child, values which it intimately associates with moral, mental, and physical hygiene.[3]

The rival values of man and woman, husband and wife, father and mother, as produced through the pages of the *Dawn* and the *Bulletin*, are values which both magazines connect with discourses on the nation and the national type. In this sense they are issues which are bound up in important ways with the political strategies of nationalist interests of the period, and the subsequent mythologisations of the national identity which characterise this country's cultural history. The question I wish to address then is what happens to our reading of the work of Henry Lawson, a figure who has been central to both nationalist accounts of the period and discussions of the national identity, when we examine it as a textual enactment of the man/woman debate.

Lawson's stories, and in particular those stories which deal with madness, are intimately concerned with the key values of the man/woman debate of the period. The ideology of the family produced through the pages of the *Dawn*, for example, is a major theme in the representation of Bob Baker's mental and physical degeneration in Lawson's story "Telling Mrs. Baker." Baker is a man's man in the *Bulletin* sense of the term, one whose predilection for alcohol leads to his death "in the horrors". Baker's weakness for drink is represented as a threat not just to his own life, but to those of his wife and children as well. His drinking places him within a male cultural group which is clearly identified with the single man. The family responsibilities of the married man make his participation in this single man's cultural practice a morally reprehensible activity. Baker's drunken behaviour threatens the respectability of his family. When he eventually dies, it is his mates' job not just to protect the name of their friend, but that of his family as well. They do this by rewriting the sordid story of Baker's death as a comforting, respectable tale. The "real" Bob Baker resembles closely that criticised by the *Dawn* and associated with the *Bulletin*, while the "fictitious" Baker resembles the ideal described in the *Dawn*.

The aetiology of Baker's madness is familiar in the work of Lawson. The vicissitudes of the Bush have led to professional failure. This failure has then led to drink, and the drink to madness and death. Baker's madness is clearly associated with sunstroke and alcohol, common causes according to the medical literature:

> Perhaps the boss hadn't been quite right in the head before he started drinking: he had acted queer for some time, now we came to think of it; maybe he'd got a touch of sunstroke or got brooding over his trouble anyway he died in the horrors within the week.[4]

The form his madness takes locates the cause within the conflicting values of family debated in the pages of the *Dawn* and the *Bulletin*:

> Sometimes, towards the end, he'd be sensible for a few minutes and talk about his "poor wife and children"; and immediately afterwards he'd fall a-cursing me, and Andy, and Ned, and calling us devils. He cursed everything; he cursed his wife and children, and yelled that they were dragging him down to hell. He died raving mad. It was the worst case of death in the horrors of drink that I ever saw or heard of in the Bush.[5]

The blame for Baker's destruction is divided. There is an implication that the Bush is an environment in which a man is unable to guarantee provision for a family. The pressure to do so in the face of misfortune is represented as the cause of personal and mental degeneration. The conclusion, of course, is that the bush is no place for a family, no place for a woman, and therefore, no place for a married man. This makes the bush the domain of the single, independent, nomadic bushman, the male cultural hero which Lake associates with the *Bulletin*.

Lake's association of the *Bulletin* with the eulogisation of this mode of life, in opposition to that of the family man, is interestingly offset by the events of this story. It is, for instance, the bushmen who move to protect the family from the potentially destructive truth. This move comes not just out of loyalty to their mate, but admiration and recognition for his wife and family. In addition, they entrust their secret and the role of protector to Mrs. Baker's sister, "a pretty, bright eyed ... Sydney girl" who "had been educated ... and wrote stories for the Sydney *Bulletin*" (416). In doing so they earn the admiration of this woman, who responds by celebrating them and their type: "You are good men! I like the Bushmen! They are grand men — they are noble!" (420). This generalisation, as Colin Roderick suggests, rings hollow when it is remembered that Bob Baker and the avaricious shanty keeper are also bushmen.[6] Both points run counter to the value of "man" produced through the *Bulletin*. The suggestion, however, at least in this story, is that the concept of the bushman eulogised in the *Bulletin* is the romanticised construction of educated Sydney sophisticates. This, of course, is precisely the argument put forward by Graeme Davison in "Sydney and the Bush: An Urban Context for the Australian Legend".[7]

The destruction of the bushmen is not merely the result of vicious environmental conditions, however, for the narrative clearly ascribes a measure of responsibility to the individual. The failure of Bob Baker and those of his ilk is as much a failure of moral courage as of environmental determinism:

he'd been a jolly, open-handed, popular man, which means that
he'd been a selfish man as far as his wife and children were
concerned, for they had to suffer for it in the end. Such
generosity is often born of vanity, or moral cowardice, or both
mixed. It's very nice to hear the chaps sing "For he's a jolly good
fellow", but you've mostly got to pay for it twice — first in
company, and afterwards alone. I once heard the chaps singing
that I was a jolly good fellow, when I was leaving a place and
they were giving me a send-off. It thrilled me, and brought a
warm gush to my eyes; but, all the same, I wished I had half the
money I'd lent them, and spent on 'em, and I wished I'd used the
time I'd wasted to be a jolly good fellow.[8]

The narrator here takes the form of a reflexive bushman,
who retells the general experience of his past as an
explanation of the present predicament, which is only
glimpsed in personal asides such as the one quoted above.
This narrator is retrospectively aware of the parallels
between Bob Baker's behaviour and fate and his own. This
connection implies that the Baker story is representative.
What this passage also demonstrates, however, is the
identification of personal responsibility in the
individual's failure to resist the seduction of the male pub
fraternity. In the battle between the rival values of man,
the ideology of family and the ideology of the bachelor-
bushman, the bushman narrator has clearly lived that of
the *Bulletin* (bushman), but he endorses that of the *Dawn*
(family).

The representation of madness in Lawson is consistent
with the domestic ideas produced through both the *Dawn*
and the medical discourses of the period, in that it is
frequently connected to the pressures placed upon the
family by the inability of the Bush to provide for them.
"No Place For a Woman", for example, tells the story of a
bushman who goes insane when his wife dies in childbirth
because of the isolation of his property. "The Selector's
Daughter" tells the story of a mother and daughter who
are driven to madness and death by the failure of the men
in the family to fulfill the roles required of father,
husband, brother, and betrothed. "The Babies in the Bush"
describes how Mrs. Head goes mad, and Walter Head
becomes an introspective melancholic, after the death of
their two young children when lost in the bush. It is Walter

Head's burden of guilt because of his absence "on a howling spree" at the time of the incident which is responsible for his "heavy trouble". In this story it is once again the figure of the independent bushman who helps to protect the woman's fragile peace of mind by confirming a comforting fiction in the place of the revealed truth. The representation of madness as the destruction of the domestic is also the central narrative strategy of "Water Them Geraniums", and I want to pursue the representation of madness, and its connection with the man-woman debate in this story, in some detail.

Madness in "Water Them Geraniums" is represented through the theme of the destruction of the family caused by the poverty and isolation of the Bush. The story tells of the Wilson family's move from Gulgong to a rural selection in the Bush in an effort to circumvent Joe's weakness for alcohol. It is divided into two sections: "A Lonely Track" and "Past Carin'". The first section deals with the Wilson's removal to the selection, and indicates the likely repercussions of such a move; while the second explores these repercussions through the figure of Mrs. Spicer. The story of Mrs. Spicer is a study of the effects of life in the Bush on a wife and mother, and prefigures the future destruction of Mary Wilson. It is Joe Wilson's responsibility for this destruction which is the cause for his madness. It is the destructive effects of the Bush which excite Mrs Spicer's malady.

"A Lonely Track" opens with the Wilsons en route to their selection, and moves quickly into a detailed description of their modest but "respectable" material possessions. These possessions operate as the apparatus of the domestic, and as Joe describes the contents of his household he effectively delimits the boundary of a family which can only be defined and located within a space organized as the domestic. The careful, detailed and complete description of the Wilson's simple yet treasured sticks of furniture, perched precariously upon the back of the wagon as it moves into the isolation and monotony of the Bush, effectively signifies the fragility of the domestic within its new environment.

The domestic is set in opposition to the Bush. If the domestic is both structured and signified through the presence of the domestic apparatus within the domestic space, then the Bush is located through the absence of not just the domestic or public, but the possibility of making any of the distinctions which might be associated with civilisation:

> It was a dreary, hopeless track. There was *no horizon*, nothing but the rough ashen trunks of the gnarled and stunted trees in for the coarse, brownish tufts *dead* grass, as *bare* as the road....[9]

Concern for the effects of the Bush on the civilised character of the pioneers in the 1880s is demonstrated in "Burying a Woman." (*Bulletin* 17 Sept. 1881). This article reports the burial of a woman with as "little ceremony ... as one would bury a dog!" It claims that such incidents are common in the bush, and that such behaviour is "inseparable from the colonial life of the Australias [sic]. If this be one of the marks of its advance, it is not a promising prospect. We may well doubt the efficacy of our plans for the spread of civilisation through our vast interior, in the hands of pioneers such as these". The Bush is absence, the absence of civilisation, the absence of home, the absence of the personal. The Bush lacks the apparatus to sustain any of the roles provided as normal by the culture producing the selectors. It is therefore no place for the normal. The description of the hut which is to house their possessions and be their home provides a graphic image of the inability of the Bush to sustain the sort of the familial values associated with "civilisation".

The bush hut is a depleted and insufficient domestic environment. It lacks the domestic structures required to locate and reaffirm the subject positions which deploy the body and bodies of the Victorian family. The absence or dilapidation of the domestic apparatus means that Joe and Mary Wilson are not brought together through their deployment as husband and wife within culturally-produced and ideologically-sanctioned patterns of communication and interaction. The Bush hut is clearly a structure which is unable to sustain such a deployment. The inability of the Bush to sustain these cultural structures, and the values located by them, means that the Bush is constructed as individually and socially destructive. This destruction is then presented in the human dimension as the alienation of husband, wife and family through the replacement of the healthy interpersonal relations of family with the brooding introspection of the hysteric:

> As we went along — and the track seemed endless—I got brooding, of course, back into the past. And I feel now, when it's too late, that Mary must have been thinking that way too. I thought of my early boyhood, of the hard life ... all for nothing. The few months at the little bark school, with a teacher who couldn't spell. The cursed ambition or craving that tortured my soul as a boy ... I thought of these old things more than I thought of her (Mary). She had tried to help me to better things. And I tried too — I had the energy of half-a-dozen men when I saw a road clear before me, but shied at the first check. Then I brooded, or dreamed of making a home — that one might call a home — for Mary... And what was Mary thinking about ... of her girlhood. Of her homes — not the huts and camps she lived in with me.[10]

This introspection is characteristic of both the reflexive gaze of the narrator in the text, and the onset of hysteria as described in the medical discourses. The personal history supplied by Joe Wilson's reminiscence reproduces the preconditions described in the contemporary medical accounts of hysteria. The itinerant lifestyle, the lack of home, poverty, poor education, and the "disappointment of a purposeless or misdirected life" are characteristic predisposing causes of hysteria.[11] These medical discourses not only match Joe's history, they go on to describe his reaction to this history:

> There is not only a tedium vitae, but this is intimately mingled with vain regrets, ideas of faults of omission and commission, and these in the face of a declining life and lack of opportunity to make good may take on an exaggerated and pathological aspect.[12]

> The patient presents a change of character, or rather mood ... she is no longer able to apply herself to her accustomed avocations; she cannot concentrate her mind; hence she cannot read or sew or attend as usual to household duties. It is observed by others that the patient is abstracted, self-concentrated, depressed or absorbed in reflections. She shuns the society of others, and if approached may be irritable, repellant, and not inclined to make confidences.[13]

The pressure associated with exciting Joe's hysterical disposition clearly stems from the guilt he feels at being the reason for the family's move into the Bush. Joe feels guilty because it is a move which promises to, and eventually does, destroy the character of his wife, Mary. Joe's inability to resist the lure of drink in the city, then, becomes the reason behind the destruction of his wife and family in the Bush. The study of Mrs. Spicer in "Past Carin'" prefigures this destruction, and therefore represents the deployment and reinforcement of the pressure associated with Joe's hysteria. Mrs. Spicer's fate is to be Mary's. And the responsibility for it lies with Joe and his inability to "be a man":

> I didn't feel like going to the woman's [Mrs Spicer] house that night. I felt — and the thought came like a whip-stroke on my heart —that this was what Mary would come to if I left her here.

> I turned and started to walk home, fast. I'd made up my mind. I'd take Mary straight back to Gulgong in the morning ... I'd say, "Look here, *Girlie* (that's what I used to call her), "we'll leave this wretched life; we'll leave the bush for ever! We'll go to Sydney, and I'll be *man*! and work my way up." And I'd sell the wagon, horses and all, and go.[14]

The location of Joe's madness in his inability to be a "man" demonstrates the importance of the social value associated with this identity in the construction and representation of madness in the 1890s. The argument which ensues between Joe and Mary upon their arrival at the selection clearly demonstrates that the mental struggle within the introspective selector is bound up with the rival concepts of man described above, and the cultural values associated with them.

Joe incites the argument when he discovers Mary crying over the poverty of the selection:

> "Now, what is it, Mary?" I asked; "I'm sick of this sort of thing. Haven't you got everything that you wanted? You've had your own way. What's the matter with you now?"
> "You know very well, Joe."
> "But I *don't* know," I said. I knew too well.
> She said nothing.
> "Look here, Mary," I said, putting my hand on her shoulder "don't go on like that; tell me what's the matter?"

"It's only this," she said suddenly, "I can't stand this life here; it will kill me!"

I had a pannikin of tea in my hand, and I banged it on the table. "This is more than a *man* can stand!" I shouted [My emphasis]. "You know very well that it was you that dragged me out here. You run me on to this! Why weren't you content to stay in Gulgong?"

"And what sort of a place was Gulgong, Joe?" asked Mary quietly. (I thought even then in a flash what sort of a place Gulgong was. A wretched remnant of a town....

"Well why didn't you come to Sydney, as I wanted you to?" I asked Mary.

"You know very well, Joe," said Mary quietly.

(I knew very well but the knowledge only maddened me ... Mary was afraid of the drink ...

"But Mary," I said, "it would have been different this time. You would have been with me. I can take a glass now or leave it alone."

"As long as you take a glass there is danger," she said.

"Well, what did you want to advise me to come out here for, if you can't stand it? Why didn't you stay where you were?" I asked.

"Well," she said, "Why weren't you more decided?" I'd sat down but I jumped to my feet then. "Good God!" I shouted, "this is more than *any man* can stand [My emphasis]. I'll chuck it all up! I'm damned well sick and tired of the whole thing."[15]

The interchange between Mary and Joe is supplemented by the retrospective narrator. Different concepts of man are clearly at issue in the different arguments. Joe's argument is that it was Mary who wished to move to the selection, and that as a man he needs to take control and reassert his male authority. Mary's and the narrator's (reflexive Joe) argument is that the reason for the desperate move to the selection is that Joe was unable to be man enough to resist his weakness for alcohol and to work hard to provide for his wife and family. The poverty of the selection and the fate which awaits Mary, therefore represent an indictment of Joe's manhood. Joe's reaction to this pressure is to take refuge in a more assertive and domineering concept of man; a concept of man which the mature Joe (the narrator) now discounts, and holds responsible for his wife's eventual death and his mental collapse:

If I don't make a stand now," I'd say, "I'll never be master. I gave up the reins when I got married, and I'll have to get them back again."

What women some men are! But the time came, and not many years after, when I stood by the bed where Mary lay, white and still; and, amongst other things, I kept saying, "I'll give in," and then I'd laugh. They thought that I was raving mad, and took me from the room. But that time was to come.[16]

The "masculine" concept of man stands in opposition to the domestic man, and is linked to the dominating, misogynist, individualist value of man produced through the *Bulletin*. By opposite here, I mean the binary relationship which the different concepts have within the semiotics of the *Dawn* and the *Bulletin*. I do not mean to suggest that the domineering, controlling man is incompatible with the man in the home. Patriarchy, of course, describes precisely such a power structure. "Water them Geraniums" therefore becomes a story of Joe's inability to be a father and husband, a provider and protector, that is, a "domestic" man. Compare this, for example, to the ending of "The Drover's Wife", when the woman's son places the blame for the vicissitudes of her life on the absence of her husband and his father: "Mother, I won't never go drovin'; blast me if I do!".[17] It is interesting to note that Joe's alcoholism is associated with the town and the city rather than the Bush. The Wilson family, it appears, has the choice of destruction by alcohol associated with a male pub fraternity, or destruction by the isolation and deprivation of the Bush. The importance of the Bush therefore lies in the specificity of its process of destruction. This specific is domestic. The destructiveness of the Bush is focused firmly on the domestic and its associated values. This includes the value of the domestic man. While the narrator clearly endorses the domestic value of man, the implication remains clear, that the Bush is the place of the single man, the outdoor, the independent, the male. For the family and the domestic The Bush represents a process of gradual mental destruction. This does not mean, however, that the individual male is immune to the destructive effects of the Bush. Mrs. Spicer's tale of the suicide, and the hatter in "The Bush Undertaker", are but a few of the many "independent" bushman who succumb to the Bush in the stories of Lawson. This process is fully explored in the study of Mrs Spicer developed in the second section of the

story, "Past Carin'". Here, Mrs Spicer's mental destruction
is played out through the representation of the increasing
dilapidation of her domestic space and its civilised
appointments. This in turn deploys the pressure on Joe's
sense of guilt for his failure to protect his wife and provide
a home for his family — a failure, that is, to be a man. It is
a pressure which we now know will ultimately cause his
own mental collapse.

The events of many of Lawson's stories of bush madness
can thus be seen to tell of the consequences of the pressure
placed on men by their insufficiency within the Bush
environment. It is an insufficiency to be a "domestic" man,
and it leads to the destruction of family, corruption,
disgrace, and madness. What emerges from Lawson's stories
of madness, then, is the representation of madness as the
binary opposite of the domestic. Such a representation is an
important feature of the medical texts of the period. In an
article entitled "The Causation and Prevention of Insanity"
published in 1880, Dr Frederick Norton Manning identified
isolation and nostalgia as the leading cause of insanity in
the colonies. He wrote:

> This isolation, which is something terrible to the new emigrant,
> and which lasts often for years, is kept up by the disparity of the
> sexes ... and to some extent prevents marriage; and it is *fostered*
> *by the peculiar mode of life both of the miner and the bushman*, by
> the shifting from place to place with the seasons in search of
> work, and by the restlessness which seems an inherent feature of
> colonial existence at present.[18]

For Manning, the key features of the onset of mental
collapse are the lack of a wife, a home and a family:

> The absence of the near home ties and all active sympathy,
> together with the constant change of associates, leads on the one
> hand to a dwarfing of all those better feelings which are
> fostered and flourish in home life, and on the other to the
> development of a miserable selfishness, to a suspicion and
> distrust of ever-changing comrades, and at last to evil habits, to
> introspection, to hypochondriasis, and to the development of
> delusions of suspicion and fear, which are prominent symptoms
> in this class of cases ... *A system of family, instead of isolated,*
> *emigration, would do much to prevent this cause of insanity*.[19]

Manning's stress upon the importance of the values of the
family as a bulwark for sanity is a common emphasis in

both the medical and social discourses of the period. The enshrinement of this ideology of family within the institution of health ensures its production throughout the colonial society of late nineteenth-century Australia as the normal, the healthy, and the civilised. The *Dawn* operates as a prime example of the dissemination of this domestic or family ideology of mental hygiene for, as I pointed out earlier, health is a characteristic feature of its domestic interest.

The inability of the Bush to sustain family life, then, predisposes bush men and women to mental illness. Because the bush is no place for a woman, it is also no place for a family, no place for the civilised, no place for the healthy, no place for the sane. At least, that is, according to what the *Bulletin* would see as the conservative, colonial, English or imperial logic of domestically-located women. For the *Bulletin*, the Bush is no place for the family man because it is no place for the Englishman. It is instead the domain of the independent bachelor bushman, the domain of the Australian masculine hero, a territory for the emergence of a new national identity.

Precisely because it is no place for the family, The Bush can be seen as offering the emerging nationalist interests of the late nineteenth-century in Australia a place in which it might contest the power of the Imperial culture. By establishing a defensive resistance to the madness, which the imperial identifies with the loneliness of the Bush, the national is able to register an authority which eludes the power of the Imperial. The Bush is a geography beyond the edge of the Imperial. The madness associated with the Bush is the madness which stems from the absence of imperial civilisation and the domestic space within which it is deployed. It is because the Bush represents the limits of this civilisation, and therefore the point beyond which these imperial values cannot progress, that it represents a space for the potential deployment of rival values, the values of the nation. If the national is to do this, however, it must resist the logic of the imperial, it must resist, that is, the madness which comes from living beyond the edge of the civilised. The diagnosis of this madness is the deployment of an imperial power which dismisses that which exceeds the logic of its own cultural values as the mad. To resist this madness is to resist the Imperial, and to deploy the rival values of nation. To give in to the madness is to become a part of the story of the Empire, to become the object of both the medical and the colonial subject.

My reading of Lawson has left little room for such strategies of national resistance, and appears therefore to run counter to the logic of those accounts of him as the centerpiece of a nationalist tradition organised through the institution of the *Bulletin*. For in the conflict which Marilyn Lake describes between men and women for control of the national culture, Lawson's work endorses the logic of the women, the logic of the *Dawn*, the ideology of the family. Lawson's representations of madness endorse the conservative, English, imperialist, values of the domestic, which the *Bulletin* contests in its production of a masculinist, separatist image of national identity. It is perhaps for this reason then, that A. G. Stephens declares the work of Lawson is often characterised, not by the voice of independent Australian manhood, but by the "womanish wail of someone who needed a sturdy Australian backbone".[20]

Female and Juvenile Meanings in Late Nineteenth-century Australian Popular Theatre

Veronica Kelly

As far as the current narrative of theatrical history goes, the 1890s are significant mainly for the effect of the Depression on entrepreneurial practice: by putting an end to most of the local stock companies and enabling the capitalist reorganisation which gave the J. C. Williamson touring chain an almost unchallenged Australasian monopoly. Yet, at the same time as this internal and international imperialism was forming in mainstream professional theatre, with "original" London or American shows touring Australasia and ousting local professional input, local production continued to flourish. From around the mid-80s such actor-managers as Bland Holt, Alfred Dampier, William Anderson, Dan Barry, E. I. Cole, Kate Howarde, George Darrell and Bert Bailey toured their popular repertoires, much of it locally-written and on Australian subjects. Theatre in this period still serviced the working-class audience, both urban and rural, who were enthusiastic patrons of Australian-interest drama. But by the mid-1920s the talkies, a new Depression, and the "commercial Empire-minded middle-class theatre", by cultural self-definition British or American-oriented,[1] had completed that gentrification of live theatre which since around the 1860s had slowly encroached upon Western societies' first and last mass popular live performance art.

The 1890s were thus in the midst of this transitional phase. The 1882 union of J. C. Williamson, Arthur Garner and George Musgrove in the first "Firm", and Musgrove's Australian tour of the London cast of *La Fille du Tambour Major* in 1880, had already signalled the end of the colonial phase of theatre established three decades previously at the time of the gold rushes.[2]

Despite the growing embourgeoisement and imperial interests of managements and audiences the local working class still ruled the theatre economically by force of numbers. In 1885 Dion Boucicault found that the cheaper seats still predominated. "The result is a popular audience", he concluded, while the "rowdy element... wants no better drama than *The Lights o' London, Struck Oil, The Shaughraun* and *The Silver King*".[3] The "rowdy element" — native-born single youths and courting couples — ensured the success of Dampier, Holt *et al* with their bushranging and sensational repertoire; a trend which was initially observable three decades earlier but which continued through this time. However, the gallery larrikins did not rule theatre unchallenged. The rapid late-century expansion of industry and commerce in the colonial cities provided both middle and working-class women with some means and leisure to attend theatre, and to form in consequence an extremely strong pressure group whose interests astute managements did their best to woo. *Camille, The Factory Girl of Melbourne, The Worst Woman in London* and the perennial *East Lynne* were typical plays catering for various class factions within the female audience. The muted role in Australian myth-formation of women and the young — or, more specifically, of those cultural elements which have been designated "feminine" and "juvenile" — now requires further examination.

The neglect of colonial theatre in recent revisionary cultural studies of Australia is a puzzling feature of otherwise challenging and innovative analyses. While the work of theatre historians has attained visibility in the 1980s, their findings are rarely considered in overviews of the construction of colonial culture.[4] In her feminist rereading of Australian literature, *Women and the Bush*

(1988), Kay Schaffer proffers an explanation of the gendering of cultural phenomena which suggests that the grip of aspects of the 1890s nationalist myth is still strong, even on its most radical critics:

> Within discourse, in relation to the masculine-feminine dichotomies, that which is demeaned in value is also feminised. So, the city, urban life, morals, intellectual and cultural pursuits come to be represented as derivative, inauthentic, unnatural and thus "feminine".[5]

Colonial theatre — urban, moralistic, intellectually eclectic and combative, both a despised and a prestigious cultural form — exactly fits within Schaffer's list of marginalised areas. Its relative neglect by cultural commentators suggests that it is still seen as alien, irrelevant, "feminine", even within the current reconstructions of nationalist discourses; an urban, class-stratified and class-contested, sometimes imperialist presence which fits comfortably neither into the male bush-*Bulletin* legend nor its recent contestations.

Besides this consignment to alterity of the entire enterprise, there are also generic difficulties. As Susan Sheridan and others have pointed out, the *Bulletin* legend of a matured "Australian" identity marginalised and displaced the older Romantic "colonial" literary forms by labelling them "immature" or "feminine": "the norm — in this case, the egalitarian, the realist, the vernacular Australian culture — requires as a condition of its articulation the suppressed Other — in this case, the class-bound, the romantic, the popular 'colonial' culture".[6] The romantic and popular theatre, more tenacious than its literary counterpart, maintained a robust presence long after such innovators as Louis Esson deemed its existence unnecessary. Yet colonial theatre was created by and bound to its audience by more than the powerful ties of its romantic mythic and folklore material, or the vibrant communality of live performance. It was I believe consonant with, and retrievable by, the lived experience of urban audiences during this stage of colonial expansion: its discourses could "fit" with "reality" and offer variant readings of their historical condition.

Since the urban population of early Australia constituted the audiences of our thriving metropolitan theatre, it is vital to restore something of the social and hence psychic and emotional texture of their lives. The historical experience of the Australian urban populations can not be claimed as being unique to this country, as it could be paralleled in other settler and migrant communities within expanding capitalism. The same industrial revolution in Europe which uprooted traditional rural populations and relocated them as alienated and impoverished wage workers in the exploding urban trade and manufacturing centres also, by the logic of expanding imperialism, sent millions of these displaced persons in fragile boats across vast oceans to take their chances of subsistence or success in the "new" or "empty" lands. Many however did not even arrive. On Sydney's South Head stands the memorial of the wreck of the *Dunbar* in 1857 where sixty-three intending migrants and fifty-nine crew drowned when their ship was dashed to pieces on the very shore of their new home. Such wrecks litter our coastline, memorials to the precariousness of even an industrialised society's relationship with the sea. Death by water is a folk theme active in our cultural symbolism, yet often overlooked in favour of the mystique of the interior with its particular myth-formations: the lost child, the inland sea, the perisher, the battling selector. But shipwreck memories were kept alive on the Australian stage by the topical re-enactments of sensation drama; as late as 1887 Alfred Dampier wrote a play around the already much-mythologised *Dunbar* story, while spectacular wrecks were part of the attractions of Bland Holt's English-derived but Australian-interest 1880s and 1890s melodramas.

Fantasy and folk-lore themes, of which I pick out death-by-water as one which demonstrably had wide circulation in colonial theatre, are as Fredric Jameson states in *The Political Unconscious* "the primal motor force which gives any cultural artefact its resonance", yet they must always pass through "a determinate social and historical situation", and so find themselves diverted to the service of various ideological functions. Melodrama can then serve a political and Utopian function as well as an ideological and regressive one, just as Lévi-Strauss saw myth and cultural forms as projecting imaginary solutions to real contradictions.[7] Communal discourses informed by specific historical experience are seen in this mediated form in melodrama's narrative and symbolism, while its capacity for searching out the contradictions is particularly evident in its generic tendency to swing abruptly between tragic and comic inflections. A basically idealist and mythologising form, melodrama promises deliverance, justice and the restoration of lost love, while villainy frequently wears the face of class oppression. Part of its fascination and co-optive power is the intricate and opportunistic way in which the topical interweaves with the mythic and psychic structures, each guaranteeing the dynamism and "novelty" of the other. Themes of renewal, regeneration, self-division, loss and return surge through the stage narratives of the nineteenth century in complex and ambivalent ways, as the restless energies of melodrama attempt to render into never-quite-finalised structures the contradictions of a society in rapid transition.

As the industrial revolution with its disruptions and relocations originally created the urban audiences for melodrama, so too it created the Australian urban populations, and stamped their psychic life with these experiences. At the heart of nineteenth-century melodrama lie pervasive discourses about family, domesticity, hearth-and-home. But here is a seeming contradiction between construct and experience: this homely haven was being maintained as a central value at a time when subsistence poverty, migration, disease and the ruthless exigencies which frontier capitalism exerted on its labour force wrenched apart families and communities and scattered them across oceans and continents. The melodramatic fascination with disruptions and restorations of family relationships needs to be seen in the context of the pre-sewerage death toll,[8] the perils of shipwreck, and the oceans separating communities from each other — communities fragmented not only by distance but by history, as disparate experiences eroded further class and regional identifications and so turned kin into strangers. The frequent stage device of blood relatives failing to recognise each other can be seen to display an essential perception about such a world; a world in transition which was simultaneously and perceptibly changing British peoples into new historically-conscious beings who began to construct an identity as "Australians".

Albert Facey's *A Fortunate Life* (1981), dealing with the early post-Federation period, movingly depicts the power of the image of the mother from whom the young boy was early separated upon her remarriage when the children were split up among relatives. Sections of the story read like a tragic romance, with the mother figure variously illuminated by yearning love and hope and shadowed by a bitter betrayal and loss. It is a valuable document of the psychic effects in a settler community on family relationships wrenched apart by poverty, female economic dependence and the needs of the labour market, where the brunt is borne by men, women and children, each with their own hurts and losses which are available to be variously articulated via prevalent cultural imagery.[9] One can readily imagine, for all the stoical understatement of Facey's story, an audience of mature Alberts weeping over, say, *East Lynne*, with its famous climatic scene of the death of the child William. One can as readily imagine the Mrs. Faceys doing the same, for differing reasons: for one the bitter-sweet romance of the unattainable union with ideal beloved; for the other the guilty grief and burden of knowledge that her separation from the child, whether by death or economic necessity, can leave incurable scars. As Robertson Davies writes of melodrama, it explored "that inner world of the psyche where the unfinished business of life is to be found — the wounds that have not healed, the sorrows that have not been assuaged, the loves that have not been requited, the sense of having been used less than justly by life — and to offer the solace of chivalry, constancy and renunciation".[10] The daily texture of early Australian experience, particularly for the working class either urban or rural in the 1890s Depression, guaranteed plenty of unfinished business.

Female Australian experience was particularly so burdened. A hundred years ago in this country children before the age of five still died at rates which would now demand apocalyptic explanations. Any oldish cemetery shows family graves with inscriptions of names of numerous infants, along with, in many cases, those of their mothers and stepmothers who failed to survive repeated and unsanitary childbirth. The recent decline in infant deaths, an immemorial part of Western peoples' understanding of existence, commenced slowly here around the decade 1880-1890 when public health measures, vaccination and an improved urban standard of living slowly eroded the infant death-toll caused by infanticide, typhoid, diphtheria, measles, scarlet fever, diarrhoea, whooping cough and various forms of malnutrition.[11] According to a recent study of paediatrics in Queensland, in 1889 children under the age of five accounted for 41% of all deaths.[12] In the Sydney of the 1880s, 22% of live births did not survive to adulthood; by 1900 this figure had dropped to 15%.[13]

The absent mother, the dying child — these are also persistent motifs of nineteenth-century melodrama. Oscar Wilde notably ridiculed the famous and frequently dramatised death of Little Nell/Little Eva setpiece with his quip that only a heart of stone could refrain from laughing out loud.[14] In that many of these scenes were (as their audiences fully realised) over-heated, and shamelessly wrung sentimental tears from a real and hurtful situation which people were prepared to weep over anyway, Wilde's comment is true — as far as it goes. Responses to representations of pain and loss are anyhow ambivalent, with terror and farce as near generic neighbours. Furthermore, once-fearful scenes gradually become objects of uneasy comedy as the social realities guaranteeing their power modify such that the "past" can be constructed as a nightmare from which an enlightened "present" has awoken. It is easy now, fortunately, to laugh at the deaths of Little Nell, Little Eva or little Willie, and to deride "Victorian sentiment" in general. But these are historical assumptions, misinterpreting the cultural codes and gender interests of a theatre audience different in its historical experience and class composition from the largely middle-class live theatre of today. As Keneally writes in the "Epilogue" of his novel *The Playmaker*, "Antibiotics and plumbing have made melodrama laughable to a modern reader. It is only in our own third world, where in the one phase of time lovers are sundered, clans consumed and infants perish without once saying, 'Mother', that melodrama causes tears still to flow."[15]

There were, then, powerful factors in the social formation which induced colonial theatre-goers to seek out theatrical articulation of their lives, a practice which many have impatiently dismissed as mere escapism.[16] In the attempt to reconstruct the absent element from our early Australian theatre — the audiences and what they knew — melodrama's enduring authority can be glimpsed. We are now prepared to consider the function of apperception in the creation of cultural artefacts, and acknowledge that receivers pull out those messages which can be used in the act of reception, and shrug off the rest. This applies as much to users of popular culture as to any other receiver, and an audience's or an individual's own purposes may be far from, or subversive to, the overt or acceptable codes of the original transmitters. Hence playtexts of foreign provenance can be read as "Australian" when performed in that context. Early theatre-goers should be seen as skilled and practised decoders of their theatrical forms rather than as an inert and manipulated mass. There was nothing either supine or silent about colonial popular audiences: as countless contemporary accounts testify, the theatre was their space and they vociferously let their wants be known. The long process of somatic and intellectual regulation of the working class by its class superiors, now an integral feature of most theatrical audiences, had not yet triumphed. (This actually Pyrrhic victory was accomplished, ironically, not by cultural missionaries but by the defection of the mass audience to sound cinema in the late 1920s, leaving a defeated and demoralised live theatre to the commercial chains and the educated elite to dispose of as they would.) Far from their waiting in pious expectation for the advent of Ibsenite realist drama or of

the bush-vernacular school, early audiences, including
significantly women and young people, were getting on
with the creation and negotiation of our communal cultural
imagery.

The construction of "Australian" self-images via the
nineteenth-century stage has received scholarly attention
recently; hence one of the most pervasive cultural
mediators of its time (the other being the press) is
receiving some of the attention it requires. Margaret
Williams in her *Australia on the Popular Stage* (1983) has
traced the mutations of melodrama, pantomime and other
theatrical forms as they adapted to local conditions in
terms of plots, character types and settings. The triumph of
bush comedy-melodrama at the end of the century
dominates in Williams' account, since urban audiences seem
to have then desired to locate the lost yet ideal world of
pastoral in their country's past and in its interior. Not that
the 1890s marked the beginning of theatrical nationalism
as such: this arguably occurred not in the 1890s but the late
1860s; not in melodrama but in pantomime and burlesque;
having not a rural but a distinctly urban inflection.[17] In
later decades such actor-managers and playwrights as
Walter Cooper, George Darrell, Bert Bailey and Alfred
Dampier produced splendid late-colonial nationalistic
melodramas which form the surviving traces of the early
nativist repertoire. Of these, *For the Term of his Natural
Life* (eleven versions from 1885 to 1913), *The Sunny South*
(1883), *The Eureka Stockade* (four versions from 1891 to
1907), *On Our Selection* (1912) and *Robbery Under Arms*
(1890) are the texts best known today, through their film
versions and through Currency Press's publications. But this
strand of local theatre, so coherent with elements of the
bush-*Bulletin* nationalist discourse, is not the whole story.

In the "Introduction" to his edition of Dampier and
Walch's 1890 melodrama *Robbery Under Arms*, Richard
Fotheringham corrects the impression that only bush or
local-flavoured shows drew houses. Contemporary sources
certainly indicate that audiences, particularly the young
and hence native section, could not get enough of either the
tang of the gums or the clang of the Swanston Street tram.

But audiences are various in their age, class, factional loyalties and gender composition, as the account of Dampier's 1888-1892 Alexandra Theatre season in Melbourne shows. The financial success of the season was actually guaranteed by female box-office. The most-performed play was the "Ladies' Drama" *The World Against Her,* written by the Englishman Frank Harvey, which tops all of Dampier's locally written "Aleck" offerings in popularity, winning over *Robbery Under Arms* itself, *Marvellous Melbourne, The Scout,* the lurid *Wilful Murder, The Miner's Right,* the old favourite *Count of Monte Cristo* and his own *East Lynne* version. As Fotheringham states, "not for the first or last time the influence of women in audiences and the domestic as subject matter was underestimated and undervalued." *The World Against Her* was a financial success, even if "Authorities in these matters are bothering their wits to divine the reason thereof".[18] The pervasive bankability of the domestic theme shows that urban and female myths were powerful forces in theatre, and constructs of the emergence of any turn-of-century "Australian identity" should be prepared to incorporate such evidence along with the more male-centred discourses of dramatic nationalism.

My project is to foreground the contemporary co-existence with the bush-nationalist and "Marvellous Melbourne" repertoire of plays addressing domestic themes, whose appeal was variously to female and juvenile interests. As we know, the drama of the age incessantly dwelt on themes of marriage and motherhood, and the charismatic figure of the Mother, whether guilty or sanctified, dominates these plays. Granted that many domestic dramas were overtly moralistic, their covert mythic meanings were subversively recoverable, feeding in their audiences not only orthodox constructions but also ideas and passions either nameless or suppressed. Hence in a sense the stage Mother's literal guilt or sanctity hardly matters to her impact; she was a transfigured and transformative icon. Nina Auerbach writes of the nineteenth century's figure of the woman as empowered, particularly on the stage, even by the taboos which enchained her.[19] Kay Schaffer however demonstrates that the discourse of the Maternal occupies a central position in Australian self-imaging, arguing that "the 'damned whore' is not the predominant underside [to 'God's Police] of the code for Australian femininity. Rather, it is the bad mother".[20] Moreover, she sees the Mother as standing as a projection of white male desire for the land itself, which resists its "son's" attempts at mastery: "in Australia the fantasy of the land as mother is one which is particularly harsh, relentless and unforgiving".[21] Hence it seems that, despite their overtly non-Australian origins or subject matter, the domestic drama's stage-mother's transcendent power may have sublimated discursive connection with the Land-as-Mother construct which Schaffer discerns in 1890s and subsequent literature. Audiences read theatre through their own dominant social coding, thus producing "Australian" readings of international culture.

Motherhood is made central to this argument not only because the mother-child dyad dominates popular stage iconography, but because its centrality in feminist analyses opens the way for reading the contemporaneity of important strands of colonial culture. Dorothy Dinnerstein argues that:

> Woman, who introduced us to the human situation and who at the beginning seemed to us responsible for every drawback of that situation, carries for all of us a pre-rational onus of ultimately culpable responsibility forever after.[22]

Representations of the Mother thence are of vital interest to audience members, as all have been or will be variously mothers or children, or both. Marriage, however, in reversing the parent-child dynamic, complicates the issue. The woman was and is expected to provide maternal nurturance to the man in a grossly unequal social contract, but now without the parental immunity from retaliation. "Her transgressions, like the child's are punishable; his, like the parent's, are not" and "She thus carries the moral obligations of the parent while suffering the powerlessness of the child".[23] At the century's end Freud switched the problematic of maternity to concentrate on its effect on the (implicitly male) child; and motherhood as such becomes abstract and instrumental. Both Ibsen and *East Lynne* are pre-Freudian in this sense; they study the experience of maternity on the woman, as private and as social being. Part of the radical force of *A Doll's House*, still felt today, is a structural feature it in fact shares with the ostensibly more ideologically-bound *East Lynne*: the proposition, inherent in plot although not spelt out in dialogue, that motherhood and marriage are actually incompatible functions.

The particular dramas which I select to typify this maternal discourse are all significant to the history of late colonial theatre: Ibsen's *A Doll's House* (1879) and to a lesser extent *Hedda Gabler* (1890),[24] and the various dramatisations of Ellen Wood's 1861 bestseller *East Lynne*. That none of these plays is Australian-written[25] is partly because the contemporary Australian melodrama with its own readings of gendered potential is considered elsewhere in this collection; and partly to provoke acknowledgement that "Australian" readings are products not of the provenance of the texts but of the historical specificity of the audience, who negotiate meanings to suit their needs and situation. The difficulty is to avoid the trap of constructing a monologic "Australian audience", or even a "female audience", since this can universalise significant differences in class, age, ethnicity, religion and gender. I want to suggest ways in which these highly visible plays by Ibsen and the Wood adaptors offered different, even conflicting, possible readings to the female and juvenile audience members. Since motherhood is the dominant discourse, "juvenile" is taken to mean not only the actual young people in the gallery and pit, but a child-identified view of maternity available to a receiver of any age. It is a complex and shifting set of responses which these texts mobilise.

As Ibsen's plays are relatively well known, I shall concentrate on *East Lynne*. Ellen Wood's sensational novel was, with Wilkie Collins' *The Woman in White* (1859) and Mary Braddon's *Lady Audley's Secret* (1862) one of the age's bestsellers, whose popularity depended on the feminisation of the late nineteenth-century mass reading market. In dramatised form, much-loved and much-parodied, it held the stage from the 1860s until well into this century. With Jones's *The Silver King* (1882), itself inspired by the success of *East Lynne*,[26] it was one of the many mid-century plays relying on "child-appeal".[27] It came to stand as the classic formulation of the ultimate projection of Utopian ideal — the mother, both lost and found. Now known principally, if dismissively, for its much-satirised line "Dead, oh dead! And never called me Mother", the play was box-office magic. With *Camille, Uncle Tom's Cabin* and *The Ticket-of-Leave Man*, it carried managements over bad financial patches in endless revivals.[28] It also supplied actors with a desirable commodity which Ibsen and Shaw also exploited; a "fat" female role. What was the secret, apart from its performance values, of *East Lynne's* popular success? It is true but inadequate to see it as merely another fallen-woman play, warning and prescribing woman's place. It is that and more: its Utopian and critical discourses should be considered as well as its ideological role. The heroine, Lady Isabel Vane, does "err" in rashly leaving her middle-class marriage for a seducer and so forfeits domestic security, but the real heart of the play — as distinct from the novel — is the mother-child relationship. Disfigured in a railway accident and disguised as a governess (the usual alternative middle-class female option to marriage), Isabel, wishing to be near her husband and children and nurse her ailing son, returns to her former home, where her devoted husband has married another. Like "Squeaker's Mate" she must witness the endearments showered on the new wife. The much-parodied line indicates the outcome: close at hand but unrecognised, her alienation is compounded by the child's dying in ignorance of her identity.[29] Shortly afterwards she herself dies after an affecting deathbed reconciliation "until Eternity" with the excessively virtuous Archibald Carlyle. The motif of the disguised and disfigured heroine, believed dead, who is faithful to her loved ones even though unrecognised by them, served Furphy for the Nosey Alf romance in *Such is Life*.[30]

Given the mythic motifs of the lost mother, the unrecognised loved ones and the dying child, *East Lynne* certainly merited its tribute of tears. The stage versions, given the relative literary compactness of drama and the scope for tragic acting, are I would argue more subversive and less recuperative than Wood's novel. This initial text foregrounds an emasculated rendering of the marriage tie, obsessively emphasising Isabel's guilt and Carlyle's husbandly perfection, but dramatisation of crisis moments renders this already unstable reading very much open to negotiation. Moralising apart,

> The audience did not allow any tampering with their sympathetic identification with Isabel. When Edwin Forrest starred as Carlyle, he tried to shift the weight of the final scene by giving himself a long speech blaming Isabel for the suffering she had brought to him and to the children. The audience booed so much that he quickly returned to the ending they expected. The popular audience for *East Lynne* came to cry, and their release in tears required not only Isabel's suffering but also her virtual apotheosis. Some versions closed with a tableau of Willie and his mother enthroned on a golden cloud.[31]

Hijacking and massive reconstruction of extant fables by popular theatre is a common occurrence, of which this American instance is but one example. A performance text cannot in any case be unproblematically compared to a literary text. The volatility of the popular audience and theatre's arsenal of signifying codes, which provide countless avenues of potential resistance to dominant discourses, have earned it the distrust of the powerful throughout its existence, with suppression and state regulation as expected periodic phenomena.[32] In the 1890s the colonial stage remained a disputed and electric cultural site, with various highly-changed lines of desire, whose subversive trajectories could not be surging between stage and audience predicted or controlled even by the interpretants.

The libidinal investments in such an *East Lynne* performance could thus be various. To those of Louisa Lawson's opinion that woman the ever-submissive "sham angel" was no longer a "spectacle worthy of sympathy and reverence",[33] the gross disproportion of Isabel's suffering to her lapse confirmed that the spectacle had reached a point of ideological crisis where repressed meanings were on the verge of vehement articulation. Women in more-or-less satisfactory bourgeois marriages could vicariously enjoy Isabel's transgression, be grieved by its punishment, consoled and justified by the real or implied maternal apotheosis, or assured that marriage worked if only *they* would work at it a little harder yet. Working-class women, to whom the Domestic Angel ideal was anyhow a fantasy inappropriate to the real material conditions of their lives, could also appreciate that the bourgeois marital ideal, into which the recalcitrant colonial working class had been corralled since mid-century at least, was actually not all that liberating. Perhaps, in impulses of class revenge, they might sardonically reflect that they should be so lucky as to have only Isabel's problems![34] Single women, such as Catherine Helen Spence wrote about and for, could gain access to identification via the "governess" disguise and enter into the forbidden realms of maternity and wife-hood, and possibly be relieved to return to their single state at the end of the performance. And for "children" (as actual people or child-identified adults), *East Lynne* offered the sadistic option of vicarious punishment of the Mother for her seeming absence or withdrawal — a need which Dinnerstein sees as implanted in both sexes under current social arrangements, where the mother has sole caring role in infancy, and must bear subsequently the "pre-rational onus of ultimately culpable responsibility". Yet the "children" could also be mythically reassured: although Mother appears to be absent or to have deserted, she is really near at hand, loving and caring, her life revolving around theirs. The opposites of life and death, near and far, love and hate, have their boundaries eroded in such mythic material, where desire eludes the rational categories and ambitiously seeks total satisfaction — part of melodrama's enduring vitality to our own day.

While the "Australian sense of humour" — masculine, sardonic and under-stated — has been privileged as the topic of much comment, and the 1890s frequently located as the flowering time of this alleged typifying national trait, equally demanding of investigation is what popular audiences weep over: a phenomenon usually consigned scornfully to the realm of the Feminine. Yet numerous testimonies of colonial theatre show that male and female responses were not always differentiated, nor was "masculine" unemotionality held as necessarily a privileged stance; both sexes would shed tears openly at sad scenes. Claude McKay's tongue-in-cheek account of a performance of *East Lynne* depicts the stockbroker in the stalls and the beer-stained burglar in the gallery united in weeping over Eugenie Duggan's rendition of the famous finale. Although McKay's satirical point is that "the criminal classes are the most emotional", it is significant that both of McKay's exemplary figures at this quintessential "ladies' drama" are men.[35] Melodrama brought some of the pain into visibility and formalised its expression. The precise nature of male libidinal investment in such performances is, however, a question requiring a "masculinist" critique of our culture as vigorous as feminist critiques have proven themselves to be.

The popular *East Lynne* arguably drew as powerful and complex responses during its decades of extraordinary ubiquity as Ibsen's more famous quasi-realist plays have evoked. The three plays — *East Lynne, A Doll's House* and *Hedda Gabler* — can be read across each other, as they share a repertoire of symbolism and plot-motifs which cancels out the tendentious dichotomies of melodramatic/ realist, or popular/art theatre, and illuminates their essential partaking of similar discourses of femininity, bourgeois selfhood, motherhood and marriage. The controversial chipping apart of the ideologically unified mother/woman icon is Ibsen's most notorious contribution. "They are not all made to be mothers", he mused in his working notes for *Hedda Gabler*[36]; and *A Doll's House* provoked scandal in its splitting of the wife/mother unity, proffering also the suggestion that an infantilised woman cannot adequately mother her own children. Schaffer's reading of Baynton's "The Chosen Vessel" supports this discourse of subversion of the Maternal: "What confers the power of the Maternal as a concept, also demands the denial of the Mother as a person".[37] In Spence's then unpublished novel *Handfasted* (1879), marriage is again separated from motherhood, in a Utopian setting where the stigma of illegitimacy is removed. *East Lynne* also splits marriage from motherhood; just as Nora must leave her doll's house before she can adequately mother her children, the banished Lady Isabel must return and tend her dying child when herself presumed dead: maternity is presented, for the real woman, as a literally impossible state. Lady Isabel, like Hedda Gabler, is a déclassé aristocrat fallen into the stuffy respectability of middle-class marriage, rife with single female relatives possessive of the husband and small-town ambitions, whose constricting conventions trigger a desperate revolt (Sir Charles Levison acting as the Lovborg/Brack character). In all of the plays, then, successful motherhood is problematic: images of dead and dying children, absent mothers and inadequate stepmothers abound. The former characteristic (dead children) is equally noticeable in some current Australian theatre, and hence may be read as a distinct and still-current post-colonial motif.[38]

All these texts can be subject to a "dual hermeneutic": one critical and one which recuperates their Utopian potential — Utopian in Jameson's sense whereby popular culture's appeal may be validated even where it is reactionary by advanced liberal standards; an appeal which seeks the Utopian moment concealed in such productions and obviates despairing consignment of popular taste to false consciousness or market reification.[39] The latter manoeuvre presumes an inert and powerless popular audience, unable to appropriate or resist ideological messages. Such an approach, seeing mass culture as reified, is, as Janice Radway argues, itself a symptom of cultural alienation, reproducing the reifying tendencies of late capitalism.[40] The controversial impact of the Achurch-Charrington Australian tour in 1889 of *A Doll's House* has been amply documented,[41] and the attempts by male middle-class reviewers, both literal and reactionary, to recuperate its textual meanings for their own ideologies are on record. As J. C. Williamson suggested to James Smith:

> It struck me that after Nora's final exit as at present arranged the children should come on and ask for their mother, Helmer tell them that she has gone, the children cry out for her, and their cry bring her back again, but I am in doubt as to whether anything should be spoken after she rushes back to embrace them, though she might say "My darlings, I cannot leave you!" What do you think?[42]

If institutionalised bourgeois patriarchy could make such vigorous attempts to co-opt Ibsen, it is conceivable that the muted women of the popular and middle-class audience could be just as active in recuperating *East Lynne* for counter-hegemonic readings, remote from literate male scrutiny. In the waves of volatile communication surging between actors and audience in live performance, Utopian desire, along with what Dinnerstein ironically calls the "truly feminine" responses of "masochism and split-off fury"[43] can all find a place.

Theatre is a site of highly-charged transformative transactions, "a privileged place where our ideology, our ideological condition, is in a spectacular manner checked by the force of desire."[44] Marie Maclean writes that ideally we need to "analyse the reader/spectator libidinal input as carefully as that of the author has been studied in countless works of psycho-criticism".[45] Although this project is highly problematic in the case of colonial audiences, its necessity must be acknowledged. In 1907, for instance, the nightly capacity of Sydney's theatres was 20,300 and Melbourne's 15,600[46] — late colonial theatrical consumption was an impressive rival to the popular press, which may account for the Bohemian superiority with which the *Bulletin* for one reported this presumptuously long-lived "colonial" activity which dared to persist in competing with it for the minds and money of the urban populace.

The problematic of motherhood, Fiona Giles argues, is central to the reclamation of the female romance tradition in our construction of late colonial culture. In her reading of the novels of Praed, Spence, Couvreur and Franklin she discerns "preoccupation with the discovery of origin" as a central generic theme, and disruptions to the mother-child bond as a typical narrative device, such that these heroines "enact the uncertainties created by their unprecedented significance as important agents in an emerging culture — in another sense motherless".[47] The maternal, the romance tradition, and the colonial stage which addressed both and has been marginalised by a "feminine" ascription, are related cultural phenomena. Each appears to have suffered at times a similar fate of partial or total invisibility, which is understandable given the "feminine" discursive inter-connections argued here. In order to understand fully the complexities of late colonial culture, the role of theatre in both its imperial and nationalist inflexions should be reincorporated into an on-going critique of "Australian" self-imaging. From the viewpoint of female or juvenile meanings, neither inflection is necessarily automatically privileged; the former may in fact be as rich or richer a field as the latter, and both are in any case inextricably connected by the "Australianising" readings of their audience. Urban, topical, class-stratified, culturally eclectic, ethically and morally didactic yet with an urgent mythic underlay, and with a magpie fascination with new intellectual trends, colonial theatre was a rich, lively and pervasive phenomenon. It should not be stigmatised for seeming to provide for contemporary andocentric constructions of "Australian culture" a rejectable model of a "Bad" mother.

Postmodernism, Cultural History, and the Feminist Legend of the Nineties: Robbery Under Arms, *the Novel, the Play*

John Docker

In the last few years the cultural history of the 1890s is beginning to look very different from what it was, less concerned with a certain range of "high literature" writers and texts held to be central, or with a presumed pure rural "folk" culture. Theatre historians in particular have done marvels of recovery of nineteenth-century urban popular theatre, from pantomime to melodrama. But cultural history still occasionally suffers at the hands of the cultural theorists themselves. As I noted in *In a Critical Condition*, the two most influential post-World War II approaches, the Radical Nationalist and the New Critical/Leavisite, both anchored their view of Australian cultural history in accounts of the Nineties. For the Radical Nationalists of the 1950s and 60s, a truly distinctive literature, and an accompanying democratic, egalitarian spirit, was there for all to see and build on in the writings of Lawson and Furphy, in the work of the bush balladists, and in the Sydney *Bulletin*, a literature and spirit that developed in response to Australia's unique natural environment. The assumption was that culture in the cities in colonial Australia was similar to the culture of other world cities. It could not therefore yield a distinctive national tradition, and so was of little interest to cultural history.

The New Critics/Leavisites disagreed. Also writing from the 1950s on, they felt the Radical Nationalists were being unduly restrictive and prescriptive, wishing to confine "Australian literature" to writers such as Lawson and Furphy, and ignoring Nineties writers with obviously strong international literary affinities and "universal" metaphysical interests like Christopher Brennan. And Brennan could be seen as inaugurating the true line of "Australian literature", in the writings of Slessor, FitzGerald, Hope, Wright, McAuley, Patrick White, Martin Boyd and the like. In any case, they thought, you could argue that Lawson and Furphy also, if you tore away the wrappings of temporary social and political ideals, were metaphysical in their underlying essential interests. The spirit of the times was not robustly egalitarian and optimistic, but edged by those primary modernist values, gloom, terror, defeat, despair, uncertainty, meaning-lessness, values waiting to be discovered as much in Lawson and Furphy as readily apparent in Brennan.

Yet there were similarities between the New Critics/Leavisites and the Radical Nationalists. For both, the "lower genres", principally of melodrama and romance, on the page or stage, were of negligible interest. Only either "pure" "folk" genres, or genres recognised as "high" in this century (lyric poetry and ballad verse; realism, naturalism, the tragic), could yield the abiding qualities of a culture, the insights into a society's spirit and times that could be taken as truly representative. Shared alike by the Radical Nationalists and their opponents was the defining modernist opposition to mass culture.[1]

In the 1970s and into the 80s anti-racist, multicultural, and feminist perspectives would come to question the Radical Nationalist focus, as in Russel Ward's *The Australian Legend*, on a legendary figure (based on the outback worker, the shearer, drover, bullock driver) as the admired typical Australian — laconic, irreverent, independent, stoical, sceptical, without affectation, and so on. The ideal Australian was free of family ties, a rolling stone, nomadic: was, that is, for later commentators, exclusively male, white, Anglo. And his portrait was drawn, they thought, from far too narrow a range of texts and genres of the Nineties period, a range that especially acted to exclude "lower" so-called female genres like romance. Feminist critics in particular have pointed to the importance of neglected romance writers like Ada Cambridge, "Tasma" (Jessie Huybers Couvreur) and Rosa Praed.[2]

In this way feminist criticism has, we might say, added its voice to and become part of a much wider "post-modernist" movement. In Australia and elsewhere, in film and TV and popular culture study generally, as well as in literary studies, aesthetic postmodernism questions the necessary superior/inferior relationship of "high" and "low" cultures.[3] It questions the need for a hierarchy of genres, by which an entire genre can be judged inferior for lacking the qualities of other genres. It sees genres as having their own specific identity, their own specific aesthetic character, their own history of possibility and potentiality. It especially defends the "lower female genres" like melodrama and romance.[4] It defends and rescues for cultural history genres considered "lower" like travel literature.[5] It builds on previous theories of popular culture and genre like those of Bakhtin, Benjamin, Brooks.[6] It ... reader, I love it.

Postmodernism does not see literary or historical periods as possessing a single true spirit, a single dominating character, a single ideology or discourse, a single conflict or point of opposition, but rather as contradictory, heterogeneous, diverse, fragmented. There might be multiple oppositions and conflicts. Instead of a single coherent structure, a presumed centre, there are forces and structures with no easy "fit", either in relation to each other or to the "time" they are in.

In conceptualising historical periods, however, postmodernism and some influential recent feminist cultural history draw steadily away from each other. Here feminist interpretations of the Nineties look back to the structuralism of previous theory. Like the Radical

Nationalist and the Leavisite/New Critical approaches, feminist criticism is currently also positing a single determining force or spirit for the period. We are witnessing the construction of an essentialist, a legendary view of the literary, cultural, and intellectual life of the 1890s.

In this Feminist Legend of the Nineties, we find, in the words of major pioneering figure Marilyn Lake, that the Nineties was through and through dominated by "masculinism". The national ethos as evoked by Russel Ward in *The Australian Legend* can now be identified not as the property of rural male nomads but as the creation of the urban Bohemians of the Nineties clustered about the *Bulletin*, the "most strident of the masculinist magazines" of the time. These male Bohemians projected the values of their own lives, of bachelordom and male camaraderie, on to the Bush, translating male camaraderie as mateship and a bachelor lifestyle as the bushman's nomadic freedom from family ties. In promoting the Bushman as cultural hero, in eulogising him as heroic ideal, in all-round idealising him, the *Bulletin* and *Bulletin* writers like Lawson were promoting, idealising, and eulogising themselves. The *Bulletin*'s "masculinist ideal" became, Lake claims, "typical" in the Nineties, its "ascendancy" excluding women and also deriding men who were not hostile to women, and who might believe in the family. Women were marginalised, forced to the periphery, the despised other, victims.[7]

In *The Nervous Nineties* I take up the challenge of this particular Feminist Legend in relation to the *Dawn*, the *Bulletin*, and William Lane. Its argument has also been questioned by critics like Brian Matthews and Julian Croft in relation to Lawson and Furphy. Matthews argues that the men in Lawson's stories, far from exerting masculine dominance, feel they are always unworthy of, and fail the women in their lives; while Croft points to a submerged narrative in *Such is Life* where romance is admired.[8] If Matthews and Croft are right, then the Feminist Legend is in danger of overlooking and denying the ambivalences and pro-women and pro-feminist aspects of Nineties male writing; even the *Bulletin*'s attitudes to women were, as Sylvia Lawson argues in *The Archibald Paradox*, contradictory.

Further, in its rush to see women and women writers in the Nineties as victims of masculinism, the Legend is in danger of underestimating the degree to which women were active agents in their own history: for example, as writers and readers of the highly popular romance novels themselves. The Legend, that is, in stressing only ideological domination and oppression, is in danger of downplaying the strength and achievements of female culture in the Nineties, its vigorous feminism and feminist journalism as in the *Dawn*, its debating societies as in the Dawn Club, its rapid political organisation and respected public figures. It also is in danger of forgetting the most spectacular "symbolic" public figure of the times, male or female, the smoking, bicycling, Rational Dress and trousers-wearing New Woman. Feminism and female culture were, indeed, important and influential in the Nineties period. As I argue in *Debutante Nation* (1993), the *Bulletin*'s frequent anti-feminism and misogyny was, we could argue, a defensive and ever less influential position. Its stridency can be read as indicating fear, a sense of losing ground to new ways of thinking about the relations between men and women. Its tone on these issues will involve detailed analysis of Nineties texts, and this process is still in its early stages. In this essay I want to test the "masculinist" thesis of the new Feminist Legend by looking closely at the gender relations created in the two versions of *Robbery Under Arms*, Rolf Boldrewood's novel and its wonderfully free adaptation by Alfred Dampier and Garnet Walch as a melodrama for the popular urban and country-town stage. The two texts, we can say with Mikhail Bakhtin, enjoy a dialogic relationship, the play "conversing" with the novel, arguing with it, agreeing and disagreeing, questioning and probing, contesting and parodying.[9] I want to suggest that while feminist perspectives are helping us to re-examine such "lower genre" cultural history, the new Feminist Legend is leading us, for the while, down a false trail.

The Novel

While Rolf Boldrewood's *Robbery Under Arms* was first published as a serial in the *Sydney Mail* in the early 1880s, its popularity began with its re-issue in a single volume in 1889, after which it was reprinted frequently, and filmed a number of times. The 1889 version proved popular in part because its length had been cut; it remains, however, a very long novel, indeed tediously so. Its narrator is Dick Marston, who is in gaol awaiting execution for a life misspent as a bushranger, an interest stimulated by the discovery of gold at the Turon goldfields (near Bathurst) in 1850. Before that young Dick, along with his younger brother the genial Jim, their old ex-convict father Ben, the gentleman bushranger Captain Starlight, and Starlight's servant the "half-caste" Aboriginal Warrigal, had chiefly been engaged in cattle stealing, including the spectacular exploit of driving a huge mob of stolen cattle from New South Wales to Adelaide. The crime became known about because a prize bull, beloved by its squatter owner, had unwisely been taken along for sale. This had been at the insistence of Captain Starlight, whose taste for the flamboyant made his fame and endeared him to much of the colonial populace, but also endangered his freedom as well as that of his confreres. Whenever the police, in particular Sub-Inspector Goring and later Sir Ferdinand Morringer got too close, the gang would flee to the Terrible Hollow, a beautiful valley in the mountains fortunately known only to themselves. They also often found time to relax at a tavern run by Jonathon Barnes and his daughters Bella and Maddie. After various adventures, gaol escapes, and even some romance between Dick and Jim and the Morrison sisters Kate and Jeanie in Melbourne, where the boys were hiding out after the great cattle robbery, Jim and Dick and the Captain decide to disguise themselves as miners at the Turon, working under the very noses of the police. Here, however, Kate Morrison takes a hand in the plot. Now running a pub for the miners, she feels betrayed by Dick when she learns that he is actually in love not with her, as she had imagined from Melbourne, but with his childhood sweetheart Gracey Storefield. Accordingly, she betrays him, Jim (now happily married on the goldfields to her own sister) and the Captain to Sir Ferdinand. Nevertheless only Jim is arrested, at home with Jeanie, though he is released from his trooper captors by a daring Dick. Later, with the addition of far less salubrious and less honourable bushrangers like Dan Moran, the gang holds up a gold escort. Holed up at Terrible Hollow, the Captain, Jim and Dick feel this is not the life, and make a break for Queensland, where they hope to catch ship to California, when they would send for the women who love them (old Mrs. Marston; Jeanie; Gracey; and sister Aileen, who has fallen in love with the Captain). But betrayal dogs; Kate again pops up, near the border; Warrigal tells the police about Jim and Dick, whom he dislikes for reasons that are never given; and in any case a well-known horse of Starlight's is spotted. In a showdown with Goring and Sir Ferdinand, Jim and Starlight are shot dead, and a wounded Dick is brought to gaol so he can reflect on his life and write the novel. Fortunately, by the intervention of Grace's brother George, now a wealthy rural entrepreneur, and Mr. Falkland, whose daughter had once been saved by Jim, the sentence is commuted — though we and Dick only learn this near the end of the story.

Boldrewood's novel has clear affinities with the nineteenth-century adventure novel ("male romance"). It also has affinities with another popular genre of that century, the broadside supposedly spoken by the condemned man as his last words before being hanged (the broadsides were printed before the event; occasionally printers were caught out when the hanging did not take place). It often emphasised the wrongdoer's guilt and repentance.[10] But not always. A much admired figure in broadsides, as in popular mythology, music hall and melodrama, were the criminal hero, Captain Kidd, Jack Sheppard, Dick Turpin, admired for successfully outwitting their pursuers, but even if caught and hanged, remaining, like the music hall character Sam Hall, defiant to the last.[11] The criminal hero is clearly a carnivalesque figure, emerging from trickster tales and ballad, and festive World Upside Down traditions, that mock and overturn authority, respectability, and power.

Boldrewood's *Robbery Under Arms* wavers between the attitudes of repentance and heroic defiance. For the opening couple of hundreds of pages Dick frequently reminds us of his guilt, sorrow and anguish, his regret that he ever took up his "cross" life. Much of the novel is then spent recounting Dick and the gang's successful adventures, though tedious passages of repentance keep interrupting and slowing the pace of the narrative. The adventures, the danger, the daring, can be exciting; and Jim, Dick and particularly the rogue figure, the handsome and chivalrous Starlight, shade into carnivalesque folk heroes. Whatever comedy there is in the novel, surviving the mournful repentance, comes from respectable squatters, or upper-class New Chums, or the police being so frequently fooled, often by disguise, that stock-in-trade of the trickster and rogue, as when Goring and Sir Ferdinand are lured out of town and Starlight's famous horse Rainbow wins at the Turon races. Starlight himself feels that he is a "colonial Dick Turpin", an opinion shared by the local newspaper the *Turon Star* when it delightedly writes up the Rainbow incident, comparing Starlight's horse to Turpin's well-known steed. The *Star* also compares Starlight and Rainbow's exploits to an "enthralling melodrama", and Dick too, quite often, can bring himself to note that various comic moments of trickery and disguise are "as good as a play" — the novel here calling attention to how close its adventure passages are to legendary associations and popular stage representations. The pub run by Jonathan Barnes and his saucy, spunky, bold, sassy daughters Bella and Maddie, with drinking, dancing, singing (the "girls romped and laughed and pretended to be offended every now and then, but we had a regular good lark of it") might also bring to mind the carousing tavern that Dick Turpin could relax in, signifying a local population that was supportive of lawbreaker rather than law. At the end of the novel, however, repentance returns in a flood; we see Dick as a broken man, prematurely old, white-haired, grateful for the commuting of his hanging and his release after twelve years in prison, then making his way with the loyal Grace to North Queensland, there to end his days in honest rural work, the honest work he should always have done, and by which he would probably have steadily prospered, like Grace's brother George.[12]

In terms of the Feminist Legend, we might observe that the novel's adventure sequences are certainly dominated by the male characters, from Warrigal (also given to tricking by disguise) to Starlight. Old Mrs. Marston, from Ireland, is mentioned occasionally as off-stage crying. For long periods Grace and Aileen barely appear in the narrative, and Aileen is a particularly suffering figure, bowed in misery because of what the men have done to her family and her mother. Aileen hates and despises bushranging, as she tells Starlight, and believes Jim and Dick should work steadily and industriously in life, like George Storefield. She is, when seen, quiet, timid, pale, reproachful, bitter, wretched, miserable, sad, earnest, solemn, mournful, pleading, sorrowful, turning faint, weary of everything, quietly bearing the pain, drooping, despairing, hopeless. Once, when Ben Marston tells his daughter of some of his criminal doings, Dick comments that this "made poor Aileen a bit more miserable than she'd been before, if that was possible". Dick usually refers to his sister as "poor Aileen", and she also often has tears in her eyes, and might whimper or sob, though once she laughs in spite of herself. Aileen does become a bit more spirited as the novel goes on, once deliberately putting Sir Ferdinand, who had come to visit her, on the wrong track. But, like her mother, she was very observant of her religion, very regular in her prayers and crossings and beads, and when she learns of Starlight and Jim's death and Dick's gaoling, she tells her brother that she will not see him again because she has vowed her life to the Blessed Virgin; she would go into a convent and wear out her life in prayer because she knew she had committed a sin in pledging herself before to an earthly love. To every appearance Aileen is Victim.[13]

Yet, apart from old Ben, one of the least sympathetic characters in the novel, none of the chief male characters is contemptuous of women, derides them, or extols a female-free life. Even Starlight, who, not surprisingly in a trickster figure, declares that he will always pursue a wandering life ("An outlaw I, by forest laws, almost since the days of my boyhood, I shall be so till the day of my death"), finds that he has fallen into a kind of quiet love with Aileen, and hopes she can join him in America if he can escape. Jim is absorbed by his love for Jeanie, marries her, sets up house with her at the Turon, and is captured at the diggings because he insists on saying goodbye; later he joins Jeanie in Melbourne, they have a child together, and Jim evidently loves being a family man; when separated from her for any period he goes into a decline, fretting. Much of the repentance talk, and much of the interest of the novel, concern crime and punishment, even when not captured, and Dick accordingly expresses his torment that he has hurt Gracey and Aileen so much by his doings, and that he can not freely go home: much of his punishment, as for Jim, is that he is separated from women and family life. His freedom from capture is still deprivation. Dick indeed feels that his disregarding of the wellbeing of the women in his life is "unmanly".[14]

Nor do the sympathetic men of the novel enjoy mateship/male camaraderie either as a pleasurable existence in itself or because it excludes women.In their hiding place, Terrible Hollow, when they have to lay low, they rapidly become bored, find things dull, take to drink as solace, and then emerge either to engage in another escapade for the sake of tedium-relieving adventure, or to make their way to Barnes' pub to enjoy the company of Bella and Maddie ("Anyway, we all enjoyed ourselves. It was a grand change after being so long alone"). Dick, Jim and the Captain only really enjoy and appreciate the beauty of the Hollow when Aileen joins them there to nurse her father back to health, after he had been shot on one occasion. Here Starlight and Aileen realize their love for each other. But also Dick realizes that the presence of Aileen makes the place come alive: "Those were out and out the pleasantest days we ever spent in the Hollow — the best time almost Jim and I had had since we were boys". Only the presence of a woman makes the Hollow into

Arcadia. And in any case they feel women are their moral superiors.[15]

While Dick and Jim clearly enjoy riding a good hill-country horse (it is often a very horsey book), neither the bush itself nor bush life, except for that brief Arcadian moment when Aileen is at Terrible Hollow, is ever eulogised, as the Feminist Legend has it. Because the men are always away (legitimately shearing or fencing at the beginning of the novel), Aileen has to work extremely hard on their selection, doing all the dairying by herself. Dick appears to prefer anything to the continuous hard work of farming, whether it be adventure, or, when gold arrives, the country town life of the Turon diggings; and Jim, while he enjoys rural work, always follows older brother Dick. At Turon, as Dick says, they can escape from the "sad-voiced solitudes of the bush", a phrase that refers us to Marcus Clarke's famous evocation of the Australian bush as Weird Melancholy, as desolation, sullen despair; which is also how the bush is frequently perceived by writers in the Nineties, like Lawson and Boake — hardly empirical support for the Feminist Legend's claim that bush life is presented as ideal.[16]

Dick indeed declares that he wished he never had to leave the diggings (they only left because of Kate Morrison). He is clearly entranced with its cosmopolitan life, lovingly evoking the different nationalities on view: "There were Californians, then foreigners of all sorts — Frenchmen, Italians, Germans, Spaniards, Greeks, Negroes, Indians, Chinamen. They were a droll, strange, fierce-looking crowd. There weren't many women at first, but they came pretty thick after a bit. A couple of theatres were open, a circus, hotels with lots of plate-glass windows and splendid bars, all lighted up, and the front of them, anyhow, as handsome at first sight as Sydney or Melbourne ... all kept open till midnight ... It was like a fairy-story place, Jim said". It was also a democratic place, where none tried to "make out he was higher than anybody else". It was, Dick nostalgically recalls, a "grand time — better than ever was in our country before or since". It was "a new world".[17]

Dick and Jim particularly single out for admiration and emulation the Californian miners, big sunburnt men with beards and red silk sashes round their waists, with a sheaf-knife and revolvers stuck in them. Dick and Jim let their own hair grow long, and people take them for Yankees. For much of the latter part of the novel America beckons to them as a "new world ... a new life", its society apparently an extension at large of the exciting bustling life of the Turon goldfields.[18]

Starlight is also admired by his young friends for his cosmopolitanism, his knowledge of wondrous distant parts of the globe. Aileen, too, is an admirer of the cosmopolitan, never tiring of listening to stories of "the wonders" of great cities like Adelaide and Melbourne after the boys return home for a visit, and similarly being entranced by Captain Starlight as, in her perception, a wondrous cosmopolite. If she were a man, Aileen declares, she would go everywhere, for as it is, she has never been anywhere or seen anything, hardly so much as a church, a soldier, a shop-window, or the sea.[19]

We might, then, conclude these notes on the novel by suggesting that it nowhere presents as ideal a narrow, male-exclusive bush nationalism. On the contrary, what most excites the characters we are invited to sympathise with is urban and cosmopolitan life, preferably American, a new world that democratically and fascinatingly mixes in many nationalities. In terms of colonial society itself, characters like Dick and Aileen do not oppose a somehow unique "Australian" national identity to the identity of other societies. Dick and Jim clearly see themselves as "natives", as currency lads, meaning they are tall and can ride horses wonderfully, particularly in hill and mountain country. Aileen can also ride incomparably like a true currency lass, even with her head usually bowed in misery. But just as clearly Aileen, Dick and Jim admire Starlight (who also adopts Dick and Jim as in effect his sons — as "family" rather than "mates"), Starlight the English gentleman and English "criminal hero" figure. The novel here stresses the continuities in the new society between

Australian and English popular cultures in terms of anti-authoritarian, carnivalesque traditions.

Boldrewood's *Robbery Under Arms* is not without its many contradictions, including a frequent acceptance by Dick of class hierarchy, particularly that gentlemen like Mr. Falkland (there is also a much admired Mr. Knightly) and young gentle ladies like Miss Falkland really are gentlemen and ladies, full of honour and breeding, deserving to be above the likes of Dick and Jim in status and "rank". It is an attitude that puzzles Dick's American friend at Turon, Arizona Bill, who declares to Dick: "durn my old buckskins if I can see why you Britishers sets up idols and such and worship 'em, in a colony, jest's if her was in that benighted old England again".[20] Certainly Dick's admiration for true gentlemen and ladies contradicts his own love of the democratic "new world" of American-style goldfields society, the novel here revealing something of the conflicting attractions within Australian culture to England and America that we have become familiar with in this century.

The Play

The Feminist Legend can also draw little comfort from the play. Dampier and Walch first adapted Boldrewood's novel for the stage in 1890, and it immediately became a highly popular mainstay of the Dampier family's repertoire. As Richard Fotheringham explains in his introduction, the play as presented was a lot more than the words on the page, with its performance values, its music and expressionistic melodrama effects, its quick shifts from intense moments of pathos to comedy and burlesque. The play was a kind of mobile text, frequently changed for different audiences and conditions, and the version he reprints is from 1894.[21] The play drastically reduces the number of characters, particularly those of the admirable gentlemen, changes the character of Warrigal, and adds comic stage Irish police and a comic spinster figure. Notoriously, it allows Starlight to survive and he and Dick at the end of the play to be pardoned (they had saved Sir Ferdinand from the evil Dan Moran). In particular for our purposes, the play transforms the character of Aileen. Here is metamorphosis.

For if she is a dim, recessive, grey, sniffling and rarely appearing figure in the novel, Aileen fairly seizes the stage version, takes it over, and becomes a major player in its drama. Compared to Aileen's spectacular actions and exploits and lively romance with the Captain, Dick and Jim now hardly figure. Further, barmaid Maddie does not appear in the play, and Bella only minimally; their spunkiness, sassiness, sense of fun and mischief are clearly transferred to Aileen, who is a recognisable stage presence, the vigorous currency lass, the robust popular heroine, dashing horse-rider, independent, standing up for herself, recalling for the audience not only previous stage currency lasses but the stage presence and mythology of Kate Kelly.

As Richard Fotheringham points out, the play wishes to associate the stage Marston family with the actual Kelly family, who in sympathetic mythology were small Irish settlers brutally and vindictively harassed by the police, an harassment that turns the Kelly boys into social bandits rather than mere criminals. The play appears to assume its popular audiences would certainly know about Ned Kelly's powerful and moving Jerilderie letter denouncing the police and authorities for the persecution of his family. Chief persecutor in Ned's account was Constable Fitzpatrick, who tried to molest Kate Kelly sexually, and later was instrumental in having the Kelly brothers charged with murder, and their mother and her six-week-old baby imprisoned. He was dismissed soon after from the police force for lying and drunkenness. As Fotheringham also points out, this possible kind of police behaviour is carefully omitted by Boldrewood (T. A. Browne, an ex-police magistrate and goldfields commissioner) from the novel.

In Boldrewood's *Robbery Under Arms* judges and police, while often tricked by the outlaws, are not shown as malicious or persecutory or vindictive or brutal. Goring especially glows on the page, a genial kindly figure. When Dick is captured early in his career as outlaw at the family home, the troopers are civil to Mrs. Marston (who was keening) and Aileen (who looked "like a dead woman"), and Goring comforts the women as much as he can, recognising that it was no fault of theirs. Goring can put on an official face, "devilish stern and hard-looking", but generally he shows the human face of the Law; he had come from England, and was a "chap as liked the fun and dash of a mounted policeman's life". Dick thinks Goring shows pluck and gumption at what he does, that he is a smart, dashing chap, a good rider (though not as good as "us natives" in scrub and mountain country), and all-round a good policeman. What the outlaws do not like is civilians who try to capture them, like those who later hang around the Marston family home, one of whom tries to harass Aileen (he is shot for his pains by Ben Marston). In general, Dick says, he has "no call to have any bad feeling against the police ... and as long as they do what they're paid for, and don't go out of their way to harass men for spite, we don't bear them any malice". The only real villain in the novel is the particularly nasty bushranger Dan Moran, who is despised by Starlight and Dick and Jim.[22]

In the opening act of the play, however, we see a very different Goring, when he arrives at the Marston hut to try to capture Ben Marston; as it happens, Dick and Jim are at home, and a Mr. Beresford, Starlight in disguise, is visiting, the first time the Marston children have met him. Warned by Warrigal of Goring's approach, Starlight comments that Goring is the "smartest and most unscrupulous man in the force". Starlight then goes inside the hut. Soon after Aileen comes out for air, finding herself very attracted indeed to the notorious bushranger, though she does not know he is that, and indeed has already told him (as in the novel) that she does not like bushranging. Goring takes advantage of Aileen's being alone to harass her sexually, promising he will let go her father if she will become his mistress. In an aside Goring says he'll then "pop on him afterwards".

When Aileen angrily refuses, Goring grabs her, but the Aileen of the play struggles and breaks away, boxing his ears. Starlight enters, throws Goring down, who then vindictively says to him, "You shall repent that blow to the longest day you live", and to her: "My girl, you shall suffer for this. I'll never rest till you and yours are hounded out of the district." Dick and Jim also emerge from the hut to register the incident, Dick angry at the insult to his sister, Jim saying: "Curse you meddling police — you think you're the Kings of this country".

It is the evil policeman Goring, then, who stings Dick and Jim into being outlaws, whereas in the novel their engaging in a life of crime is largely, curiously, unmotivated. The novel's Dick indeed does not really know why he follows Ben into such a life; in part, he thinks, he and Jim are just obeying their father, in part they are doing it for the love of adventure and flash ways, in part because they can get to ride good horses, in part because the Devil is possessing them — and in part, Dick says in an unconvinced voice, because of the unfair disparities of rich and poor, squatter and small landholder. But he does not really know why. Ben's life of colonial crime is explained by his bitter memories of how brutally he was treated in England for wrongdoing when he was young. But the clear implication is that in colonial society itself there is no real reason for young men to take to crime or to resent or oppose authority, everyone can rise steadily by hard industrious work like George Storefield, the police are civil and the justice system fair. For the novel, justice in colonial Australia is not deeply tainted by Botany Bay Justice, by the harshness and brutality of English Old World law, as the contemporary *Bulletin* or Marcus Clarke's *His Natural Life* would have it.

The play chooses otherwise. And in it Goring is as good as his word, harassing the Marston family and vindictively pursuing Starlight and the Marston boys, who join their father in the gang, which is now also actively assisted by — Aileen. Her initial disapproval of bushranging, her conventional way of thinking about authority, is shown to be a pre-Goring illusion. At one point of peril Aileen dashes in on horseback and warns the gang of the troopers just in time: perhaps reminding the audience, if it needed reminding, of Kate Kelly's equestrienne feats (there was a report of official intervention to prevent Kate Kelly from appearing on stage on her brother Ned's famous white horse in one stage adaptation of the Kelly legend).[23] Another time, to try and prevent the vindictive Kate Morrison from revealing the presence of Jim, Dick and Starlight to Goring at the race meeting, she seizes Kate, takes away her pistol, throws her down and holds the gun to her head.

Neither Aileen nor Captain Starlight nor Jim nor Dick are interested in financial gain, and in this sense they are obviously not characters in any "realist" psychological mode, but are recognisably mythic "figures". In his *Australian Melodrama* Eric Irvin entirely appropriately entitles his chapter on the stage *Robbery Under Arms* "New-style Robin Hood". Starlight jokingly refers to himself in conversation with Aileen as such, while Dick and Jim are also signalled as entering a long English tradition of highwaymen (Dan Moran, for example, saying to Dick: "So you've took to the Queen's highway"). Dick is also true to such an ancestry in being in part a trickster figure, escaping the gallows: just as many a trickster of early modern Europe would escape the hangman (often by saying to that gentleman, look, you're doing this wrong, let me show you how to arrange the rope properly around your neck, and the hangman then hangs himself).[24] In cheating the hangman, and in Starlight's surviving wounds so severe that everyone thought he must be dead, Dick and Starlight are clearly not ordinary mortals, but recall a tradition, deep in the history of folk cultures, of the trickster as one who is always outsmarting death, and is overcoming the harshness and apparent inevitability of fate. Here the play extravagantly and joyously carries out a carnivalesque cosmology that the novel plays with and then at its end denies and reverses. (Interestingly, a 1980s film version, a South Australian Film Corporation production starring Sam Neill, based on the novel, with Starlight dying at the end, proved a box office flop.)

Aileen is also given a mythological history, Starlight telling her early on that she reminds him of Maid Marian. But the audience soon sees that the Aileen of the colonial play is not the pale and demure Maid Marian (or Marion) of "polite" culture. Rather she clearly belongs to a robust popular tradition. In an essay on Robin Hood and Maid Marion as carnivalesque figures, Peter Stallybrass argues that the connection of Maid Marion with Robin Hood did not establish itself until late in the sixteenth century. But long before this Marion had been an important figure in the festivities of May-games, with their plays, pageants, and morris dances. She could be played by a woman or transvestite man. She was not a "coy dame" but a "smurkyne wench", exchanging lewd jokes with the Fool who accompanied her. She could be used to signify the revolt of the powerless in subversive ways, and indeed various subversive acts were led by women or men dressed as women. In France, Marianne became a name for the French Revolution, and she figures in Delacroix's famous painting as Liberty, bare-breasted, a flag in one hand, a rifle in the other. In these ways, Stallybrass feels, Maid Marion was emblematic of the "unruly woman" of early modern Europe made well known to us by Natalie Davis in her "Women on Top" essay.[25]

The dialogue exchanges between Starlight and Aileen also suggest another context for Aileen, as heroine of romance, romance as we have come to know it since Jane Austen's *Pride and Prejudice*. In romance narratives the love relationship usually begins, or apparently founders, in conflict between the hero and heroine. The romance-hero is generally rich, commanding in manner, and older and more experienced in the ways of the world than the heroine. But he is not a tyrant, he can be made to change, to recognise the heroine's equality, and he does this because he is attracted to her for the very reason that she is independent and answers back and stands up for herself. In romance there is, that is, an exchange between his offering of confidence and knowledge (worldly and sexual), and her teaching him not to be arrogant and regard himself as superior. Much of the pleasure of the genre lies in the conflict and the conflict-dialogue.

The romance of Captain Starlight and Aileen is a feature of the play. Starlight is older, more experienced,

an educated gentleman from England (bearing, in a long
melodrama tradition, the guilt of a brother's crime). As
Aileen says, "You, a gentleman, and I only a bush girl".
Their romance, we have seen, begins in conflict, in her
telling Mr. Beresford/Starlight of her opposition to
bushranging; and she captivates Starlight by sending up
his old-world, courtly manner. She joins the gang, against
Starlight's urging, proving an invaluable member, and she
stands up to Starlight and his authority in a way not dared
to by Ben, Dick or Jim. Aileen and Starlight also engage in
comic conflict-dialogue, as when in Act One they agree to
be friends and shake hands:

AILEEN:	… Ooh! You've sprained my wrist.
STARLIGHT	(*with flask*): I'm so sorry. Let me rub some whisky on it.
AILEEN:	Is whisky good for sprains?
STARLIGHT:	Very good. Will you allow me?
AILEEN:	No, thank you.
STARLIGHT:	Then you will excuse me if I (*drinks from flask*)
AILEEN:	Did you sprain your throat?

This is not the Aileen of the novel. Nor is she the
marginalised woman of the Feminist Legend. This is no
victim.

Aileen also would have been recognised by Nineties
audiences as belonging to a long tradition of colonial stage
heroines. Margaret Williams argues in *Australia on the
Popular Stage* that there was virtually no equivalent in
Australian melodrama of the English heroine seduced by a
member of the upper classes and then abandoned to ruin.
The Australian heroine is made of altogether sterner stuff,
belonging to a tradition that can be traced back to
Geoghegan's 1844 *The Currency Lass; or, my Native Girl*.
The villain of colonial melodrama, Williams feels, never
had a chance against such vigorous and independent
heroines, beside whom the heroes themselves pale.[26] In
Dampier's stage version of *For the Term of his Natural Life*
Sylvia apparently stands up to Frere and punches him on
the jaw, the *Bulletin* describing the Sylvia of the play as
"pretty, winning, imperious, tender-hearted, fiery,
impetuous and affectionate".[27] Even Kate Morrison in the
stage *Robbery Under Arms* strikes Dan Moran when he tries

to take advantage of an alliance they form against Starlight and the Marstons. Such actions make more understandable Sybylla's notorious striking of Harold in Miles Franklin's *My Brilliant Career*, Sybylla having many of the characteristics of the romance and colonial-stage heroine.[28]

There are other elements in the play that bear on the Feminist Legend. Ben Marston is (as in the novel) a surly, unaffectionate, unlikeable figure, and we can observe that in melodrama as in much popular culture generally the Father is an object of carnivalesque dislodgement as a figure of moral authority, of wisdom and guidance, of patriarchy. Then there is the comic transvestism involving Warrigal. The Warrigal of the play is not the treacherous Warrigal of Boldrewood's novel, but rather belongs, as Margaret Williams observes, to a colonial stage convention of the Aboriginal servant as a sympathetic figure, who often by his or her resourcefulness saves from danger the heroes of the play.[29] Warrigal is still the faithful servant of Starlight, but he shares his loyalty and friendship as well with Aileen, Dick and Jim; the play stresses their affinity, white outlaws, black outcast. Characters do at times express racist attitudes. When the gentleman bushranger rescues Sir Ferdinand from Moran, the chief of police says, "Starlight, you're a white man", and on another occasion Sir Ferdinand refers to Warrigal as "the boy". Yet at most times Warrigal is near the centre of the drama's carnivalizing of usual relations, making fools of the police, scaring their horses, taking their guns, throwing stones at vulnerable areas of Maginnis and O'Hara, the comic, stage-Irish police. At one point Warrigal enters dressed as a woman. Miss Aspen the comic spinster figure, whose fearfulness and respectability contrast with currency lasses like Aileen and Grace, takes "her" (Warrigal's) arm, so she can be escorted to post a letter. Moments later she bursts back on stage shouting hysterically, "That woman was a man!" The carnivalesque inversion of man dressed as woman tells the audience, as it had told it for centuries, that the culture they are enjoying is presenting a deliberately topsy-turvy world, where relations of power, class, gender and age are being held up for scrutiny.

Conclusions

Like the novel, the play neither marginalises women nor presents male camaraderie as desirable; its final tableau, of Dick with Grace and Aileen with Starlight, hardly promises to be anti-family. Also like the novel, the play brings out for the audience's pleasure and reflection continuities in popular traditions between English and colonial culture, particularly in the legendary associations of Starlight and Aileen with Robin Hood and Maid Marian; Aileen has an added international association, with the courageous irrepressible heroine of romance, an Elizabeth Bennett or Jane Eyre. Both features, Maid Marian and romance-heroine, are developed in specific colonial ways in the currency lass. The cosmopolitanism of the Turon diggings that is so important in the novel is only lightly and comically sketched in the play; but the support for Englishman Starlight and the invocation of Maid Marian was, just as much as in the novel, a vote against a narrow male cultural nationalism.

We can certainly say that the Nineties melodrama image of woman as spunky, independent, irrepressible, unbowed, conflicts with a great deal of late nineteenth-century "high literature" texts, written under the sign of the tragic, where the heroine is a victim of unassailable male power, which can only be defied or escaped by madness, suicide, death. We can think of the fate of Lyndall in *The Story of an African Farm*, Tess in *Tess of the D'Urbervilles*, our own Judy in *Seven Little Australians*, the wife in Charlotte Perkins Gilman's *The Yellow Wallpaper*. But this is only to say that any period will be crossed by opposing discourses and genres, will be marked by cultural conflict, contestation, argument.

Finally, the Feminist Legend might have to acknowledge that there were sources of attitudes to women in the Nineties other than those contained in the *Bulletin*, in Lawson or Furphy, or the *Dawn*. It would be just as strange in our "postmodern" era to ignore cultural values in action on television, video, and film as it is to ignore pre-electronic mass entertainment, as in melodrama, pantomime, farce, music hall. Dampier and Walch's *Robbery Under Arms* reveals the importance for Australian cultural history of the "non-print media".

Romance Fiction of the 1890s

Peter Pierce

If romance fiction in colonial Australia was powerfully
influenced from overseas first by the novels of Sir Walter
Scott and later by those of Rider Haggard, Australian
authors working in this mode were still responsible for
originating some of the nation's foundation myths. In *The
Recollections of Geoffry Hamlyn* (1859), Henry Kingsley
invested Australia with a romantic, pioneering history;
pictured the local forms of outlawry; imagined adventurous
journeys into unsettled regions; and pondered the tensions
inherent in a belief in an inchoate Australian future and an
attachment to its recent British past. The veritable
treasure in his novel is to be found not haphazardly —
through prospecting or theft — but in the exploitation of
the pastoral wealth of Australia. Yet in this country,
according to Kingsley, that wealth is notional only. Its
efficient function is to buy back English land, thus to
retrieve one's British cultural heritage.

To qualify himself as one of the instigators of romance
writing in Australia, plain Thomas Browne re-christened
himself "Boldrewood" (from Scott's poem, *Marmion*) and
added "Rolf" because it had the savour of Icelandic saga.
In Australia he sought and determinedly fabricated "the
domain of legend and tradition" that would enable romance
fiction to be written here. In his famous Preface to *The
Marble Faun* (1860), Nathaniel Hawthorne judged that
"Romance and poetry, like ivy, lichen and wall-flowers,
need ruin to make them grow". In a country which lacked
the traces in stone of many human generations,

"Boldrewood" gave the semblance of historical remoteness to the events in the recent colonial past that he adapted for his fiction. Thus his most famous romance, *Robbery Under Arms* (1882-3), drew on the Turon gold rush of 1850, and Frank Gardiner's robbery of the gold escort at Eugowra Rocks in 1862, but treated them so as to make these incidents appear to be part of an age long ago.

In his short novel *In Bad Company* (1901), which "Boldrewood" wrote in the 1890s, he converted near-contemporary events into a dark, moralising historical fable. Outraged at the Queensland shearers' strike that had occurred early in the decade, he inflated it into "The Shearers' War". The unionists were transformed into "outlaws in the worst sense of the word", who even threatened the country with "civil war". "Boldrewood" was creating in the 1890s the insurrectionary, sanguinary history which the nation soon-to-be had seemed to lack. As an indigenous romance writer his endeavour was prompted by a premature nostalgia for the kind of history that Australia had not yet had time to have.

The balladists responded similarly. In the 1890s Henry Lawson was already lamenting "The Days When the World Was Wide", while A. B. ("Banjo") Paterson's purpose in "The Man from Snowy River" was to create a legendary figure to join an understocked pantheon, to make "a household word today" of a superficially unpromising representative of proto-national virtues — the stripling on his weedy pony. Another horse — the broken down animal in Paterson's poem "The Droving Days" — can take its owner back in memory to a golden, youthful time in his personal, and in Australia's national past. "Kiley's Run", a poem based on recollections of the station which Paterson's father had lost, is filled with "the stories of the days of old".

The provision of Australia with the means of historical nostalgia was still a powerful function of romance literature in the 1890s. It was in this seminal decade that Paterson wrote "Waltzing Matilda", now the national song, and the most famous of the romance tales sung and remembered here. The tone of the song summons up the defiant radicalism, the intransigent resistance to authority of legendary days in the pioneering past, but its genesis was very recent. The story behind "Waltzing Matilda" was an episode in the shearers' strike which Paterson had heard of while staying on Dagworth Station in western Queensland early in 1895. It concerned the burning of station property and the suicide of a swagman who had been harassed by squatters and police. In his novel, *In Bad Company*, "Boldrewood" had written of the same place and of some of the same events, though in a temper so far removed from Paterson's as to indicate the partisan divide in history and literary history which early opened up in Australia. For his part, "Boldrewood" did not admire the defiance of the swagman, but groaned instead about the need to defend Dagworth "against a lawless band humorously describing themselves as Union Shearers". This 1890s' contribution by "Boldrewood" would have no truck with the romanticisation of outlaws. The romance narrative was the only form in which he worked comfortably at length (though his sketches and essays are of considerable interest), but it was a form now less in tune with his political sympathies.

Although both writers are quixotically excluded from Leon Cantrell's anthology, *The 1890s*, Rosa Praed and "Boldrewood" continued their established careers as authors of romance fiction in that decade. Allegedly, "Boldrewood" was an author whose "talent had spent itself by the nineties". This is a judgment quantitatively hard to defend. During this decade, "Boldrewood" had seven novels published (one a revision of an earlier work) together with a volume of short stories. Probably no Australian writer of the 1890s was more prolific. Nor should Praed so readily have been disregarded. With Haggard's *King Solomon's Mines* (1885) and *Allan Quatermain* (1887) in view, Praed had naturalised the "lost race" romance in Australia. In his essay "The Lemurian Nineties" (*Australian Literary Studies*, May 1978), J. J. Healy showed how Praed, together with a number of other authors who had romance fiction published in the 1890s — J. F. Hogan, Carlton Dawe, Ernest Favenc,

J. D. Hennessy and G. Firth Scott — professed to believe that traces of the lost continent of Lemuria could be found in outback Australia. This ancient civilisation gave an antiquity to Australia that validated it as a territory for romantic exploits and discoveries.

Praed's novel *Outlaw and Lawmaker* (1893), one of three which she published in this decade, drew on memories of her childhood in Queensland and in part on her father's career in colonial politics. Yet — saturated as it is with the occult, with mesmerism, spiritualism, curses, superstitions — the novel is as exotic in its own ways as *Fugitive Anne* (1902) (where the lost race of the Aca is discovered in central Australia) or the numerous romances in which Praed expressed her belief in reincarnation. *Outlaw and Lawmaker* is set in Leichardt's (sic) Land, a country "wild enough for anything". And it is set in the past, enabling Praed slyly to joke about the apparition of historical distance in Australian fiction:

> These things happened a good many years ago. This strange tragic episode was felt to be a blot on the history of Leichardt's Land.

The title of the book indicates the double life of Blake, both bushranger and Colonial Secretary. To the infatuated Elsie Valliant his career seemed "like some wonderful tale of romance". For Blake, Australia is a romance precinct where — as the bushranger Moonlight — he can exorcise, chivalrously, the wild, tormented side of his nature. He labours under an ancestral Irish curse. To the colonial electors, however, Blake is "Monte Cristo. He chucks half-sovereigns to railway porters, and rides thoroughbreds fit for a king". Monte Cristo indeed: that was the name which Praed's husband fondly gave to his property on Curtis Island where the couple spent several desolate years early in their marriage.

The climax of *Outlaw and Lawmaker* occurs at a Romantic secret place, near the Rock of the Human Head. Here the fastnesses of Scott, Fenimore Cooper and "Boldrewood's" Terrible Hollow are recalled. Yet Praed has begun to corrode and to treat ironically some of the literary commonplaces with which she works. Earnest

prose has its say against romantic fancy, as dour Frank
Hallett scorns Elsie's notions of love:

> The sort of caring you mean is a romantic dream — the glamour
> that never was on sea or land, but only in the imagination of
> some romance writers'

At the rock, "a curious and romantic scene", subject of a
threatening Aboriginal legend, reached by traverse of a
forest "in which perhaps white foot had never trodden",
Elsie — soon to be abducted by Blake's accomplice Dominic
Trant — will be spoken of as "the goddess of these wilds".
Now Praed adds a daring satiric touch. Into an
immemorially romantic scene, she obtrudes an anachronism
— a young man with a Kodak who "was posing the half-
castes at a little distance from the Fall"!

Praed's satirical target may be those timid venturers
into Australia who let cameras do the office of
imagination, but the episode also shows a degree of amused
scepticism concerning the literary vehicle with which she
is working. A scrutiny of the romance fiction that was
produced in Australia in the 1890s suggests that its authors
were becoming self-conscious about the form. This did not
allay the pleasure that they took in writing romance,
despite a sense which some may have harboured that its
day had passed. The most important consequence of this
intuition was not a ceding of the literary high ground to
realism (as the literary history of the 1890s is sometimes
reckoned to have witnessed) but the sophistication of
romance narratives with satire.

Romance has always been an obligingly inclusive
literary form. In *The Progress of Romance* (1986), Jean
Radford argued that romance and realism have shown
themselves far from antithetical forms, ones capable
indeed of becoming "close and compatible literary
bedfellows". Kingsley and "Boldrewood" had realised the
portmanteau possibilities of romance. In their fiction they
took the licence to comment discursively on colonial
politics, lawlessness, the "coming race" in Australia, the
nature of riches and treasure here. Similarly, Rider
Haggard used his African romances to discuss the nature
and tenuous supports of civilisation, and the moral

relativities that travel disclosed. By the 1890s in
Australia, in the works of a small and heterogenous group
of writers, such commentary had taken on a satirical edge.
If we ask at first in vain of the whereabouts of literary
satire in the prose of the 1890s (for satire seems to have
been conceded as the province of cartoonists, leader writers
and versifiers) we can — by looking harder — find it given
life in the latitude allowed for criticism of contemporary
society within romance fiction.

In 1896, William Moore Ferrar's novel *Artabanzanus:
The Demon of the Great Lake* was published in London.
Dedicated to Arthur James Balfour M. P. (who would be
Tory Prime Minister of Britain from 1902 to 1905), the book
was subtitled "An Allegorical Romance of Tasmania".
Surprisingly turning up on their English doorstep, a very
old man tells his descendants a wonderful tale of his
holiday in the Lake District of Tasmania, "this land of
enchantment". It is a landscape (like the antipodean Lake
District popularised by the first generation of English
Romantic poets) that encourages reverie. Falling into a
"mesmeric trance", Oliver Ubertus (then a young man) is
given a beatific vision of the vast city of Eternity. So
moved is he that he recites to his indulgent hosts one of his
own compositions — a four page Jubilee Ode to Queen
Victoria. Ubertus is also vouchsafed a visit to the
Underworld. At Great Lake he encounters its demon —
Artabanzanus, a creature seven feet tall whose "robe was
the rough waterproof hide of a bunyip". Ferrar (as editor)
excuses the strange sights that follow when Ubertus is
taken down to Pandapolis by remarking that:

> Those who have read Mr. Rider Haggard's startling romance *She*
> will not be surprised at the wonderful pictures presented to my
> view in a hitherto unexplored region of the universe.

Ferrar's dream vision modulates into satire. The demon
reckons Tasmania to be very ripe for colonisation, and to an
extent Ubertus agrees. Reviving a robust local tradition of
political satire (from occasional poems attacking early
governors Arthur and Eardley-Wilmot, to such longer
productions as Edward Kemp's *A Voice from Tasmania*
(1846) and Maxwell Miller's *The Tasmanian House of*

Assembly (1860)), Ferrar has Ubertus inveigh against the colonial government. Landowners pay for public works, for urban extravagance. "We ought to be a happy people", he moans, "but we are little more than slaves". In this spirit there is a good deal more: the permissive form of romance has given Ferrar the chance to make complaints that he assumes are too little heeded in Tasmania.

In a much better known work, though one perhaps not so accurately known as it might be — Ethel Pedley's *Dot and the Kangaroo* (1899) — the satirical substance is largely incorporated within a dream vision. Dot is a lost child — that emblem, in nineteenth-century Australian literature and painting not only of the harshness of the bush but of the delinquency of parents. But Dot, unlike a small boy of the district whose fate she vaguely recollects, does not perish in the bush. "The romantic", wrote Henry James, stands for the things that "we never *can* directly know, the things that can reach us only through the beautiful circuit and subterfuge of our thought and our desire". In Pedley's romance, a sympathetic if sententious kangaroo befriends Dot, and gives her "small, sweet berries" to eat that enable her to understand the speech of the bush creatures. This awakened faculty opens her to admonishment. Humans "know no other way to live than that cruel one of destroying us all". The platypus grouches about the many books humans have written on him and looks forward to the time when, ceasing to be new creatures, humans will stop writing books altogether. The world, says the kangaroo, is a sad place because of humans, although once it was happy.

It is a fall from Edenic complicity between the human and the natural worlds which Pedley has imagined. Sleeping in the hollow of an old watercourse, Dot dreams of a court of animals (which at times turns out to be as fractious as Chaucer's "parlement of fowles"). Here she is arraigned "for the wrongs we Bush creatures have suffered". Pedley ends sentimentally, with reunion and separation. Dot is returned to her family, while the kangaroo finds its lost joey and goes back to the bush. Nevertheless, *Dot and the Kangaroo* retains sufficient intimations of what has been lost of Edenic possibility during the European habitation of the continent to darken a story that is benignly dedicated "To the children of Australia".

Besides Pedley, Cantrell had omitted from his anthology Praed, Ada Cambridge and "Tasma", thus persisting in that slapdash lumping of the careers of the three women writers which is first instanced in Henry Gyles Turner's and Alexander Sutherland's *The Development of Australian Literature* (1898). Out also was "Boldrewood", as we have seen. Cantrell also dismissed "some writers who established considerable reputations during the nineties ... Louis Becke, Ernest Favenc, and E. J. Brady". Becke's and Favenc's "tales of life in the exotic tropics" disqualified them by being "somewhat removed from the spirit of the nineties I have attempted to capture". That is, they did not suit still another tendentious interpretation of the decade. Yet Becke's writing exemplifies not only a long-secured function of romance fiction in Australia — that of colonising and mythologising the land (or, in Becke's case, the Pacific islands where he had worked as trader, supercargo and perhaps pirate) — but also the increasing satiric, analytical burden of that fiction. Becke wrote two historical novels in collaboration with Walter James Jeffery in the 1890s, and a collection of his short fiction, *By Reef and Palm*, was published in 1894.

The latter are stories that entice readers with languidly romantic, balmy island landscapes, and claim a veridicial quality on the basis of Becke's experiences there. Yet almost all of the stories have violent rather than consoling episodes at their core. Most concern marriage. By transposing his setting from urban, domestic life in Australia to the Pacific, Becke gave himself a mordant freedom. He used it — as Herman Melville had half a century before him — to castigate the role of European missionaries who proclaimed "This new foreign god, which said that all men were equal, that all were bad, and He and His Son alone good". But it is the marriages con-

ventionally made in Australia that are Becke's chief
satirical target in these anti-romantic tales of the islands.

The first of the stories, "Challis the Doubter", tells of
how a man "cursing the love-madness which once possessed
him, walked out from his house in an Australian city with
an undefined and vague purpose of going 'somewhere'".
This is a flight from domesticity more extravagant than
any Lawson was writing of at the same time. Challis
abandons his smug, flirtatious wife (the "white lady" of
the subtitle), takes a "brown woman", and is last seen
living contentedly, with no sense of being in moral or
physical exile. In such a way can marital discord be
resolved in romance fiction, and "among the Islands of the
North-west Pacific".

The titles of the other stories in *By Reef and Palm*
signal Becke's disposition to analyse the elements of
conjugal life in the less cluttered social environment of
these islands. The stories include "The Revenge of Macy
O'Shea", "Long Charley's Good Little Wife" and "The
Doctor's Wife", the latter subtitled "Consanguinity — from
a Polynesian Standpoint". The first of these stories is
Becke's rebuttal of anyone who might have suspected him
of entertaining sentimental views of married life in the
Pacific. The worst exploit of the brutal Macy O'Shea is
recalled. He has this pedigree: "sometime member of the
chain-gang of Port Arthur, and subsequently runaway
convict, beachcomber, cutter-off of whaleships, and
Gentleman of Leisure in Eastern Polynesia". One of the
brutes of Marcus Clarke's fiction has strayed into Arcadia.
In the tale, Macy's cast-off wife murders her successor. So
he has her stripped, flays her with the "serrated tail of
the *fai* — the gigantic stinging-ray of Oceana"; has her
right hand cut off and watches her die.

The views of sexual and married life by reef and palm
may be unsentimental, but Becke registers the overt
intensity of passions that are camouflaged or sublimated at
home in Australia. The protagonist in "Pallow's Taloi"
kills for love, then shoots himself when his native wife
dies. In "Enderby's Courtship", the vicious Langton is
murdered in righteous anger by Enderby, who later marries

the Scotch-Tahitian Mrs. Langton. In this way murder is palliated by chivalry and — Becke implies — hypocritical European standards of judgment must be set aside. Another aspect of that hypocrisy is dissected in the story called "Long Charley's Good Little Wife". Because he had unluckily "lost the run" of the last Mrs. Charley during his absence at another island of the group, Long Charley seeks a replacement. The narrator explains the business in the deadpan fashion that he brings to all of these tales:

> In the South Seas, as in Australia and elsewhere, to get the girl of your heart is generally a mere matter of trade.

With twelve yards of turkey twill Charley buys a new wife: "And thus without empty and hollow display, were two living hearts made to beat as one".

That sardonicism is often the note that Becke strikes in these stories of marital union and discord in the Pacific. *By Reef and Palm* avoids the easy path of titillating Australian readers with disclosures of island customs and breasts in the name or disguise, of an account of cultural and moral relativism. Becke's romance has an unyielding satirical undertone. He will, for instance, insist on how essentially alike (and demeaning to women whether brown or white) are marital transactions in Australia or Polynesia. The narrator warns "The Methodical Mr. Burr of Majuru" (in one of the grimmest of all these stories) that:

> You are not like any of us traders... it doesn't harrow our feelings much if any one of us has to divorce a wife and get another; it only means a lot of new dresses and some guzzling, drinking, and speechifying, and some bother in teaching the new wife how to make bread.

Becke also uses the freedom of the romance form to allow for Polynesian strictures on the behaviour of Europeans, as in the native woman's remarks on the marriage of cousins in "The Doctor's Wife": "I say again thy women have not the shame of ours. The heat of desire devoureth chastity even in those of one blood".

Out of a mistaken sense that Becke's work is exotic in more than its physical setting, Cantrell excluded him from *The 1890s* anthology. In *The Oxford History of Australian*

Literature (1981), Adrian Mitchell agreed that Becke belonged to "a persistent sub-stratum of Australian fiction" which — like Somerset Maugham's work — "had looked to reefs and islands". Mitchell numbered as Becke's successors Vance Palmer (under the pseudonym "Rann Daley"), Norman Lindsay and E. J. Banfield. One might argue that the centrality of the marriage theme in Becke's fiction, which he surveyed without illusion within the framework of romance, puts him in the mainstream of Australian fiction and — as work of the 1890s — properly asks for comparison with the short stories of Lawson and Barbara Baynton, and with the portraits of disintegration, of dashed hopes, loneliness and insanity in marriage which they draw.

That comparison indicates the topical uses to which the genre of romance was being put in the 1890s in Australia. If Becke is compared, less unexpectedly, with another contemporary and popular author of romance — the short story writer William Astley ("Price Warung") — then the formal development which is being traced here — the increasing vent for satire in romance fiction of the 1890s — can again be discerned. Twenty-five instalments of "Warung's" "Tales of the System" appeared in the *Bulletin* during 1890-1, some of which were republished in 1892 as *Tales of the Convict System*. Further series and books came later in the decade. The first of the tales, "How Muster-Master Stoneman Earned His Breakfast" was published on 24 May 1890. It begins "Warung's" reconstruction, which he performed with relish and in detail, of the dark era in the Australian past, the period of convict transportation. This is the temporal setting of Marcus Clarke's novel *His Natural Life* (1870-2). Historical romance is pointedly bound up with satirical commentary as "Warung", with reference to the murderous convict escapee Glancy, speaks of "the mild discipline with which a genial and loving motherland had sought to correct his criminal tendencies".

"Lieutenant Darrell's Predicament", published late in 1890, was set at Hell's Gate, Macquarie Harbour, the sombre place of abandonment that is the second and worst of the four convict prison locations depicted in Clarke's novel. Clarke had given a romantic hue to this desperate coast, and other authors noticed. In "Boldrewood's" *The Ghost Camp* (1902), it has become one of the few Australian spots worthy of romantic sight-seeing, one able to inspire a *frisson* from such a vicarious venture into the past. The hero of this romance (an Englishman who has just made a fortune in silver mining in Tasmania that will permit his return home, and his marriage) organises "a large, fashionable party to the weird, gloomy solitudes of Macquarie Harbour". The creation of a Tasmanian tourist industry around the history of convictism is here foreshadowed. "Warung" tried to make his revisiting not a matter of homage, but a black recycling and revision of Clarke's subject. Gabbett the cannibal is back, though unnamed, as an escapee who returns to the settlement at Macquarie Harbour with a "plump appearance ... and a certain slavering of the mouth". The gaoler Darrell, like Clarke's Maurice Frere ("Warung" prefers the comparison with John Price, a commandant at Norfolk Island, with history, rather than romance) "formed intimacies with the convicts in order to ascertain their mode of thought, their secret practices, and their mysterious modes of communication". As "Warung" comments heavily, "altogether, a very promising youth, Lieutenant Darrell".

The romance fiction of "Warung" is always tinged with the sardonicism of hindsight. His stories depict a faithless, barbarous age, that labours under the oppression of institutions conceived in the old world. The stories constitute a bleak and overly insistent satirical portrait of the mentality that created the convict system. They are no kind of celebration of origins in a country which had just observed its centenary, and was less than a decade away from political federation. For these extra-literary reasons, "Warung" reinforced his attraction for the *Bulletin*, which advocated an anti-imperialist, pro-nationalist line for Australian life and writing. The magazine's sponsorship of realist fiction (though this was never the pure literary form that it might have suspected) was linked to its campaigning for political independence. Literary and political chronologies have ever been confused in Australia.

As Barry Andrews suggested in *Price Warung* (1976), the stories are animated by "his vehement desire to show that the convict system was an unmitigated evil which blighted the growth of the colonies and went a long way toward explaining the problems of pre-Federation days". "Warung" professes little of the contrived historical nostalgia that an earlier generation of romance writers in Australia had believed to be necessary. Beavering away at his archival research, part of "Warung's" project was to bury romantic falsifications of the national past. At the same time, he profited from the dozens of stories with historical settings that he produced and from the unwitting and perhaps disingenuous publicity that these stories gave to the convict era in Australia.

Authors of fiction in the 1890s made no decisive break with the romance tradition. Some successfully continued into the 1890s, and beyond, careers which they had begun earlier: Praed and, for a few years into the next century, "Boldrewood" among them. As Fiona Giles pointed out in her essay on "Romance" in *The Penguin New Literary History of Australia* (1988), this form of fiction remains "the largest-selling section of the publishing industry". Rather than extinguishing fiction set at convict Port Arthur, "Warung" may have encouraged it, as James Hebblethwaite's *Castlehill* (1895), Roy Bridges" *The Barb of an Arrow* (1909) and William Gosse Hay's *The Escape of the Notorious Sir William Heans* (1919) attest. Moreover, such a work as Patrick White's *Voss* (1957) must to a significant degree be analysed within a local tradition of romance journey, or quest.

Giles contends that a realist literary opposition to romance in Australia is discernible as early as James Tucker's *Ralph Rashleigh* (written c1845), and Catherine Helen Spence's *Clara Morison* (1854). Perhaps this is better stated as a realist opposition to certain romantic notions that are entertained within the accommodating form of romance. This is a distinction that Giles implies when she discusses Miles Franklin's *My Brilliant Career* (1901) as a work "which professes to distance itself from romance fiction", yet:

> traces the quest of a heroine who, while rejecting the conventional romantic option of love and marriage, proposes her own romantic future as the splendidly isolated literary outsider.

That a revisionist, sometimes satirical use of the romance form became more pronounced in Australia in the 1890s has been suggested above. Such revisionism never feels obliged to sever all affiliations with romance fiction, as the career of an assiduous, combative reader within that tradition shows.

By 1896, Joseph Furphy was ready to write out a fair copy of his novel *Such is Life*, on which he had worked for a decade. Notoriously, the book assaults the conventions of romance fiction. "The life of stock in Riverina", he comments, "was not as cheap as the life of the common person in the novels of Robert Louis Stevenson, Rider Haggard, Rudyard Kipling, and some other modern classics". Tom Collins, Furphy's narrator, ponders on "the quality and quantity of Australian-novel lore": "The outlawed bushrangers; the lurking blackfellows; the squatter's lovely Diana-daughter, awaiting the well-bred greenhorn ... how these things recalled my reading!" Furphy purported to take particular offence at Kingsley's *The Recollections of Geoffry Hamlyn*. The fun that he had in inventing an alternative fate and reputation for the Buckleys has obscured the affinities of theme which *Such is Life* has with Kingsley's romance.

Sam Buckley — who would be the Buckley of Clere in England — is transformed by Furphy into "Hungry Buckley of Baroona — a gentleman addicted to high living and extremely plain thinking" who loses his property after foreclosure. His daughter, having passed for a time as "a veritable heroine of romance" marries thrice — first to a hyphen, then to "an aitchless property owner", last to an Honourable, who is "a social refugee from Belgravia". It is a progress that Barbara Baynton may have admired. Kingsley and Furphy, however, write with equal earnestness, setting aside the other business of their books, of the "coming race" in Australia, and of the ways in which it is now being peopled. Thwarted romantic love quests can be found in each book. Both involve struggles to survive at the margins of civilisation (though these are observed at some remove). Each novel — if from different pre-suppositions — imagines heroic national types. Collins' comic, fuddled, deluded viewpoint disguises these likenesses of theme (which admittedly have different weight and centrality in each work).

The tradition of romance fiction in Australia pivots in the 1890s. Some authors continue the work of mystification, find more lost races, more previously undiscovered traces of remote civilisations in the interior of the continent. Others find the flexibility of romance narrative handy for critical and satirical appraisals of Australian society on the eve of its political federation. Still others — notably Furphy — assail the romance heritage in Australian literature without relinquishing its impulses to dream of a national future, to quest after self and past as well. It is in this way, perhaps, that Furphy — whose work seems to have had so few inheritors and imitators in Australia — is most truly influential.

"The same itch ..." : Poetry by Women in the 1890s

Patricia Barton

We are really becoming an astonishing race of rhymers — especially in the bush. In the cities there are more distractions of thought and occupation; but in the vast interior, away from the cities, you seem rarely to meet men who have not at some time or other written doggerel verse. The women have the same itch, but not to the same degree ...

"Says and Hearsays" Bookfellow 29 April 1899.

Such pronouncements by A. G. Stephens, editor of the influential "Red Page" of the Sydney *Bulletin*, linger stubbornly in the annals of Australian literary history and criticism for nearly a century, bolstering the popular conception of the literature of the 1890s as written by bush men about bush men. It was not until the feminist revisions of the 1980s and 90s that this view was seriously challenged,[1] from the position of gender, class and race.

In the *Commonwealth* in 1901,[2] shortlisting the nineteenth century Australasian poets he thought worthy of notice, Stephens noted that only eight of the forty poets included were women. He explained the anomaly as the "ocular representation of the literary inferiority of the female sex ... The women are less notable; their work has (naturally) neither the mass nor the quality of the men's work ... [but, of them] Ada Cambridge is strongest, M. H. Foott sweetest, Jessie Mackay [a New Zealander] keenest, clearest; M. J. Gilmore the most passionate; Louise Mack the most distinguished". Essentially the same list was trotted dutifully forward on the rare occasions in the following decades that poetry written by women in late nineteenth-century Australia was discussed. Of these women writers Gilmore and Foott in particular became most closely synonymous with the spirit of the 1890s. In fact, though all were published in newspapers and periodicals during the decade, only Mary Hannay Foott published a verse collection, *Morna Lee and other poems*. Issued in 1890, the collection was actually an enlarged edition of her most famous work *Where the Pelican Builds & other poems* published in Brisbane in 1885, the much anthologised title poem dating back to 1881. Ada Cambridge's last two volumes of poetry, *Unspoken Thoughts* and *The Hand in the Dark*, were published in 1887 and 1913 respectively. Mary Gilmore's first volume, *Marri'd and Other Verses* was not published till 1910 and she was overseas for the latter part of the nineties, much of the time with William Lane's New Australia Settlement in Paraguay. Louise Mack, perhaps least known today, has probably the strongest claim to be considered part of the 1890s *Bulletin* school, most of her work being originally published within its pages, and her first collection *Dreams in Flower* being issued as a *Bulletin* Booklet in 1901. Yet in his Personal Note to that volume, Stephens described her as a lyric poet, comparing her to Will Ogilvie and Roderic Quinn,rather than Henry Lawson and the bush school of realism for so long associated with that journal and others such as the *Lone Hand*.

The literary currents of the 1890s were much richer and more varied than was reflected in prevailing Australian literary criticism, at least until the 1980s, and especially in the criticism of women's poetry. Within the pages of the *Bulletin* itself, verse written by women was consistently published and reviewed, while in every major centre, particularly Melbourne, a variety of literary influences persisted and flourished which stimulated contributions by women. Of the women who have been remembered, some such as Ada Cambridge made their reputations mainly as writers of fiction, and others as journalists. Both Mary Gilmore and Louise Mack, for instance, worked extensively on newspapers and periodicals, while Mary Hannay

Foott's reputation is probably due more to one or two of her frequently anthologised poems on exploration and the bush, and her years as literary and social editor on the *Queenslander*, than to her total poetic achievement.

Newspapers and periodicals were in fact one of the major avenues for the publication of poetry by both men and women in nineteenth-century Australia, but particularly for women who more often lacked the financial, social and educational resources to publish independently in the very limited Australian publishing market.[3]

Effectively the interests of gender, race and class coincided to exclude women of non-Anglo-Celtic middle-upper class origin, education or pretension from publishing poetry at all in nineteenth century Australia. The relatively privileged élite who did unquestioningly universalised their culture's concerns and history in a way no longer uncritically possible.[4] Nevertheless they voiced a range of styles, concerns and experiences which at times reinforced the matronising and colonising interests of the British Empire[5] including Australian nationalism, but in other instances, questioned and subverted them.

As women writers they were themselves restricted by their context and the acceptable modes of gender representation. Many, for instance, relied on earnings from their writing to support themselves or supplement marginal incomes, but the "sweat" of the poetic labour is rarely visible. While a gentlewoman might write verse she did not engage in a desperate battle for survival.

Indeed, even after the 1890s, the majority of women poets were invisible to critics intent on the construction of a distinctive Australian literature, a task which pre-occupied them for at least the first half of this century. The argument that females generally lacked contact with the vital force of nationalism flowing through the leading social and intellectual circles of the period is by no means applicable to all women, and neither were such nationalist circles necessarily paramount or exclusive during the 1890s themselves.[6] Put very simplistically, until recently literary reputations depended most on whether a particular school of poetry and poets became identified with the newspapers and coteries which gained literary, social and financial prominence in twentieth-century Australia. In practice, as the nationalist spirit of a newly federated and independent Australia became attached to its literary productions, those features which could not be connected with visible or material differences from other literatures were de-emphasised.[7] The 1890s was selected in retrospect as the decade in which national self-consciousness was consolidated in verse celebrating the isolation and harshness of the bush and masculine bonding in the guise of "mateship". Such criticism generally repudiated or ignored the intellectual traditions, soft beauties and home comforts associated with "mother" England, and by extension the lyric and feeling qualities associated with the image of the English woman constructed over the centuries. This gradual exclusion of the traditional subjects of women's poetry from the definition of Australian verse, and the concentration on poems with explicitly Australian subjects has, as Elizabeth Webby said of nineteenth-century women's verse in general, "worked against the recognition of women poets who, perhaps from choice as much as obedience to the conventions of the period, preferred to celebrate the joys and sorrows of love, domestic life and religion rather than the camaraderie of the campfire'".[8] Poems on the delights of motherhood, babies, and the doings of small children occur in almost every verse collection published by women. This is scarcely surprising, as it was the role in which social expectation and lived experience coincided most closely. Such "domestic" writing was generally outside the concerns of "serious" art, and antipathetic to the myth of the solitary bushman, but nevertheless allowed the celebration of relationships, home and intimacy. It enabled women to construct a relationship to the land and emerging nation as "home" rather than alien adversary.[9] A mode of creative existence in the imagination was as essential for women as men, yet women also had to stay within a much stricter code of social, literary and publishing conventions.[10] Perhaps as a result, domestic writing was the most difficult in which to escape the predictable and the sentimental.

An unusual vantage point is offered by Jennings Carmichael, a nurse who wrote poetry and prose sketches based on her personal and professional life and her love of the Australian environment. Her *Poems* (1895) were well received in Australia and England, especially those dedicated to the sick children whom she had nursed and those lamenting the passing of the natural bushland. "The Old Bush Road" and "A Woman's Mood" were both frequently anthologised, the latter lamenting the plight of a woman left to wait alone at home for her wandering husband. Another interesting variant was provided by Ruth Bedford who was only eleven years old when the first edition of *Rhymes by Ruth* was published in 1893, and fourteen at the time of the second enlarged edition in 1896. In addition to a couple of delightful little verses on "Thomas the Cat" (who cares more for food than for his mistress) and "May and the Duck" (on a present to her four-year-old niece), the books are mainly concerned with family occasions; the advent of a new cook in "What Was She Thinking Of"; and the deaths of other children.

Death was as much a reality in a woman's life occupied with bearing and raising children as it was for any man exploring the interior of the continent; but these more frequent and "everyday" griefs fell outside the concerns of a literary criticism allied with nationalism and masculine self-construction. In addition, the feminine griefs were frequently formulated in conventional Christian religious language, increasingly alien to twentieth-century critics. Loss of faith was a preoccupation of late nineteenth-century European culture, disrupting accepted beliefs and supplying the inspiration for some fine poetry by writers such as Ada Cambridge. Nonetheless for several centuries religious writing, in poetry and prose, had provided women with a balm for life's hurts and an apparent reason to accept the sufferings and injustices of their social lot. Paradoxically, it also allowed them to speak of those very sufferings and injustices in a form sanctioned by an authority beyond secular male institutions — God himself (*sic*).

At its most imitative, piously spiritual and resigned, this poetry is truly mind and sense numbing. The seemingly relentless connection between death and religion suggests at times that the only good woman was literally a dead woman, or that "goodness" was intimately linked to death. Certainly verse which portrayed death as the desired state for women abounds. Nor was it limited to religious verse, as shown by a reading of Louisa Lawson's work, particularly "A Dream" and "Lines Written During A Night Spent in a Bush Inn" collected in *The Lonely Crossing* (1905). Generally the feminine desire for death is overcome only by the need to care for the family.

Some women were able nonetheless to survive the boggy paths of religiosity. The crudely vigorous lyrics of the South Australian Baptist poet, Mrs Hannah Fry, for example, are interesting both sociologically and as examples of the translation to Australia of the popular verse forms of lower middle-class Britain. Her *Poems* (1900) reveal a confidence increasingly rare for the period, echoing variously the rhythms of the Bible, Baptist hymns and traditional ballads, and ranging from the wearyingly clichéd, through the bathetic to the shockingly powerful. Many of her religious verses show little original imaginative thought, some obviously intended as hymns, others as sources of consolation or instruction — including a mnemonic, "The Books of the Bible". More interestingly "To the Reverend Allan Webb" deals with the Baptist Church's need for clergy, and laments the desertion to the Church of England of one of their number, revealing in the process some of the social distinctions between the congregations. Other verses celebrate the women's temperance union and the departure of several female missionaries overseas. A series of poems illustrating the terrible deaths (railway crossing smashes, shark attacks) awaiting those who fail to observe the Sabbath recalls the female tradition of instructive religious verse while employing the rhythm and style of the popular tabloid press, from which they were probably culled. One however, "A Fatal Scene", is especially notable for a combination of the steady inevitability of balladic structure with the ferocity of the subject — a father's murder of his children and his own suicide.

The climate of religious uncertainty also encouraged some writers to attempt to reconcile their beliefs with an active social concern. Florence Emily Todd's *Christian Socialism (In Verse): Twelve Socialistic Poems,* published in 1896, announces its purpose proudly in the Preface as

> an essay in verse divided into sections on social and religious matters ... to show poor people, workers, and earners (women especially) who have little time or inclination for reading or opportunity for interchange of thought with people who understand or study social questions etc, that Socialism and Christianity are ... *identical* ... I have chosen to versify my ideas and opinions because the subject matter of rhymes is much more easily and lastingly impressed on the memory ... [and] is much more attractive than matter-of-fact prose to numbers of people, especially *women,* whose attention and interest I particularly wish to secure or arouse

Her stated preference for rhyme over metre, and the occasional sacrifice of both for clarity, do hinder the smoothness but insists on a conviction which carries the verse.

The poems "Distribution", "Equality", "The Land", "Woman", "Labour, Wages, Talents etc", "General Charity", "Careless Pastors", "Master & Servant", "Poverty & Riches", "Life", and "Guidance" expound the redistribution of wealth and labour based on biblical principles which she supports. Her verses on "Women" proclaim their right to equality because it was:

> women who came to the sepulchre,
> Before the men He had loved ...
> Men surely have read Christ's teaching
> To little purpose and vain
> When they are eternally preaching
> That women have no claim
>
> To exercise their influence
> Their powers of thought and speech;
> Save in the home, or the province
> They say she may reign in or teach.
>
> Woman! thy God hath made thee
> Equal to functions great;

> Queen of the home, and worthy
> To move in matters of state.

And in "Poverty and Riches" she refutes the passive
acceptance of the status quo preached by so many religious:

> The sins of the opulent really outnumber
> Those of the poor, who are said to encumber
> The earth — and a difficult problem present
> To wise-acre thinker, and crass government
>
> But sooner or later their greed and their wrong
> Will o'er balance the scale and the poor'll become strong,
> For tho' they be sinners, yet they have merit
> As children of God his gifts to inherit.

Of course writers of religious verse were particularly prone
to the "damned whores and God's police" stereotype
applied so successfully to the image of woman in Australia,
but some of them were able to use the stereotypes
themselves to question the assumptions and apparent
certitudes behind them. Inez Hyland, for example, wrote a
considerable body of poetry and several short stories before
her death in 1892 at the age of 28. Published in 1893, *In
Sunshine and In Shadow* displays a number of different
modes and strategies, especially humour, which broaden
the scope of her poetic voice. Perhaps the most
immediately striking is her colloquial first-person verse
ridiculing rigid fundamentalism and sectarianism, as in
"The Sinner Speaks". She also challenges the edicts of
strict religion, especially male-dominated religion, in
poems such as the satiric "St Catherine's Votary"; and
decries social passivity in poems such as "The Will o' the
Lord" (which was, she insisted, to provide drains not to
lament the spread of sickness).

Hyland was not restricted to religious themes. In
"Disloyalty", for example, she recounts an early squatter's
refusal to demolish the hut in which he and his deceased
wife first lived, despite his daughters' desire to do so for
the Duke of Edinburgh's visit. She was also capable of
more serious social questioning, several of her poems
examining (with varying degrees of success) the plight of
the fallen — as in "The Scarlet Feather", "A Fair Fable",
even "A Schoolgirl's Story". Her voice ranges through the

gentle tones of "womanly" faith and love, the cadences of children, and the authority and intellect more commonly associated with the male poet of the period. "In Memoriam: Francois Rabelais", for example, urges breaking the bonds of guilt with compassion. Hyland essays nearly all the set pieces of the period, even entering the arena of local politics in "Knock at the Government Door", a comic disquisition on the consequences of an MP's refusal to request a government grant for a cooking school, and " "Why Do Women Wilt?" (Andrew Lang): The Reason Why" which lays the responsibility at the feet of the men who cause them to labour for countless hours without relief. Hyland also wrote occasional verse. Her twelve poems on "The Seasons", celebrating the changing landscape in a South Australian vineyard, were also being issued separately in 1917 as *A Book of the Months*.

Perhaps the most outstanding commonality within poetry written by women in the 1890s was the often avowed and almost always implicit need to connect it to a purpose — a feature also found in earlier poetry written by Anglo-Celtic women about the Australian experience. Caroline Leakey for example, best known for her convict novel *The Broad Arrow*, prefaced her 1854 book of verse, *Lyra Australis, or, Attempts to sing in a strange land*, with the hope that through its publication "some shipwrecked brother may take heart again ...." These earlier poets wrote on diverse subjects and employed an often bewildering range of metrical and verse forms; many volumes were introduced with apologies for inelegance of phrasing and rhythm. Their authors may have experienced "seasons unfavourable to composition, of severe domestic calamity, and bodily suffering ... [and] singular reverses of fortune" as Fidelia Hill relates in the preface to her *Poems and Recollections of the Past* (1840), but the writing generally conveys a sense of identity and security of selfhood not as evident later in the century especially, I would suggest, in the 1890s. This confidence may have arisen partly from the small number of books written and published earlier in the century, and from the relatively high proportion representing the collected work of a lifetime. But more pertinently Australia's colonial status was still by and large unquestioned, links with England were valued, and not generally experienced as divisive. And woman herself, in theory if not in practice, had a more clearly defined role and position in society.

The questions affecting woman's place were especially complex in the 1890s when so many competing forces were at work. As pressure for federation mounted, increasing numbers of women were seeking the right to vote and to influence public policy, as well as continuing the battle to enter university and the professions.

Examples of explicit suffragette verse seem almost non-existent in the readily accessible sources, though there are enticing hints, as for instance in the *Sydney Mail* of 14 November 1891 with Janet Lee's "In Change, Unchanged": 'Back to thy place'" cries man in fear, as Woman fain would rise". Louisa Lawson's the *Dawn* also offers poems of unity in sisterhood, but they are almost invariably generalised rather than offering a specific vision or platform of independence. Women generally focussed their attention on conditions affecting the domestic sphere. Sometimes their interests coincided with those of men and at others they did not.[11]

In her otherwise fairly unexceptional volume, *Verses at Random* (published in 1901 but largely composed before 1900), "Thistle" Anderson notes an exchange of correspondence in the *South Australian Register* during March 1900 when "The author advocated a women's contingent for South Africa — gentle satire, of course! — and the idea, being taken seriously, evoked a heated discussion in the leading dailies". There follows "The War and Other Things" spoken by a young woman reared in the bush to ride and shoot, who with her love gone seeks death in fighting for her country. A Mr John Howell responded by denouncing her idea in verse, to which she replied lightly in a further poem promising that he would pay for denying her sex the right to fight when he was wounded and she a nurse! At the very least this material shows an unexpected side to the usual conventionally patriotic response to war — deflated by humour; but it also illustrates the protection of comedy in skirmishes for equal rights, especially in a sphere held sacred by men and in absolute conflict with the expected role of women.

Increasingly in the 1890s, social discourse presented the role of respectable wives and daughters as adorning the private sphere and thus enhancing the status of husbands, fathers and brothers. Social distinctions multiplied. The latitude of behaviour that had existed for many people in earlier days when hardships, distance and difficulties of communication created a certain leniency was much reduced. At the same time, especially after the financial collapses of the late 1880s and early 1890s, legions of women were deserted by their "husbands" and fathers (who may have gone bush to figure in the stories and poems of Lawson and Paterson as the wandering solitary male!). These women were forced to support themselves and their children at any number of harsh and demeaning jobs where considerations of social and even personal niceties were all but irrelevant.[12]

The range of poetry at the time reflects a little of this range of women's experience but as noted above it was necessarily skewed by the educational, financial and social restrictions which made it impossible for all but a few to publish poetry collections. Nevertheless, as we have seen with religious poetry, there were ways of negotiating the contradictions dictated by role, social expectations, political and survival needs. Poetry portraying famous women (European nobility and Joan of Arc were very popular) was one attempt to find models, or to express sentiments that had no acceptable contemporary voice. Other poets with the old certainties gone found their purpose by participating vicariously in male activities and thus contributing to the development of the nation,[13] as Eliza Berry did in *Australian Explorers (from 1818 to 1876) In Rhyme* (1892). Berry, head teacher at Kangaroo Point State School for Girls and aware of the "beguiling" nature of verse especially for the young, wrote — as she said in her Preface — in the hope that it "may induce, even in a few, a warmer interest in the bygone labours of those gallant men, to whose devoted efforts we owe the early development, and much of the subsequent progress of our native, or our adopted land".

Others increasingly saw a special role for women. A collection by "Jenny Wren" (Nellie Cruttenden), *Leaves of Love*, appeared in 1890 with a respectful dedication to the youngest daughter of Lady Carrington, the Governor's wife. (Dedication to the Governor's wife was a tradition followed by many 19th century Anglo women writers, perhaps to clothe their entry into the public sphere with establishment respectability, but also because the Governor's wife was often the recognised patron of women's culture, and as such could affect not only their status but readership and sales.) Jenny Wren's more interesting pieces include "Flakes of Marble or The Words of 'The Angel'" (on Michelangelo and the role of the artist); "The Silence that Speaketh" and "The Flower-Wreathed Cross" (on religion); "Golden", "No Rent to Pay" and "Eight Hours A Day" (on work, poverty and social equity). In the uneven "Lines on the opening of the Women's Industrial Exhibition 1888" she portrays woman awakened by social distress to use her heart and her mind, combining science and love for the benefit of all:

> Man in the power of his glory and pride
> Saw not the angel who walked by his side,
> Knew not the strength of those delicate hands,
> To compass the world with love's glistening bands;
> Thought not that woman the saviour might be,
> Of all that was human, fraternal and free ...

Political involvement of a more overt kind was the purpose for others. Helen Orr Campbell (Mrs Jackson) published *The Marriage Contract: in four acts* in 1899, a satirical verse-pantomime of the Australian Federal Campaign featuring Mistress Enness Doubleyou and her suitor Victor[ia], Mr Barton and Mr Reid and the other state leaders. The acts consisting of The Consultation; The Contract; Equal Representation; Braddon's Blot; Bounties; Inland Rivers; Federal Capital; The Secret Conference; and Amendments and Conversion cover the essential features of the campaign both thoroughly and humourously. Campbell's conclusion retreats disingenuously into the traditional role allotted to her sex, though her disclaimer is completely undercut by all that she had so ably contained in her work:

> And I no counsel may impart, for, being but a woman,
> My head surrenders to my heart, my judgements are but human,
> My lips are not for loud demand — "tis mine to soothe — caress —
> To pray a Mighty Unseen Hand to guide, control and bless.

Interestingly, while the image of women was invoked continually in the Federation debate,[14] it appears that engagement by an individual female writer still required apology and disguise — using the acceptable image to cloak her actual presence. Campbell's second book *The Marriage Contract & Other Poems* (1902) includes the original title poem with some explanatory notes for the British market, plus a number of interesting new verses revealing interests as diverse as the Indian famine, racism and monopoly powers among NSW country store-keepers. In "The Kollickville Temperance Union: (An Australian Enterprise)" she questions one of the most widespread, active and long-lived political organisations of women in Australia. While apparently supporting the wowser stereotype, Campbell uses it sophisticatedly to stress the plight of many women and children in Australia. Verses on the misery caused by alcohol abound. Louisa Lawson, for example, in "The Song of Bacchus" from *The Lonely Crossing*, laments the ruined lives and families stemming from drink: "I curse the land, and I curse the sea, / While the poets my praises sing". "Agnes Neale" (Caroline Agnes Leane) includes a verse "Died Drunk" in her 1890 collection *Shadows and Sunbeams* describing the death of a woman in an Adelaide cell while drunk, and calls on those tempted by alcohol to resist and to help their fallen sisters.

An unusual subject calls attention to Ida Lee's *The Bush Fire & other verses* (1897). The volume's title piece first published in the *Sydney Mail* Christmas number for 1896 was typical of the increasingly popular concern with the bush, and is powerfully evocative. It is, however, "The Forest King's Lament" which introduces a subject treated more rarely in poetry by women in the period, the sufferings of the Aboriginal people and their doomed resistance to invasion:

> From over wide seas the white chieftains had come
> To rest in our mountains and claim our dear home;
> 'Twas morn in the vale when we rose up to fight,
> Twas darker than darkness, that fell ere the night.
> Our farewells were short, as thro' thicket we sprang,
> All armed with sharp spears and the curved boomerang;
> My people loud shouted their battle-cry old,
> A quick answer came, by the bullet soon told!
> I prayed as I fell, "May I speedily die
> With those who, around me, now silently lie
> Like reeds in a tempest, struck low by the rain,
> Who never to life will awaken again!" ...
> For bitter is life to me, sweeter is death ...
> Do yearnings increasing disturb the strong breeze,
> That moans in the brushwood and grieves in the trees?
> Its sob overcomes me, no more can I sing,
> But bend low in anguish where once I stood king!

Her sympathetic depiction of Aborigines in this heroic lament is undercut by the associations of this verse tradition with a dying race, a conviction expressed overtly in "The Homestead", where the advent of western civilization is seen unquestionably as an advance. This conviction was increasingly typical of the 1890s and the sense of white Australia's growing destiny. Lee here adopted existing literary traditions to portray Aboriginal experience with compassion, but in finding a place and a mode from which to speak her language necessarily reflected the interests and assumptions of the prevailing Anglo-Celtic colonial culture. Representations of the "noble but doomed savage" race helped assimilate them into existing power relations and modes of social control which in twentieth-century Australia resulted in what was effectively an attempted diaspora. While socio-political interests do not necessarily obliterate the universalising potential of language[15] (such as portraying human dignity and empathy), they do require that a consideration of nineteenth-century Australian women's poetry include them. Appropriately, A. G. Stephens may provide us with an insight into this insubstantiality. Shadowing his pronouncement on women poets ("the same itch, but not to the same degree") is the sexed female body which, other than in safely contained maternal or companionate forms, is largely invisible — even (especially) in women's own published works.[16] In daring to write themselves into the public realm of linguistic expression as determined by the prevailing social order, and in using existing language traditions and codes to speak their experiences publicly, these Anglo-Celtic women poets of 1890s Australia also paid the price of their own work being limited by and assimilated into those same codes and conventions. The cost lay in what was unable to be publicly named or spoken in their culture, the absent and unheard. Not only their own bodies/sexuality/desire/power but the bodies/voices of: black women; working women;[17] lesbian women; women of difference; and their anger, humour, inter-racial love etc. Yet, particularly in the emerging freer verse forms, poetry remains liminal. In the pleasures, absences and inversions of its forms it continually evokes the unexpressed. It attempts both enunciation and connection, yet is never "the same" as the experience to which it refers. It is essential, particularly in reading and evaluating women's poetry of this period, to retain an awareness of what is missing as much as what is voiced.

Amidst this poetry of purpose, women were also experimenting with freer verse forms as exemplified in the work of Queenslander Lala Fisher. Her verses were published liberally in Australian newspapers and journals, and in *A Twilight Teaching and other poems* (1898), *Grass Flowering* (1915) and *Earth Spiritual* (1918, an enlarged edition of *Grass Flowering*). Fisher left for England in 1897 and her first collection was published there to a very kindly reception, but it was after her return to Australia in 1901 to work in radical and later dramatic journalism that she did her finest work. Stylistic difficulties and hesitations seem to have been common to women's lyric and free verse, at least until 1905 or so. It is as if a new form had to be found before women would express other visions fully or satisfyingly, free of the verse forms, rhythms and conventions explored and possessed by the traditional Anglo-Celtic male poet. It was this spirit which Stephens admired in Louise Mack. The independence of her poem "To soar as a wild white bird"; the unexpected reversals of "Vows' and "I take my life into my hand', the songlike qualities of many of her verses show why they were published in the *Bulletin* and later collected. But as a whole there is a curious flatness or insubstantiality, a general lack of that concentrated presence which supports the freer forms used more successfully by poets such as Mary Fullerton and Lesbia Harford in later decades.

I have tried to suggest here a few of the ways in which women publishing in the 1890s used existing traditions, roles and stereotypes to support and to undermine particular beliefs about themselves, their relationships, their social, political and religious lives, and their art. But these suggestions themselves need to be interrogated and expanded before women's "itch" to write can be gauged in either quantity or degree.

Under Two Flags:
Ada Cambridge and
A Marked Man

Robert Dingley

Writing enthusiastically of *A Marked Man* six years after
its first appearance in book form, Desmond Byrne noted
with approval that Ada Cambridge's "good taste" had
excluded from her novel "the bustle and commoner interests
of colonial life" in order to intensify "dramatic quality and
a richly sympathetic study of character":

> The natural beauties surrounding the home of the Delavels at
> Sydney are not less delicately and poetically described than the
> village life they have left behind in the mother country ... but the
> view given of Australian society is, in keeping with the relation
> to it of Richard Delavel and his household, of the slightest kind.[1]

Although Byrne's remarks certainly oversimplify a
complex issue, they contain, I think, a sufficient degree of
truth to constitute a useful starting-point for discussion, and
I want to begin by examining what seems to me a very real
discrepancy between the book's evocations of its English
and of its Australian milieux.

A Marked Man's opening chapter contains a minutely
detailed   description   of   the   coastal   village   of
Dunstanborough, a description in which visual particulars
(the outer walls of the manor, for example, "encrusted with
crumbling shields chiselled with the numerous quarterings
of the Delavel house"[2]) have been carefully selected in
order to locate the place and its inhabitants within a nexus
of distinctive social and economic conditions and within a
clearly defined historical continuum. The village, as the
book   begins,   appears   "ideal"   (p.2)   in   its   feudal

obsolescence. Church and mansion, the twin axes of traditional rural life, are both firmly controlled by members of the ancient Delavel family and "the lower classes knew their place and kept it" (p.2). This venerable polity, however, is conspicuously failing to respond to the age's demands: the church, we are told, seems more suited to the pompous monuments of deceased Delavels than to its living congregation, while the squire embodies "a condition of things that had gone by without his knowing it" (p.5). The Hall may be "a museum of treasures to the artist and antiquary", but this, ironically, is because "for several generations the Delavels had been hampered for money" and so have been unable to modernise; the rooms are, in fact, "so comfortless and inconvenient as to be unfit for the requirements of nineteenth century life" (p.4).

As the book proceeds, this early established sense of a tension between continuity and change is carefully consolidated. Landlord and tenant, for example, appear united in their efforts to keep Victorian England at arm's length: "though the hum of steam machinery was not unknown in the village", farmer Morrison spurns all innovation, preferring to "walk in the benighted old paths generally" (p.75) and thus earning the approval of the squire, in deference to whom the "vulgar and levelling" railway stops twelve miles short of Dunstanborough (p.132). Even so, that parenthetical admission that there *are* steam-powered machines working on the estate does hint at its likely future transformation, while the reference to old Mr. Delavel's intransigence over the railway is followed by a proleptic glimpse at the very different regime of his son, who will permit the "sacrilegious" intrusion and so foster the conversion of the village into a fashionable (and profitable) watering-place.[3] Dunstanborough's air of immemorial permanence is thus seen (like that of the rural communities depicted by Hardy) to be a deceptive one; the village is, in fact, visibly poised on the brink of major change, and the first signs of the direction which that change will take are the events that initiate the book's action — Richard Delavel's conscientious refusal to take holy orders and his equally conscientious determination to marry the daughter of one of his father's tenants. What, indeed, is especially impressive about these opening sections of the book is the way in which the private concerns of Richard and Annie are so fully integrated with Cambridge's depiction of the larger society they inhabit. The relationship between the two lovers could never have evolved if Richard's loss of religious belief at Oxford had not already led him to question the value of other orthodoxies, or if the growing prosperity of Annie's parents (concisely signified by their "best" parlour and by the primly bourgeois antimacassars which adorn its furniture (p.16)) had not resulted in her education as a "lady". Their transgression against traditional order is both symptom and result of more general changes which are beginning unobtrusively to amend the structure and ideology of their world.

If, however, we compare this intricate fusion of plot and setting in the novel's English chapters with its later depiction of Australia, a sharp difference becomes, I think, at once apparent. Our first view of Sydney occurs at the beginning of Chapter 21, "Five-And-Twenty Years After", when Sue Delavel looks out over the Harbour from Dawes Point (to which she has come, although we do not yet know this, in the hope of meeting a strange woman to whom she feels drawn):

> The funnels of the P and O and the Messageries and the North German Lloyd boats smoked gently side by side almost under her nose, while the current Orient liner, in a noble company of fellow voyagers, spread her gigantic length along the opposite quay; and they were as dignifiedly quiet — or seemed so — as the old Nelson in Farm Cove. No noise, no dust, arose from that busy neighbourhood, which was a mart for the world's wares. There was just the sense of strong and stirring human life underlying the outward serenity of things, enhancing the charm of it, as the mighty unseen forces at rest in their long hulls enhanced the impressiveness of the tranquil ships. On the two little grassy tongues of land immediately enclosing the inner port no moving thing was visible. Fort Macquarie, so dwarfed by contrast with the mighty warehouses close by, was as blank and silent as an old tombstone. Fort Denison, islanded in the placid waters, was an inert mass of sandstone rock again. (p.142)

And so on. The description is, of course, extremely precise, almost cluttered with place names and with the titles of shipping lines. But it is also, I think, essentially a picturesque description, in which Sydney is offered to the reader as a source of aesthetic response rather than as the location of a particular social and economic life. The scene is a static one ("No noise, no dust, arose from that busy neighbourhood"), but there is just enough "sense of strong and stirring human life" to enhance the "charm" of the "prospect". Sydney in this passage is, and remains throughout the novel, a place which exists solely in the present moment of perception and which consequently seems to lack any identifiable past (or, for that matter, any easily conceivable future). We are, to be sure, told that Constance's house in the Rocks dates from "historic times" and belongs to "old Sydney" (pp.183-84), but these epithets merely serve to augment its attractiveness and are not being deployed to signify a unique past which has determined a distinctive present. The situation is very different when, on the book's first page, Cambridge quotes at length from Dunstanborough's eleventh-century Latin charter and remarks that "there were old families at the farms, whose tenancy of their lands was hereditary, and, in a way, historical" (p.1). History in England is still going on; in Australia it happened an indefinite time ago.

It is tempting, and perhaps not wholly unjustified, to suggest biographical reasons for the distinction I have been trying to define. Cambridge's depiction of English village life in the 1860s is clearly drawn from her exceptionally sharp memories of a childhood in which "Parsons and squires — Church and State — combined to keep the lay person in his place"[4] and which she recorded in vividly minute detail in *The Retrospect*. When she wrote *A Marked Man*, however, her acquaintance with Sydney was confined to a single idyllic holiday in July 1887, from which she emerged, feeling like an ousted Cinderella ("I left my glass slipper on the Redfern platform"), with improved health and a firm conviction that the city was "an earthly Paradise", the "Eden of the South".[5] Those seem curious phrases to use of an urban environment and they are, I think, strongly suggestive of the principal reason why Cambridge selected Sydney (rather than the more familiar Melbourne, of whose social life she was an acute and critical observer) as the locus for *A Marked Man*'s Australian scenes. For her, Sydney functions almost as a version of pastoral, a place in which it is possible, if not fully to resolve, then at least to disentangle, the problems — sexual, spiritual, social — whose very inter-relatedness in the more densely realised English milieu is itself the central source of perplexity. And inasmuch as Sydney represents the potential for a fresh beginning, it has to be seen in terms which will not compromise that freshness by a too specific location within historical time. The novel, moreover, is primarily concerned with the extent to which Delavel and his daughter are able to liberate themselves from the burden of their English heritage, and is therefore reluctant to complicate the clarity of its exploration by providing anything too distinctive (and distracting) in the way of an Australian present. For Cambridge's purposes in this book, indeed, Australia is still essentially *terra nullius*, a place for a new start untrammelled by any relevant identity of its own. The only social pressures which are visibly exerted there are exerted by Delavel's first wife and they, of course, are directly derived from the couple's English past — specifically from Annie's snobbish compulsion to assert the genteel status to which she has elevated herself through marriage. Interestingly, Delavel attempts to evade even this vestigial reminder of the world he has left by creating a remoter pastoral enclave within the more general Sydney pastoral he already inhabits. His "camp", presided over by the Bo'sun and looking "out upon the great gateway of the Heads" (p.163), has been contrived as a "refuge from fashionable society, from all the boredom of conventional life ..., from the fret and chafe of the matrimonial bondage" (pp.163-64). Annie, inevitably, disapproves of this *plein air* haven and "would have liked a bush fire to burn it up, or land buyers and builders to oust it" (p.164). For Richard and Sue, however, the camp represents in miniature what I have been claiming that Australia represents for the novel in general — a place for renewal through simplification: "They had the feeling of escaped prisoners, secure from pursuit, when

they had put those few miles of water between themselves
and Darling Point" (p.164).[6]

But to simplify problems is not, I have already
suggested, to resolve them, and the virtue of the Australian
Eden is rather that it permits difficulties to be isolated
from one another in a manner not available to
Dunstanborough or London. In England, for example, the
formation of private relationships is perceived as
inextricably entwined with issues of social status and class
solidarity. The liaison between Annie and Richard,
because of their difference in degree, is misconstrued both
by other people and, more importantly, by themselves.
Buxom Rhoda leaves the pair alone together in the parlour
and is convinced that they have "taken advantage of her
absence in the manner she believed customary with young
Oxford gentlemen and village maidens when thus
conveniently thrown together" (p.34). Richard's mother,
more histrionically, can only suppose that her errant son
has decided to emulate Arthur Donnithorne or Alec
D'Urberville: "'Oh, my boy,' she sobbed, embracing him, 'if
I see you taking to evil courses — ruining poor innocent girls,
and our own tenants too — it will break my heart!'" (p.57).
Her fears are groundless, of course, for Richard has already
adopted a quite different model:

> She was the village maid of romance — the ideal farmer's
> daughter; and she had grown up here in Dunstanborough
> without anyone finding her out — until he, Dicky Delavel, came,
> like the Lord of Burleigh, with the seeing eye and the
> understanding heart, to make the interesting discovery. (p.31)

Rhoda, Lady Susan, and Richard himself all see the
relationship with Annie in terms of literary stereotypes
(whether melodramatic or Tennysonian) because the social
distance between the young people is felt to preclude any
more mundane and natural scenario. I will return to this
point later, but for the moment it is enough to notice the
crippling entanglement of sexual and social proprieties
which the novel detects in English life.

In Sydney, on the other hand, this fatal collision of
class obligation and private desire is no longer seen to
constitute a serious dilemma. When Sue engages herself to

the phlegmatic Rutledge, she quizzes him ironically about his ancestry. His inability to come up with anything more exalted than an auctioneer and a doctor will, she knows, elicit resolute opposition from her mother (already appalled by Rutledge's unrespectable agnosticism). But the form this opposition takes — incarceration and domestic espionage — despite its ultimate derivation from Clarissa's treatment at Harlowe Place, can nevertheless be presented in lightly comic terms, largely because it is not shown to have the powerful support of an oppressive social code (as was the Delavels' earlier disapproval of Richard's misalliance). Annie's tyranny is anyway of short duration and is almost providentially terminated by her drowning in Sydney Harbour, after which Richard at once throws decorum to the winds and goes off to find Constance, careless of offending the "senseless prejudices of shallow people" (p.269).[7] Both incidents — Sue's betrothal to a lapsed clergyman and Richard's refusal to act a grief he cannot feel — are enabled, ethically and aesthetically, by being made to take place in a milieu whose superficial depiction implies the absence of any very formidable social and ideological coercion. The reason, that is, for the appearance of a greater degree of personal freedom in Australia than exists in England is only partly that the two are seen as different societies at different times in which different possibilities exist; it is at least equally important that the two countries are perceived and evoked in essentially different terms. The depiction of Dunstanborough, with its detailed suggestions of a particular kind of social and economic life developing through time, belongs firmly within the conventions of nineteenth-century realism; Sydney, on the other hand, a city without a distinctive past in which complex problems can be clarified and personal choice can be liberated from social custom, is primarily the site of romance.

Romance, indeed, with its "appearance of freedom from the details of place and time", its presentation of the "hero's quest for spiritual values", its "concern with origins",[8] seems an especially appropriate term for the Australian sections of *A Marked Man*, and Cambridge in fact draws specific attention to the heritage of which her novel is the partial beneficiary. When Constance nobly leaves Richard for the second time and tries to escape without seeing him, he gently chides her: "So you were going to play Jane Eyre to my Rochester again, were you?" (p.216). When the two lovers are finally reunited, we are told, they "understood each other ... 'to the finest fibre of their being', as Jane Eyre says" (p.312). It can hardly be coincidental that when Cambridge, early in the book, notes the resemblance of the rocks on Dunstanborough beach to the table tombs in an old church-yard, she should add parenthetically "say Haworth, in Yorkshire, for instance" (p.21).

But if allusions to an earlier tradition of fictional romance can be used without irony of Richard and Constance, who are able to withdraw into a private paradise of feeling, analogous allusions cannot be so innocent when applied to the earlier courtship of Richard and Annie. When Richard attends Rhoda's wedding feast and is unable to see Annie among the merrymakers, he asks "Why is she drudging in the house, like Cinderella, instead of dancing with the rest?"(p.79). Annie, for her part, thinks of Richard as a "princely young man"(p.109). Romantic reminiscence in this case is actually a trap for the two people involved, not only because it gets in the way of mutual understanding, but because it leads them to assign to one another roles which the obtrusive facts of their world will not allow them to perform. The false English "romance" of Richard and Annie is a disaster, and allusions to Cinderella and Prince Charming measure that disaster's extent; the true Australian romance of Richard and Constance is, in its own terms, a triumph, for which the union of Jane Eyre and Rochester affords an appropriate parallel. The distinction comes about very largely because in the novel's version of Australia romance can be reality, while in England the two modes are not only distinct but inimical.

One important consequence of this counterpoint between realism and romance, however, is that it tends to reinforce England's position as the book's centre of gravity. This occurs not so much because readers are culturally conditioned to privilege the realistic, as because a very considerable part of the dialogue between the principal characters is taken up with the exploration of possibilities for social, economic, and intellectual change, and these discussions — which are clearly of major concern to the novel — have little apparent relevance to the Australian milieu in which they are conducted; it is only when they are applied to the more palpable realities of England that they seem to acquire substance and meaning. When, for example, Sue explains to Rutledge, as they row back to Darling Point from the camp, her notions about the future of capital ("wealth will go out of fashion amongst well-bred people ... and life will be more simple and sincere, more intelligent and refined" (p.238)) we are, as Debra Adelaide points out, intended to respond not only to her youthful enthusiasm but also to her naivety and ignorance (p.xii). When, on the other hand, Sue returns from her wedding trip to England, her "visionary" (and she uses the word of herself) economic projections have acquired a sharper focus through being exposed to concrete facts:

> Then the talk fell upon the hopeless state of the agricultural interest, and how the Dunstanborough property, with its mortgages and dower charges, would have been bankrupt over and over again had it not been for the new watering-place; and Sue rushed into the burning land question with her characteristic ardour, and then into a moralising account of her uncle's splendid establishment, and the impressions she received from her sojourn therein. (p.327)

The "characteristic ardour" is undiminished, but it is now tempered by a knowledge and experience which can, implicitly, be acquired only in England. Moreover, although there is much vague talk of the obligations owed by the rich to the poor (the recurrent theme of "paying back"), the only practicable scheme canvassed in the book appears after Richard, on his deathbed, has unexpectedly inherited the Delavel estates. Sue at once proposes a return to Dunstanborough, where a real duty needs to be performed and which is, anyway, "home": "we will go home, my darling, to your own old home, and do all that splendid work that is waiting for us. Do you understand? You could pay back all then" (p.346). Although Richard seems already too far gone (and too caught up in his private grief) to respond to this appeal, his own thoughts, in his last moments, turn back to his English past, and his final words suggest a sardonic amusement that his dreadful cousin Max will now be left in possession of Dunstanborough. Cambridge hints that this dying utterance — "Max stands next" — may merely be random and coincidental ("It is seldom that last words are so *à propos* to the occasion as novels and deathbed gossip imply" (p.346)), but that ultimate reversion to English concerns is, as we have seen, fully consistent with the book's pervasive tendency.

Superficially, of course, *A Marked Man* differs from earlier novels of colonial life like *Geoffry Hamlyn* or *The Caxtons* inasmuch as there is, for the protagonist, no happy and predestined return to the mother-country loaded down with antipodean wealth. Even though that convention has been abandoned, however, the juxtaposition of romantic Australia with a realistically detailed England still tends to consolidate the latter's hegemonic position in Cambridge's narrative.[9] For the earnest projects of Richard and Sue, and their assiduous study of Mill and Arnold and Morley, are directed to the solution of problems which are not shown to exist in their adopted country, and which appear to be of pressing urgency only in that old world from which they might otherwise seem so completely divided.[10]

Realism and romance, that is, cannot simply be isolated as distinct narrative modes, but must inevitably entail different ways of perceiving, ordering, and judging experience. Just how different will perhaps emerge if we examine in some detail Cambridge's treatment of one of her book's chief concerns — Richard Delavel's lack of Christian belief. We first hear of this in Chapter Two, when Richard refuses to take Anglican orders "on conscientious grounds" (p.7), and Cambridge carefully locates his decision within a recognisable intellectual context by inserting a reference to the current notoriety of Bishop Colenso. Even at this early stage, however, there is an element of ambiguity about Richard's agnosticism or, rather, about the extent to which it has been the outcome of anxious soul-searching. He has, we learn, been instigated to heterodoxy by the example of "a curate-missionary to the Oxford slums" whose ostracism by the established Church has in itself increased Richard's allegiance to his beliefs:

> Dicky, if he had been anyone *but* Dicky — 'marked' himself with the seal of a distinct individuality — would have dropped the discreditable acquaintance. Instead of that, he cherished it more and more as it became less and less socially desirable, and naturally became more and more like-minded with the friend beside whom he stood and fought, and for whose cause he suffered. (p.7)

There is more than a hint there that Richard's loss of faith in fact derives chiefly from a psychological predisposition to champion victims — a trait that surfaces again when his determination to marry Annie increases in proportion to the resistance of his family. What, then, we are presented with in this chapter are two possible sources for Richard's unbelief which differ not in degree but in kind. On the one hand, there are conscience and Colenso — the "hard struggle" of a painful spiritual evolution; on the other, there is the "seal of a distinct individuality", an inherent tendency to the rejection of conventional pieties which appears, like the blackness of the black sheep, to owe little to heredity or environment.[11] The first possibility belongs to what we might roughly describe as a "realistic" mode of perception, in which character is shaped gradually and by interaction with what is external to the self; the second might broadly be categorised as "romantic", for it implies that character, essentially, is innate, given rather than formed.

The ambivalence I have been attempting to define in this early episode continues unresolved for the remainder of the novel and is, indeed, at its most conspicuous in the final chapter, in which Richard dies without the consolations of orthodox Christianity. In one sense, this scene forms an interesting addition to that extensive corpus of Victorian fiction which explores contemporary problems of faith and doubt, for the agnostic Richard is sympathetically shown facing death with undaunted courage, and his only regret is for the shortness of his life with Constance. His stoic fortitude in the face of extinction is, indeed, favourably contrasted by the narrative voice with the maidservant Hannah's conventionally pious regard for "sacred use and etiquette in the hour of death", and we are clearly intended to align ourselves with Sue's verdict: "What are names? ... There are good heathen and bad Christians — good men and bad men. He is a good man — that's enough for me" (p.343). Even the reservation that Richard's single-minded devotion to his life with Constance has culpably eroded his sense of social responsibility is partly mitigated by his own clear-sighted awareness of the fact ("I should have paid back more" (p.346)). We are, in short, being presented with the non-believer's equivalent of holy dying (the sacred nimbus of traditional Christian iconography has even been replaced by the accidental illumination of a neighbouring lighthouse), and Richard's capacity to confront his own mortality without hope but with equanimity is, and is intended to be, impressive.[12]

It is, however, impossible to view the hero's death only as a challengingly favourable account of agnostic fortitude, because the manner of that death — or rather, its mode of presentation — is so obviously remote from the immediate realities of late nineteenth-century intellectual controversy. Despite Sue's topical reminder to her father about "Arnold's paper in the *Fortnightly*" (p.345),[13] Richard's dying scene has far more in common with that of Heathcliff than with the last days, say of Robert Elsmere, "his worn and scored Greek Testament always beside him, the quick eye making its way through some new monograph or other, the parched lips opening every now and then to call Flaxman's attention to some fresh light on an obscure point".[14] For Richard, speculation on the ultimate mysteries comes a very poor second to the overwhelming consciousness of lost love. He dies because the death of Constance has deprived his own life of meaning, and Sue's attempts to rally him with talk of Matthew Arnold or of his possible future as a reforming landlord in England seem beside the point, irrelevant intrusions from what is, in every sense, an alien world. The novel seems uncertain about its response to this romantic self-absorption and, as elsewhere in the book, that uncertainty is reflected in a statement which can be read as either partial or objective:

> It did indeed strike even his daughter, so like himself as he had made her, that it was dreadful to be overwhelmed in such an hour with an aspect and result of life that was comparatively so ignoble. To have the faculty to discern the proportions of things, to stand as he stood now with the Infinite around him, and to concern himself only with this local detail — it showed how, in the moral as in the physical world, thwarted nature was but another name for disease. (p.345)

It is impossible to decide whether the second sentence there, for all its apparent conclusiveness, expresses the judgement of the narrative voice or only registers the limited viewpoint of Sue. That reference to the death of Constance as a "local detail", indeed, seems not only harshly incompatible with Sue's ready sympathy but also with the novel's general (though not unqualified) endorsement of Richard's all-or-nothing second marriage. It is as though the book is attempting to distance itself, at this point, from the romantic momentum of its own narrative, to relocate the action in a wider context in which the death of a wife might indeed be perceived as a "local detail" and in which the world is not necessarily well lost for love. But this attempt to restore balance (one of a number in the last chapter) actually results in the creation of a deep ambivalence about the novel's final scene. Just as Sue and her father, the one pressing the claims of social and intellectual responsibility, the other enclosed in a private emotional space, are no longer capable of full communication, so the novel's two dominant modes — which, at the risk of gross oversimplification, I have been labelling realism and romance — have finally become irreconcilable, each serving only to expose the limitations of the other, and neither acquiring sufficient authority to inform a conclusion about the worth of Richard's life or the exemplary value of his death. For in the end, as I have already suggested, the two modes are not only different ways of recording but of judging experience, and of ordering priorities within it. The attempt to integrate them within a single narrative structure — an experiment in many ways characteristic of late nineteenth-century fiction[15] — is both what energises *A Marked Man* and what limits it. If an Australian setting enables Cambridge to simplify the intractable problems of English experience, that very simplification means that they are no longer the same problems. Richard's retreat into a world of private and exclusive love, a conclusion to which *Jane Eyre*, say, feels able to give unequivocal assent, now seems problematic in its evasion of larger responsibilities, but those larger responsibilities themselves seem crudely obtrusive when set against the tender idyll of Richard and Constance. The novel's consistent effort to sustain a counterpoint between conflicting perspectives on the history it chronicles ensures that its judgement on these and other matters must remain suspended. But that, perhaps, is appropriate, for it is not only, as we've seen, at the formal level that inconclusiveness pervades *A Marked Man*. The final event in the book is, of course, Richard's death, but its real ending is arguably the last significant remark made by a major character, and that, typically, takes the form of a question to which the narrative provides no answer:

> 'Oh, *what* does it all mean?' wailed Sue, in an anguish of bewilderment, overwhelmed by the terrible mysteries with which she was confronted. (p.347)

Catherine Helen Spence: Suffragist At Last

Helen Thomson

To consider where Catherine Spence was situated in the last decade of the nineteenth century is to uncover a tangle of paradoxes. The key to unravelling them is the thread of steadily developing radicalism in Spence. It is almost certainly more typical of women than men that youthful conservatism should be replaced by mature-age radicalism. The constraints placed on nineteenth-century young womanhood were legion, and even an unmarried woman could find increasing age became itself a form of liberation. The staunchly Presbyterian young Catherine Spence of the 1840s, who engaged herself so passionately on the conservative side of state aid in the education debates then raging, could hardly have foreseen her later self, liberal, Unitarian, a suffragist and in all things a reformer.

Spence has always represented something of a problem to feminist scholars hoping to claim such an outstanding woman of her time for one of their own. I would suggest that it is not until the mid-1890s, around about Spence's 70th birthday, that her opinions can justifiably be seen as having moved definitively beyond nineteenth-century liberalism. Making an assessment of her development in the late 80s and 90s has always been difficult, since it is precisely then that her output of printed material drastically declined. Her novel-writing days were over, for reasons to which I will return. Her journalism was not taken up again after her long absence overseas in 1893 and 1884. Her major form of expression became public speaking, but almost exclusively on one subject, proportional representation, a preoccupation with democratic process which dated from 1859 when Thomas Hare's system of proportional representation first came to her notice.

The effect of this concentration on a single reform was, I think, to hamper the development of Spence's political opinions. She constantly maintained that this reform of the exercise of democracy must precede any other, even, in her youth, failing to see the importance of the secret ballot.[1] It is true she published numerous leaders and articles in the Adelaide *Register* advocating social reforms of all kinds, from Henry George's land tax to easier divorce and improved maintenance provisions. Yet every time an attempt is made to measure Spence's radicalism, it tends to founder on a contradiction. One such is her involvement in setting up South Australia's boarding-out scheme for orphan children. This represented a crucial shift away from private philanthropy towards a reform of state intervention, a humane replacement for the grim asylums of the time. But as Kay Daniels has pointed out, it also preserved, in the volunteer inspection system, a middle-class imposition of moral standards on the households of the poor.[2] There was a similar contradiction behind her advocacy of proportional representation which had to wait for its resolution until the 1890s and the introduction of female suffrage.

When the 1890s dawned Catherine Spence was 65, today's official age for retirement. In fact she was beginning the most active and public decade of her life. Hitherto, her public life had consisted of her journalism, her lectures and sermons, her novels and pamphlets and her official role in South Australia's boarding-out scheme. She was to take up a number of public positions in the next decade, in many cases being the first woman appointed, to the Board of Advice to the Education Department, the State Children's Council, the Destitute Board, the Effective Voting League, the South Australian Co-Operative Clothing Company, the Kindergarten Union — all this in her sixties and seventies. For a woman of the time it was an extraordinary "old age", rich with achievement and respect. It was also, if we take her

Autobiography as evidence, a life Spence was profoundly grateful for, looking back at the age of 85 to a triumphant breaching of the narrow social and sexual barriers of its beginnings. A modern feminist reading of the same text, however, can see all too clearly that the triumph had its source in the steady overcoming of gendered disadvantage, and that the space for achievement had to be found from the competing claims of domestic duty.

Single women, then as now, had dependants, and Spence had assumed a bread-winner's burden as early as seventeen, after the death of her father. She was 53 before she had her first regular employment as a journalist, and although she published a prodigious amount in the Adelaide *Register* and *Observer* as outside contributor, she was never made a staff journalist, and never given professional recognition or remuneration for the work she did. She was 62 when her beloved mother died, by which time she had also raised two families of orphan children, and was to take on a third in her seventies. Spence in fact assumed the double burden so commonly the lot of an unmarried daughter of the time: prohibited from the masculine world of paid employment, but required nonetheless to support the elderly and the young and helpless members of her family. Under such conditions it is hardly surprising that radicalism tended to develop, and that what we would today call sexual politics was a constant and growing theme in Spence's work.

It was only at 62 that Spence acquired the kind of freedom which almost any young man of her class might have claimed at twenty. "Henceforth", she says in her *Autobiography*, "I was free to devote my efforts to the fuller public work for which I had so often longed, but which my mother's devotion to and dependence on me rendered impossible".[3] Unsurprisingly, that freedom found its form primarily in travel, and the remainder of Spence's life saw her constantly on the move. In 1893 and 1894 she toured America, Canada, Scotland, England and Europe, preaching the gospel of proportional representation, while in the years leading up to Federation, she travelled around Australia on the same mission. Her lectures on proportional representation met with an enthusiastic reception, particularly in the United States, where she also gave literary lectures and preached sermons. The effect of this overseas tour on Spence was to broaden immensely her interests and opinions, to introduce her to the leading liberals and reformers of her day, to give her a much more informed context in which to argue for reforms in Australia, and to raise her consciousness still further on feminist issues, this largely through contact with American and English suffragists.

The translation into an activist after so many decades as a theorist seems to have charged Spence with energy extraordinary in anyone her age. This was consonant with her lifelong optimism, the constitutional inspiration for all her reformist activity. And here she parts company with what many have described as the zeitgeist of the nineties — its prevailing pre-occupation with failure. Leon Cantrell, for example, says, "My view of the 1890s sees a sense of alienation and loss as a principal literary hallmark".[4] Repudiating this was a completely conscious choice on Spence's part: "The one-sided pessimistic pictures that Australian poets and writers present are false in the impression they make on the outside world and on ourselves".[5] She was still further in opposition to prevailing literary subjects in her treatment of the bush. In Spence's fiction it is simply neutral territory where hard work and loneliness were no more a problem than in the towns. For a single woman with a living to earn from her pen, the town was the only possible environment. Further distancing her from the Lawsonian and *Bulletin* ethos was a sturdy anti-romanticism on the one hand, and a South Australian's relative unfamiliarity with the particular tragedy of the selectors, on the other.

There are a number of other factors which put Spence outside the mythology which the 90s constructed for itself and which we have inherited. One was the matter of class. If the icon of the times was the bush battler, male or female, then Spence distanced herself further by never attempting to speak for those who had only their labor to sell. She herself thankfully drew upon the capital of her excellent Scottish education when it came to earning an income. Sympathetic to the hardships of the working-class, Spence's middle-class Cinderella Clara Morison is rescued from her kitchen, while in the same novel the incorrigible ignorance of Mrs. Tubbins precludes sympathy for a genuine member of the labouring poor. Spence's solid good sense, however, dictated social action in the practical form of her journalism, as well as less directly in her fiction, and she consistently argued for law reform, particularly as it impinged on women and children. Her theology, too, had long since moved away from Calvinism's determinism and Original Sin, to the point where, in 1897, she published a lecture given to the Adelaide Criminological Society, "Heredity and Environment", a humane argument for the amelioration of the appalling social conditions which produced crime, and a thorough-going repudiation of hereditary determinism.

As a writer of fiction, Spence wrote from a contrasting position to many of her contemporaries, particularly the male writers. Her novels are domestic in focus, realistic in mode, conventional in their romance plots. Where a more strongly imaginative writer such as Barbara Baynton (whose work Spence admired immensely) turned the bush and its inhabitants into the scarifying, the haunting and the tragic through the symbolic intensification of reality, Spence moved to the more intensely rational mode of utopianism to improve an unsatisfactory reality in her fictional writing. By the 1890s Spence had abandoned fiction, judging her journalism to be more effective; it was certainly better paid. Even journalism was effectively given up after her 1893-4 overseas trip. I would suggest that the progress from domestic romance to utopian fiction to journalism also indicates Spence's developing awareness of the need for women to abandon the restrictions, and the seductive pleasures, too, of the private sphere, the usual point of closure in romantic fiction. As she grew older Spence must have become aware of the inappropriateness of the bourgeois courtship and marriage romance plot to her social reform purposes. Her one attempt, in her novel *Handfasted*, to combine romance conventions with radical social reform of the sexual double standards that so disadvantaged women, had such a hostile reception from a panel of novel-competition judges, she simply put the manuscript away.

In the 1890s the purchase of an annuity meant that Spence could concentrate her time and energy on proportional representation, free at last of the need to generate an income. Her zeal for voting reform certainly placed her in the midst of the 1890s enthusiasm for democracy. Effective voting, as she called it, was not merely the tinkering with a faulty voting system that it may have seemed, but to Spence was the necessary precursor to any form of democratic reform, for unless democracy was made as fair and effective as was humanly possible, unless political equality was made genuine, then citizens might as well have been unenfranchised. This was her defence when it came to explaining her rather late enthusiasm for female suffrage. Her exposure to suffragists in America and England, and her return in 1894 on the eve of the vote being given to women in South Australia, made her an ardent supporter. The culmination of her public political life came with her standing, in 1897, for election to the Federal Convention, the first Australian woman to stand for such a political position.

Spence's political opinions can be found not only in the newspapers, but also in the utopian novels which replaced the domestic romances in her fiction writing. Her earlier novels were peppered with conversations and opinions on social questions of the day, but they were not overtly political. *Handfasted*'s account of a radical sexual politics remained, alas, unpublished in Spence's lifetime, so we will never know how it might have been publicly received. The 1888 *A Week in the Future* was far less original, in that it closely followed Jane Hume Clapperton's book *Scientific Meliorism and the Evolution of Happiness*, but this later book is more politically advanced. It is worth noting that 1888 was also the year of the formation of the Women's Suffrage League, and saw the first issue of the *Dawn*. The Social Darwinist ideas Spence adopted in her account of life in a transformed London in 1988 emphasized the emancipation of women as the basis of its genuinely egalitarian society. Internationalist in perspective, the book still preserved Spence's nationalist preferences, and was even unobtrusively republican, with a gracefully retired royalty earning an honest living as ordinary citizens. Oddly enough, Spence did not use *A Week in the Future* as a platform for her advocacy of proportional representation, and there was no overt reference made to female suffrage.

The feminism of *A Week in the Future* was dependent upon mastery of biological destiny as a necessary precursor to social and political emancipation — that is, birth control was successfully practised. Not only did this prevent Malthusian predictions from fulfilling themselves (there was a legal limit of three children per couple in this fictional 1988), more importantly, it freed women for fully professional or other working lives. In the earlier *Handfasted*, women were given sexual and economic equality, the one through trial marriages, the other through land grants to all citizens, regardless of sex, but large families were still the norm. In the later utopian work the problems of conventional marriage had been ameliorated by easy divorce, and an uninterrupted working life ensured economic independence for women. Child care in cooperative homes minimised domestic duties. The judges' hostile reception to *Handfasted*, it might be noted, resulted in a falling back from the radical and revolutionary concept of trial marriage, to the reformist position of easier divorce.

These utopian books of Spence's place her firmly within what Marilyn Lake has described as one of the greatest political struggles in Australian history: "The contest between men and women at the end of the nineteenth century for the control of the national culture".[6] For the masculinist context, we need go no further than the *Bulletin* of the time, or Lawson's later stories, particularly those in which Mitchell addresses "The Woman Question". Catherine Spence's public speaking voice was not, apparently, marginalised in her own lifetime (if we set aside the silencing of *Handfasted*), as perhaps the title of "grand old woman of Australia" given on her 80th birthday, testifies. Yet to speak as a woman was of itself limited by the "otherness" of woman in a masculinist ethos.

Nothing demonstrates this so graphically as Lesley Ljungdahl's 1988 re-issue of Spence's *A Week in the Future.*[7] Beautifully produced, this edition frames Spence's serious and high-minded text with cartoon illustrations, chiefly from *Punch* and the *Bulletin*. All the illustrators are male and their work is often amusing, but also irreverent, racist, larrikin, satirical, politically biased and consistently misogynist. They perfectly demonstrate both the necessity for a text such as Spence's, and its inevitable marginality in a masculine world. As Sylvia Lawson describes it in *The Archibald Paradox*, "that derisive and defensive anti-feminism which amounted then, throughout the English-speaking world, to an inexhaustible source of journalistic humour".[8] Lesley Ljungdahl's text of Spence's work precisely demonstrates the gendered struggle for control of the national culture that Lake sees as so central to the 1890s.

It is in this context that I want to examine what can be considered a key document in Spence's developing radicalism. For politically aware women, 1896 was an even more important date than Federation was to be four years later, for this was when South Australian women voted for the first time in an Australian election. Shortly before this election Spence had a letter published in the Adelaide *Register*, engagingly subtitled "A Few Plain Words to the Women Electors of South Australia by One of Themselves". It appeared in the *Register* on the 24th March, 1896.

The Approaching Elections
A Few Plain Words to the Women Electors of South Australia by One of Themselves

> Many of us did not expect the vote, not a few of us did not desire it, but now we have got it we are pressed on all sides to use it. Most of us no doubt will vote on the same side as our husbands, father, and brothers, but there is a limit to this amiable course. If our male relatives, for party purposes, ask us to vote for men whose moral character or political platform we disapprove of, we ought not to do so. If we elect bad men to Parliament we will have a bad Government. If we elect good and able men we will have a good Government. I say good and able, because a man

may be respectable and agreeable, and yet may be so ignorant that he does not know what is best for the country, or he may be so persuadable that crafty politicians may twist him round their fingers for their own purposes.

I know that the choice will be limited to four or five, and that in many districts there may be no man offering who is a heaven-born legislator. This is why I want to enlarge the districts and give a wider choice to all electors. But generally speaking there will be two men whom you prefer to the others. There is at the present time a very distinct difference between the two main parties, and those who have given thought to politics will have no difficulty in making a choice. Those who think the colony has gone too far on democratic lines will vote for the Conservative candidates, even though they may not agree with all the platform of the National Defence League. Those whose interests and sympathies lie with labour will vote for Labour candidates when they offer, and for Radical or Democratic candidates favourable to labour when no direct representative is in the field. The temperance advocates — the W.C.T.U. and their friends — will give support to candidates who promise aid to their cause. But many voters, especially among the women, have no strong opinions or convictions, and they can be persuaded to promise their votes to any one who takes the trouble to canvass them. This is partly because they are pleased to be solicited, but chiefly because they do not feel the importance of the duty of voting intelligently.

I am not surprised at the apathy and indifference of so many of my sisters. They have been kept out of politics, and considered it was no business of theirs. Even when suffrage was given it seemed at first sight that it would only increase the number of votes at the poll, but would in no way change or modify the results. I should much like if the ballot-papers given to women were of a different colour, so that we might see how far this is true. If women took to heart their responsibilities we ought to see some change. In the first place character should count for more than it has done in the past. Women do not want to be represented by drunkards, libertines, gamblers, or political adventurers. And character should embrace more than this. Political consistency and integrity are indispensable in a representative. And, as in old days, there were men who devoured widows' houses and for a pretence made long prayers, so now there are men who occupy church pews and support the churches who are greedy and grasping and cruel in their business transactions. These men are as little to be trusted as men of open bad character, for their own interests are always foremost with them, whereas we women want laws to be for the good of all. Do not vote for any man, however respectable and clever, whose politics you disapprove of. His cleverness will enable him to do more mischief to the cause which ought to be yours than if he were stupid. In the second place, women who are the housekeepers ought to support economy in the housekeeping of the State. Our lives are a constant war with dirt and with waste. We want a clean and wisely economical Government. We should set our faces against reckless borrowing, which causes heavier taxation. Every candidate, of course, professes economy, but when any retrenchment is proposed by a Ministry the opposite party says that this particular retrenchment is cruel, unjust, and unwise. If the retrenchment touches a relative or a personable friend, if it affects our district or our class, it is opposed from whatever quarter it may come. Now, let us women put fair play and common sense into the national housekeeping.

As to the act of voting, that is simple enough. Mark with a cross the candidates you prefer in the squares opposite their names. *Do nothing more. Do not sign your name.* If only one man seems to you worth voting for mark only his name.

In order to vote intelligently you must learn exactly what each candidate intends to do, and you must enquire into his past political history. If he has been false to his promises do not trust him. After the election is over you must watch the conduct of the representatives of your district in Parliament whether you voted for them or not. We do not need our members to be always making speeches, but we want them to support right measures in a right way, and to be able to give reason when needed for their actions. We have no right to expect our local members to subscribe to local objects. This is a growing evil in South Australia. We have no right to ask him to push our local interests at the expense of other districts, or at the cost of the whole province of South Australia. We ought to be able to further our honest interests and to call attention to any grievances we may have. But he is our representative, not our slave. He is not merely the representative of a district, but a member of the South Australian Parliament, charged with the interests of the whole community.

The eyes of the world are upon us, and we owe it to ourselves and to South Australia to use the vote conscientiously.

Catherine Helen Spence[9]

Here we find Spence positioning herself *as* a woman (whereas she had carefully assumed a gender-neutral position in her other writing), speaking specifically *to* women (an audience of value at this particular point of history, as a separate category of readers, newly empowered by enfranchisement). For these reasons this little document seems uniquely suitable for a feminist analysis. It also can well stand for the radicalism of Spence in the 1890s, particularly as it affects her lifelong concerns, voting and women.

It seems to me that at this point Spence significantly closes the gap between bourgeois liberalism and the kind of feminism to be found in the pages of Louisa Lawson's the *Dawn*. The common ground is the shared perception of the need for the feminisation of public life. As Susan Sheridan has pointed out, such an aim requires a prior awareness of a gendered speaking position and readership.[10]

A careful reading of this letter of Spence's reveals within the unexceptionable, commonsense prose familiar to the *Register* readers, a sub-textual construction of the male legislators and voters of the time which is almost totally damning, and a contrasting picture of the female voter which flatters her by making clear her moral and intellectual superiority. This is a relatively new note in Spence's writing. Earlier in her life she had shared George Eliot's pessimistic opinion of women in general as being incapacitated for public roles by their disgracefully poor education. American experience in the 90s made more of a democrat of Spence, and more of a feminist as well. On the other hand, it further disenchanted her with party politics, which made the possibility of a non-party, gender-directed vote an exciting possibility for the woman reformer. The disappointment of this hope had to wait until after the election.

The two significant premises underlying Spence's advice in this letter were the secret ballot itself, and the new power of the female vote, all the more powerful because of its legal anonymity. Thus her first point stresses that the moral character of the candidate is of more importance than the persuasions and directions of male relatives with dubious motives: "If our male relatives, for party purposes, ask us to vote for men whose moral character or political platform we disapprove of, we ought not to do so". Note already that "party purposes" are of no relevance to women. Respectable and agreeable men, she goes on, may in fact be ignorant men, or simply gulled by "crafty" politicians. The "good and able men" seem a faint hope when even respectability and agreeability cannot guarantee worthiness. As this subversive undermining of the male legislator and voter continues, the gap it creates can of course, in a gendered world, only be filled by someone who must be, given the terms set up, both superior *and* of the other sex; in fact superior simply by virtue of her sex. Female representation was not yet an issue, but Spence was to act in the following year by accepting nomination for the Federal convention. This was no more than the logical extension of the advice given in this letter. R. B. Walker has pointed out that female representation had acquired almost accidentally a de facto legality, untested until Spence stood for election:

> In the adult suffrage bill of 1894 there had originally been a clause barring their election, but this had been negatived by the joint votes of the supporters and opponents of the female vote. Presumably the opponents hoped that with this *amplification ad absurdum* the bill would not pass; E. Ward for instance painted a picture of females debating in the house while their husbands nursed the babies at home.[11]

The second paragraph of Spence's letter appears merely to disavow party affiliation: it is not her intention, she says, to instruct any woman to vote for any particular party. On the contrary — although she makes clear that a Conservative vote will be an anti-democratic vote, something of a contradiction in terms in this particular election. The negatively constructed reference to the National Defence League should give us a clue, however, to Spence's own opinions on this. Established in 1891, the National Defence League (later renamed the Australasian National League), was set up to defend the interests of property against socialism and radicalism, a political position with which the younger Spence may have had sympathy, but certainly she had moved well beyond this position by the 1890s. More interesting, at this point in her letter, is her construction of the woman voter without party allegiance or even political opinions as vulnerable to flattery and unaware of the significance of her vote. Once again, the underlying danger is in the possibility of a new and hardly won power being subtly appropriated by men. Spence hastens to shift the blame from women themselves, a reversal of her own earlier position, to those to whom it really belongs — the men who excluded women for so long from politics. Her suggestion that votes should be visibly gendered by different coloured papers is as challenging as it is intriguing. It would in fact increase the power of the women if they could be persuaded to vote in their own, and not only their menfolks', interests.

The remainder of this paragraph constructs an even more strongly negative picture of the male in political life. The terms she uses — "drunkards, libertines, gamblers, or political adventurers" — are exclusively male, as are the church hypocrites who tyrannize over women ("devouring widows' houses") for their own "greedy and grasping and cruel" purposes. Even the clever and respectable man can do more harm if his moral character is faulty, than the ignorant and respectable man earlier warned against. This second attack on the merely respectable is in contrast, again, to the youthful Spence, to whom middle-class respectability had been a guarantee of superiority. In contrast to the selfish interests of men are "we women" who "want laws to be for the good of all". The subtle valorisation of women continues with the suggestion that women's domestic economic experience better fits them for national housekeeping, than men. The deliberate transference of terms (domestic\state) reverses the usual binary opposition weighted towards the masculine domain. Further, male economics are subverted by sectional or personal interests, Spence maintains. It is women who must bring "fair play and common sense" to the national arena: that is, these things are missing from the existing masculine power structures. Again, it is in an absence that we must look for meaning. It is precisely women's previous exclusion from political power which makes them more honest and far-sighted than men.

Subversion requires secrecy: Spence's reminder to women voters not to sign their names on the ballot-paper may, at first sight, seem unnecessarily condescending. In fact it is a reminder that women's voting power depends upon the prior condition of the anonymity of the secret ballot. Finally, a reminder that their voting responsibility is an on-going one, a reiteration of the fact that the vote means the power to lobby effectively as well.

Without scaring any horses in Rundle Street, or, one presumes, any male voters, Spence has inserted into the discourse of politics and economics carried forward in the press, a consciousness-raising document which achieves much more than its "plain words" so ingenuously promise.

As a journalist, Spence had taken part in the public, masculinist discourse, by speaking from within it, urging reform of injustices to women by appealing to male responsibility. The historic 1896 election allowed her to speak as a woman, to point out to women their potential as a political group transcending other sectional interests.

The radicalism of this step needs to be measured against Spence's earlier political position. Her advocacy of proportional representation, for example, had always had as its aim the fairer representation of minorities. But the particular minority whose interests she wished to protect, were the educated middle-classes, whose votes, once manhood suffrage was introduced, could be swamped by an ignorant majority. R. B. Walker refers to an 1860 letter to the *Register*, from Spence: "South Australia must not follow the erring path of her sister Victoria where a depraved democracy, rendered omnipotent by the ballot box and the simple majority rule, had taken control to the detriment of talent and respectability".[12] Walker points out that by 1892, when a party system was in place, Spence's fears shifted from the possible tyranny of the majority to the harmful effects of the conflict between labour and capital.[13] As far as female suffrage is concerned, there had been a complete change from Spence's attitude in the 1860s, tantalisingly referred to in a letter from John Stuart Mill, dated 1862, which ends: "I suppose I am to understand the sentence in your letter which includes giving the suffrage to women in the category of "absurdities" as ironical".[14]

Thus Spence's 1896 letter to the women voters is a very significant document indeed. The nearest thing I have found to its frankly feminist tone is in the latter part of Spence's *Autobiography*, the section written by Jeanne F. Young after Spence's death in 1910. The fact that the same words are recorded in Young's own later book about Spence seems to verify their authenticity.[15] "We women are accused of waiting and waiting for the coming man, but often he doesn't come at all; and oftener still, when he does come, we should be a great deal better without him".[16]

Such a comment, along with Spence's 1896 letter, suggests that we should give the older woman more credit for radical feminism than she has commonly received. More work needs to be done on Spence in the last two decades of her life, on her relationships with better-known and more radical feminists like Vida Goldstein and Rose Scott. Spence's letter to some extent echoes Goldstein and Scott's writings on pacificism, as her recording of their sorrowful and disgusted retreat from the Mafeking Day junkets in Sydney, in the seclusion of Scott's home, testifies.[17] It is a great pity that the autobiographical account of Spence's later years had to be taken up by Jeanne Young at the precise moment in Spence's life which was to see an acceleration of her development as a thinker and activist, for she died just after she had reached the point in her story of her mother's death in 1887.

Tom Collins and Work

Julian Croft

"UNEMPLOYED at last!", the first three words of *Such is Life* (*SiL*, 1/1)[1], are justifiably some of the most famous words in Australian literature, but what do they mean?

Contained in the phrase is the tension between two entirely different meanings of "employment". The most immediate, and the one most current readers would respond to, is that of work in the sense of a labour input into the economic system. Unemployment then is the denial of the opportunity to participate in the cash economy through the sale of one's labour. What unfolds as the introductory paragraphs are read, though, is the older meaning of employment as the opposite of idleness, as the morally elevating "works" which lie behind Tom's reference to Isaac Watts' lines

> In works of labour or of skill,
> I would be busy too;
> For Satan finds some mischief still
> For idle hands to do.

The two meanings of the word have class affiliations. Unemployment as dispossession from the labour market is that of a working class with little or no capital; unemployment as idleness is that of a Protestant middle class with sufficient "Congealed Ability" (*SiL*, 263/328) to countenance a moral dimension to free time. Tom Collins' attitude to work and leisure is, I believe, both middle-class and Calvinist in origin.

Conditioned as we were until recently by the notion that unemployment is a disaster, and full employment the goal of democratic governments, the sense of delight and expectation, of the fulfilment of a long-awaited boon in Tom's opening words, would make us think more of retirement than forced redundancy. It would seem that for Tom his unemployment is temporary, has been saved for, and is more in the nature of a vice than penance. His attitudes are not those of the "wage-slave" of contemporary socialist and liberal economists,[2] but that of the minor capitalist who is between "specs". This is at odds with most of the traditional interpretations of *Such is Life* as an epic of the proletariat. In fact, as the opening words indicate, nothing could be further from the truth.

Many of the attitudes which inform Furphy's works are those of Christian Socialism, which was probably the most wide-spread and influential leftist thinking in Australia in the latter part of the nineteenth century. These ideas stem in part from Protestant, in particular Calvinist, thinking, mediated by the liberal tradition in Britain during the nineteenth century. It was not a collection of beliefs which sprang from the unskilled workers, but from the class of journeymen, skilled workers, and minor entrepreneurs. If we look at the range of occupations of the characters in Furphy's work, it is apparent that most of them are of this class, or of higher class allegiances. The main group of characters in *Such is Life*, the bullockies who are at the centre of Chapters I, IV, V, and partly VI, are minor entrepreneurs in the sense that present-day "truckies" are minor capitalists. At the nodes of Chapters II, VI, and VII are the workers on Riverina sheep stations — mainly Runnymede — but many of these are in "genteel" occupations: the narangies (jackeroos), the store-keeper, the squatters themselves, the itinerant self-employed, and the boundary riders. The latter are certainly wage-earners, but they have an independent existence in which they are responsible to themselves in the main, and are certainly of a different class from the manual labourers whom Tom Collins sees as aliens and outsiders — for example, at Runnymede, Sling Muck the gardener, and Vandemonian Jack, the old lag who is a representative of the best-forgotten *ancien régime* of the penal colonies. Tom does not depict those quintessentially heroic workers of the 1880s

and 1890s, the shearers, but shows us instead the fate of the
broken-down, unlucky manual worker in Andrew Glover,
with his deafness and encroaching blindness, in George
Murdoch, with his fatal total blindness, and in the lost and
perishing stranger in the Wilcannia shower. The main
protagonists, unlike Lawson's, are not these sufferers, but
the confident and aggressive self-employed bullocky. The
one bullocky who does not conform to this profile, the mad
and distraught Elijah Peterson, was dropped in Furphy's
re-write of the 1897 version of *Such is Life*.

Furphy came late to socialism. He had returned to
Shepparton to become a skilled labourer in his brother's
foundry in 1883 after going broke as a long-distance carrier.
Up to this point in his life he had been a minor, if
relatively unsuccessful, capitalist. As a teenager he had
worked the diggings for himself. He had at various times
run a pub, dummied for land, worked as a mechanic on farm-
machinery, been a selector, and finally he had set up as a
carrier on the tracks between Hay and Nyngan. He was a
product of his age: a minor entrepreneur, an auto-didact,
and a self-improver. Samuel Smiles would have been proud
of him. But in 1883 drought and disease destroyed his
bullocks, his three year winning streak as a capitalist came
to an ignominious end and, at the age of 40 he had to turn to
his elder brother for help and charity. For the rest of his
life he worked for wages and became at the same time a
committed Christian Socialist. He seems to have had scant
savings, and spent the little excess income he had on
tobacco and occasional trips to Melbourne.

Furphy's political beliefs before his conversion to
socialism in Shepparton were mostly conservative. They
would have been on one side or other of the great political
debate of the time — Free Trade or Protectionism. Furphy
lived and grew up in the garden of Protectionism, Victoria,
but he was a business success (and failure) in the open
plains of New South Wales, where Free Trade held sway
and Victorian meanness and greed seemed unheroic and
parochial:

> Victorian poverty spoke in every detail of the working plant;
> Victorian energy and greed in the unmerciful loads of salt and

> wire, for the scrub country out back. The Victorian carrier,
> formidable by his lack of professional etiquette and his extreme
> thrift, is neither admired nor caressed by the somewhat select
> practitioners of Riverina. (*SiL*, 7/8)

His family were Protestants from Ulster, and the inheritance of Calvinism, though often attacked, is evident in his work and in his ideas. Protestant groups, including the Loyal Orange Lodges, which Furphy pilloried in *Such is Life*, were Free Trade Supporters, as well as Single-Taxers, following Henry George's vision of a single Land Tax as the most equitable form of taxation, and the best way of ironing out the wild swings of the business cycle.[3] I think it likely that before he embraced socialism he was probably a Free-Trader as well as being a half-hearted believer in the Godliness of individual work and works. His elder brother, as befitted a Victorian manufacturer of the time, was probably Protectionist.

His experiences in his brother's foundry, friendship with young disciples of Socialism who worked there, and weekly exposure to the *Bulletin* moved him from his conservative inheritance to a labour theory of value, and thus to become an enthusiastic supporter of the rights of the worker, the necessity of union organisation, and the evils of capitalism and imperialism. For Furphy, though, these beliefs could be only be followed as extensions of the message of Christ in the Sermon on the Mount, so that throughout his life he remained a Christian, a Protestant, and a Dissenter.

When Furphy returned to Shepparton to work as a labourer, he had a freedom which he had not had as an entrepreneur. His work was predictable and regular. He worked for eight hours, slept a little in his lean-to which was divorced from the house and its distractions, and spent most of his time reading, writing, and talking. He had a lot of unemployed time, yet he still held down a job, which might explain some of the ambiguity which lies in his novel's opening sentence.

But those words are not Joseph Furphy's. They are written by Tom Collins. What then of Tom Collins at the same time that Furphy was writing *Such is Life* in the early 1890s? When Tom sat down to annotate his diaries a recession was wide-spread, the famous shearers' strike was under way, unemployment was a very unpleasant prospect for many people, and the economic conditions of that time were the background for the first great clash of labour and capital in the Australian colonies.[4] Yet unemployment in those famous opening paragraphs of the novel is treated not as a personal or social disaster, but as a creative opportunity, for Tom is not one of the lower orders. At the time of the action of *Such is Life*, Tom has passed beyond the heights Joseph Furphy reached of being a carrier — Tom seems to have given up that "profane profession" in 1880 — and is now a member of the New South Wales Civil Service, most probably in the Lands Department.[5] This is definitely a step out of the worst consequences of the curse of Adam. What was in Furphy's mind when he made Tom a civil servant?

The New South Wales Civil Service in the 1880s and 1890s was a by-word for nepotism and patronage; in fact these abuses were the subject of a Royal Commission in 1894. That Commission found that over a third of all appointments were "temporary", that is, they were appointed directly by the minister and were made without the usual examination and without reference to the Civil Service Board. James Fry's memoirs of forty years in the New South Wales Civil Service, spanning the 1880s and the 1890s, confirm Tom's description of his work[6]

> ... I may remark that I was at that time a Government official, of the ninth class; paid rather according to my grade than my merit, and not by any means in proportion to the loafing I had to do. Candidly, I was only a Deputy-Assistant-Sub-Inspector ...
> (*SiL*, 4/5)

We are not told whether Tom is a "temporary" or not, but if he were he could only have been dismissed by the minister. Furphy would possibly have wanted his ideal contemporary reader to have come to the conclusion that Tom, as a member of the New South Wales Civil Service, was probably a Free-Trader, that he might have had some acquaintance with Masonry or some other line of influence to the minister, and that he is definitely not a state socialist.

Although Tom's political opinions are not clearly expressed in *Such is Life* (many of the most political statements are made by his pipe), in *Rigby's Romance* there is no doubt in anyone's mind, including his own, that Tom is on the side of the conservatives. Talking of Rigby, Tom makes an unambiguous distinction between himself and the American prophet:

> "I'm a Conservative; and he is — well, not to mince matters, he's a State Socialist. In other words, I adapt myself to the times and the seasons, whilst he thinks the conformity ought to be on the other side." (*RR*, 12)

It is fitting that Rigby should be the mouth-piece for the arguments for state socialism, and for the integration of the Christian ethic into the socialist platform, for the ideas he expresses come mainly from American sources — Henry George's *Progress and Poverty*, Laurence Gronlund's *The Cooperative Commonwealth*, Edward Bellamy's *Looking Backwards*, and Ignatius Donnelly's *Caesar's Column*. Kate Baker tells us that Furphy's Scottish friend William Cathels provided the model for Rigby, and that the relationship between the two, seems to have been close to the relationship between Tom and Rigby:

> It was an education to hear the two men discuss a problem — to listen to Mr Cathels' polished pronunciamentos given in measured rather staccato utterance, and Joseph Furphy's deep Irish-burred tones bringing forth some brooded-over originality. Anyone who knew William Cathels would suspect where Joseph Furphy had found his Rigby. He had fitted His type — his "antitype", as Furphy would insist was the right term.[7]

That seems significant to me. There is no doubt that Tom is a figure of fun and is sent up numerous times over the course of the three novels and the short stories, but then so is Rigby. I have written elsewhere on the binary oppositions in Furphy's work,[8] and it would seem to be confirmed by this remark of Kate Baker, and of Furphy's use of the word "antitype". Furphy seems to have consciously set up a dialectic in his treatment of political economy in his work (as he does with other issues). The tension between conservatism and radicalism in his works is, I feel, a reflection of a tension within himself. It surfaced in the use of a conservative narrator who has to give us a radical message. It is particularly the case in the way work and labour are treated in the fictions.

It is hard to ignore the passion which lies behind the Christian Socialism of the symposium of the rewritten *Rigby's Romance*, but it is equally hard to ignore Rigby's personal emotional desiccation and his inability to love at the intimate level; likewise it is hard to ignore Tom's play-acting and his conservatism in *Rigby's Romance*, but equally difficult to discount his numerous acts of kindness and charity in *Such is Life*. The ethic of responsibility is an obvious preoccupation in Furphy's fictions, but we have to balance this against Tom's self-interest, and an equal capacity to act irresponsibly — most notably in Chapter III of *Such is Life*. This ambivalence in Tom was most probably a result of Furphy's own divided loyalties to his conservative family and to his radical friends and members of the *Bulletin* set. The conflict between the two is seen most poignantly in the confused presentation of work in his fictions.

Furphy's belief system, along with his hand-writing and reading habits, were probably inherited from his mother, and were based on the Christian precepts which the family brought with them from Northern Ireland. Although the family seems to have been at different times Methodist and Church of Christ (and Joseph in later life was to have Spiritualist leanings like many others in the latter decades of the nineteenth century), nevertheless I think I sense a strong thread of Calvinism running through Furphy's ideas. Extreme interpretations of Calvinist doctrine, such as those of Jonathan Edwards, are mocked in Chapter III of *Such is Life*, but the Scottish tradition of Knox came down to him not only within the family, but from without, through the writings of Thomas Carlyle.[9] For example, Carlyle's view of labour, that it supplied the emotional needs of a people bereft of the traditional support of Christianity, and that it was necessary for individuals to act and to work in an heroic way to change this world's nature so that the absent God might be manifested in our works, is a Romantic development of basic Calvinist attitudes to Works, and in a slightly changed form underlies much British socialist rhetoric.[10] Likewise a belief in Providence, which is one of the recurring common-places among the characters in Furphy's novels, has a fundamentalist Protestant origin. In *Such is Life* material success occurs because of Providence; and luck, or the lack of it, makes and breaks fortunes throughout Furphy's fictions. Thompson has a curse which ensures that he will never be able to keep two teams of bullocks at the same time; on the other hand he never goes completely broke, even when cleaned out by the genial remittance rogue, Dick the Devil. Even Mosey Price, the sans-culotte and iconoclast, believes in the workings of Providence. The saintly squatter Stewart is obviously one of the elect because, beyond all his other virtues, "his *mana* never failed" (*SiL*, 165/206), while Ida's battling selector father who hangs himself is obviously not elect.

While Carlyle would have argued against election, and have stressed the heroic nature of the supernatural struggle with the powers of chaos in this world, Calvin's teaching is that we must accept our position and make-do under the mysterious and unknowable providence of God. The pipe argues against this inhuman doctrine in Chapter III, while Tom, being at heart a Protestant conservative, realises he must accept his position in life as a Deputy-Sub-Inspector because of the youth of his superior, and because of his superior's inability to be promoted, thus blocking Tom from the bright reversion he sees for himself in the New South Wales Civil Service. Tom's nineteenth-century belief in a rigid determinism, metaphorically drawn for the reader in the parable of the locomotive and the railway lines (*SiL*, 70-1/87-8), is not so much scientific Darwinism as good old-fashioned Calvinist theology.[11]

Carlyle's elaborately mysterious meditation on clothing and man, *Sartor Resartus*, with its dialectic between "The Everlasting No" of despair and "The Everlasting Yea" of the will, between the world of social clothes and the world of the naked soul, and its rousing call for the expression in work of that naked soul, is an antidote to the Calvinist notion of work as an expression of acceptance — for Carlyle work was revolt, and a cry of the individual will:

> Be no longer a Chaos, but a World, or even Worldkin. Produce!
> Produce! Were it but the pitifullest infinitesimal fraction of a
> Product, produce it, in God's name! 'Tis the utmost thou hast in
> thee: out with it, then. Up, up! Whatsoever thy hand findeth to
> do, do it with thy whole might. Work while it is called Today;
> for the Night cometh, wherein no man can work.[12]

But Tom seems incapable of carrying out Carlyle's injunction. He has plans and projects. He has three notebooks full of jottings for a planned series of Shakespearean studies, and is waiting for the leisure to develop his ideas (*SiL*, 206/257); his natural indolence, however, allied with an obsessive but debilitating desire to bathe, robs him of his achievement. We should not be surprised. The progress of the novel shows the gradual deterioration of Tom from the energetic and charitable being of the first chapters, to the dandified conservative of the last chapter, whose callous but necessarily selfish treatment of Andrew Glover is the final glimpse we are given of him in this novel. Clothes are the signs of this deterioration. Chapter III marks the climax of the hero's moral progress. After an involuntary bath in the Murray, he is a naked soul alone, property-less and lost in the underworld of Victoria; but by the end of the novel he has accumulated a bell-topper (symbol of the bloated plutocrat in the musings of Tom's pipe (*SiL*, 87/108)) and a long alpaca coat to go with his coloured glasses — and in this guise he appears to the workers at Runnymede station like a financier come to buy the station (*SiL*, 283-4/353-4). We also find out that the pipe, the moral conscience of the work, is an accessory acquired by stealth, if not theft. Tom's final action in the novel is to give the glasses (which at least belong to him) to Andy Glover under the guise of mateship and a concern for the man's ophthalmic eyes. It is one of the few times the word "mate" appears in the novel, and its use seem strongly ironic, for Tom's charity is compelled by a sense of deep guilt for a crime for which Andy has been blamed. Tom does not confess to it, for he is an actor — a man with no centre of identity — whose

desperate search for clothes to hide his essential
nakedness in Chapter III leads him to assault, arson, and
robbery. His disguise leads also to mistaken identity.
Quarterman the magistrate believes that Glover has burnt
the hay rick which Tom has fired, and Tom Armstrong
believes that Tom is actually a fellow Scot when Tom
intervenes to save Warrigal Alf's bullocks from the pound.
Both disguises are nearly penetrated in the final scene of
the book, but Tom the consummate actor is left unmarked,
free to muse "Such is Life, my fellow-mummers" (*SiL*,
297/371). The irascible Scot, Armstrong, and the deaf and
blind Glover, both itinerant manual workers, are open and
frank about their situations — there is no duplicity or rôle-
playing in their characters, and perhaps the message is
that honest manual workers are not hypocrites.[13]

And Tom is not a worker. As he sits on the verandah at
Runnymede in a debilitated state after yet another bath,
he watches the labours of Vandemonian Jack, Sling Muck,
"Joey Possum" the itinerant saddler, and that most
shocking of all examples of the futility of labour, Priestley
the Roman Catholic bullocky with thirteen children. But
Priestley is a self-employed man, and the moral Tom draws
from Priestley's industry and his lack of success is that:

> ... to everything there is a time and a season — a time for work,
> and a time for repose — hence you find the industrious man's
> inveterately leg-weary set of frames in hopeless competition
> with the judiciously lazy man's string of daisies... The fact is,
> that the Order of Things — rightly understood — is not
> susceptible to any coercion whatever, and must be humoured in
> every possible way. In the race of life, my son, you must run
> cunning, reserving your sprint for the tactical moment.
>
> (*SiL*, 215/268)

The Order of Things, *mana*, Fate, Providence determine
what the worker gets out of life, not the amount of effort
put into it. A revealing comment in one of Furphy's letters
shows very clearly what might have been in Tom's mind
when he used the phrase "Order of Things" and how close
his position is to that of traditional Calvinism:

> And the squalid element of life [work] rightly regarded, is but a
> necessary part of the complex machinery which was in motion
> when the Constadt people discussed these things over a bit of
> baked hyena. But it mustn't be *too* squalid in any individual

instance. This is an outrage on the Order of Things; and the Order of Things is the another [sic] name for the Will of God. It is a question of opposition or co-operation — and we safely put our bit on the latter policy.[14]

The distinction Furphy makes is between the "squalid" and by inference the noble aspects of work. In two other letters he returns to this theme. The first is to Cathels in 1898 during the flush of enthusiasm for the composition of *Such is Life*. The second is to his mother, when later in life his inability to find a publisher for *Rigby's Romance* produced a depression concerning his literary life:

> To Cathels, 30/6/1898. Shepparton.
> Beginning with the good old Sheol of our fathers, I had reasoned step by step, in my shallow way, till at last I was landed in the belief that, after death, nothing remained of the human skunk except the work he had left behind — call it Materialism; Positivism — anything you like. Seemed to me that the purpose of our life was to make this world somewhat less of a disgrace to its alleged Creator, that done, the most desirable thing was a thorough good sleep.[15]

To his mother he always professed himself a Christian — though not a sentimental, conservative one. Writing to her from Western Australia in his weekly letter, he confessed that work, intellectual work, was now impossible because of the demands put on him by his family, and that "sordidness", the squalid drudgery of manual work without any higher purpose was all that engaged him:

> To Judith Furphy. Dec. 7 [no year. no place]
>
> It is good to have some interests beyond the daily round of work — in fact, it is just there that the superiority of one man over another is made manifest. Nothing in the world is more to be avoided than sordidness. In reality I am no more sordid than at any former time; but I have drifted into a kind of eddy or back-water — drifted, Mam, drifted.[16]

> To Judith Furphy.
> W[estern]. A[ustralia] Nov. 15 [no year]
>
> (After quoting from *Rigby's Romance*) ... which is another way of saying that I sincerely — and I hope, intelligently — believe in the Holy Spirit. And not all the canting hypocrites, and temporising frauds, and brainless fanatics ... have been able to disturb my own confidence in God whom they ignorantly insulted.[17]

There is a confusion here brought on by two different audiences. To his male socialist friend Cathels he confesses himself as a materialist, to his beloved mother, he confesses his depression and his view of himself as the failed hero-artist (definitely not one of the *canaille*), but a believer in the Holy Spirit. There is no doubt that Furphy was a passionate democrat and materialist, but, as we have seen, there were also parts of his belief system which remained unreconstructed after his exposure at Shepparton to socialist materialism. Those unreconstructed parts of his beliefs were those which he had learned from his mother's Protestant evangelical faith. The tension between the two can be easily seen in the debate on political economy in *Rigby's Romance*, and might explain why this unattractive novel was considered by Furphy to be his masterpiece, and why such a personally heartless and unsympathetic character as Rigby should have appealed so strongly to Furphy. Indeed he believed that "80% [of] masculine readers will long to be like Rigby, and that feeling will disarm criticism."[18] One can sense in the letter that the feminine side of Furphy realises that Rigby is a failure — which he is as a character in a fiction, and as a moral hero; while the masculine side wishes the reader to respond to the agitator's ideas, rather than his actions.

What then are Rigby's ideas about political economy and work?

The first thing we should know about Rigby is that he is of Puritan descent, and Tom sees him in terms of the Earl of Moreton's tribute to John Knox: "There lies one who never feared the face of man" (*RR*, 36). That inheritance can be seen in Rigby's argument with Lushington, the clergyman, who sells insurance policies which Rigby claims are a form of usury and thus un-Christian. Rigby's development of his argument with Lushington turns on his belief that Nature is God: "The Earth is the Lord's — Nature's ... The Power behind Evolution — the Power which controls the million operations of natural law ... is beyond man," and, one might add, beyond insurance policies. "But man's moral nature ... is his own, without any reservation whatsoever." Rigby then goes on to cite the example of Canute, who could by his own volition "damn himself ... though he couldn't dam the tide; his soul was his own, the tide was God's" (*RR*, 156). Jonathan Edwards, the spokesman for Rigby's Massachusetts forbears, could not have put the proposition of free-will and pre-destination any better — Man proposes, but God disposes.

Christ's teachings are teased out by Rigby in Chapter XXXI to show their clear message of social justice, and according to Rigby, as they were to many Christian Socialists of the time, Christ's prophecies are in fact those about to be fulfilled by Socialism: "Is that a forecast of Socialism — or is it not? I tell you, boys, Orthodoxy is doing its best to make Christ a false prophet" (*RR*, 175). There has been a perversion of Christ's message by concentrating on individual salvation rather than the general good, and this is particularly evident in the:

> various branches of the Wesleyan cult, where the pathetic effort to serve God and Mammon is reduced to a system fortified by the accumulated sanction of millions of holy and money-making men who, by Divine grace, are purified from every unprofitable sin. Compulsory poverty, with its endless train of evils, they hold to be a Divine institution — which it is every man's duty to oppose tooth and nail on his own private account. (*RR*, 185-6)

While poverty is man-made, although attributed to the deity by the deluded, goodness is not. Showing his Puritan background, Rigby's fundamental point is teleological — that is, there is a destiny, a Providence, which, once articulated by prophets such as Christ, and socialists like himself, can be used as guide for progress toward a social system based on humanity's innate goodness (*RR*, 186-7). The tone of these passages and much of what Rigby has to say is derived from Henry George's *Progress and Poverty*, with its powerful combination of traditional Biblical diction and contemporary illustration and the passionate conviction of George's single answer to the complex problems of the trade cycle, human ethics, and the Protestant amalgam of individualist theology and scientific determinism.

If the inheritance of Puritan, Calvinist orthodoxy lies behind Rigby's State Socialism, other American influences run through his thoughts. Although he is a Yankee, his attitude toward equality does not extend to race. He vigorously supports the White Australia policy on the ground that Indians and Chinese may be equal as men, but judged on the standards of their "progress-potency" and the fact that they have sold their birth-rights as men by accepting their exploitation for generations, they cannot have free access to the advances to be made by State Socialism in Australia (*RR*, 212). Readers of the 1897 version of *Such is Life* will therefore not be surprised to find that Rigby was in Charleston before the Civil War, and attended a sale of slaves.[19] On matters of equality before Christ, Rigby argues vigorously against Binney's conservative argument that inequality is innate in humankind, but his defence of a closed shop for white Australian labour, and Furphy's belief in an open market for a freed black labour force in America, are examples of an unresolved conflict, not only in Furphy, but in Australian and American progressive ideologies in the nineteenth century.[20]

Tom is the conservative Mutt to Rigby's socialist Jeff. Much of what he has to say in *Rigby's Romance* is a caricature of the opinions which occasionally surface in *Such is Life*. There is little doubt, though, that from the first we see of him in September 1883 until the dateless time in the future when he is unemployed and writing his realist account of life in the Riverina, Tom becomes a more and more vigorous spokesman for conservatism.

In the rewritten sections of *Such is Life*, the theory of alternatives is developed. These are the main insights we have into Tom's belief system. Its first articulation is in Chapter II, one of the two chapters written for the 1903 version of *Such is Life*. There Tom attempts to define by literary illustration (*Hamlet, Othello, Macbeth*), parable, and allegory his notion that there is a teleological imperative, a determinism or destiny, within which are made the aggregate of human choices. The model is one with which we are familiar; it is the one Milton exploits in *Paradise Lost* and *Paradise Regained* (which Tom significantly has recommended as an unitary work to

Thompson in *Rigby's Romance*); it is the one Jonathan
Edwards endorses in his essay on "Redemption" (which
Tom is reading in Chapter III of *Such is Life*); it is the one
which lies behind Rigby's sermon on State Socialism; and
it is one which Joseph Furphy drew from his Protestant
environment.

There are major distinctions between Tom's position and
that of a true believer. He does not necessarily admit that
there is a deity. He sees divinity as being subject to destiny
— destiny being the state of affairs at this moment. From
these present alternatives we make choices with our free
will, which is in turn influenced by our moral centre.
Perhaps, though, he has fudged the issue, and merely
pushed the Deity further back into the mist of the first
efficient cause, and called It Destiny. In his development of
the ideas of the "controlling alternative" (*SiL*, 68-71/85-
8), Tom recognises that the individual does not follow the
line of least resistance, and that although s/he may have
a moral centre, this does not necessarily mean that choices
are made which will produce happiness, peace and honour.
The situation is exacerbated when we realise that no
decision is made without an effect on, and an interaction
with, others. When considered in the mass, human choices
are "more often wrong than right", and thus history is a
"record of blundering option, followed by iron servitude to
the irremediable suffering thereby entailed" (*SiL*, 71/88).
That certainly is the case with Tom at this point in the
narrative. He does not stop to hail the swagman he sees
under the tree, and as a result the swagman dies.

The chance to redeem himself comes in the next chapter
of *Such is Life*, where Tom, deep in his reading of Edwards'
On Redemption, meets another swagman down on his luck,
and debates with his pipe on the nature of poverty, social
justice, and the Christian message. We find out after Tom's
meditation (*SiL*, 94-5/117-9) on the pipe's message (*SiL*,
85-91/106-13), that his reason for thinking about justice and
poverty is that he wanted to take his mind off the deaf,
blind, and indigent swagman and the ample money in Tom's
pocket, which despite the pipe's moralising still remains
there.

Tom we realise from these two digressions is at heart a conservative. He believes in a Whig view of history, and sees humanity's progress as one of decline, while the pipe argues for optimism and radical change — an effort of will based on the teachings of the New Testament. It is quite fitting that Tom should be reading Jonathan Edwards, and although he dislikes him, Edwards' thinking has left its mark on Tom's musings. There are those whose *mana* is out; whose poverty is the outward show of their being shut out from grace. Even Tom himself might have reached his highest point — as Deputy-Assistant-Sub-Inspector — and be faced with the prospect of being "'a swagman, bluey on shoulder and billy in hand ... Such is Life'" (*SiL*, 94/117). There is no guarantee that we have any idea of the working of fate or of God's mind, and Tom struggles with the awful realisation of the basis of this belief " — that the poor shall never cease out of the land. And no man knows when his own turn may come" (*SiL*, 95/118). Even Tom may be "UNEMPLOYED at last!"

That, one feels, is Edwards speaking. The paragraph which follows is a sudden change in mood for Tom, and one in which we sense that Tom perhaps speaks with passion of his rejection of determinism and his belief in the operation of collective human will to change things. The Divine may be manifested to us, by clear-sighted prophets — Christ, current socialist thinkers — and we can follow that "Divine Idea [which] points the way, clearly apparent to any vision not warped by interest or prejudice, nor darkened by ignorance; but the work is man's alone, and its period rests with man" (*SiL*, 95/119). But we cannot take this seriously. As I pointed out above, Tom's reverie, of which this is the rousing conclusion, has been indulged in to allow him to forget his simple duty to give alms and relieve the suffering of a fellow human being.

Tom is the epitome of that Wesleyan ethic which Rigby attacked, and which Joseph's elder brother John, epitomised — a committed Christian who nevertheless is quite happy to accumulate while others starve. In their varying degrees, Lushington, Binney, Furlong, and Tom are the conservative Christians, while Rigby is the flawed

Christian Socialist, the man for whom ideas are more important than feelings. If there is any person in Furphy's fiction who represents a proper example of the new order, it would be Sam Brackenridge. He has married, he is a committed socialist, and he is a happy, energetic worker — but he cannot think for himself.

Such is Life, Rigby's Romance, and *The Buln-Buln and the Brolga* certainly put the case for socialism and egalitarianism but an analysis of the ideas in the novels, and their method of presentation through a conservative narrator and a flawed spokesman for state socialism compromise the force of those ideas, and confuse the readership of the novels. This came about from Furphy's difficulties in trying to make Protestant Christianity conform to the optimistic and progressive ideas of state Socialism. He came to the latter late, after a failure as a minor capitalist, and his status in the world of male aggressive capitalism was not high. He lived in his successful brother's shadow, but he also lived in the darker shadows of puritan Protestantism, which I suspect he learnt at his mother's knee. As much as his letters indicate that he accepted willingly and totally the socialist messages of Henry George, Laurence Gronlund, Edward Bellamy, and Ignatius Donnelly, the novels themselves are fraught with ambiguities, contradictions, and ironies, which perhaps are the result of a structure, erected for one purpose — to explore the nature of romantic and realist fiction — which has escaped from the control of the author.

That is certainly the case with work and workers. *Such is Life* is not an epic of the proletariat. It is about property, land, and profit, and the criminal acts needed to survive as a self-employed businessman. *Rigby's Romance* shows us an agitator at work in the promotion of Socialism, but he is also someone who is so divorced from the world of action and a prisoner of the world of ideas, that he will not (and does not) accomplish anything. The symposium which Rigby addresses is not a collection of workers, but middle-class landowners, carriers, a clergyman, a watchmaker, and a socially ambiguous kangaroo-hunter. *The Buln-Buln and the Brolga* is more a comedy of manners, in which social pretence and social masks are scrutinised, and the self-deception and fantasies of individuals are analysed and exposed. There is no hero of the working-class in this novel. Tom, Freddie Falkland-Pritchard and his wife are all members of the mercantile middle-class, while Bob Ross, the "real" Australian from the back-blocks is a flawed representative of heroic frontier. Barefoot Bob is a boundary-man, who has dummied for land, and who has been the boss's creature for many years. He is a first-rate bushman, but he cannot read men as well as he reads the bush, and is cheated by his boss.

In none of Furphy's novels can we see work in a positive light. For Tom Collins to be "unemployed at last" is to be away from a treadmill of lies and duplicities, to be free from responsibility, and to have enough time to write up the truth about work: that work has little to do with success, and has no bearing on our *mana* or our destiny, which is, in turn, controlled by some inscrutable process somewhat similar to Calvin's God. The contradictions in Furphy's personality and in his belief system were the subjects of his fictions and can be seen in the words he chose to open his major novel, and in his attitude to one of the nineteenth century's major intellectual preoccupations, the nature of work.

"The Yellow Peril", Invasion Scare Novels and Australian Political Culture

Neville Meaney

Yearly the condition of affairs became more serious and the hatred of the white masses for the yellow enemies more bitter. When our story opens in the winter of 1908, it only needed a leader to light the flames of racial war.
> — "Sketcher" (William Lane), "White or Yellow? A Story of the Race War of A.D. 1908", *Boomerang*, 18 Feb 1888.

The Mongols after a sleep of centuries, had awoke at last. Still brave as lions, enduring as dogs, and rapacious as wolves they had shaken off their death-like stupor and again taken up their glorious tradition of the past ...Strong as ever in their belief in their absolute superiority to all mankind, and armed with the very weapons which in the past had brought about their humiliations, they were coming under the old banner of blood and fire to avenge past insults and win new possessions.
> — Kenneth Mackay, *The Yellow Wave,* London: Richard Bentley & Sons, 1895, p.214.

But it is the problem which in initial importance overshadows all others. For the alienated extreme Northern corner — Australia irridenta — is flourishing with a hostile civilization. Under lenient British rule a new Japanese empire is in the making ... A truce has been called until 1940 A.D. Till then the Commonwealth must get ready for its relentless march to the North to save the purity of the race by sweeping the brown invaders back over the coral sea.
> — C.H.Kirmess, *The Australian Crisis* , (Melbourne: George Robertson, 1909), p.335.

From the 1880s to the first World War, the fear of an Asian invasion, whether migratory or military, was a major theme in Australian literature as it was in Australian politics. It excited the imagination of utopian socialists, bush balladeers and radical reformers, and was a central, if misunderstood, motif in the "Legend of the Nineties" which strove to define a "National Culture."[1]

This literary preoccupation, which amounted almost to an obsession, expressed itself through cartoons, short stories,[2] plays,[3] films,[4] and most substantially of all, novels. Of the latter the three most important were "White or Yellow? A Story of the Race War of A.D. 1908", written by William Lane under the pseudonym of "The Sketcher", which appeared in the Brisbane weekly the *Boomerang* from 18 February to 5 May 1888; *The Yellow Wave: A Romance of the Asiatic Invasion of Australia* by Kenneth Mackay, which was published in 1895; and *The Australian Crisis* by C.H. Kirmess, which came out first as a serial entitled "The Commonwealth Crisis" in the Sydney journal the *Lone Hand* between October 1908 and August 1909, and was turned into a book in 1909 under the more nationalistic title.[5] These three novels responded to three successive phases in the Australian saga of "The Yellow Peril", firstly Chinese immigration, secondly Chinese invasion and thirdly Japanese invasion. And each had something to say not only about Australian perceptions of Asia but also about the consequences of a perceived Asian threat to Australian political culture. In all the novels it is possible to detect a search for a vision of community in a newly-established, modernising society.

The invasion scare novel was a relatively new fiction genre which took off following the Franco-Prussian war. In an era of technological progress, mass nationalism and collectivist idealism, such cautionary tales had widespread appeal. The newly self-conscious "nation" or "race" — and the terms were often used interchangeably as colour and culture were compounded — saw itself engaged in a struggle with other nations or races for survival or supremacy, and the language of Social Darwinism lent a pseudo-scientific authority to this view of international politics. The prospect of technological marvels being harnessed to the chariots of war added a frightening and fascinating dimension to this scenario; indeed science fiction appeared simultaneously with the war novel and was often merged with it. The romance of peoples striving to triumph over rivals and to fulfil their historic destinies stirred deep emotions.

The invasion scare novel was in origin an English creation, and it was in England that the genre was most successful. From George Chesney's *The Battle of Dorking* (1871) to William Le Queux's *The Invasion of 1910* (1906), most of these stories told of French or German invasions of the British Isles. They had a clear purpose, namely to alert the nation to its defenceless position, to turn the people from their feckless, indolent ways, and to convince the country of the necessity of increased defence expenditure and disciplined military training. It was a popular, even populist literature. In this first age of mass literacy, writers were using novels to influence public opinion on the questions of the hour, whether social reform or foreign danger. The invasion novel aroused hostility to the national enemy. Inside Britain they uncovered nests of spies, generally foreigners, who were bent on sabotage and subversion. While the consequences for the political life of the nation were not always drawn out, it was frequently the case, as in *The Invasion of 1910*, that parliamentary institutions were found wanting, and a strong new leader, embodying the true spirit of the nation, emerged out of the old ruling class to rally the people and save the day.

Though the small European countries, unlike the great powers, did not follow the English example and produce their own invasion scare fiction — perhaps reflecting their sense of helplessness[6] — Australia produced a number of creative works which spoke to the nation's peculiar geo-political circumstances and racial anxieties.[7] Australians, as proud Britons, avidly read English novels such as *The Invasion of 1910,* and performed English invasion scare plays such as Guy Du Maurier's *An Englishman's Home.* Yet, despite their attachment to Britain and the British Empire, no Australian author wrote an invasion novel, or for that matter a play or film script, in simple imitation of the English model. None of the plots of the Australian novels were set in Britain. Nearly all — including the most significant and influential — took for their story line what was a distinctively Australian concern, namely an Asian threat to white Australia. Australian novels, like the English ones, reflected their nation's strategic vulnerability and political culture. Indeed a common sub-theme running through the Australian novels was Britain's indifference to Australia's plight, and its inability or unwillingness to help Australia resist the Asian menace.

The Australians also drew very different political lessons from the national crisis created by the threat of invasion. Whereas English authors, such as Chesney in *The Battle of Dorking*, attributed Britain's failure to rise to the challenge of foreign threats to "power ... passing away from the class which had been used to rule, and to face political danger ... into the hands of lower classes ... untrained to the use of political rights and swayed by demagogues",[8] the Australians found that fault lay not only with the unsympathetic British who left the colonies to fend for themselves, but also with the local ruling class who toadied to the imperial authorities and lacked the virtue, will and energy of the common people. The heroes of white Australia in these stories were depicted in the nationalistic guise of "The Legend of the Nineties". They either rallied under the Southern Cross banner of the Eureka goldfield rebels of 1854, or were the true sons of the Bush and therefore best fitted and able to devote themselves to Australia's welfare.

If it is true, as Vance Palmer has asserted in *The Legend of the Nineties*, that William Lane's "New Australia" experiment in Paraguay "covered the substance of the Australian dream itself, the idea of a closed continent, of building up a free community apart from the world",[9] then this dream was concocted not out of an Australian bush experience but from English and American radical ideas, and in this ideal society racial purity was at least as important as the democratic equality. In "White or Yellow?" as much as in "New Australia", race was the principal basis of community.

It is difficult to trace the intellectual origins of Lane's racial view of the good society. Unlike Mackay and Fox, Lane was not Australian born and bred. He had grown up in Bristol and did not arrive in Australia until 1885. He had spent some time in North America and while a journalist in Detroit had acquired radical sympathies. He was much influenced by Henry George's *Progress and Poverty*, Edward Bellamy's *Looking Backward* and Laurence Gronlund's *Cooperative Commonwealth*. But it is difficult to see how these American writers could have shaped his racial views.

Most commentators have tended to dismiss the question by claiming that Lane was merely reflecting the ideas of the Australian labour movement, which when organised as the Australian Labor Party adopted as its first objective "the cultivation of an Australian sentiment based on racial purity". But the religious intensity with which he held this racial belief would seem to belie such an easy explanation.

Perhaps Michael Wilding's suggestion that Lane was an heir to the Ranter-Leveller tradition of the English Civil War and the fact that that tradition contained elements, especially in the late nineteenth century, which lent themselves to the development of racial notions of community, might be helpful here. The English revolutionaries had justified their right to rebel on the basis of the historical myth that the Norman Conquest had replaced an egalitarian, self-governing, Anglo-Saxon society with a monarchical and aristocratic despotism. Lane at times invoked such arguments to justify resistance to the ruling class: "Our parliamentary system is ... only a degenerated survival of the assembly at which in primitive times our Teutonic forefathers gathered, free and equal, to make for themselves laws for their governance". The good society which had been subverted by a foreign invader was an Anglo-Saxon Teutonic tribal one, and by inference, the good society was to be attained by restoring this lost world.[10] Lane's "Race War of A.D. 1908" would seem to have had such a goal in view.

The story begins with a flashback to 1888 when "imperialist traitors" undermined the independence of the Australian colonies. By agreeing to the 1887 naval defence scheme, under which the colonies subsidised the local British squadron rather than build their own, they took a first step towards crushing Australia's spirit. Shortly afterwards "British troops garrisoned her ports, British ships watched her coasts. British interests dominated her parliaments, British diplomacy fanned the local jealousies that kept the colonies apart". In 1889 the British government had quashed the colonies' anti-Chinese legislation, and as a result "the gates of Australia had been thrown open to the yellow men". Through a generous distribution of titles and honours, the local elite was suborned, and the scattered resistance easily crushed. In the subsequent twenty years the number of Chinese in the colonies grew to twelve million, or over a quarter of the total population. Chinese competition reduced the great majority of whites to a status inferior to that of the European masses. The "Plutocracy and Landocracy", whose white members fraternised freely with their yellow counterparts, imposed their will on the common people. By 1908 the racial tension arising out of dispossession and alienation had reached a critical point.

Against this background the narrative recounts how the Queensland premier, Lord Stibbins, a native born son of a mining speculator, sought, by marrying his daughter Stella to Sir Wong Hung Foo, "the head and fount" of the Chinese community, to establish an imperial dynasty to rule over Australia. At his palatial mansion, Taringa Park, in Brisbane's best suburb, Stibbins laid out his plans before Wong. Using the well organised, docile Chinese and the officials who depended on government patronage, he intended to carry out a coup against the "'white trash', this braggart mob which is at once unreasoning and uncontrollable". Wong, enthusiastically entering into the conspiracy, believed that they could hoodwink the British until the Chinese government could send cruisers to protect their new regime from outside interference. At first Stibbins would act as viceroy for China, but once they had consolidated their position they would announce their independence and proclaim "a dynasty that in the future will rule the world".

Stibbins' daughter was both repelled and attracted by Wong. As she watched him "within her leapt up the instinct of race ... involuntarily she felt repelled by the tawny skin, rounded forehead and flattened nose, even while the glittering eyes and brutal mouth possessed for her a strange fascination". But seduced by the promise of imperial pomp and power, she fell in with her father's wishes.

On the very day of the wedding, however, Wong ravished and murdered the daughter of a white farmer, John Saxby, who was adventitiously the leader of the Anti-Chinese League: "sensuality was stamped upon his heavy lips and drooping eyelids and upon the expressionless mask wherewith, Mongol-like, he veiled his face". This fiendish act became the signal for a rising against the Chinese usurpers and their white collaborators. "War to the Yellow devils! War to the bitter end", cried Bob Flynn, the girl's fiancé and Saxby's right-hand man. The League's pre-arranged signal was given, the alarm bell was rung and the great majority of the whites rallied to the cause. This latest outrage "had awoken the Anti-Chinese instinct, had driven to madness every man who was crushed down and injured by the competition of the aliens, and had filled the land with a fanatical indignation". In Brisbane alone ten thousand men sprang to arms, and it was expected that the whole of white Australia would follow their example.

The white vigilantes attacked the Chinese quarters, Taringa Park and ultimately Parliament House. In the heat of the battle it became evident that race, not class, was the critical issue at stake. At Taringa Park, Stibbins' wife and daughter, after learning of Wong's infamous crime, repented their race folly. Lady Stibbins herself shot down Wong, and when the Chinese tried to retaliate, the white officers and men in the government forces turned on their erstwhile "Turanian" allies and threw in their lot with the Anti-Chinese League. The cry of "law and order" could not suppress the imperatives of blood and race. Similarly in the Queensland senate, the conservative white politicians rejected Stibbins' appeal for support in putting down the rebellion. He had "misjudged the intensity of the white instinct which existed among his own caste". Isolated he had to face alone the wrath of the Chinese, who hacked him to pieces.

With White Australia united, the Anti-Chinese League carried all before them. The victory bells "told of a successful revolution and of the race battle well begun". The vanquished Chinese were sent north "like great droves of cattle", and expelled from the country "as fast as fear could drive and ships could carry". Australia declared its independence, and the United States, which had excluded the Chinese in the 1880s, sent a fleet to prevent Britain from attempting to restore its rule. The concluding message was that "when the race-fight came and when the whites shook off the trammelling of the traitors who ... cared only for gold and greed, and nought for the white race, Australia was true to her destiny. In spite of white Chinamen, she stayed white".

The story was inspired by the contemporary controversy over Chinese immigration in Brisbane, Queensland and Australia. From the opening of the northern goldfields in the mid-1870s, revived fears about the Chinese presence in the colonies gathered strength. The mining, maritime, market gardening and cabinet-making industries evinced a pronounced dislike of their "celestial" competitors. By the mid-1880s this hostility to the Chinese, though still based primarily on the union movement, was acquiring a cultural and intellectual character. At a time when the modern social fabric was being constructed, when ideas of the organic people were at the centre of political discourse, the racial challenge was felt acutely. Many European settlers were asking themselves whether it was possible to achieve a new social order when aliens, who did not share the same common assumptions about life, labour and leisure, about morality, mores and manners, permanently resided in their midst. As Lane's *Boomerang* editorialised on 27 April 1888, while the instalments of "White or Yellow?" were still being published, "It is more than a social or national movement that is upheaving around us ... it is a true racial struggle".[11]

Soon after Lane arrived in Queensland, anti-Chinese agitation gained a new lease of life. Troubles on the northern goldfields in 1886, the influx of large numbers of Chinese into Darwin, including the entry of one thousand in

December 1887 alone, the tour of Imperial Chinese Commissioners in the winter of 1887 for the purpose of investigating the treatment of their fellow countrymen, all combined to stimulate the formation of a network of Anti-Chinese Leagues, firstly in Queensland and then in the other eastern colonies. These associations were obviously the model for the Anti-Chinese Leagues which in "White or Yellow" fomented the race war. Lane had a rich experience to draw on. In August 1887 the Brisbane League had organised an anti-Chinese conference with representatives coming from ten Queensland groups and from Sydney. By January 1888, the anti-Chinese bodies had agreed on a common programme which aimed, through punitive poll and residential taxes, not only at discouraging new Chinese emigrants, but also at encouraging those Chinese already resident in the colonies to return home. Taking advantage of an inter-colonial trade union Congress in their city, the Brisbane Anti-Chinese League in March 1888 — as the *Boomerang* serial was reaching its climax — held a packed meeting at which the president of the Melbourne Trades Hall Council, who was also president of the Melbourne Anti-Chinese League, the Vice-President of the Sydney Anti-Chinese League, and representatives from South Australia and Tasmania, supported a resolution which demanded that "in the moral, social, political and commercial" interests of the colonies, measures should be taken "to bring about the entire prohibition of Chinese immigration".[12]

In Queensland first and then in the other colonies, the anti-Chinese movement and the Anti-Chinese Leagues were winning greater respectability. Though the Brisbane League had been set up by European cabinet-makers who were hard pressed by Chinese craftsmen, its leadership, by mid-1887, had passed into the hands of a contractor and the owner of a large tailoring establishment. The anti-Chinese cause was becoming increasingly a populist one.[13]

Lane gave a similar social character to his Brisbane Anti-Chinese movement. Though he had made John Saxby, the president of the Farmers' Union, secretary of the Anti-Chinese League, he put "a big shopkeeper" at the head of the Committee of Public Safety which had responsibility for controlling the rebellion. The composition of Lane's League, while not identical with the Brisbane League of 1887-8, nevertheless had a similar mixture of unionists and non-unionists, employees and employers, propertied and propertyless. In its ranks were on the one hand miners, seamen and building labourers, and on the other, landowning farmers like Saxby and shopkeepers. The anti-Chinese agitation was supported by an even wider social spectrum. After the League's call to arms, manufacturers and merchants threw in their lot with the white rebels. Even some squatters, mine owners and planters, who were the backbone of Stibbins' party, immediately joined the white forces. Lane hailed this evidence of racial solidarity: "It was gladdening to see that here and there blood proved stronger than self-interest". Moreover at the height of the crisis, the military officers and troops deserted the government and went over to the whites, and the conservative politicians who represented planter and pastoral interests refused to cooperate with Stibbins and his Chinese allies. Though Lane, in his authorial voice, rejoiced at the overthrow of the "white Chinamen" who "cared only for gold and greed and naught for the white race", only Stibbins, at the end of the story, was left in this category. All other whites, even if for some it was a reluctant decision, had accepted that race was more important than caste or class.

By positing that Britain had rejected the colonists' anti-Chinese legislation in 1888, and thereby allowed the Chinese to become so numerous by 1908 in Australian society, Lane was echoing well-established fears about British attitudes to the colonies. The British government's decision to disallow the Queensland Goldfields Amendment Act of 1876 because it violated the Anglo-Chinese Convention of 1860 had left a bitter memory. Indeed in 1887 and early 1888 many of the anti-Chinese zealots believed that Britain would not renegotiate the Anglo-Chinese treaty to remove the legal obstacles to exclusion, and that Britain would use the treaty as an excuse to nullify further colonial attempts to oust the Chinese. Lane made the claim that if the colonies had had such men as Saxby and his anti-Chinese supporters in 1888, "the white man's Australia of 1888 could have held her own against a banded world". It was a declaration to Lane's fellow colonists that, if the Anti-Chinese Leagues acted with sufficient determination, the British could be compelled to bow to their demands that the "Chinese must go".

At the end of "White or Yellow?" it was clear that, given Britain's betrayal of its colonies, Australia had to become a republic. Lane gave colour to this point by having his rebels fight under the Eureka emblem, the 1854 symbol of colonial resistance to British tyranny and of Australia's first attempt to become an independent republic. "Since we have no hope in England and because her aid will be given to the Chinese against the whites", Saxby asked his followers to swear that "Australia shall be free and that the Chinese shall go". With the hoisting of the Eureka flag, "Men grasped each other's hands and turned aside to hide their moistened eyes". A venerable survivor of the Eureka Stockade incident was present to add his blessing to the undertaking.

But what was to be the character of this White Australian republic? The novel in fact pays little attention to this question. It was as though once the Anti-Chinese Leagues, all "good men and true", had gained their victory, a pure, selfless and just new order would emerge naturally. Lane had little use for parliamentary government. By 1908, in his telling of it, parliamentary politics was about privilege and plunder. While Stibbins' constitutional party stood for British supremacy and Chinese equality, the opposition consisted merely of the dissatisfied who were waiting for their turn to exploit the fruits of office. Admittedly Lane explained that the British had corrupted parliament and concentrated power in the upper house, which was dominated by property holders, at the expense of the people's assembly. Nevertheless there was no hint that a reformed parliament might be installed under the new republic. During the rising, the white rebels had established a Committee of Public Safety to control the revolution, and the body was clothed with complete powers:

"Absolutism sprang up, an absolutism to which men yield an unhesitating obedience". As a result of the insurrection, "the people were at last the government ... and the whites of Northern Australia had now no rulers but themselves alone". This was all the reader was vouchsafed. The republic appeared to be a self-fulfilling ideal. The "good men and true" who were entrusted with its governance could not but bring about a new and better world.

It must be wondered whether Lane was not gratified to learn that on Saturday, 5 May 1888, as he was bringing his story to a triumphal conclusion, Brisbane's anti-Chinese enthusiasts were, as it almost seemed, taking the "Sketcher's" advice and resorting to direct action to secure a racially pure society. On that day Brisbane's whites launched their own modest campaign in the real race war. Crying "Down with the Chinese" and "the Chinese must go", a one-thousand strong mob attacked the shops, factories and houses of the race enemy in every part of the city. It was the largest anti-Chinese riot ever to take place in Brisbane. The *Courier* commented that "The real reason of the demonstration is hard to tell, but it is generally believed to have been at least encouraged by persons whose social position should have placed them above such behaviour".[14]

Race was the key condition for Lane's good society. For him the selflessness of purity was all: purity in sexual relations (he was unequivocally opposed not only to sexual intercourse between the races but also to any form of sexual relations outside marriage), purity in physical health (he was, in addition to being a teetotaller, a severe critic of Chinese opium smoking and their supposed racial diseases such as leprosy and plague), purity in political and economic life (he was a stern enemy of the monopolist, speculator and influence peddler). Above all, he stood passionately, even pathologically, for racial purity.

Through his whole career as communitarian and journalist he was loyal to the racial ideal of "White or Yellow?" In drawing up the plans for "New Australia" in Paraguay, he made it one of the founding principles that no coloured person should be admitted to membership of the utopian society. It has been alleged that one of the reasons why he left "New Australia" and established Cosme in 1894 was the fear that many of the original settlers would not be able to resist "the admixture of the native"[15.] At Cosme, the toasts on Foundation Day set out the order of importance of the principles underpinning the grand adventure, first "The Race We Spring From", second "Cosme and Communism", and last "Sweethearts and Wives."

After becoming disillusioned with the Paraguayan experiment, and accepting a post as leader writer in 1900 and then as editor in 1914 of the New Zealand *Herald*, Lane became a prophet of British race patriotism. Selfish interests were still abhorrent to him. He showed, at this time, no more sympathy for the rights of individuals or the materialism of capitalism than he had when he wrote "White or Yellow?" In his editorial at the outbreak of World War One he saw "the red blood in war" as the British people's "redemption from the canker of selfish and unwholesome peace. Today the British are brothers. Wealth counts for less than it has done for a hundred years, and clan counts more. All that is noblest and best in us rises to the challenge of circumstances. We know that we are the custodians of a sacred trust, the guardians of the national life of the British".

Looking back to the era of "White or Yellow?", he contended that "It was the dread of Asiatic invasion that brought the Australians into line, that tamed the growing class-hatred of the Commonwealth by the knowledge that the poorest and richest in Australia had much to lose and much to defend ... War with all its evils and horrors teaches the great lesson of nationality". Still conscious of the issues which had separated the colonies from the mother country in the 1880s, he reproved "the British at home" who "forgot that the British should be brothers, that they should help one another to better things and stand by one another against the world".

The ambition to achieve the good community remained, even if it was now defined somewhat differently. He remained a social visionary to the end. The war would bring about a new community for the British race: "We shall root out the slum conditions. We shall see that no child lacks in a civilization bursting with riches. We shall teach them to be in peace as in war, helpful brothers to one another, loyal and loving children of a world-wide Britain that can only live while for her they are glad to die".[16] In giving up his republicanism Lane had not renounced the ideals of his earlier years. The essentially racial view of the good society which informed "White or Yellow?" was fulfilled, not denied, in his latter-day crusade for a visionary British Empire of white, Anglo-Saxon brothers.

Kenneth Mackay, author of *The Yellow Wave*, was also an archetypal representative of the "Legend of the Nineties". Unlike Lane, Mackay was born in Australia and brought up on rural properties. He was a bushman and balladeer, a celebrator of the values of the outback. He had an affinity with both the land and those who worked it. His first book of poetry, *Stirrup Jingles from the Bush and the Turf*, which was dedicated to Adam Lindsay Gordon, received the *Bulletin's* proudest encomium, as showing "quite enough talent to go a lone hand". Thus, in contrast to Lane, he was inspired more directly by bush mythology than social ideology.

Mackay's invasion scare novel, which centred on a Chinese military invasion of Northern Australia, was set against a quite complex picture of international politics. The salient features of this threatening world, however, were taken from the foreign policy issues of his time, from the perceived threat of China to Australia, and of Russia to the British Empire. By the end of the 1880s the fear of a Chinese military invasion in support of a migratory invasion had become a major concern of colonial Sinophobes. Rumours that the Chinese Commissioners who visited the colonies in 1887 were spying out the land preparatory to founding a colony fed this anxiety. Moreover, the great number of Chinese pouring into the Northern Territory at the end of the year was taken as palpable evidence of these more ambitious intentions.[17]

Sir Henry Parkes, the Premier of New South Wales, gave respectability to such opinions, and became the major purveyor of the Chinese imperialism thesis. In 1888 he declared that Chinese settlement in Australia was assuming

"a form entirely new". He adjudged that "the Chinese
Government was privy to what was taking place in the
Northern Territory" and thought that there might be a
"design of a considerable number of Chinese to form a
settlement in some remote part of the Australian territory ...
where they might become strong enough to form, in the
course of time, a kind of Chinese colony".[18] Parkes
subsequently made this prospect of a Chinese invasion the
cornerstone of his appeal for federal union. Taking an even
stronger line on the possibility of a Chinese invasion in his
Presidential Address to the first federal convention in 1891,
he repeated his warning: "I think", he said, "it is more than
likely that forms of aggression will appear in these seas
which are entirely new to the world. We have evidence
abundant on all hands that the Chinese nation ... are
awakening to all the power which immense population
gives them in the art of war, in the art of acquisition, and
all the other arts known to a European civilisation ... and it
seems to me ... that if we suffer in this direction at any time
... it will be by stealthily ... effecting a lodgement in some
thinly-peopled portion of the country, where it will take
immense loss of life and immense loss of wealth to dislodge
the invader".[19] The Australian federation movement was
formed in the shadow of the fear of Asia, and Parkes, "the
father of federation", was also in the same sense "the
father of the Yellow Peril". Mackay's concept of "The
Yellow Peril" might well in broad outline owe something to
Parkes' portrayal of the Chinese menace.

Mackay's fears of a Chinese invasion were associated
with Russian threats to the British Empire and set against
a changing balance of power in Europe and the Far East.
During the 1880s and early 1890s Russia was challenging the
British Empire in Afghanistan and the Balkans. Its
ultimate aim was to seize Constantinople from Turkey and
so gain direct access to the Mediterranean and the Near
East. Thus from Pendjeh in 1884-5, to Bulgaria in 1887 and
Pamir in 1894, British relations with Russia were troubled
by one crisis after another, each of which raised the spectre
of war. During these war scares some Australians expressed

alarm that a Russian squadron might raid their ports and commerce.

In *The Yellow Wave*, Mackay projected these circumstances forward to 1954 and gave them an eccentric twist. According to Mackay, the strategy of the Czarist Empire was to launch attacks simultaneously against India and Australia. By tying up British military and naval resources in these conflicts, the Russians would be able to capture Constantinople almost unopposed. For the purpose of carrying through the Australian side of the scheme, the Russians entered into an alliance with China, and Philip Orloff, an Australian-educated son of a Russian merchant, who was masquerading as an American adventurer, had the responsibility for turning the Chinese army into a modern fighting machine. When the day came, the Russian fleet, in cooperation with the fleet of its French ally, drew off the British Far Eastern squadron. In Australia the invaders linked up with Russian agents, who, while pretending to be railway builders and merchants, had gained control of much of North Queensland and prepared the way for Chinese domination of the interior of the continent. Though the Russian interest in Australia was merely a function of their European strategy, the Chinese, having been blocked by the Russians and Japanese in Asia, sought an outlet for their growing population in a southward advance. It was their intent, once the Australians had been routed, to rid themselves of their Russian commanders and advisors and take possession of the conquered territory.

For Mackay, the dangers which Britain and Australia faced in the international arena were not just a sensational setting for the romantic drama of a star-crossed love match between Orloff, the Australian traitor, and Heather Cameron, the daughter of a "dauntless bushman". Rather they were real and enduring, and through his novel the Australian people were to be shown the seriousness of their situation. In his own public life he demonstrated his belief in Australia's peril. As a member of the New South Wales Legislative Assembly and as a volunteer military officer, he spoke again and again of the lowering cloud descending on Australia. Addressing the house on the Coloured Race

Restriction Bill in 1896, he warned that the time was coming when "we shall have to defend our position against some of these Asiatic nations ... I believe that unless some step is taken, racial troubles will take place in Northern Queensland. Unless some step is taken to prevent an invasion of coolies and aliens into that territory, it will be a very poor buffer to put against an invasion of Asiatics in the future".[20]

At the end of 1897 during his campaign to raise a five hundred strong volunteer cavalry regiment from the ranks of the bushmen — the first such light horse regiment in Australia — he gave interviews to a number of Sydney newspapers in which he enjoined the lessons of *The Yellow Wave*. He told them that it was "only from the East that I have ever anticipated danger". The increasing influence of Russia — itself an Asian power — over China would "Russianise China" and enable Russian officers to create a modern Chinese army. Australians should not be misled into judging the Chinese fighting ability from "the poor specimens of coolies" who had migrated to the colonies. Drawing perhaps on the knowledge of his father, who before coming to Australia had been engaged in the Chinese tea trade, he pointed out rather inexactly that the Chinese had a military tradition dating back to Tamerlane. "Chinese" Gordon had shown conclusively that Chinese soldiers, if properly led, were as brave as any others. The Japanese victory over China in 1895 had encouraged the Australian public to think that the Chinese were impotent, but their defeat was the result of poor leadership not of shoddy material. With Russians in command, the Chinese would be a very different proposition.[21]

In terms very similar to those used in his novel, Mackay asserted that, while the Russians themselves were not interested in the permanent conquest of Australia, the same could not be said of the Chinese. The Chinese considered "that they owe a debt of vengeance to Australia". Mackay believed that the Chinese Commissioners at the end of the 1887 tour of Australia had vowed that "China would yet find a way to repay Queensland for the indignities heaped upon her countrymen".[22]

When, as *The Yellow Wave* described it, a Russian-led Chinese army landed at Port Parker [Burketown] in North-West Queensland, they at first carried all before them. The ground had been well prepared. Chasing imperial honours and deferring to foreign investors, Sir Peter McLoskie, the colonial premier, the "high priest of land-grant railways and cheap alien labour",[23] had permitted British and foreign capitalists to buy up most stations in the Northern Territory and North Queensland, and to replace white workers with cheap coolie labour, and, as a result, the invaders encountered little resistance. Indeed the local Chinese turned on their white masters and joined the invaders. Mustering their forces at Charleville, they stood poised to launch themselves against Brisbane and the southern colonies.

The conservative colonial politicians were ill-prepared to meet the emergency. Heedless of the Asian menace, they had placed their faith in the British fleet and neglected Australian defence. When the blow fell, they were aghast to find that the British Admiral in command of the Sydney station refused to help. Russia had simultaneously moved against India and Turkey, and so the Admiral explained that since "Interests affecting England's very existence were at stake ... the colony must rely for defence solely on themselves".[24]

In the event it was left to the bushmen in the outback to mount the only serious resistance to the "Yellow Wave". The bushman hero of the story who led the resistance, Dick Hatton, was a man after Mackay's own heart. Like Mackay he was skilled in bushcraft and horsemanship, as well as in sketching and balladeering.[25] Driven off his small Northern Territory station, he found it difficult to stick to any one line of work. Before any other, he had suspected the Chinese and Russian designs on Australia, and he used his popularity with young bushmen to form "Hatton's Rangers", a volunteer body of light horse. After news of the enemy landing reached Hatton and his men, they concentrated at Fort Mallarraway, the only property run and worked by white men, which stood in the path of the oncoming alien hosts. Outnumbered, Hatton's men retreated towards

Brisbane. There they linked up with volunteers flooding in from all the other colonies. In the ensuing battle, the whites' lines, despite the valiant efforts of Hatton's cavalry, were broken by Orloff's disciplined Chinese soldiers. At this point Orloff, who had taken Heather Cameron captive, began to feel some remorse for the part he had played in the subjugation of his native land. At Heather's insistence he abandoned the leadership of the invading force, hoping to escape with his love to start a new life. Such race infamy, however, could not be permitted to enjoy a happy ending and so when a vessel, possibly of a British fleet coming to the rescue of Australia — this is left strangely unclear — rammed the boat in which the lovers were fleeing, they were sent to a watery grave. The future of Australia was left unresolved.

Mackay, like Lane, was a public figure caught up in the political life of his times. He was elected to the New South Wales Legislative Assembly in 1895 as the member for Boorowa, a rural constituency, and from 1899-1933 he was a member of the Legislative Council. During these years he was a minister of the Crown and held numerous other official positions.

In many respects Mackay agreed with Lane about the ills that beset colonial society. They were at one in identifying the villains who had corrupted the good community. Mackay's Sir Peter McLoskie, like Lane's Lord Stibbins, was the villain responsible for fostering and protecting the interests of absentee capitalists who had bought up large tracts of land and brought in coloured labour to work their investments. Such actions had forced Australian squatters and farmers off their properties and denied white men their proper place in the economy and society. These colonial leaders had no sympathy with the producing classes in the colony. They tacitly conspired with the plutocrats to sell out white Australia's inheritance. As a result of their activities Mackay complained that the intent of the Land Acts of 1861 to divide up the great leaseholds had been defeated: "shadowy syndicates sprang into life among the festering garbage of broken oaths and shameless trickery. Stations grew larger and fewer; millions of improved acres became as complete a blank in respect to human existence and national well-being as a mangrove swamp or a worked out mine. All signs both of family life and local wealth disappeared".[26]

But there were also differences of emphasis in the two authors' social analyses. For Mackay, aspiring labour no more than ascendant capitalism offered the answer to national problems: "Neither alone possessed the right of shaping the nation's destiny." Rather he believed that the country's surest hope resided in the "vast number of people who, in the popular sense, were neither capitalist nor yet labourer", but who nevertheless comprised "the real intellectual and creating power of Australasia".[27] It was these people who possessed the capacity to regenerate colonial society and to restore the wealth of white Australia.

Mackay, perhaps influenced by Lane's "New Australia" experiment, established in *The Yellow Wave* a small-scale cooperative which was organised in accordance with his visionary ideals. Fort Mallarraway, planted in the midst of the vast territories dominated by overseas proprietors, stood as an exemplary rebuke to those outsiders and their colonial collaborators. Fort Mallarraway was founded as a "cooperative settlement" in reaction to a political culture rent by the conflicts between capital and labour. As a result of their disquiet with the tendency of colonial society, "100 men belonging to that class who stand between capital and labour, and who set more store by brains than either money or muscle", purchased a property which they could run as a community according to their own lights. Under the constitution the station was governed by a committee of three elected by members every twelve months. All shared the manual tasks. No one was paid a salary or fees. Each man as a producer held an equal share in the increasing value of the property. The cooperative was a great success. In raising sheep and breeding cattle it proved itself superior to the syndicate-owned properties that were worked by cheap coloured labour. Fort Mallarraway remained, in good times and bad, independent of the government, the banks and the labour unions. Despite its antipathy to unions, it is nevertheless difficult to see how Mackay's cooperative differed in substance from Lane's "socialist" utopia.

Mackay's ideal Australia was, however, unlike Lane's, based avowedly on the bush legend. Fort Mallarraway was not only set in the bush, but the men who worked it were of the bush and the principles which regulated it came out of the bush experience. Like Hatton's Rangers, these men were resourceful, self-reliant and held together by bonds of mateship, which meant that each was willing to sacrifice himself for the other. They represented the values celebrated in Mackay's bush ballads. In Mackay's novel it was the men of the outback, not the urban-based Anti-Chinese League, who formed the core of the resistance to the Asian invasion.

On the other hand Mackay's view of the role of parliament in colonial political life was quite similar to Lane's. In *The Yellow Wave* parliament had nothing to offer the country. The leaders of the government and the opposition parties were equally responsible for selling out Australian interests to overseas speculators. Politicians were depicted as stupid and self-serving, their sole aim being to plunder the government's coffers and to bedeck themselves with imperial honours. Even after they were faced with the crisis of the invasion they continued to squabble among themselves.[28] The New South Wales parliament was unable to take prompt action in support of its neighbour because the politicians insisted on debating at length the question of whether they had constitutional authority to send troops across the colonial border. The troops, not the parliament, broke the impasse when they volunteered to a man to go to Queensland's aid.

The people were the heroes of the story. They refused to tolerate the ineptitude of their political leaders. Capital and labour put aside their differences in order to combat the "supreme racial peril".[29] As in Lane's "White or Yellow?", social classes were united in a racial community for the purpose of defending white civilisation. When news of the invasion had reached Brisbane, angry crowds had stormed parliament and even threatened to lynch the premier. They demanded action from their leaders or their replacement.

Hatton's Rangers was the supreme embodiment of the spirit of the people. Created in the backblocks it formed the nucleus of a new organic community. Hatton's leadership, which gave unity and harmony to the whole, was not derived from his class origins, his official appointment or formal qualifications, but from the respect in which he was held by his men: "Beloved by the men he had gathered around him, he in return treated them as comrades, who having tacitly acknowledged him as their leader, were prepared, while calling him friend, to obey him with unquestioning promptness".[30]

The Yellow Wave, like the other two novels, was also a tract in favour of Australian federation and independence. From a number of aspects, Mackay attacked the British connection. Britain failed to protect Australian interests. It drew off Australia's best men to help fight the Empire's battles in India—implied here is a criticism of the New South Wales contingent which was sent to the Sudan in 1885.[31] While the ties remained, Australian political leaders would sacrifice Australian interests in order to please British authorities and financiers. Many of them had forsworn their earlier republican ideals in order to win favour and titles from the Mother Country.[32] Finally the novel had claimed that it was the British absentee landlords and investors who had destroyed the settler society and brought in Asian labour in place of the independent white man. Mackay, as a politician, was somewhat more diplomatic in dealing with the British relationship, but, even so, when the issue of race was at stake he indicated he was willing to countenance the consequences. It was, he said, "our first duty to keep our race pure, let the consequences be what they may".[33] Mackay had come to the opinion that Australia had to rely on its own resources for its defence. He was himself a keen advocate of military and political federation. His own cavalry regiment of bushmen was intended to show the way. "Among its ulterior objects" he said, "it aims at fostering a national spirit among men in the country districts".[34]

Mackay, like Lane, was certain that race was the foundation of community. But he, again like Lane, was never clear about the limits of that community. Despite the republican tone of *The Yellow Wave,* Mackay in late nineteenth-century Australia found it difficult to unscramble the loyalties to Australia, Britain and the British Empire. All three shared in different ways the same notion of race. And Mackay, like Lane, found that when it was tested not against the local challenge of a "Yellow Peril" to Australia but against a foreign challenge to the Mother Country, it could embrace the whole white British Empire. At the time of the Boer War he led the New South Wales Imperial Bushmen's Contingent to fight in South Africa. The bushmen's cavalry, which had been raised to defend Australia against a Chinese invasion, saw its first action in a British Imperial War in a distant continent.

Charles Kirmess, the author of *The Australian Crisis,* also came under the spell of the "Legend of the Nineties," and his invasion story was informed by the same romantic vision. Unlike Lane and Mackay, he was not a public figure. Indeed very little is known about his background, education and occupation, or about what caused him to write the novel. *The Australian Crisis* may owe something of a debt to Mackay's *The Yellow Wave.* Looking at them in a broad perspective there are a number of similarities in the plots of the two novels. In both novels the "Yellow Peril" manifested itself through a clandestine Asian landing in the Gulf of Carpentaria; the coloured invaders had planned the enterprise very carefully and executed it most efficiently; the British failed to come to the colony's aid; and a force of mounted bushmen, who had spontaneously responded to the call, offered the only resistance to the violation of White Australia. Kirmess's work was, however, the most powerful and complete of all the Australian invasion scare stories, and its exploration of the crisis of political community was more comprehensive and penetrating than that offered by either Lane or Mackay.

Kirmess's tale, written twelve years after Mackay's, addressed what was, by general consent, a much more dangerous and immediate foreign threat. Kirmess, in making Japan the enemy at the gate, spoke directly to the anxieties of the time. Following Japan's victory over Russia in 1905, the first Asian victory over a European nation in the modern era, it became the dominant power in the Western Pacific. At the same time Britain, answering Germany's challenge in the North Sea, withdrew its capital ships from the far East, and Australians came to fear for their safety. They had no faith in the Anglo-Japanese alliance, for since it was not based on a mutual exchange of benefits. Moreover it was known that Japan bitterly resented the "White Australia" immigration policy. Australia seemed vulnerable to a downward thrust of Japan into the South Pacific.

Between 1905 and 1909, the year in which *The Australian Crisis* appeared in the book stores, Australian political leaders reached a consensus about the Japanese "Yellow Peril". Alfred Deakin, who was Prime Minister for most of this period, recognised clearly the meaning of Japan's victory over Russia for Australia. It opened up "wider possibilities for all Asian nations", but most of all for Japan. As a result of the Battle of Tsushima, "Instead of two fleets in the China Ssea belonging to separate — even opposing powers — we shall now have one fleet, only it will be as strong as the two former fleets, and will operate under one flag". Allan McLean, who was deputy prime minister in the Reid Government, made the point even more sharply: "The stupendous struggle in the East must awake the people of Australia to the fact that we have been living in a fool's paradise ... Japan has astonished the world ...We now find one of the great naval and military powers within a very short distance of our shores".[35] A Labor spokesman on defence, Senator George F. Pearce, was equally apprehensive; "Japan has shown she is an aggressive nation. She has shown that she is desirous of pushing out all round ... Is there any other country that offers such a temptation to Japan as Australia does?"[36]

The Australians were not reassured by the British renewal of the Anglo-Japanese alliance in 1905. It was in their view no substitute for a British Pacific fleet. The Liberal prime minister Joseph Cook told the Colonial Office that Australia "should not be left to depend upon the

continuance of such a delicate security as an alliance".[37] So
great was the Japanese threat, surpassing as it did all other
previous invasion scares, that the political leaders pressed
for the introduction of compulsory military training and for
the creation of an Australian navy. A National Defence
League was formed in November 1905 to persuade the public
of the necessity of adopting these measures, and Frank Fox,
the editor of the *Lone Hand* who was responsible for
serialising "The Commonwealth Crisis", became the co-
editor of the League's journal, the *Call*. Kirmess's work, by
rendering a fictional dramatisation of the Japanese menace,
made a major contribution to this campaign.

As Kirmess put it in the preface to the book, the novel
was meant to rouse the Commonwealth "to a sense of its
danger". In contrast to Lane and Mackay, he placed his
invasion scare not in the distant future but in 1912: "I know
what is possible under the known circumstances of the hour
almost, today or tomorrow. And I think if that has no power
to compel the citizens of the Commonwealth to seriously
consider their position, no dreadful vision of a distant future
will".[38] The prospect of a Japanese invasion was in the air.
Japanese merchants, fishermen, tourists and circus
performers were reported by the press to be engaged in
mapping the country and spying on Australian defences. In
early 1907 a rumour was even circulated that Japanese
settlers had illegally landed in the Northern Territory and
established a little colony.[39]

Though the reviews were overwhelmingly favourable
—the Sydney *Bulletin*, *Sydney Morning Herald* and the
Sydney Star being particularly positive —[40] the influence of
the book is hard to gauge. Kirmess, in drawing up a circular
to promote his book noted that since its publication, the
Commonwealth government had "hurried forward some
vital safety measures", namely legislation to acquire the
Northern Territory from South Australia, to introduce
compulsory military training and to establish an Australian
navy.[41] Yet while ministers and members supporting these
bills employed arguments which could have been taken from
The Australian Crisis, no mention was made of the novel in
these debates.[42] Similarly following a tour of Northern

Australia in 1913, three senior naval and military officers submitted reports to the Commonwealth Government in which they maintained that Japan posed a major threat to Australia's northern perimeter and that all defence planning should be directed at once and exclusively to counter this grave possibility. If not prevented from gaining a foothold, Japan would use its occupation of northern lands to extort concessions from the Australian and Imperial governments.[43] It was as though they had written their reports after reading and digesting the lessons of *The Australian Crisis*. Rather than influencing the politicians or the professional officers Kirmess probably provided no more than a fictional account of what in official circles was becoming the conventional wisdom.

In his novel, Kirmess related how the Japanese Government had secretly despatched a convoy containing soldier settlers to establish a colony on the uninhabited coast of the Northern Territory —just west of Burketown. When eventually the Australian people learnt of this alien occupation, "there arose the cry from the slopes of the Pacific to Cape Leeuwin, that the Japanese must go". The Commonwealth Government appealed to London to intercede with the Japanese on their behalf. But the British, preoccupied with combating the German naval challenge, did not wish to offend their ally, and they tacitly accepted Tokyo's explanation that the colony was the work of a private philanthropic organisation which sought to help poor Japanese who were victims of famine. While the Japanese government indicated that it would release these citizens from their allegiance so that they could swear an oath of loyalty to the British Crown, it gave no indication that it would tolerate their forcible expulsion.

The British authorities were in a quandary. They desired to support their Dominion but could not afford to incur Japan's hostility. Since vanquishing Russia, Japan had begun to construct a navy which would "overawe even the Mistress of the Seas", and by this means it hoped to force the British to accept its position in the Northern Territory.[44] Though the Royal Navy was still superior to Japan's at the time of the invasion, the Admiralty could not risk sending a significant proportion of its Home Fleet to the Pacific for fear that the remaining elements "would not be strong enough to guarantee the safety of the Heart of the Empire against the ambitions of European rivals." Moreover Britain depended on Japan for the protection of its extensive economic and political interests in the Far East.

Australians at first could not but believe that Britain would insist on the Japanese evacuation of the occupied territory: "There was too much at stake for Great Britain, for Anglo Saxondom and for White Humanity, to allow of any lukewarmness".[45] When, however, the British imposed a blockade preventing both parties from having access to the disputed lands, and then arbitrarily proclaimed a protectorate over a greater part of the Northern Territory — and so used the Pax Britannica against British Australia — the Commonwealth recognised that they would have to rely on their own resources to safeguard their national sovereignty. Even their sister dominions, which had initially protested against Britain's failure to support Australia, were induced by financial pressure to turn a blind eye to Australia's predicament.

The British betrayal angered the Australian people. Looking for scapegoats, they found it easy to vent their frustrations on the coloured residents in their midst. In the riots that followed many Asians were lynched. Anticipating the action of the street mobs at the outbreak of World War I, the Chinese quarters of Melbourne were attacked and property destroyed. In the feverish atmosphere, new elections were called. During the campaign Moderates who urged caution were not only silenced but often physically assaulted. The national fabric was unravelling. The Japanese had planted a colony in the Northern Territory, the Commonwealth and State Parliaments had lost their authority, the financial system was in trouble and, after the victory of the extremists in the Eastern States, Western Australia, which did not wish to sever ties with the Mother Country, seceded from the Federation.

Yet while urban Australia was wracked by internal dissension and social disorder, the bushmen, who, living closer to nature, understood better that "force, brutal force" was in the circumstances the only path to salvation, determined to act. The bushmen "bore an undying hatred against an enemy who contested the white supremacy and who was doubly loathed because of his inferiority of race, environment and ideal".[46] They spontaneously formed themselves into an irregular mounted corps, called aptly the White Guard, for the purpose of engaging the intruders. The White Guard relished the elemental nature of their task. The extinction of the invaders was their aim: "That was after all was said, the only way to punish and to end the intrusion of the alien race on Commonwealth soil." No quarter would be given or expected in the fight for racial supremacy. Regretfully the Japanese women, like their menfolk, were to be slaughtered. Yet, despite their gallant efforts, the White Guard was defeated by superior Japanese numbers and organisation. Only a handful out of the original 1200 escaped to Darwin to tell the tale.

By the end of 1912 the Commonwealth was left with little choice. The British had no sympathy for the Australian cause; liberal humanitarians were revolted by the ruthless treatment of the Asian residents and conservatives were "resigned to the thought that Communism — as they termed it — must run its full course in Australia." They were convinced that "the helpless and demoralised Commonwealth was now less than ever worth the risk of exposing the Heart of the Empire to danger". In order to put a stop to Australian provocations, the British government, after consulting the Japanese, demanded that the Northern Territory be handed over to them. To force the issue the British blockaded Australia's main ports and imposed a complete boycott on trade, causing depression and riots. The Commonwealth government succumbed to the pressure and accepted the British ultimatum. Under the terms of the agreement the Commonwealth handed over the Northern Territory to Great Britain and received an assurance in return that the Japanese colony would not be granted independence before 1940. As a result, the narrator concluded grandiloquently, "A truce has been made until 1940 A.D. Until that time White Australia has to prepare itself for a final struggle to determine whether the White or Yellow Race shall gain final supremacy".[47]

Kirmess's treatment of the consequences of an Asian invasion for political culture was more probing and perceptive than either Lane's or Mackay's. For him, as for the others, the challenge to national survival and integrity created a political crisis and called into question the nature of political community. Parliament, which continued to dispute technical points, to play to party interests and to obstruct necessary action, made itself irrelevant. In the author's view the Long Parliament, by acting in this manner, had brought about the English Civil War. The United States Congress similarly had allowed Fort Sumter to spark off the American Civil War, and in the French Revolution, the National Convention had made possible the rise of Robespierre's reign of terror.

At one level, Kirmess pursued his analysis as though he was a detached sociological observer; but at another, more fundamental level was a partisan in the story he unfolded. In the latter role his sympathies were with the triumphant "Extremist Party" which emerged out of the popular protests against the orthodox parties' timidity and indecision. The Extremist Party had a pronounced radical bias. It incorporated the Labor Party, which had gained in popularity during the crisis, because it had, from its inception, been unqualifiedly for a White Australia, and had taken a stronger stand than its moderate rival against British domination. Moreover, Labor's policy of paying for national works from income tax and graduated land tax, rather than from British loans, was now seen to be for the common welfare. "Behind the Government the Labour Party is fighting. None of their responsible leaders would think of taking mean party advantage now. The people outside regard them with friendly eyes. They have always stood for White Australia."

Caught up in the hysterical urgency of his own story, Kirmess exclaimed "But, why restate these things? It takes time even to tell the truth and time is precious". It was as if the author's political reflections, like the politicians' shilly shallying, were an obstacle to the people taking action to save themselves.

Kirmess despaired of parliament, for parliamentarians could not help themselves. It was "with the best of intentions ... settling down to raise points", and as a result, a whole week was lost. The people, who knew that their existence was at stake, became impatient: "Outside the people cry with one voice: Dissolution! New elections! The Sovereign of Australia wants to take his fate into his own hands".[48] At the polls, the Extremists swept away the old party system and achieved a great victory. The Extremists were not properly a new party. They arose at the demand of the people. They incorporated many from the old parties into their ranks. They were elected to represent the whole nation.

In accordance with the "Legend of the Nineties", Kirmess had envisaged Australia as an idealised community, as Bernard O'Dowd's "Delos of a coming sun god's race." But the alien invasion blasted these hopes. Before Australia's

> congenial blue skies a new Greece was arising, a more perfect Athens, scorning slavery and conferring the sacred rights of citizenship upon its entire manhood and womanhood, and which, even as in Athens of old, those deserving citizens had been ostracized who monopolized political favour, would dare to ostracize Old-World monopoly and injustice.

Australia's vision had faltered because Australians had neglected to look to their own defence and relied on others to protect them. Only by assuming this prime responsibility of community would Australia once again be able to recapture the dream, to be "in the vanguard of humanitarian progress". For this purpose "Everyone of thy sons shall be a warrior, everyone of thy daughters a warrior's helpmate ... Then, only then, thou mayst safely continue thy triumphant march. Then thou will enter into thy proud Twentieth Century Nationhood, which will be a joy, not an oppression".[49]

Yet, even if Kirmess's dream had descended into a nightmare, nevertheless the experience of the Australian crisis clarified much about his good society. Even if some of the consequences of the people assuming their sovereign powers, such as the lynching of Chinese and the destruction of their property, and the intimidation and harassment of Moderate Whites, did not altogether merit his approval, they were condoned as a necessary price to be paid for the survival of the good society. The dissolution of the parliament of parties at the behest of street crowds, and the creation of a one-party populist state was part of a natural purging and purifying process in the interests of the racial community, which was the necessary core of the good society.

The racial character of the good society can be seen most strikingly in the White Guard. It was the bushmen who, after parliament and politics had failed, epitomised the idealised will of the people and took direct action to save the people. Those who responded to the call were "the typical Australian: the hardy pioneer who wrestled with and conquered hostile nature and the heart of the Continent, the selectors, stockmen, miners, drovers, carriers and other bushworkers". Kirmess commented that "A finer body of men never took the field to do battle for Aryan ideals". In this portrayal of the White Guard one comes closest to his vision of society. The core of his ideals was neither socialist nor radical, neither environmental nor political, it was first and foremost racial.

Though Kirmess did not acquire either intellectual or political recognition through his writing, nevertheless *The Australian Crisis* did make a profound impact on Frank Fox, the editor of the *Lone Hand*, who was also a leading member of the National Defence League. And it is through Fox that the broader significance of Kirmess's novel can be best understood.

Like Lane, Mackay and Kirmess, Fox embraced the "Legend of the Nineties". Born in South Australia in 1874 he had learnt his journalist craft on the *Bulletin*. He was also a friend of Mackay's and shared the latter's idealisation of the bushman as the Australian type.[50] Fox's first book, *Bushman and Buccaneer*, was a defence of, or at least an apology for Harry "The Breaker" Morant, who personified the authentic Australian of Fox's imaginings.

For Fox *The Australian Crisis* was a tract for the times. It addressed some of the most persistent themes running through the *Lone Hand*: the lack of a white population in Northern Australia; the fear of Asia, especially Japan; the suspicion that Britain might not assist Australia to repel a Japanese invasion; and the need for Australia to look to its own defences. Fox had turned the *Lone Hand*, which originally was intended to be a literary adjunct to the *Bulletin*, into a vehicle for his political preoccupations. The first issue contained a story, "The Secrets of a Prime Minister", presumably written by Fox, the plot of which revolved around the problem of how to deport a "colony of Asiatics" from the Northern Territory. In August 1908 Fox used the occasion of the visit of the American Fleet to write a homily about Japan, "the not altogether trusted champion of the Yellow Race", which propounded "a policy of aggressive Asiatic Imperialism" and challenged "the long accepted principle of the hegemony of the White Race". If war came, Australia would be "quite unable to strike any blow to justify our position as the garrison, the lonely outpost of the White Race in these seas". In his monthly column he regularly expatiated on the Northern Territory, "Our Unguarded Gate" which was "far nearer to the naval bases of Asia than to Sydney and Melbourne". It was "Australia's fate to be pushed into the van of the certain conflict" since Australia was territorially "the southern part of Asia, the natural outflow for surplus population". With British leaders convinced that a war with Germany was inevitable, he wondered whether Britain, in order to keep Japan's goodwill, might put Australia "into the bidding as a disposable pawn".[51]

Given Fox's view of Australia's strategic predicament, it was natural that he should have a high opinion of Kirmess's work. In an editorial footnote to the first instalment of Kirmess's "Commonwealth Crisis", he declared that this "forecast romance" was "something more than a novel". In order to bring it more quickly before the reading public, he had not included illustrations. Fox desired to use the novel to further the cause of national defence. Fox, who had numerous political friends in the ranks of the Labor party and among the radical protectionists (most notably Alfred Deakin), had intended, according to Kirmess, to use his contacts to have the message of "The Commonwealth Crisis" discussed in the federal parliament at the end of 1908, but the Deakin government had fallen before this could be effected.[52] In March 1909 Fox travelled to London for the purpose of founding a newspaper which would awaken Britain to its responsibilities for the British-settled empire overseas. As part of this campaign he published *Problems of the Pacific,* in which he argued the case that "The Continent [Australia] must be held by the British race", and that it was "almost as certain that it must be attacked one day by an Asiatic race." To bring home the point he summarised the plot of "The Commonwealth Crisis", commenting that the idea of a "colonising invasion" of Australia by Japan was quite possible.[53] No other literary work was cited for this purpose.

Though Fox, shortly after his arrival in England, had written to Deakin that "I look on life here as exile", such provincial nostalgia did not survive the experience of living at the centre of the Empire. He quickly made himself at home in Britain, and with the passage of time his Australian mission withered on the bough. Following the outbreak of the First World War he joined the British army. In the post-war period he became a leading figure in the Imperial Press Association, devoted himself to Imperial causes, and was knighted for services to the Empire. It was as though he had betrayed the land of his birth and the aspirations of the "Legend of the Nineties". Indeed it might be considered that when in 1923 he published the novel *Beneath an Ardent Sun,* which was also centred on an Asian invasion of Australia, he was rewriting *The Australia Crisis* to suit his new loyalties and the Empire's new circumstances. In the later work, the Asian invaders were more tactfully "Cambodians" rather than "Japanese". The "Feverish Party" — the counterpart to the Extremists — stirred up public opinion in favour of the interlopers' forcible eviction. The hero of the story, however, — now a Moderate — spoke up for soundness and sense in solving the Australian crisis. Henry Trent "pricked the government of the day and let out the rank gases of the bombast". With the support of the bushmen — "for at bottom the Australian has a good fund of sober earnestness" — Trent became Prime Minister. When Britain urged caution out of concern for Germany's ambitions in Europe, and a minister denounced Australian jingoism, the cry went up that Britain was ready to betray Australia and sacrifice the White Australia policy.[54] Trent, however, stood fast and refused to be pushed into a confrontation with the Mother Country. Instead he set out on a compromise path which would "secure all that is necessary for the safety and racial purity of Australia ... without being offensive to a chivalrous, friendly nation".[55] His quiet diplomacy was very successful. The "Cambodians" were cooperative and the Commonwealth helped finance their repatriation.[56] The crisis faded away almost as quickly as it had appeared. Statesmanlike leadership had reconciled British and Australian interests, and the British Empire emerged from the ordeal stronger than ever.

Lane, Mackay and Fox seemed over their lifetime to have moved from a belief in Australian nationalism to a commitment to British race patriotism and the British Empire. In explaining this transformation it would be easy to say either that they simply became conservative with age, or that they were seduced by the hope of imperial recognition and distinction. But such a reading misses what was most important about the "Legend of the Nineties". Lane, Mackay and Fox did not betray an exclusive Australian national dream. The assertion of Australian independence in these novels derived not so much from a search for an autonomous nation based on a bush idyll or a utopian ideal, as from resentment at Britain's rejection of the British Australians. Even the most reluctant of the three, Kenneth Mackay, was firm that Australia must declare its independence, if Britain vetoed the colonies' immigration laws, and so threatened the British character of their society. As they worked through these problems in changing personal and international circumstances, they all came to equate the good community with the British "race", though in this respect it is worth noting that the most conservative, Mackay, was the least passionate about his

Britishness. The upshot was not so much a recantation of an earlier vision embodied in the "Legend of the Nineties" as the realisation of its more fundamental meaning, that of race.

For Australians at the end of the nineteenth century and in the early twentieth century the great social and political question was the defining of the good community. The novelists were unwittingly engaged in working out through their invasion scare stories the issues surrounding this question. They employed their imagination to explore the consequences flowing from a crisis brought on by the prospect of invasion. At the end of it all it was clear that the religion of race as culture was more important than respect for traditional institutions or the rights of man. In the hour of national peril there was no room for diversity or dissent. The Anti-Chinese League, and even more Hatton's Rangers and the White Guard — the forerunners in a sense of C.E.W Bean's Anzacs, Jack Lang's Labor movement and Eric Campbell's New Guard — personified the heroic values of the "Legend of the Nineties". Frank Fox in 1926, after the social disorders of the Great Strike in England, took up the old questions in a book entitled *Parliamentary Government: A Failure.*[57] Once again, in a crisis, parliament had failed the people. Parliament was inherently corrupt, and unless there was reform the British Empire, like the Roman Empire before it, would die of "bread and circus" politics. He looked to the example of Italian Fascism adapted to the British tradition to find the answer. The new Fascist principle which he wished Britain to accept was that "the governance of a self-respecting community can be organised on the basis of setting up as the primary assumption the duty of the individual to serve the community not the right of the people to share in the community". The attraction of Fascism for Fox was not so much a product of his conversion to British Imperialism as an adaptation to new circumstances of the Australian "Legend of the Nineties".

D.H. Lawrence, in bringing fresh eyes to bear on Australia at the end of World War I, perceived that the central problem of the country and its political culture was community. In a new society it could not be taken for granted. As British settlers built new cities and farms and civilised the land, so they felt a need to find community. In his novel *Kangaroo*, Lawrence's two protagonists, Willie Struthers, the socialist leader, and Kangaroo, the nationalist leader, were locked in battle over different conceptions of community. Both sought, in Lawrentian language, "the new ties between men, in the new democracy...the new passional bond in the new society." *Kangaroo* offered the continuation of the A.I.F. camaraderie; for Lawrence's Diggers "the war was the only time they felt properly alive". Struthers on the other hand offered a class community, a socialist community based on the solidarity of labour. But even when united with the world's workers in spirit, Struthers assured his followers that this would not mean they would "take the hearts out of our chests to give it to Brown Brother to eat. No, Brown Brother and Brother Yellow had on the whole best stop at home and sweep their own streets rather than come and sweep ours".[58]

What then these novels have suggested is that race, viewed as culture as well as colour, was the common denominator informing the Australian vision of the good society contained in the "Legend of the Nineties", and that "race" in this same sense was its most important and enduring legacy.

"Useful Practice — Blooding the Pups" Australian Literature and the Boer War

Rick Hosking

In April 1988, the South Australian Minister for Education, Mr. Crafter, approached the Adelaide City Council with a request that Harry "The Breaker" Morant's name be added to the South African War Memorial, just outside the main gateway to Government House on North Terrace. Mr. Crafter had been asked by Mr. Lewis Fitz-Gerald (who had played Lieutenant George Witton in Bruce Beresford's 1980 film *Breaker Morant*) to support the case for the inclusion of "The Breaker's" name on the Memorial. Given that the memorial says "to commemorate the valor" Mr. Crafter told the *Advertiser*, "I think that fits Morant's contribution and it isn't a matter of judging innocence or guilt ... Although Morant was very nomadic, he did enlist in SA and was one of our men who put his life on the line".[1] Through May and June of the Bicentennial Year, South Australians followed the ensuing debate in their morning *Advertisers* about a sorry episode in a "forgotten war".[2] Council voted to endorse its Policy and City Development Committee's decision to take no action. William Wilks, and eight other Year Ten signatories from Kingston South East Community School, passionately supported "The Breaker's" case ("We ... believe that he was a courageous and considerate person. We ... believe that he and Peter Handcock were used as scapegoats by the British Army to prevent the Germans from entering the Boer War on the Dutch side. We admire Morant, and think that if more Australians knew about the unjust way he was treated they would be disgusted".[3]) B. J. LeLeu, Registrar of War Memorials (SA), argued that Morant's name should be included on a proposed local war memorial at Burra, where Beresford shot most of his film.[4] And on 24 May 1988, "The Breaker", Handcock and Witton were acquitted at a mock trial eighty-six years after the original, in the Burra Town Hall, an event which attracted international attention. T. A. Goodwin had the last say. He responded in early June with the notion that:

> The edifice on North Terrace should be bulldozed and broken up. Australian participation in the Boer War was a disgraceful episode in our history ... Those named on the war memorial did not fight for home or liberty, but to aid the richest and most powerful country of that time to promote its mining and business interests ... From a distance of nearly ninety years we should not be whitewashing the past or attempting to make heroes of criminals, but coming to terms with a darker side of our history.[5]

The extraordinary thing about the controversy is that this supposedly forgotten war could still inspire such passion after nearly a century, and that the issues that drove thousands of Australian men and women to cross the Indian Ocean to fight in an imperial war should still be strongly felt enough to inspire public pronouncement.

Throughout the nineteenth century, British armies were engaged in "over two hundred"[6] minor wars, fought mostly as police actions, and usually on the borders of the inexorably advancing Empire. Australians, however, fought in only a handful of these one-sided conflicts: there had been some involvement in the Maori wars in New Zealand; in Egypt and the "Soudan" between 1882 and 1888, when members of a New South Wales contingent spent their time building railways, scrub cutting and fighting fever rather than fighting the Mahdi's troops; and a small naval presence at the Boxer Rebellion in China in 1900, when South Australia's only warship, the Protector, sailed away to fight the Mongol hordes. The number of men who served in these theatres was too small to excite either much attention or enthusiasm. The Boer War, however, was a different matter entirely.

The Boer (or South African War) lasted from 12 October 1899 to 31 May 1902, when the Treaty of Vereening was signed. It was a complex, nasty little war, and astonishing for its foreshadowing of things to come. To read about it ninety years on is to realize how significant it was. It was the first war to be fought by men in drab khaki, by men carrying new weapons. The Boers used the German-made, highly efficient .276-calibre magazine Mauser, which could kill at 2,000 yards. The British used the .303 Lee-Metford and Lee-Enfield, the rifle of World War One, and much of World War Two, the rifle kept in many a wardrobe through much of this century. The Maxim gun, although first used with devastating effect against the Matabele in 1893, and in the Sudan at Omdurman in 1989, was used extensively in the Boer War: in its later modified form it became the Vickers gun, the machine gun of the trenches. Both sides used the new smokeless powder cordite, which made it possible for a man to hide himself behind a rock or in a trench and kill from a mile away, without revealing his position. It was the first war fought where the fire zone, the area between two armies, was a place where movement was very dangerous, and the only defence was to dig in. It was the first war fought with revolutionary new artillery: with rifled barrels, brass cartridge cases, with new explosives like lyddite, thanks to Alfred Nobel's nitroglycerine. Furthermore, improvements in military communications, such as the widespread use of the heliograph, the telegraph, and even the wireless telegraph, as well as observation balloons for artillery spotting, forced changes in strategy. As the South African historian Rayne Kruger put it, the Boer War would see the testing of these new weapons, and the realization that there would need to be "changes in military thought more far-reaching than any required since the invention of gunpowder",[7] changes not fully comprehended until the bloody and futile battles of fifteen years later.

Not only was it a war of new technologies, but it was also a war of new strategies prompted by those technologies: "pacification", "police duty", the burning of enemy houses and crops and the killing of livestock, the rounding up of survivors, mostly women and children, and their incarceration in what became known as "concentration camps", "block houses", fortified posts linked by miles of barbed wire, and endless patrolling, with mounted infantry chasing the elusive Boer commandoes around the veldt — all sinister echoes of things to come. It was the last war fought mostly on horseback, and at tremendous cost to the horses. And it was a peculiarly political war, fought only by white troops, and never on Sundays, for the Boers respected the Sabbath, with one side seeing it quite plainly as an imperial conflict, and the other as a civil war, fought over a very simple principle, pungently captured by a Pretorian Boer: "In the future I must either take my hat off to an Englishman, or he must take off his hat to me."[8]

There were many and complex causes for the war, which broke out when the Boer Republics' armies invaded Natal and the Cape Colony, after the British ultimatum that the Boers must offer concessions to the Uitlanders had expired. Obviously the Kimberley diamond fields, and the goldmines of the Rand, had much to do with it, as had the British belief that as much of the African map as possible should be painted red; but the issues were much more complex than the Empire supporting the Randlords, economic and territorial interests in southern Africa. "England was guided into war by many currents and many pilots: in short, by the entire epoch of the late nineteenth century".[9] And perhaps the strongest of those currents was the cross-class acceptance of the ethic of "British paramountcy".[10] Post-colonial and post-imperial spirits in the late twentieth century may find it hard to understand why that ethic alone might have been enough to inspire Australians to queue up to volunteer for the Boer War, and to line the streets to cheer the departing contingents (more Australians did the latter than the former). But a more recent war Australia fought in was to uphold American paramountcy in South East Asia, and Australians in the middle and late sixties could well have remembered the

Boer War and why it was fought, and why it would not have been. Vietnam is well on the way to being forgotten, too.

While the imperial forces were struggling to subdue the rebellious and intransigent Boers in South Africa, and the Boxers in China, the Americans had taken up their own version of the white man's burden and were fighting their very own colonial wars in Cuba and in the Philippines. All these little wars of the late 1890s were fought with an enthusiasm, an ardour and a brutality which, post-Vietnam, we might find surprising. Charles Carrington, Kipling's biographer, states that by "sweeping away such cob-webby anachronisms [as the Boer republics and the Spanish colonial possessions] ... [the British and the Americans] conceived themselves to be releasing the life-giving processes that would make the twentieth century, and, in America as in Britain, the people supported them".[11] Who is right? Was the Boer War for Britain and Empire the ultimate experience of the nineteenth century, or, was it rather a foreshadowing of the brave new world of the twentieth?

Those who remember how influential the camera men and women and the journalists who worked in Vietnam were, might well have expected the many writers who saw the Boer War at first hand to have made much of this point. But the "campaign created no great literary event",[12] as Gerster puts it, speaking of the Australian contribution, but he might as well have been describing the British literary response as well. Rudyard Kipling, Rider Haggard, John Buchan, Winston Churchill and Roger Casement all played active roles, but none left any enduring literary record of his experience of the war, let alone any discussion of its significance for the new century. "Banjo" Paterson wrote his best prose in, and about, South Africa, but it is largely forgotten today. The Boer War was the first to be covered extensively by journalists and writers from all round the world, when "Our Correspondent at the Seat of War"[13] was a household name, and people could talk knowledgeably about the progress of the conflict, and throw around all those Afrikaans words which, for a decade or two, meant something: laager, drift, spruit, nek, dorp, kopje and donga. The much-vaunted new journalism of the late nineteenth century finally could not find much to say about the nature of modern war, and about the Boer War in particular. Some writers, however, did manage to communicate something of what was happening, and in letters home, showed that simple, direct observation and reflection were possible, whereas it was difficult, if not unimaginable for the more public writers to attempt such honesty, bound up as they were with the conventions of writing about war. The *Bulletin*, keen to tilt at such conventions, searched hard for honest reportage, and printed it often:

> We have commandeered a large number of horses, sheep and poultry. The boys kill the fowls by running them through with lances. It is rumoured that one of the Landers came across 400 pounds in one of the houses the other day on the Modder River. I would not mind striking a few myself. The houses are beautifully furnished, lovely pianos and organs. The boys break up the organs and vehicles for firewood.[14]

It is, however, hardly surprising to find the writers of the handful of poems, short stories, memoirs and journalism about the Boer war taking a position about the nature of Australia's relationship with Britain. The imperial connection was "obvious",[15] but just as "undeniable" was the "strength of the new nationalism"[16] which had been developing through the 1890s. The decade was, in hindsight, one of seemingly conflicting national and international imperatives, when many, like Alfred Deakin, thought of themselves as "Independent Australian Britons" and saw no difficulty in building the new nation as a component of the Empire."[17] Such attitudes infuriated the *Bulletin*: "In Australian sentiment, Australia should be a home and not a boarding-home — for the benefit of the Empire. Pity it should be necessary for departing U.S. Consul Bell to tell us that. The Home Party and the Boarding-house Party. Good!"[18] The *Bulletin*, however, did not speak for all Australians when it ridiculed the imperial relationship. Deakin observed that "We are now able to see that the supposed agitation for independence was of the most superficial character and of the narrowest dimensions".[19] And Field contends that:

> Australians acted more like imperialists than nationalists in 1900, so the essential thing to them was the supremacy of British arms. Therefore, they could react with almost unbelievable fervour to the relief of Ladysmith ... they could turn the relief of Mafeking into a riotous public holiday ... They were also ready to revere Roberts and Baden Powell above [the Australian military leaders] Tom Price and Charlie Cox.[20]

Australians like to think that they shared in that excited feeling of belonging to a great and powerful tradition, much as a child might feel proud of a family name and a family history. The metaphor of the adolescent out to prove himself was much used: lion's whelps, cubs,[21] pups of the old British bulldog, fresh green shoots from the old tree, "stalwart slips of the ancient stock",[22] the literary progenitor Spenser's Red-crosse knight struggling to control his fiery steed. War would test the young man, enable him to show his mettle, and by so doing, demonstrate the strength of the family relationship. It would not have occurred to very many Australians that the individual should do anything other than answer the call, and have a go. Most wished to demonstrate a loyalty, and, by so doing, to feel able to share in, and be a part of the "devastatingly effective style"[23] of the British, and their concomitant belief in their paramountcy. The style was supported and promoted by a propaganda machine of particular effectiveness: the imperial honours system alone was enough to move politicians to act in the Empire's interests, and just about every area of public and private life had been affected. Schools, the Churches, public and private entertainments, the publishing industry, youth movements:

> became the servants of the dominant ideology of the age, patriotic, militaristic and imperialistic. They celebrated the excitements of an expansionist age — exploration, colonial campaigns, and missionary endeavour. They allied such activities to entertainment, the mass entertainment of music hall, Bank of Hope, and missionary meetings; public lectures, slide and cinema shows, and the new opportunities for home entertainment provided by cheap music, cheap journals, and even cheaper ephemera.[24]

Most of the daily newspapers in Australia reflected the prevailing "Jingo" line about the war. The *Bulletin*, however, took every opportunity to ridicule the journalistic rhetoric of the papers, and quotes verbatim a speech given by a departing contingenter in Sydney:

> Well, chaps, I'm going ter fight for me Queen. When I reads in the newspapers (and after all we have ter go to the newspapers for information) how them Boers slaughter innercent wimmin and chindren me blood biles, and I want ter get at 'em. I'll go straight for old Kreuger; I'll go to that place where he is now — what d'ye call it? Well, never mind wherever it is — I'll go there and get 'old of 'im, and bring 'im back in a cage. (This with a withering look in the direction of a crying youngster.)[25]

Within a week of the declaration of war, Kipling wrote "The Absent-Minded Beggar", the most famous literary statement about the war, which was published in the *Daily Mail* on 31 October 1899, and then set to music by Sir Arthur Sullivan. It raised a quarter of a million pounds for the wives and children of the thousands of "Tommy Atkins" who served in South Africa, and within a month Kipling was offered a knighthood, which he declined.[26] Lord Roberts, who became the British Commander-in-Chief in the same week as his only son was killed at Colenso during "Black Week", "was perhaps the first general to appreciate the importance of the press in warfare and to take journalists into his confidence".[27] The war became the first in history to be widely reported not only by journalists and writers, but also photographed, both by still and movie cameras. The relatively inexpensive Eastman Kodak camera was freely available after 1888,[28] and "Banjo" Paterson took his with him, capturing many images of the war, which, on his return to Australia, he showed to his audiences when he was touring the country giving illustrated lectures about his experiences. "Banjo's" photographs were hardly controversial, but others recognised the significance of the photograph in influencing public opinion: famous images from Spion's Kop, Natal, taken on 26 January 1900, of trenches filled with Boer and British dead, were used by the Boers, but banned from publication in England, such was the awareness of the power of the glass and paper image.[29]

Australians were manoeuvred into feeling more aware of the imperial connection in 1899, even while they were pondering the federation of the colonies. The world, as they saw it, was shrinking, and this made them all the keener to strengthen those silken bonds. Even though British imperial expansion through the last quarter of the nineteenth century had painted most of the map with those "rich splodges which ... lay across five continents like spilled claret, or shed blood",[30] the comfortable feeling of being tucked away at the edge of the world was passing. A. P. Haydon draws a connection between the new imperialism and the completion of the overland telegraph in 1872, linking Australia with Europe, which meant that the news read in Australian morning newspapers was "almost as fresh as that in London itself".[31] His point is a useful one, for whereas most of the small wars and police actions before 1872 must have been over by the time news reports reached Australia a month later by sea, the telegraph meant, that, for the first time, Australians must have felt themselves in touch with the Empire, and able to witness the day-to-day business of its running, and the processes of attendant decision-making. But the political realities of the shrinking world, and especially a fear of Great Power rivalry in the Pacific and of the rise of Japan as an industrial and military power, encouraged most Australians to support Britain, not just for the sake of the relationship, but because of the fear of standing alone on the edge of Asia. "What do we care if she is right or wrong? Our mother is attacked," said a Victorian parliamentarian when the war broke out.[32] But another, a South Australian MP F. W. Conybear, recited a few lines of verse to describe the quandary of some of his fellows during debates in the House about sending troops:

> As for the war, I go agen it,
> I mean to say, I kind of do —
> That is, I mean, that being in it,
> The best thing is to see it through.[33]

To understand this ambivalence is to feel something of the pull of imperial sentiment, which can be perceived in George Essex Evans's patriotic song "The Lion's Whelps", written shortly after the disastrous "Black Week" in December 1899, when British forces suffered three humiliating defeats at the hands of the Boers:

> There is scarlet on his forehead,
> There are scars across his face,
> 'Tis the bloody dew of battle dripping down, dripping down,
> But the war-heart of the Lion
> Turns to iron in its place,
> When he halts to face disaster, when he turns to meet disgrace,
> Stung and keen and mettled with the life-blood of his own,
> Let the hunters 'ware who flout him
> When he calls his whelps about him,
> When he sets the goal before him and he settles to the pace.
> ...
> Beaten! Let them come against us,
> We can meet them one and all,
> We have faced the world aforetimes, not in vain, not in vain,
> Twice ten thousand hearts be widowed,
> Twice ten thousand hearts may fall,
> But a million voices answer: "We are ready for the call,
> And the sword we draw for Justice shall not see its sheath again,
> Till we break their strength asunder
> And the Lion's whelps are round him and the Old Flag over all".[34]

The silken threads that bound the colonies to Britain were never spun from a "complex and sophisticated theorizing".[35] The "new imperialism" had evolved after the 1870s through a potent, if unspecific mix of chauvinism, an aggressive and rejuvenated militarist tradition, a monarchy which enjoyed widespread cross-class support, an expanding economic sphere, "an identification and worship of national heroes, together with a contemporary cult of personality, and racial ideas associated with Social Darwinism".[36] All of this served to create a genuine mass enthusiasm for Empire which transcended class boundaries, and offered a complex set of evangelical, philanthropic, political, military and economic possibilities, and concomitant self-aggrandising wish-fulfilments for "Establishment, parents and children alike".[37]

Late nineteenth-century militarism was a remarkable and enduring phenomenon: three generations of young men had to face its implications, and although the Vietnam War eventually did much to dampen down its dying flame in Australia, the conflict between Britain and Argentina over windy sheep pastures in Las Malvinas did much to fan the embers in England. It was born out of post-Darwinist ideas about nationalism, and the assertion of national rights in a competitive Europe. A strange assortment of bedfellows advanced the view: militant and muscular Christians, social engineers and educationalists who believed that the inculcation of a martial spirit was a way of creating a more unified and disciplined society, and, naturally, the military caste and its supporters in industry. This

> popular military activity was matched by an appropriate ideology. War came to be seen as a "theatrical event of sombre magnificence", while theories of the inevitability of warfare emerged from the social application of Darwinism. Warfare was endemic to civilisation, it was argued, both in the competition of rising States and in the conflict between them and their decaying counterparts. In naval building, the manufacture of armaments, and the soaking up of excess labour, it was crucial to the modern industrial economy. It was, moreover, a source of personal and national moral regeneration.[38]

War was the necessary, unavoidable and invigorating test of the individual's worth, and the nation's calibre and standing. Given the close link between this attitude to war, and late nineteenth-century popular fiction for boys, it is hardly surprising that at least some young Australians should have been keen to test themselves shoulder to shoulder with their British "chums". It is easy to ridicule the poems that were written to celebrate this desire, for these days the attitudes of mind which produced such effusions of sentiment and bombast are not only vitiated but also irrelevant, and dangerously so. Nevertheless, it is important to remember how the Empire was seen by its poets. John Sandes ("Oriel"), in the Preface to his *Ballads of Battle*, said "I desire at the present brilliant moment in Britain's history to furnish a small memento of the stirring events in South Africa, and of the glorious achievements of those Australian troops who have on many a battlefield cemented with their blood the unity of Empire". The poems themselves are predictably flowery. "The Bushman's

Question" at least tries to explain why so many volunteered.

> My son, there is a Motherland, and far away it lies
> 'Mid the tumult of the seas that know not peace,
> And on its shores the thunder of the ocean never dies
> And the songs of the wind never cease:
> But wind and wave together through the sunshine and the rain
> Of each fleeting season as it runs
> Have sung and thundered ever with the same glad, great refrain,
> Of liberty for England's sons.[39]

There are many such statements. Earl Beauchamp, the Governor of New South Wales (who was to help Henry Lawson to return "home" to further his literary career) wrote the following lines on the departure of the First Contingent:

> Like young lions to help the old one,
> Swift of footfall, and firm of poise,
> By jove, that foeman will be a bold one,
> Who'll face us banded, my boys, my boys.[40]

The Victorian Premier, McLean (the *Bulletin* dubbed him "Make Lean") was "moved to song by the events of the war. On Sunday, having a few hours' leisure, he gave play to his fancy" and produced these lines:

> O'er Austral lands the bugles blow,
> And rolls the martial drum;
> Their warlike strains like magic flow,
> They reach the Bushman's home.
> From hills where snow-fed rivers flow,
> From forests deep, from mountain's brow,
> From out each darksome vale below,
> The hardy Bushmen come.
>
> With iron thews, the tracker's eye,
> Though somewhat slouching mien,
> Those horsemen bold, 'neath southern sky,
> Have sun and weather seen.
> They heard their cherished country's cry,
> With eager rush to arms they fly,
> With stern resolve to do or die,
> For Empire and their Queen!

The *Bulletin* observed that "the Premier Poet makes it evident that one can be a bad poet and an extremely commonplace politician. A good politician may be excused for being a bad poet, but two wrongs should never make one write".[41]

The federating of the colonies also gave the bards a chance to dwell on the significance of the Boer War. George Essex Evans, in his prize-winning "Ode for Commonwealth Day", saw Australia's "birth" as, instead, a marriage:

> ... the New Day hath won for bride
> This Austral Land!
>
> Free-born of Nations, Virgin White,
> Not won by blood nor ringed by steel".[42]

In his "The Crown of Empire", written on the Coronation of Edward VII, Evans notes that Australia had been:

> First to draw sword, when, with a single heart,
> From every frontier line of Empire rose
> New Britons armed to meet Britannia's foes,
> Whose voices thunder, as the joy-bells ring
> Loud from ten thousand spires: "God Save the King!"[43]

John Bernard O'Hara, in his "Australia's Call to Arms",[44] summons Australians to "Wake! [and] arise!" to "maintain the glory" and light up the "star of ancient Britain" with "a glow of fiercer shine/O'er the burning sands of Afric". He finds a variation on the theme of Australia as the child of Britain:

> Shall we falter, while the fires
> Still are glowing on the altars
> From the ashes of our sires?

Buried deep beneath the euphemism and the empty rhetoric can be sensed a much more powerful and enduring legacy of the Imperial style, the cult of manly behaviour, which manifests itself, so the belief went, in its purest form in war. The cult expressed itself through metaphors from sport and business as well as from war: play the game, get the job done, respect a fearless foe, honour the team of the brave and just, and all that. It can be found in various guises in the popular fiction and poetry of the second half of the nineteenth century, and in the "literature of mass literacy and democracy"[45] in particular. Rider Haggard, Rudyard Kipling, Edgar Wallace, Arthur Conan Doyle and John Buchan, some of the most influential of the writers who catered for this new market, all worked (the verb is deliberate) in South Africa during the Boer War, and most wrote widely about the conflict, explicitly projecting the cult of mannishness in their works. Kruger describes the "mystique" as the search for:

> a sensitive masculinity midway between the effeminate and the "muddied oaf at the goals" A man of action who needed something more than brawn to reach "beyond the skyline where the strange roads go down" was such a mean ... expressing the yearning of a generation whose restlessness ... was one of the mainsprings of imperialism. Mannishness and imperialism were therefore beats of the same pulse.[46]

George Essex Evans wrote at length about this mystique: his poem "The National Builders" describes in Kiplingesque terms the handful of workers and heroes who have conquered a continent; explorers, settlers, fishermen, miners, and so on, the men of action who leave the cities and get things done. John Sandes's "Left, Right, Listen to the Marching" proposes a metaphor for responding to the call to fight which says much about the cult:

> There's a harvest on the Modder if of work you're not afraid,
> And already on the plain the sheaves they're reaping;
> There's a crop at far Colenso that is waiting for the blade;
> Oh, won't you go and take a job of reaping?[47]

And Sandes's "The Bushman's Farewell" contains the following description of a young man hearing the call of Empire:

> And I felt the sudden manhood in a stirring of the blood,
> And an impulse that within me burned like flame.
> Oh, dearer than all beauties that are found in distant lands
> Yon homestead that is hidden from my sight,
> But the reasons why I leave it — ah, the brave heart understands,
> Good night, my native land, a last good night.[48]

There is an explicit sense here of the sexual gratification offered by war, at least to the bard safe at home and enjoying the vicarious thrill of daydreaming. A poem by Morgan Hawkes, "His Mother in Australia", purports to describe the lamenting of a mother whose son has been killed on the veldt.

> It was little he knew of soldiering,

And nought that he knew of war,
But his joy and pride were a horse to ride,
And to gallop fast and far.
And all his chums were going,
The old schoolmate, clubmate band;
In many a match they had played and won,
They had followed the founds in the stiffest run —
And now he must take a hand.

It was nothing he cared for politics,
Nor who was wrong or right,
'Twas the blood of his dad, that was in the lad
That sent him out to fight.
He longed to be in a battle,
Neither shot nor shell he feared,
And he joked at having a "snipe" at Steyn,
And promised to bring me home again
A hair of Kruger's beard.[49]

The hearty rhythms and the schoolboy sports field rhetoric hardly assist the threnodial intention, but what works against the successful communication of a mother's feeling is the poet's desire to describe the nature of the warrior caste, and one young man's desire to "take a hand" and be a part of getting the job done. Furthermore, there is an indication of middle-class, rather than cross-class feeling here, supporting Connolly's contention that Australian involvement in the Boer War was promoted most strongly by middle-class Australians who most valued the imperial connection,[50] for there is little in this poem (or for that matter, in the others quoted) that we would associate with the twentieth-century "myth" of the digger that has so coloured our perceptions of Australians at war.[51] On the other hand, we can speculate: can a chum be a mate? Is mateship anything other than not letting down the side? It may be that the evolution of the digger myth owes much to the grafting of the middle-class cult of the warrior caste to the proletarian bush ethos. "Rolf Boldrewood", writing retrospectively of the Marston boys as if they had really existed, observed that:

they bore eloquent testimony to the genial Australian climate, as concerning the development of the Australian race. Well above the ordinary standard of height, they were ... "pretty men", being good with all weapons of which they had knowledge. Strong, active, enduring, intelligent, "'twas the pity of them" that so large an endowment of every manly quality should have been diverted from the right path in life. Had the South African war broken out before they were fatally compromised, none who knew them doubted that they would have distinguished themselves at the front as did so many of their compatriots.[52]

George Essex Evans wrote "Eland's River" after a famous skirmish, when 300 Australians and 200 Rhodesians defended a staging camp for twelve days against a much larger Boer force, who fired more shells into their camp than into Mafeking during the much more famous siege.

> They called us to surrender, and they let their cannon lag;
> They offered us our freedom for the striking of the flag —
> > Army stores were there in mounds,
> > Worth a hundred thousand pounds,
> And we lay battered round them behind trench and sconce and crag.
> > But we sent the answer in,
> > They could take what they could win —
> We hadn't come five thousand miles to fly the coward's rag.[53]

There is little here of the stuff from which the digger legend was later to be made, simply a pedestrian presentation of the manly virtues of "courage" and "loyalty" to caste and class, which hints at the middle-class, public school, sporting ideal. The predictable metaphor of winning the game is there, as is the excited recognition of the monetary worth of the Army stores they defended so doughtily.

Henry Lawson wrote many poems about war: he reflected more strongly and more often than most writers of his time the view that it would take a war to "bind together the hitherto diverse but nonetheless complimentary strands of the Australian experience".[54] His first poem about the Boer War, "Our Fighters (From a Worldly Point of View)", expresses his belief that, even though "the cause seems cronk", the fact that "our boys are going" is "in accordance with the things that have to be", but he seems at least ambivalent, if not disappointed, about the "worldly point of view" that has taken the contingents across the Indian Ocean:

> Then climb and crawl as long as nail hangs on to toe or claw,
> And fire and strike, and strike and shoot, as long as muscles draw!

For the girls you took to Manly Beach, who'll wait on the Quay
for you —
For the honour of old New South Wales from the people's point
of view![55]

"The Blessings of War", Lawson's best-known poem about
the Boer War, reasserts the obsession with the rightness of
war, and with the need for change and novelty:

I'm in favour of the war, and of half-a-dozen more;
And I think we should have had one long before —
There is nothing to deplore; I'm in favour of the war
Independent of all statements made by Briton or by Boer.

'Tis a healthy stirring up of the dregs of sorrow's cup;
'Tis a joyful thing, as I have always held,
For it brings us something new ... [56]

Jack Cornstalk, says Lawson, has gone to war, and perhaps
the most significant outcome will be that he

Shall be copy now at home both in story, sketch, and "pome"
In the new Australian drama he'll be great.
Both in letters and in art he will play the paying part
(And 'tis farewell to the swagman and his mate.)

Lawson was right, of course, in the long run, but it would
take fifteen years or more to realise how accurate he was.
His "Ballad of the Cornstalk" maintains the notion he
broadcast in "Concerning the Awful Contingent"[57] that
bushmen were "tired of the Bush and ... off for a spree" in
South Africa: the regret for Lawson is not the war itself, or
imperial militarism, but simply the thoughtless and
carefree spirit of the contingenters.

It might be expected that those individuals who
actually endured the war at first hand might have
attempted to test the received traditions of writing about
war and violence against the imperatives of direct, hard-
won experience. Some did, at least in their letters home.
Trooper J. J. Perkins reflected on the scorched-earth policy:

Our men are disgusted with this kind of business; the only thing
we seem to have strict orders about is to burn everything in
sight, leaving defenceless women and children to starve and
perish, and I can assure you that is the kind of thing that makes a
man feel ashamed of being a white man. I have seen women and
children appeal with uplifted hands for protection and not to
burn their old homes down; but we have our orders, and down
they must come. The other day our regiment refused, and walked

back, saying they could not burn the place down; the Yeomanry were sent up and did the job, and there was no more about it. That is one thing about the Australians, they one and all object to this kind of thing, and are of the opinion that it only tends to make the Boers more bitter; but of course it is war, and war is a new thing to Australians, and a terrible thing too.[58]

A.A.G. Hales went to South Africa as a war correspondent for the London *Daily News* and *John Bull*, and his writing "won him a reputation as a critical and daring front-line reporter which was enhanced after his wounding and capture by the Boers at Rensburg.[59] He published *Poems and Ballads* in 1909, which includes a sequence "Battle Songs", which were written out of his South African experience. They are more detailed, often colloquial, but also more even-handed than poems on similar "jingo" lines written by non-participants: Hales even writes sympathetically of the Boers in at least one poem, "In a Boer Laager: A Tale of the British Boer War: Dedicated to General De La Rey". His poem "Round the Camp Fire: Private Maloney's Story", with its description of a yarn-telling session, immediately promises something at least of the typical narrative poem the *Bulletin* might have published:

> They didn't talk as soldiers talk
> In books that I have read,
> About their noble mothers,
> Or the great and glorious dead;
> They didn't drift to poetry,
> Nor waste their time on tears,
> Nor drag up recollections
> Of pure maiden's parting prayers.
> They mostly talked of cricket,
> Of horse-racing, or the ring,
> And didn't seem to care a straw,
> For Parliament or King!
> When they spoke about the "girl they'd left,"
> And the boys used to wrangle,
> They mostly hoped she's saved enough
> To buy herself a mangle![60]

There is some evidence here that Hales was prepared to transcribe direct experience, especially when that experience seemed to run counter to the prevailing orthodoxies of martial verse; and certainly anyone seeking out early intimations of the immortal archetypal digger, could find material here. But Hales wrote much more verse which is as ponderously martial and imperial as any armchair warrior back in Australia. "The Burial of Wauchope" is a remarkable example, a poem describing a Scottish regiment's discovery of one of their officers killed by the Boers:

> Then once again the pipes pealed forth to the strains
>   of the "Flowers of the forest,"
> Now ringing proud and high, until the soldiers' heads
>   went up in haughty defiance, and eyes flashed
>   through tears, like sunlight on steel;
> Now sinking to a moaning wail, like a woman mourning
>   for her first-born,
> Until the warriors' heads drooped forward, till bearded
>   jaws rested on heaving chests, and manly tears
>   ran down the furrowed lines of war-scarred cheeks,
>   and deep-drawn sobs broke through the solemn
>   rhythm of the march of death ...
>
> Then, as if stirred by the magic of one thought, the
>   soldiers turned their eyes from the still forms
>   in the shallow graves, towards the heights where
>   Cronje's burghers stood.
> Then every cheek flushed crimson, the strong jaws set
>   like steel, the veins on the browned hands that
>   grasped the rifle barrels, swelled almost to bursting
>   with the fervour of the grip.
> Like hounds that strain upon the leash, the Scotsmen
>   stood with necks outstretched, and hard-set jaws
>   pushed forth; with shoulders squared, and feet
>   braced to the earth,
> Snuffing with wide expanding nostrils the breeze that
>   reeked with the strong scent of battle they
>   had fought and lost.
> No need for words; the look upon every stony face
>   was vengeance petrified, and every eye asked
>   silently for blood.[61]

"No need for words", says Hales. A later poem in the sequence "Battle Songs", "Driscoll's Ride", contains the following advice for his fellows:

> If we're cornered, fight like blazes,
> Never let the Dutchman brag,
> That the scouts who rode with Driscoll
> Had to hoist the old white rag.
> Keep your eyes and ears wide open,
> Don't go dreaming as you ride
> Of the girl you should have married,
> Or the little lad who died.

That's the poetry of sorrow
That we cultivate in camp,
When the stars are preaching sermons,
And we think ourselves a scamp.
Let it slide now; get to saddle,
Trust in God and shoot like sin.
We have started on this business,
And we've got to fight and win.[62]

The *Bulletin*, finally, was right. Perhaps the best weapon at the disposal of the imperial forces was not lyddite, or the Maxim, or even rogues like "Breaker" Morant, but the jingo poem. "His Conqueror"[63] makes the point. A horseman brings "something neatly rolled up" to Kruger, who reads it:

"All is lost," he murmured;
"Boys, the game is up.

"We can face their cannon,
Never flinch nor fly —
When they sool their bards on
We can only die."

The extraordinary thing is not that so few Australian writers produced the "poetry of sorrow" about the Boer War, but that the lessons the conflict had to offer were ones that it would take fifteen or more years to learn. There were a few voices raised in opposition, representing the vocal minorities in Australia (as there were in Britain) who opposed the war and who did so publicly, even though there was considerable risk in doing so. William Holman, the Labour Member for Grenfell, Billy Hughes and Arthur Griffith all made their stand, as did the *Bulletin*, and other papers like Holman's Grenfell Vedette. The best-known and most notorious of the "Pro-Boers" was the Challis Professor of History at Sydney University, George Arnold Wood, who debated the imperial involvement in South Africa with his colleague, the Professor of Modern Literature, Mungo MacCullum.[64] The issue in question, however, was not war itself, and the militarist spirit, but whether or not Britain was always in the right. Wood could not support this particular imperial war, even though he was a passionate imperialist, and his very public "Pro-Boer" stand nearly led to his being disciplined or even dismissed by the University Senate. But in 1917, when in his fifties, he (with Christopher Brennan) joined a university military group which trained three days a week.

Very few writers expressed a pacifist point of view in reacting to the Boer War, for such was the power of the imperial "style" that very few indeed saw fit to challenge the prevailing militarism and its manifestation in South Africa. Brennan's sequence *The Burden of Tyre* is well known.[65] But there were, here and there, lone pacifist voices raised in protest: John Farrell, in his "Australia to England: June 12, 1897", written for Queen Victoria's Diamond Jubilee, bravely asked the British:

> Be sure the safest time of all
> For even the mightiest State is when
> Not even the least desire its fall!
> Make England stand supreme for aye,
> Because supreme for peace and good,
> Warned well by wrecks of yesterday
> That strongest feet may slip in blood!
> Your way has been to pluck the blade
> Too readily, and train the guns.
> We [Australians] here, apart and unafraid
> Of envious foes, are but your sons:
> We stretched a heedless hand to smutch
> Our spotless flag with Murder's blight ...
> Your pride of deadliest armament —
> What is it but the self-same dint
> Of joy with which the Caveman bent
> To shape a bloodier axe of flint?

And Joseph Furphy was one writer who did more than simply challenge imperial militarism, in his "The Fly in the Ointment", where he sardonically comments on the Social Darwinism that underpins nationalism and British style, and which has led the Empire to fighting a war to protect the interests of the Randlords:

> When the great Creator fashioned us, and saw that we were good,
> He commissioned us to dominate the planet as it stood;
> Yet his ordinance meets denial still, and peace remains unknown,
> For the Boer is always with us, calling certain lands his own ...
>
> Bravely sings the longhair'd Alfred, "Forward, forward let us range!

Let the great world spin for ever down the ringing grooves of
    Change!"
O be sure the Good Time Coming shall achieve its glorious birth
When the patriot owns his blunder, and the boodler owns the
    earth![66]

"R." wrote "Red-handed" for the *Bulletin*, trenchantly
condemning Australia for its "vulture-lust" in South Africa:

We had a dream — it seems but yesterday —
That dream is dashed — to direst darkness hurled:
For where our Commonwealth, a virgin lay,
A Wanton fronts the world.[67]

J. K. McDougall wrote a savage parody of Kipling's "The
White Man's Burden" in 1900, and of the Christian
endorsement of militarism:

Take up the White Man's burden,
Lift high the blazing cross;
For Greed must have his guerdon
Whoever counts the cost.
...
Ride down — ye have the horses —
Strike down with lances keen;
Fill up the gap with corpses,
Between each still machine.
Drive home the mob like cattle,
Take ye the spoiler's pay;
Ride grimly into battle
And slay and slay and slay.

Ye are the White Man's engines;
Ye fight and force for him;
Fill up his cup of vengeance,
Yea, fill it to the brim.
Paid bullies of the robbers,
Your murders are not sin;
Kill for the trusts and jobbers —
Sock ye the bay'nets in.
...

Ye are the sordid killers,
Who murder for a fee;
Ye prop, like rotten pillars,
Trade's lust and treachery.
Hog-souled and dirty-handed
Ye sell yourselves for gain,
And stand forever branded
Red felons after Cain.

Ye are the fools and flunkeys;
Ye die to serve the great —

The rooks and gilded monkeys
Who eat the fat of State.
Ye fall in alien places,
On foreign wastes ye lie,
Stiff-limbed, with putrid faces
Turned livid to the sky.[68]

McDougall's poem was notorious in the early decades of this century. It was parodied by the Nationalists in an election campaign in 1919, and used to suggest Labor's contempt and hostility towards the diggers. McDougall, a farmer-poet and politician (he held the Federal seat of Wannon for Labor 1906-1913), was tarred and feathered by a gang of returned servicemen in Ararat for his views expressed twenty years previously.

The *Bulletin*'s role in opposing the Boer War, and jingo militarism in particular, is well known. To read its pages from mid-1899 to late 1902 is to find some of the liveliest and most enduring writing about the war, from poems and satires by Victor Daley ("Creeve Roe"), Randolph Bedford, "Banjo" Paterson and Henry Lawson, to paras (in very plain and pungent English, probably mostly by Archibald) ridiculing the patriotic excesses of governments, the military, the contingents and the people who supported them. The paper's role is well understood, but a measure of the energy of the writing can be gained from a list of the epithets hurled at the contingents: "swashbucklers", "a filibustering band", "Boer-murderers", "disinterested man-slayers", "the local slashers", "the piratical band", "the Dingo-Jingoes", "Transvaal goat-hunters", "bushrangers", and so on. The *Bulletin* offered a brief history of the conflict:

> But when Britain invited sundry Australian politicians to go to London and have a lovely razzle-dazzle and holiday at Jubilee time, these politicians rose up unanimously and said that blood was thicker than water, and that owing to the deep affection which Australia bore to England, they felt it their duty to go and have a good time. And when sundry politicians found an opportunity to advertise themselves and probably get titles, by sending a contingent to the Transvaal; and when a lot of people saw the chance of a free trip, and the pleasant excitement of travel, and good pay, by being a contingent; and the sporting instinct of a community which loves to go out and shoot something saw some excitement in view; and there was the joy of wearing a uniform and a feather, and letting off a gun with a

loud bang; and the commercial community saw in the contingent a good opportunity to put in a claim for fat army contracts — Australia's alleged love for Britain blazed forth anew.[69]

There were even a handful of Returned Australian Contingenters who came back from the Boer War, and were prepared to write about a change in attitude to war brought on by their personal experiences. M. Grover's "I Killed a Man at Graspan" is an unpretentious but affecting statement that says as much about the personal dilemmas brought on by killing, and the role of poets and priests in driving individuals to war, as any other single literary response to the conflict:

> I killed a man at Graspan,
> I killed him fair in fight;
> And the Empire's poets and the Empire's priests
> Swear blind I acted right.
> The Empire's poets and Empire's priests
> Make out my deed was fine,
> But they can't stop the eyes of the man I killed
> From starin' into mine.
>
> ...
>
> If the Empire asks for me later on
> It'll ask for me in vain
> Before I reach to my bandolier
> To fire on a man again.[70]

A final estimation of the writing of the Boer War must allow for the observation that the best stories are still to be told, or, that the writers of the day could not see the "copy", so dazzled were they by the imperial style. These include: Corporal Ben Harkus, of the Landers returned ignominiously to South Africa after being called a coward, only to die of the enteric at Bloemfontein. Dozens of nurses served in the hospitals with their "all-pervading faecal odour".[71] Private James Steele, of the Fifth Victorian Mounted Rifles,made the remark that he would not go out with one General Beatson again, after the General had described his mates as "a fat-arsed, pot-bellied, lazy lot of wasters ... a lot of white-livered curs."[72] Major Fiaschi, of the New South Wales Army Medical Corp, asked to be excluded from meeting the famous "Bobs" (Lord Roberts), as he was busy operating. A Queensland Bushman called a British Colonel "matey", and when reprimanded, gave his

name as the Man from Snowy River.[73] An un-named
Aboriginal black-tracker was taken to South Africa by one
of the Australian contingents, and got lost. Corporal
Kirkpatrick, an ex-teacher from Leichhardt, was killed at
Slingersfontein, and lay on the veldt dying from multiple
wounds; his body was found next morning with the word
"cold" scratched in the dirt beside him.

The two most significant literary products of the War,
Abbott's Tommy Cornstalk[74] and "Banjo" Paterson's
dispatches, collected now as Boer War,[75] are both
remarkable in their own ways as private statements, more
in keeping with late-twentieth century attitudes to war in
their low-key, dispassionate subjectivity and seemingly
randomly accumulated impressions, details and responses.
But even in these two works there is little real awareness
of what might come in later wars. The experience of
combat, or even of witnessing combat, did little to erode
militarism, possibly because there were so few casualties,
and because it was fought with some semblance of
"civilised" behaviour, the "Breaker" Morants on both sides
notwithstanding. Memories faded quickly. By 1914 just
about everyone was ready to start again. The Empire
finally did little to equip its members with the necessary
preparation for war, twentieth-century style. A loose mix
of ideas about race, nation and empire, a popular culture
which extolled certain manly virtues, a propaganda
machine which inculcated such hazy beliefs into people's
minds made it difficult for people to do anything other
than volunteer, and give it a go. Perhaps it is expecting too
much for war writers to be blessed with such prescience, but
for us, nearly a century on and fearful always of what
might happen in the next Great War, there is still the
desire to ask, as I can, why did my German-speaking third-
generation Australian grandfather, Johannes ('Jack') Adolf
Pahl enlist in 1916 and serve four years in France, where he
was wounded twice, and gassed once, while his elder
brother, Friedrich ('Joe') August Julius Pahl, was interned
on the notorious Torrens Island, just for refusing to allow his
children to salute the Union Jack at Murrayville Primary
School in the Victorian mallee?

Formation and Creation
Norman Lindsay's 1890s

Joy Hooton

Norman Lindsay joined the staff of the *Bulletin* as a black
and white artist in 1901. He arrived at a time when the
Bulletin was still in its heyday under the editorship of
Archibald, and when most of the familiar figures of the
nineties were still writing. Lindsay finally left the journal
in 1958, at a time when its cultural relevance had vastly
diminished, although Lindsay himself barely noticed the
change. At the time and in retrospect, he regarded joining
the *Bulletin* as one of the most important events in his
destiny. It "lugged" him out of the "muddled Melbourne
days" as a struggling student-artist on the fringes of that
city's cultural life and settled him in Sydney "where all
active movement in literature and plastic art was cen-
tralized in the personalities of two men, J. F. Archibald
and Julian Ashton".[1] Most importantly, it made him a part
of the struggle to forge a national identity for the
Australian-born, retrieving them from the "limbo begotten
by a nostalgia in the early settlers, who called England
'home'":

> the *Bulletin* was not only the national Australian journal; it
> was Australia in concrete form ... [it] initiated an amazed
> discovery that Australia was "home", and that was the anvil on
> which Archibald hammered out the rough substance of the
> national ego.[2]

There is no doubt that Lindsay had a strong affinity with
the rough substance of this nineties ego as it was hammered
out weekly by Archibald's cartoonists and writers, and
that the word "home" in this context had strong emotional

associations. Like the *Bulletin's* implied reader, he was fiercely nationalistic and suspicious of foreign influences, contemptuous of anything British, intransigently racist and anti-semitic, unashamedly sexist, and committed to a form of mateship in the easy-going camaraderie of journalists, poets and artists. Lindsay's life-history is littered with visual reminiscences of him by friends and family, often perceived as archetypal, and with photograp. Of the latter, one of the all-male Ishmael Club, composed of such figures as Randolph Bedford, Percy and Lionel Lindsay, Will and Ted Dyson, grouped around a male totem and including Norman in the back row's combined gesture of solidarity (each man leaning an elbow on his neighbour's shoulder) is one of the most eloquent of this period.

Lindsay's unsubtle but vivid style of cartooning was also a perfect complement to Archibald's polemical style as an editor, and his preference for the energetic, the irreverent and the racy. At their first meeting, Lindsay was entranced by Archibald's enthusiasm for the "humours of character" and "mad gambits of personality" offered by the Sydney scene, welcoming his interest in "the great human spectacle" as a kindred absorption.[3] In an article written in 1950, "A Mislaid Art", Lindsay expands on this interest in the "whole cavalcade of Australian types ... from the company promoter to the rabbit-oh, from the Potts Point dame to Jiggity Jane of the slums", describing the *Bulletin* files of this period as the reflection of a generation.[4] Although he worked under a series of editors and for several subsequent generations, Lindsay never forsook the nineties decade, remaining unchanged in the attitudes he brought from the Creswick of his youth, and perpetuating the same nineties types, if in different costume. During the First World War, his xenophobia and his preference for starkly expressed moral polarities found a natural outlet in the overheated conscription debate, while in the post-war period his strident racism and instinctive dislike of communism found a ready audience. If the *Bulletin* became a reactionary, anti-Labor weekly after the war, it was an adjustment in Lindsay's political direction, which had always favoured ideas of class and hierarchy. Politics, of course, were of no interest to Lindsay; he worked according to editorial direction, for some decades relying on the weekly telephone call to substitute for the newspapers he never read. By employing the same emotive devices, he achieved some curious effects, swaying public opinion against a hanging, when he himself favoured capital punishment, and inspiring opposition to the Boer War notwithstanding his own irritation with "a lot of wowseristic Bible-thumping Boer farmers ... obstructing a Roman occupation of the earth's surface".[5]

In one important respect Lindsay might be said to differ from the literary values promoted by Archibald's *Bulletin*, that is in his rejection of the bush legend and his substitution of a pagan Arcadia, which drew loosely on Greek mythology. One of the most sizeable planks of the *Vision* aesthetic of the 1920s was a repudiation of the bush as an emblem of Australia. But Lindsay was never more a representative of his youth's generation and never more Australian than in his preoccupation with female nudity surrounded with satyrs, centaurs and fauns. As Bernard Smith comments, the pagan frolics of the *Vision* school had nothing in common with the spirit of classical mythology, they were "ersatz rococo variations, little pre-Disney fantasies to amuse an antipodean cult".[6] In the rejection of European modernism, the flouting of middle-class morality, the opposition to all that was seen as suburban, the emphasis on male (sexual) enterprise, and above all in the image of Australia as a new Arcadia, Lindsay was merely adding an idiosyncratic but derivative decoration to the familiar topography of the nineties. Assertively independent in the trenchant selection and mingling of such oddly assorted figures as Sandys, Rabelais, Pepys, Boccaccio, Beethoven and Shakespeare, Lindsay's aesthetic makes a virtue of colonial provincialism in the same spirit as Archibald's *Bulletin*. Smith also underlines Lindsay's debt to English aestheticism of the same decade, and his affinity with the decorative, eclectic, reversionary art of Beardsley. Art for art's sake took longer to die in Australia than in England, due partly to Lindsay's extraordinary genius for stasis and personal charisma, and partly to Australia's isolation during the First World War. A more quirky reason was the arrival of the young and energetic Jack Lindsay in Sydney at a time when Norman had already withdrawn from the city's cultural life. P.R. Stephensen, for instance, has recorded the impact of Norman's dionysianism on his own 1920s generation, unaware of the paganism of the 1890s: "These ideas, fresh during Norman's adolescence ... were not part of the Zeitgeist of our generation, adolescent during the First World War".[7] Thus, the stream of time flowed around the rock that was Norman Lindsay.

Such commitment to the style and spirit of a period implies deep psychological causes, and indeed there is a vast amount of evidence suggesting that this was the case. The Lindsay family's addiction to autobiography and reminiscence, combined with Norman's own excursions in that area and his concern to nurture his legend, have resulted in rich deposits of material on Lindsay's early years for the biographer.[8] In addition, there is the series of novels dealing with his childhood at Creswick and his student days in Melbourne. The Creswick childhood (1879-96) is the subject of *Saturdee*, first published as a series of short stories from 1908 in the *Lone Hand*, and as a book in 1933 *Redheap*, written during the First World War, published in England and America in 1930 and in Australia in 1959 and *Halfway to Anywhere* (1947). *The Cousin from Fiji* (1945) is set in Ballarat but it shares *Redheap*'s decade and clearly draws on the same memories. *A Curate in Bohemia* written 1904-5 and published in 1913 deals with Lindsay's years in Melbourne from 1896-1901, as does *Rooms and Houses*, his last novel, published in 1968. Other novels, such as *The Cautious Amorist* (1934), *Pan in the Parlour* (1934) and *Miracles by Arrangement* (1932), which are not ostensibly based on the adolescent years include elements of them. As Jack Lindsay remarks, the novels provide "astonishing proof of the way in which [Norman's] emotional life was tethered to his early years and above all to the family house at Creswick".[9] When they are considered along with Lindsay's factual autobiographies, *My Mask* (1970) and *Bohemians of the Bulletin* (1965), his extensive extant correspondence and the reminiscences of other members of the Lindsay family, it is possible to see the seminal period for Lindsay's creativity as extending to 1909, the year that he left for London. If the Creswick years merge into the Melbourne ones as a period of carefree adolescence, the years in Sydney under the aegis of Archibald and the *Bulletin* are almost as much a period of youthful male freedom, notwithstanding marriage to Katie Parkinson, fatherhood and the responsibility of a full-time occupation. It was the visit to London which suddenly jettisoned Lindsay into adulthood, by depriving him of home and the protective figures of his youth and exposing him to unsympathetic critics. Hetherington's biography describes the negative experiences that England provided in contrast to the consistently enthusiastic reception of his work in Australia hitherto and the consequent withering of his creative vitality during this "time of exile".[10] When the *Bulletin* made another of its periodic rescues of his affairs by offering him his old position, he lost no time in returning, refusing another more lucrative offer from America.[11] After his return to Australia, he fell seriously ill, an event he later attributed to the "collapse of a special faculty in the ego", and to English criticisms that his art was derivative, no more than the slick skill of an illustrator.[12] On this occasion it was Rose who rescued him by establishing a retreat in the Blue Mountains. In 1911 he began to lead the reclusive life that continued with only brief intermissions until his death. At this time there also occurred that shift in his work towards escapist fantasy that Jack Lindsay has analysed. It was a shift away from real life to the untrammelled life of the imagination. Writing to Lionel Lindsay in 1919, for instance, he declares: "For me, I have done away with any conception that life is action, emotion. Life is lived in the mind."[13] Jack Lindsay, the most perceptive and informed of his observers, sheets the split in his father's career to his growing horror of the First World War, and presumably his shocked rejection of his previous conviction that war was the supreme opportunity for heroism and a magnificent stimulus to artistic creation.[14] The war, however, appears to have been a culminating event, confirming Lindsay's perception, gained in England, that the world was a "Bedlamite planet".¹⁵

Lindsay is perhaps the most paradoxical figure in Australia's cultural history, but the greatest paradox he presents is the contradiction between his public or received self as the influential vitalist, the charismatic standard-bearer of a pagan aesthetic, flourishing the ideals of beauty, gaiety and sexual freedom, and his private self, the isolated, alienated artist afflicted with a Puritanical work ethic, abstemious habits and scant faith in reaching minds of equal calibre. His letters and autobiographies abound in statements of contempt for the common herd, and his determination to keep aloof from human society. "Get away from all cities", he advised Hugh McCrae, "The mind loses itself in the dust and noise of affairs and the cries of common minds." To Bertram Stevens he described the world as a "plague-stricken hole ... as for man, the aggregate human animal, I turn to my dog for company in preference". In a private letter to John Hetherington forty years later he congratulated himself on having cut out the socialising third of life so that he achieved two working lives in one, and on another occasion described solitude as having "a charm that no other system of existence can give". In *My Mask* he complains that forced contact with human beings at large drove his soul "into a marsh where frogs dwell". *Creative Effort* erects this antipathy into artistic elitism: "intellectual man lives as an alien amid a horde of animals, made in his likeness. The difference between man and man is the difference between man and ape." If he increasingly regarded life as a period of probation to be endured until the welcome end, he wasted as little regret on ruined relationships: "I never indulge sentiment over broken friendships. We have extracted all we need from a friend, and so get rid of him on the same terms as he gets rid of us".¹⁶ Given the distaste for human society that overtook Lindsay after his return from Europe in 1911, it is not surprising that the period from the Creswick years until 1909 appeared to him in retrospect to have almost an idyllic colour and a seamless unity, to be, as it were, a magically extended "nineties". In fact, he frequently referred to the period as if it were a single decade, and mingled memories of the Melbourne years (1896-1901) and the Sydney years (1901-9) indiscriminately. Memories of the Creswick years were particularly ecstatic, but life in Melbourne of the 1890s and Sydney of the 1900s had an irretrievable quality. Writing to his brother Lionel in 1914, Lindsay confessed:

> I don't know particularly why it should be so, but I find my mind throws back to the unconscious observations of my early youth for a clarified sense of character. Any trifle of memory of that period strikes me as having some quality of ecstasy about it.[17]

In *My Mask* he describes the Sydney of his youth as having a charm and a diversity that "will never again be seen on earth". A "sailor-town city, a free-trade city, a pre-mechanized city", it had a population that was sharply differentiated by class, unlike the cosmopolitan modern Sydney with its "uniform mob".[18] And in *Bohemians of the Bulletin* he gives full vent to his nostalgia for the nineties, notwithstanding the fact that the period was culturally, apart from the *Bulletin*, a "moribund limbo":

> As a section of space to exist in, it was the best of all possible worlds. It was still the era of the horse and buggy, the inferno of a mechanized age had not arrived, class distinctions divided mass humanity into its proper orders of upper, middle, and low, and a tradition of existence, stable for centuries, was still extant. The earth was safe to dwell on; no bureaucratic Gestapo harried our lives with its incessant exactions and interdictions on freedom of action, what money we made was our own to spend as we pleased, the pubs remained open at all hours and whores promenaded the pavements at nightfall openly soliciting for custom. No better world could have been invented in which to spend the feckless years of youth. . .[19]

It was in short the world of the Victorian village on a larger, more exciting scale. Indeed, to Leon Gellert, Lindsay confessed with singular imagery that his real affinity was with the mid-Victorian years of his father's youth: "The old century died in the nineties. There was a clean break, like a knife cut".[20]

In his novels, autobiographies and children's fiction, Lindsay returned to the simple world of his youth as a refuge from the depression of his thoughts: "thinking can become damned oppressive for one who lives so much alone", he confessed to Hetherington.[21] Thus *Redheap*, his favourite recreation of Creswick, was written as a relief from the horrors of the First World War. This fictional world is primarily and determinedly comic, and the comedy is crude and slapstick. It is peopled by "characters" who are as physically distinctive and energetic as the figures in his cartoons, but who are universally presented from the single-minded perspective of the adolescent youth or the small boy. Lindsay delighted in his ability to present what he called "an exclusively male earth" and his girls are purely sexual commodities who may or may not be induced to participate in a "bear up". Wheedling sex from a girl is an extension of wheedling toffee from a "Chow"; both require skilful manipulation of another who is clearly inferior but also possessed of innate cunning, and both provide temporary physical relief. Meanwhile in the community of male peers, life is either a matter of warfare between competing tribes or concerted attempts to relieve the boredom of a quiet country town. School teachers, parsons and parents are to be circumvented if possible and if not, endured. Most dreaded of all is the ubiquitous and inquisitive Ma, the natural enemy of all that is good in the eyes of a boy. This boyhood world is a slapstick one of pratfalls and blows, usually to the posterior, of physical proving and sensual enjoyments, a Hobbesian world of animal pleasure and pain, which has no room for sentiment: "All decisive gestures are acts of growing up. An act done by you: an act done to you; a bunged-up eye or a bunged-up love affair".[22] Operating according to simple schoolboy logic, it discounts the moral opprobrium usually attached to cheating, stealing, vandalism or tormenting those who are weak, socially inferior or old.

Reactions to the novels have been mixed. Although some readers have hailed Lindsay's interpretation of the boy's world as superior to Twain's, others have been dismayed by the narrator's obvious enjoyment of crudity and violence. Richard Coe, for instance, describes *Saturdee* as "one of the brashest, most vulgar and ... most mindlessly cruel of all the *Childhoods* in Western literature".[23] *Saturdee*, however, is the most light-hearted and inventive of the childhood trilogy, far removed from the stale repetitions of sexual pillage that characterise *Halfway to Anywhere,* and relatively uncomplicated by the physical adult drives that make the hero of *Redheap* a consummate ocker. Relationships in this early novel have some suggestion of inner life, whereas in the succeeding novels even relationships between close friends are merely a matter of aligned interests.

Lindsay himself found this rediscovery of boyhood irresistible, frequently reading aloud from the novels to visitors with great hilarity. During his years in Sydney he also tried more direct re-experience of boyhood by frequently employing a telescope to spy on children at play, watching their antics for hours.[24] He appears to have found boyhood a period of instinctive vitalism, of "true innocence of the senses" and unthinking "concretion of personality", to use the terms of *Creative Effort.* Boyhood was a precious period of freedom from what he later called "the malady of thought" as well as from externally imposed rules and laws. If Robert Piper is minimally governed by the strictures of Ma, he nourishes an instinctive contempt for adult values, which is heartily endorsed by his author. The mother-figure is clearly the first wowser in the Lindsay eschatology. It is partly Robert's frank acceptance of himself and his friends as hedonist animals that Lindsay admires:

> They played cards, smoked, drank, sang, and were uplifted. To Robert, this was Life transfigured. *There was not a doubt in his universe.* Happiness was as concrete as a beer bottle.[25]

The same simple male confidence characterises Lindsay's memory of his brother, Lionel:

> He was the perfect prototype of the big brother, a dominant figure among his fellows and a competent exponent of the life crudely masculine. As such, he was the perfect boy. In him were compacted to excess all the worthy attributes of the junior male ego. *There were no cloudy complexities in the forthright statement of his needs and aspirations. Those were sacrosanct.*[26]

A figure of unremitting, uncontrollable activity and natural authority, Lionel is seen as effortlessly impressing himself on his world; he is the perfect expression of the self-absorbed, self-contained "male dominant" to use Lindsay's characteristic term. Like Perce, his indolent brother, and Dr Lindsay, his father, he has the quality of "aplomb" which Norman admired and longed to emulate.[27]

It is curious that Lindsay's accounts in *My Mask* and *Bohemians of the Bulletin* of the later years of his nineties youth when he first joined the *Bulletin* share many of the features of the novels. Once again the community is, as Lindsay explicitly remarks, a village one: the writers of the *Bulletin* are "a group in which all prominent identities are known to one another, as they are in a village, or a small country town."[28] Once again it is an exclusively male world; the only women to figure are down-trodden or unsympathetic wives or "useful" models, although there is a brief glimpse of the young Miles Franklin, characteristically described in cheesecake terms: "a superb mass of black hair in a cascade that reached her pert rump, to match a pert nose with fine eyes and arched black eyebrows, and an alluring pair of lips".[29] Male camaraderie, however, may depend on agreement about the female sex, and Lindsay devotes one chapter to his unnecessary quarrel with Dorrington over a girl friend, while his enthusiasm for Archibald is cemented by the latter's courageous struggle in the cause of men wrongly accused of rape. As in the novels, figures are sharply individual and energetic, graphically seized in moments of self-absorbed action. Like the boys of Creswick, they lead competitive, roistering lives filled with physical and verbal abuse, male proving and sexual pursuit. Lawson is pictured hitting Bertram Stevens over the head, A. G. Stephens as scampering back to his office to avoid a beating, Bedford as perpetually spoiling for a fight, Abbott as provoking and winning a fight when drunk. If Lindsay has great admiration for the self-possessed man of action like Paterson, who "compacted in himself all that is best in the Australian national ego", anticipating the tough outback fighting men of Gallipoli, he has nothing but contempt for Lawson's alcoholism. Comparing the self-images of both men, he expatiates on the inevitable conflict between those who function "on the higher levels of consciousness" and the underdogs who threaten society with their simmering resentment. The most dangerous underdog of all, of course, is Christ, described here as the "Messiah of a Communistic rabble". Life at the *Bulletin* and at *Redheap* is also similar in that relationships appear to have little depth. Lindsay presents himself as a detached observer of these male "types", interested in their idiosyncrasies but removed from any intimate knowledge. Hop keeps him at arm's length, Paterson tolerates him as a riding companion, but keeps "a distance between these easy exchanges", Stephens turns into an enemy after a ridiculous incident with a horse which detracts from his masculinity. Towards Rod Quinn and Steele Rudd, Lindsay is distinctly patronising; for the failings of Lawson and Stone he has a great contempt. Edmond is careful to keep their relationship at a professional level, but predictably wins Lindsay's approval for his "rejection of any sentimentality for the stresses of life and a delight in its spectacle". Stone is initially praised because he wrote "with the clinical detachment of a psychologist immune from any personal association with the people he wrote about." The treatment of Stone's nervous breakdown is a transparent and painful illustration of Lindsay's inability to sympathise with inward difficulties. Dismissing his illness as a "wilful collapse", designed to avoid facing up to the challenge of his talent, he describes his last encounter with his old friend in a hotel, ignoring Stone's silent appeal as he watched him in the bar mirrors.

One of the most overused words in Lindsay's vocabulary is "spectacle". The most admired books are those which reflect the polyglot spectacle of humanity, Stone's "visual reality which brought [Sydney's] people vividly before the reader's eye", or Dyson's creation of picturesque slum types in *Fact'ry 'Ands*. The stress on the visual appreciation of reality is characteristic for Lindsay distrusts any other way of knowing. In *Bohemians of the Bulletin,* for instance, he remarks:

> What a man thinks, or writes about himself, has very little validity. It is by his speech, gestures, actions, the very intonation of his voice, by the contour and expression of his face, that his contemporaries decide what sort of man he is.[30]

And in the Preface to *My Mask* he suggests that a writer's statements about his state of mind are "not to be accepted as valid". The inner life can not be known for the writer is as much the "dupe of his 'mask' as any of his contemporaries"; only by watching himself act can he guess at himself: "Much better to let reminiscence stay at the spectacle of life itself. There was some fun to be got out of that, anyway". The whole tone of this short Preface, dated 1957, is remarkably weary, betraying not only a hopeless acceptance of the world as a "lunatic asylum" but a wry sense of bewilderment at the lived life, and distance from the acting self: "This [autobiography] I have written to extract what entertainment I can out of the spectacle of myself as a puppet jerked about by the strings of an irresponsible destiny". It is no surprise to discover that Lindsay found Browning's "Childe Roland" a fascinating poem, describing it in *My Mask* as saying everything that can be said about the quest of "that dark tower of the self; the self that you have dedicated yourself to finding in the blind, Bedlamite struggle to retain your foothold in that river of life, 'so petty and so spiteful'".[31]

This bewilderment about the self, incidentally, casts an interesting light on Lindsay's development of the concepts of "consciousness" and the "concrete personality" in *Creative Effort* and *Madam Life's Lovers.* As with so much else in his credo, his individual psychological anxieties and needs are the real basis of his intellectual affirmations; *Creative Effort* is well titled for it is literally an act of faith, a struggle to transform doubts into certainties, to translate what *should* be as what *will* be, to find some consolation for the barrenness of actuality in the mind's imaginings.

Jack Lindsay has traced his father's "extraordinary degree of alienation" to his lengthy experience of a skin disease in childhood and his consequent imprisonment inside while his brothers enjoyed the outdoors: "He resented his mother's control, grew deeply dependent on her, and looked resentfully and excitedly at life outside the window".[32] Hetherington's description of Norman's memory of the period is another of those illuminating word-pictures which keep cropping up in the Lindsay family's reminiscences: a sickly child, he compensated for his inactivity by sketching battle pieces in which knights clashed in deadly combat or Assyrian charioteers hurled themselves against the Babylonian hosts. His only other diversion was to watch his older brothers, particularly Lionel, at play.[33] The experience, I believe, is profoundly illuminating of Lindsay's life and work.

In *My Mask* and elsewhere Lindsay describes his acquiescent domination by Lionel during his "nineties" years. Always the central figure in any group, Lionel effortlessly and unselfconsciously accepted his position as leader. At school, when Norman finally arrived there, he protected him from bullies; at home, he taught him to read; in Melbourne he introduced him to his circle of friends, provided him with work, took a hand in his intellectual development. The relationship between the two was maliciously caught by Low, who caricatured Norman as sitting on Lionel's knee while the latter instructed his brother in his artistic credo. It is of course Lionel who is the hero of *Redheap*, just as his personality is the basis of the ideal small boy celebrated in *Saturdee* and *Halfway to Anywhere*. In the poem "Joe to Joe" written in 1918, Lindsay expresses his admiration of this burly lad's courage, as he watches "behind a window pane".

JOE TO JOE

[Written by Norman Lindsay to Lionel Linday after L.L. had sent him "The Ferns", about 1918. "The Ferns" was published in *Discobolus*, (Melbourne, 1959).]

This, I recall.
How once, upon a Winter's day
At evening's fall
I saw a burly lad at play.

Without, it rained.
Within, behind a window pane
Is at enchained,
And watched my burly lad
Bound in the rain.

He scaled the fence.
Each tree in turn he scaled
And from a height immense
Myself he hailed.
Then rushing hence,
A prop he seized
And walked upon the fence.

This I recall
As something grand — immense;
This burly lad
Gymnasting on the fence.

And this might be,
Of all the days that I recall
The epitome.
In each, a lad, robust and tall,
Has gone before
Along the road of life, where opens wide
A mystic door,
And pausing in his stride
Reached for the key
Of that dark alleyway of men's ideas
Wherein we see
The measure of our secret hopes and fears.

While I, it seems to be,
Have somewhat lagged behind
This fine activity.
Have been content to find
The spoil thrown down to me
Have been content to see
A path made free.
Perhaps perforce, behind a window pane
Have thrilled at those who have no fear of rain.

Norman also drew on the memories and experiences of his brothers Reg and Percy, but Lionel's experience was most directly exploited and in *Redheap* incidents, and even letters, recorded in Lionel's schoolboy diary are reproduced.[34] This tendency to draw on life at second-hand is also present in *A Curate in Bohemia*, which according to Lionel describes events which occurred in his circle of friends long before Norman arrived in Melbourne.[35] The early experience of observing activity from behind glass

obviously explains the visual bias of Lindsay's imag–
ination and his continued interest in "spectacle". The
experience also obtrudes into his oil paintings, I suggest,
which again and again are composed around a central
figure, posed in an attitude of responding to being watched,
both by other figures in the painting and by the implied
observer or artist. Another of Lindsay's favourite themes
for a portrait, especially when using his model, Rita, was
of the sultry, mysterious woman watching the observer of
her portrait under half-lidded eyes. The period of
seclusion may also explain his reliance on literary sources
for his art's themes and his lack of interest in the natural
world.

The last stanza of "Joe to Joe" also emphasises another
aspect of Lindsay's early years which appears to
contradict his fascination with physical activity, that is
his memory of his own timid passivity: secure behind his
window pane and "content to find the spoil thrown down",
he had "thrilled at those who have no fear of rain". This
impression is reinforced by Norman's memories elsewhere
and by the reminiscences of others. Lionel, for instance,
frequently refers to his quiet, background role both at
Creswick and in Melbourne, Darryl Lindsay's most
glutinous memory of his brother is of Norman at thirteen,
sitting inside on a cold day and being fed buttered toast by
old Ellen, the maid. In *Bohemians of the Bulletin* Lindsay
recounts, still with retrospective amazement, his skill in
countering a threatening larrikin, while his account of
Abbott is ruffled by the memory of his terror of the latter's
reckless driving. Fear is also one of the most persistent of
his childhood memories:

> I remember a constant preoccupation with the sense of terror,
> though in my case, I believe it was less a desire to test my own
> courage than the intrinsic desire to feel an emotional thrill... I
> was a horrid little coward of blows as a kid, though I believe
> the worst part of those fears was the degradation of being
> hammered publicly, and thereafter exhibiting the shame of tears.
> I still think that we suffer most in pain an outraged sense of
> decency, and that a man strives in bodily agony to preserve his
> self-respect by an air of stoicism.[36]

Lindsay's actual ambivalence about the rough world of boyhood is also illustrated by his description in *My Mask* of the happiest time of his childhood as the six month period when he secretly expelled himself from State school and spent the time drawing in solitude: "happiness remained the substance of every breath I drew the moment the horizons of quartz and mullock cut off evil communications from the earth beyond them".[37] Amongst the biographical metaphors which express the paradox that was Norman, one of the most potent is the memory of him contentedly crafting his ship's models as a refuge from "the malady of thought". Becalmed in a bottle, the ship's model is a perfect image of his enduring land-lubber's interest in the sea and swashbuckling seafarers, his fascination with the life of action from a safe distance, and his persistent attempt to tame everything that teased his imagination by freezing it in art.[38]

Similarly the bohemian life that Lindsay celebrates in his art bore no resemblance to his real life. As Jack Lindsay remarks, "Norman's experience of life was slight".[39] Norman himself frequently admitted in his letters and autobiographies that he never had any capacity for debauch in actuality.[40] It is the imagination of debauch that fascinates him, and the titillating experience of anticipating physical love. Nor did alcohol play a prominent role. for despite his tolerance of drunkards in his novels, Lindsay was as wowserish on the subject in daily life as his Methodist grandfather. Beverley Nichols recalls the contrast between Norman's praise of wine "as though he were a Bacchanalian" and his actual tasting of a mouthful "taken with pursed lips, as an old lady takes her tea".[41] As always the personal ambivalence is erected into a philosophical shibboleth. In *My Mask* Lindsay remarks that "Desire as an image is more potent than its febrile gratification in the flesh", while the love affair foregone has value in creating "the illusion that life could have been the thing it never can be".[42] The importance of desire and love of the ideal is, of course, one of the main tenets of *Creative Effort*, but Lindsay makes it clear that the ideal can never be found in the actuality of life, only

suggested via the work of the elect, great artist who
responds to the symbol of perfection already implanted in
his mind. As Mr Bandparts, his mouthpiece in *Redheap*,
puts it: "We never realise that the conception of desire is
its realisation and the effort to achieve it by the gesture of
action a mad fantasy".[43]

As Bandparts's comment implies, the other side of the
coin of such idealism about women and sex is cynicism, and
indeed Lindsay gave frequent indications that he had
little interest in women as individuals, and nourished a
great contempt for the "feminine". If he prided himself on
transcending the individual in his art in favour of woman's
mysterious essence, he generally equated the feminine
with sentimentality and even stupidity. In *Creative Effort*
he is contemptuous of "those feminine half-minds" who
find an answer in religion, and describes Christ as a "half
intelligent, a feminine mind, excited, suffering and
sentimental";[44] "feminine" as a term denoting female
attitudes is always denigratory in Lindsay's writing
although male interest in the female is a qualification of
manhood.[45] Meanwhile he is devastatingly frank on the
subject of the female as a fecund field of otherworldly
qualities waiting to be ploughed by the male. Since "all
consciousness in the male mentality has its genesis in the
mystery of sex", women "are a first essential in the
adventure of the male ego". The male ego "reaches its
supreme awareness of masculinity by contact with a
feminine earth", for by bestowing sexual experience on the
male, the female bestows "the complete accolade of
manhood". If they are to "perform their function on the
male ego [girls] must be viewed from an exclusively male
earth". Sex is "the most vital of all issues, the stimulus of
Life's rebirth",[46] and sexually responsive women are
symbols of the Life Force. (Women who are not
accommodating to the male sex urge are dismissed as
"harpies", or frustrated spinsters, doomed to misery). Thus
the female is absolutely essential as a passive resource for
the male's development of "consciousness", although she is
literally a physical resource; Lindsay's concept of Mind
seems to exclude any notion of a female intelligence, just as

his artist's heaven is an exclusive male club. If on the one hand, woman is invested with tremendous power in that man is seen as incomplete without her, on the other she is shorn of power in that she is reduced to a force of nature, the semi-sentient, mindless "She". It is not surprising that Lindsay's nudes have often been described as "impersonal", embodiments of all that is mysterious in their sex. Douglas Stewart, for instance, praises Lindsay's evocation of the "strange timeless calm" of the female, which he believes to be "the very heart of the mystery of women.... Could you offer her love? Perhaps, but the secret of her being would elude you; she could never be possessed body and soul; she is beyond us, the eternally unattainable".[47] Put differently, his nudes express the familiar function of the earth mother, they are expressions of all that the male feels is awesomely and powerfully other to himself; expressing on the one hand threat of engulfment, on the other they offer all the riches of life. Simone de Beauvoir has described this age-old response to woman in terms that perfectly dovetail with Lindsay's artistic aspirations:

> "Embracing her, it is all the riches of life that the lover would possess. She is the whole fauna, the whole flora of the earth; gazelle and doe, lilies and roses, downy peach, perfumed berry, she is precious stones... the blue of the sky, the cool water of springs, air, flame, land and sea... Nothing lies deeper in the hearts of men than this animism."[48]

If Lindsay's nudes are often presented as embodiments of all that is desirable, they are also flirtatious figures, potentially withholding their gifts; in any event, it is they who are in command of the situation. Sometimes they are threatening. In some paintings, as Jack Lindsay has pointed out, they are figures of oppressive power and demonic purpose, creatures from a Bosch-like hell. This aspect is well illustrated in the self-portrait on p.310.

Female impersonality is expressed rather more crudely in the novels. Girls are "pieces" who differ only in bodily shape, hair colour and class, while the physical delights they provide are comforting at an almost infantile level: contemplating the house of the Reverend Kneebone, Robert is possessed by the thought that "several yards of ill-kept garden and a brick wall was all that lay between himself and a charming girl, plump, soft, and warm as a cat". Watching the unresponsive housemaid, Maggie, he is frustrated by the social structure that erects a barrier between master and servant: "Would its trivial economics never learn that even a scrambled embrace in a little hot back bedroom, close with the peculiar odour of servant girls, was well worth having".[49] Critics have sometimes remarked on Lindsay's inability to move beyond adolescent passion, but the preferred sensual experience seems to be even more regressive still. In the novels the threatening aspect of the female is confined to the mother figure, bent on subduing the libido of her son; fathers are either ineffective or the agents of this virago. She is the physical disciplinarian, invariably waiting, whip in hand, behind the door for the errant teenager and even the nineteen-year-old Robert Piper has to submit to her undignified punishments.

This figure accords with the mother that Lindsay presents in *My Mask*. Frankly siding with his pleasure-loving father, Lindsay presents his mother as a "satanically strong-willed" woman, inveterately opposed to pleasure, puritanical on the subject of sex and committed to a narrow, spiritually impoverished religion. His father, on the other hand, emerges as a rather older boy, a more charming Robert Piper, reluctantly subject to his wife's disapproving strictures and finding a natural relief in alcohol and possibly extra-marital affairs. Even his financial difficulties, which eventually required the help of his children, are seen as an admirable avoidance of the curse of money-grubbing. Dr Lindsay enjoys the freemasonry of the road, and the adventurous, hard-riding life of outdoors, whereas Mrs Lindsay is predictably a "Her Indoors".

Both Lionel and Darryl Lindsay have repudiated this picture of their mother, who emerges in their auto-biographies as the uncomplaining mainstay of the family; Lionel suggests that Norman resented his early dependence on her and irrationally blamed her for the years of illness spent indoors. One does not have to be much of a psychologist to understand the effects of this early ambivalent experience of the powerful mother. Both attracted and repelled by the masculine life outside the window, and dependent on the comfort provided by the mother figure, it is likely that Norman invested her with his own fears of the outside life and his own contempt for those fears. Certainly, he appears never to have recovered from the infantile ambivalence commonly generated by the mother. Dinnerstein and others have described the child's perception of the mother as an inchoate, all-embracing, quasi-natural presence before she becomes a person with a subjectivity of her own. Even when she does become a person she retains much of this awesome power, and when it is clear that she is a female in a world of males and females, femaleness may continue to be the embodiment of these inchoate, all-embracing qualities. In Dinnerstein's terms, Lindsay could be seen as permanently avoiding the knowledge that the mother was human, and as perceiving all women in consequence as "quasi persons, quasi humans", while reserving "unqualified human personhood" for the male.[50] Investing the powerful female with all his own longings for beauty, poetry, harmony and relationship, while simultaneously neutralising her power by transforming her into a mindless, impersonal force of nature, Lindsay made himself hostage to his own neurotic anxieties. Ironically, his dilemma was no doubt exacerbated by his constant struggle to surmount despair; as Jack Lindsay has commented, "Norman revealed both an extraordinary degree of alienation and a ceaseless struggle against it".[51]

The split in Lindsay's sexual self is marvellously illustrated by the painting of Ajax's rape of Cassandra by the Victorian painter Solomon J. Solomon. Introduced to the painting in the Ballarat Gallery by his Methodist grandfather, a man with whom he had some affinity according to Lindsay himself and others,[52] the young Norman thoroughly shared the old man's unlikely enthusiasm, spending long hours in studying Solomon's style. Nearly every autobiography of the Lindsay family

Solomon J. Solomon (1860–1927), *Ajax and Cassandra* 1886, oil on canvas 335.3 x 152.4 cm, purchased 1888, Ballarat Fine Art Gallery, Victoria

Norman Lindsay, *Self Portrait*, 1930, Lin Bloomfield Galleries, North Sydney

mentions the influence of the painting, and Lindsay describes its impact at length in *My Mask*. George Enyi sees *Ajax and Cassandra* as standing for "what Lindsay lastingly sought: statuesque beauty, the flowing curve of limbs, the light and shadow of moulded forms".[53] But the painting is far more interesting as an anticipation of Lindsay's perception of the self as incomplete. That Solomon's *Ajax and Cassandra* is the expression of a male fantasy of dominance by an efficient, unconcerned Rambo-like figure is obvious. There is no doubt about Ajax's "aplomb", the quality that Lindsay so admired in the male. Equally obvious is the dehumanising of Cassandra into a haunch of female flesh; conveniently faceless, contrastingly white and ineffectively protesting, she anticipates Lindsay's impersonal nudes and his repetitive treatment of dark/white figures. Most interesting of all, the figures are welded into one, even though Cassandra is perched on her ravisher's shoulder in a most unlikely fashion; the powerful male, certain of his right and indifferent to the individuality of the female, appropriates her mysterious, beautiful essence as his complementary half, solving the sexual split in a way that Lindsay longed to emulate. In the iconography of Lindsay's career it as if this painting stands at one, optimistic extreme, while the self-portrait, portraying the artist as manacled and oppressed by his antithetical male/female figures, stands at the despairing other.

The whole fascinating subject of Lindsay's sexual ambivalence, and its relationship to his aesthetic, is as yet virtually untouched, but it appears that the sexual antithesis was the source of most of the antitheses that structured his thinking. Projecting his own conviction of a severed self on to the world, Lindsay was perpetually locked into binary patterns of thought: art versus money-grubbing, culture versus the mob, vitalist versus wowser, the solitary life of Mind versus the confusions of the human city, classicist versus modernist, Anglo-Saxon versus Negro or Jew, matter versus spirit, "man the image-bearer" versus "woman the child-bearer", celibacy versus promiscuity, the Blonde Venus versus the Dark Lady, satyr versus alabaster nude, ideal versus real. Both his epistemology and his ontology are rooted in antithesis: "All imagery of life is based on a conflict of antithesis. To know what a thing is, one must also know what it is not." In 1957 he could still maintain that war provided "the whole spectacle of life at its supreme point of antithetical conflict".[54] The same pattern of thought is at the heart of *Creative Effort*, where the struggle of the creative mind for Truth is said to depend on experiencing antitheses. In this defiant credo Lindsay transforms his doubts to certainties, consoles his fears and griefs with a private system of religion and labels his dreams truths. Leap-frogging to his affirmations of immortality over the backs of a series of breathtaking non sequiturs, he invests his emotional proclivities with the dignity of "philosophical" reasoning.

"I am always surprised to find how much the emotions of childhood have to do with all the serious efforts of later life. I believe I have never tried to experience or accomplish a thing that I had not long ago prepared for by striving to experience it in youth", wrote Lindsay in 1917 with unusual insight.[55] Preoccupied as he was with the golden years of his youth, even he did not realise how much his "nineties" had determined his future.

A. W. Jose and the Nineties: Living, Remembering, Constructing a Decade

Teresa Pagliaro

A. W. Jose's *The Romantic Nineties* (1933) has been described as one of those works which "fostered the legend of the Nineties".[1] Jose himself anticipated the objection that he was idealising the past, and addressed the notion that he was romanticising:

> Sometimes one pauses to wonder, Were the Romantic Nineties really romantic?" There is no doubt about the answer. They were, not merely to us looking back on them, but to us living in them.
>
> *(The Romantic Nineties, p27)*

This essay will consider his life and literary career in the 1880s and 1890s in order to arrive at some understanding of why the final decade of the last century seemed special to him; it will also examine his construction of these years in *The Romantic Nineties*.

The romance of the 1890s for Jose derived from his personal circumstances as well as the variety of projects in which he was engaged. Angus & Robertson employed him part time as publisher's reader and reviser from about 1893. In this capacity he saw himself as contributing to the birth of Australian literature; he also devoted himself to the task of cultivating an audience for the new writers through his educative projects and activities. These included his histories, *The Growth of the Empire* (1897) and *A Short History of Australasia* (1899), and his work with the University Extension Movement.

Before we consider these we need to look at the personal circumstances of Jose's life from the 1880s until the turn of the century. Various factors marked off the Nineties as a turning point. It was not until then that Jose was to find stimulation and a cultural milieu in Australia similar to that of England. He had arrived in the colonies late in 1882 after a year spent in Oxford. The contrast between his life there and the emptiness of his first emigrant years is brought out in a letter where he writes of "the terrible weariness that comes of intellectual and spiritual isolation".[2] Even allowing for self-dramatization, the impression Australia made was stark and bleak. References in letters to occasional encounters with people interested in literature reveal his pleasure at such events, and more importantly that these are an exception, not the rule. Remembering Oxford friends, he writes, "I would give my right hand to have but one hour of talk with the circle around Carter's fire".[3] The Eighties were a low point in Jose's life. The memory of those "dull years" was with him still in the 1930s. Indeed these later, quieter years, might well have brought them back to him, casting a glow on the 1890s. For it was then that Jose had met a wide circle of friends and acquaintances at Angus & Robertson's and the University of Sydney — various writers and artists, colleagues and people in the publishing world: Christopher Brennan, R. F. Irvine, D. H. Souter, George Lambert and George Robertson among others.

In Jose's need for an immediate circle of acquaintances to share ideas, we can see a desire for a wider and richer cultural world in Australia. The Nineties seemed romantic to him because in the increased literary activity he saw the beginnings and promise of such a world. He saw the birth of what he identified as Australian literature:

> Here we were experiencing rather a naissance than a renaissance; ... Assuredly the songs of young Australia were not always tuneful, and her art was anything but languorous and dreamful ... Every one sang. Everything Australian was worth writing about, in verse, if possible.   (*RN*, p.28)

There were political implications here for he saw the birth of Australian literature as an indispensable precondition for the birth of a new nation. Jose's dream for federation was central to his vision of Australia. He shared the nationalistic fervour of the *Bulletin*, but his was an imperialist not a republican nationalism.

The literature which Jose saw developing and which he so valued was influenced by a combination of the literary movements of the nineteenth century: realism (of the Kiplingesque sort) which exacted precise and personal observation of details of the writer's world; romanticism which emphasised the landscape either in an ideal or a Gothicised form; and nationalism itself. This combination of canons of overseas thought, realised in the work of Australian writers like Paterson, Lawson and Dyson, created the impression for many of a golden age in literature. Nor was the intense literary activity merely an Australian phenomenon. Hobsbawm has observed that during the 1880s and 1890s the "arts flourished remarkably and over a wider area of civilization than ever before".[4]

In Australia, Jose, working at Angus & Robertson, was at the heart of the literary activity. The publication in book form of many of the *Bulletin* writers must have seemed a milestone, giving their work an air of permanence. Jose revised the work of a number of writers in the 1890s: among the well known are J. Brunton Stephens, John Farrell, Henry Lawson, "Banjo" Paterson, Edward Dyson and Victor Daley. Authors' reactions to his editing varied, but they were mainly favourable. In the 1890s his editing was conservative and non-interventionist and marked by a wish to favour the author's intentions. Two chief aims become apparent: to ensure the work was of a professional standard and to enhance the authors' desires to prepare their work for the English market.[5]

But one of the problems Jose faced in editing was linked with one which was inherent in writing poetry (in particular) in Australia, the problem of the audience. Vivian Smith has observed:

> Poets who identify too easily or too exclusively with what they interpret to be the stream of high culture often run the risk, or yield to the temptation, of the literary, the mannered, the poetical or the rhetorical; while the popular poets sometimes give the impression of machines churning out reams of poetical jingle ...

> But it is probably true to say that a poet needs to keep his
> distance between extremes ... the poet has to find his way
> between too close an identification with an easy and complacent
> audience, or between too stifling a sense of remoteness from any
> audience at all.[6]

There was a polarization of styles among Australian
writers in the 1890s: those like Christopher Brennan,
Brereton and Daley, revealing the influence of French poets
and aesthetic preoccupations, while others, like Dyson and
Lawson who adopted colloquial English, partly because
they thought they would thus be comprehensible to the
people of whose lives they wrote. Just as it was the poet's
task to find the middle ground, Jose, particularly in his
editing of popular poets, saw as his task to revise in such a
way that the writer's style neither distracted, or jarred,
nor lost its unique appeal. As E. A. Badham indicated,
there was a danger the audience would become restricted if
broad Australian were adopted.[7]

But the problem of a sense of audience was aggravated
where England was concerned. Writers had to consider not
only a changing Australian audience but also one which
was hypothetical or imaginary, of which they knew
nothing. The ignorance in Australian literary circles of the
English audience was typified in the Nineties by the
surprise at English indifference to Daley's *At Dawn and
Dusk*.[8] Jose may have written in 1933 that the London
critics' neglect of Daley "broke forever the old bad
tradition that London's approval was worth something"
(*RN*, p.13); but, if there was annoyance at the time,
underlying it was a desire to receive critical acclaim in
England. In 1900 A. G. Stephens and Jose set up the
Australasian Literary Agency in London. The English lack
of interest in Australian literature was summed up by
Daley in his "When London Calls":

> The story-teller from the Isles
>   Upon the Empire's rim,
> With smiles she welcomes — and her smiles
>   Are death to him ...
>
> And when the poet's lays grow bland,
>   And urbanised, and prim —
> She stretches forth a jewelled hand
>   And strangles him.

The central problem for the Australian author writing for two audiences was the problem of style. Daley questions whether Australians, in their attempts to accommodate English taste, were not robbing their style of its essential individuality.

The basic technical problem confronting Jose in his editing of Dyson and Lawson was that of language. His revisions were all the more critical in the Nineties for it has been noted that during this decade Australian writers were beginning to adopt colloquial and idiomatic speech.[9] There was as well a degree of linguistic experimentation, a search by writers for a natural voice. Jose's comments on proofs reveal that he was sensitive to this: his aim in revising the various stylistic elements was to convey a natural effect. This can be seen in his editing of Dyson's *Rhymes from the Mines* and Lawson's *While the Billy Boils,* the two works whose extant drafts and proofs provide the most information concerning Jose's revisions in the Nineties. One of the linguistic experiments which had more unfortunate effects, and which Jose sought to modify, was the fashion for using phonetic spelling. Jose saw that in both Lawson and Dyson there were two categories: that which did indicate a different pronunciation to standard English (whether dialect or broad Australian); and that which he termed "useless" misspelling. In his Notes to Dyson, Jose wrote:

> **General Note.** I believe Mr. Robinson has said something about the spelling. I was talking to Henry Lawson about his, & he agreed that a) there ought to be no *useless* mis-spelling (i.e. "sez", because it doesn't indicate a mis-pronunciation) b) it is simpler to leave the g's in: people will drop them in reading if they usually do so. His tales are g'd almost everywhere in the book.[10]

The comment is important because it reveals his dislike of a frequently used nineteenth-century device: the writer presumes that the reader, in observing the misspelling, would identify the character as an ignoramus. It has the quality of an ironical joke shared between author and reader, and was employed by Dickens and further popularised by Kipling. For Lawson and Dyson to adopt this device would have been particularly inappropriate, since they identified their characters with the lives of ordinary people and sought to accommodate their language to them; parody clashed with the overall intention.

Furthermore Dyson's attempts to represent the vernacular by misspelling become monotonous. Jose apparently felt, too, that Dyson's inconsistency with spelling even with one character (for example, "'n'", "an'", "and" for "and") was weakening rather than strengthening the dramatic impact of his poems. So in many cases Jose recommended that Dyson adopt orthodox spelling.

Jose took something else into account in his editorial revisions of style. He distinguished carefully between narrator and characters. Whereas technical ineptitude was revised universally, there is a greater toleration of the unorthodox in the speech of the characters than in that of the narrator. Where the author is narrator Jose preferred the use of orthodox language, believing that "It spoils the effect of dialect pieces if stories told as by you personally are badly spelt".[11] But Dyson has often fused the roles of narrator and character, and Jose probably felt that he failed to create a convincing workingman-narrator. That was a task beyond his command of the vernacular, over which Lawson possessed a much stronger grasp.

Jose's different approach to Lawson's work contributed to the creation of the narrator as "bush-yarner". As elsewhere he opposed the presentation of the narrator as semi-literate. In this he anticipated the English critic who wrote in his review of *Joe Wilson and His Mates* :

> These stories are so good that (from the literary point of view of course) one hopes they are not autobiographical. As autobiography they would be good; as pure fiction they are more of an attainment. We think the author will see what is meant here ... The Australian poet's name was surely Kendall, and not "Kendel" (p.61) "She was always impulsive save to me sometimes" (p.96). If the author will think that over he will decide that he did not mean to use the word "impulsive", or not, at all events, without some qualification. "A character like what 'Kit' might have been" (p.160). This phrase must be amended before the book goes into a second edition, as the reviewer hopes it will. Also, on p.313, the awkward reiteration of "bush fashion" requires correction.[12]

The reviewer, in citing various "mistakes" and expressing his wish that "from the literary point of view, of course one hopes the stories are not autobiographical", is touching on the technical problem central to the stories' acceptance in England. Jose recognised that Lawson would have to combine the two roles of omniscient author and "bush-yarner" carefully in the persona of a single narrator to satisfy an English public. The bush-yarner was to be only apparently artless — not really artless. The author must supply the art. His omniscience must be evident. Unintentional mistakes would have to be deleted, and phrasing altered to avoid clumsiness. In addition, Jose thought that for the narrator the removal of slang, the heightening of the natural quality of the language, and the revision of over-formal language were desirable. Several points should be emphasised. Lawson vetoed alterations he did not think suitable: his style was in a state of flux in the mid-Nineties, and there are indications that he thought the publication of his stories in book form required a more formal presentation.

Most of all, Jose bore in mind the natural and simple quality which was part of the narrator's character, a fact overlooked by one critic who has described Jose's style as mechanistic.[13] In "Across the Straits" the last sentence of the fourth paragraph had read "... and the "John Smith" (Newcastle) goes down with a "swoosh" before the cook has time to leave off peeling potatoes and pray".[14] Jose altered "and pray" to "and take to prayer", which is more like Lawson than Lawson. The opening of the second paragraph, "Last year", Jose altered to "A year or two ago" which is perhaps more natural and colloquial by virtue of its vagueness. In "The Drover's Wife" there are two important instances of Jose's revisions exhibiting a simplicity more in keeping with Lawson's anecdotal style. Jose altered:

> She has a keen, very keen sense of the ridiculous; and sometime or other she will amuse bushmen by relating this incident.
> She was amused once before in a manner similar in some respects.

as follows:

> She has a keen, very keen, sense of the ridiculous; and some time or other she will amuse bushmen with the story.
> She has been amused before like that.[15]

Lawson adopted the changes in both *While the Billy Boils* and *The Country I Come From.*

Jose also revised a tendency towards the over-formal in Lawson's work, particularly of the early 1890s, which seems to have been part of his search for an appropriate literary persona. Archaisms and Americanisms bearing an English influence are to be found . In "Remailed", Lawson had written:

> The paper is generally "bespoke" in the following manner, to wit:[16]

Here Jose deleted "to wit". There is a similar revision in the seventh paragraph:

> Or, mayhap, it might be a good joke — or the notice of the death of an old mate.[17]

Jose deleted "mayhap" (and altered "might" to "may"). In "The Union Buries its Dead" "an hotel verandah" is altered to "a hotel veranda". In "The Man Who Forgot" it is possible that Jose thought the phrase "try their larks" carried English overtones in sharp contrast with the colloquial Australian language surrounding it:

> ... but Tom interfered and intimated that if they were skunks enough to try their larks or chyack or try on any of their funny business ... [18]

He suggested the phrase be deleted.

Like J. F. Archibald, Jose manifested a preference for a sharpened, incisive style. Once more he anticipated the reaction of the London critics: a reviewer in the *Manchester Guardian,* (30 January 1901) wrote of *On the Track,* "Mr. Lawson's positively strong points are his terseness, concentration, and economic use of language." The reviewer of *The Country I Come From* and *Joe Wilson and His Mates* in *Blackwood's Edinburgh Magazine* (December 1901) wrote:

> But we see no reason why the writings of Mr. Lawson, already favourably regarded in his own continent, should not attract

attention wherever the English language is spoken, so keen is his eye for the essential, so brisk and business-like his faculty of presentation.[19]

From his experience revising at Angus & Robertson, Jose seems to have understood that one of the key problems affecting the development of Australian literature (both writers and audience, and the interaction between the two) was the low level of education, and its neglect in outback areas. Its effect on writers may be construed from comments we find on a manuscript:

> The other I had a good deal more to do with in the way of polishing the English & making it concise and readable. When submitted to me it was distinctly worth working up as the ideas of the stories are good. But it was longer winded, & very rambling, & the English was all over the shop — so to speak. I think it's readable now.[20]

Of another he wrote that it was an outstanding piece of work, but would not pay.[21] This was one factor which led to that sense among writers of a polarized audience. An important long-term and indirect method of encouraging Australian literature, he felt, would be the improvement of the existing education system to develop a middle range of readers.

Jose had taught from 1884 to 1887 at All Saints' College, Bathurst. Edwin Bean, the principal, was an acquaintance of his father, presumably from their mutual association with Clifton College, Bristol, upon which All Saints' was modelled, and where Jose himself had been educated. Jose expressed his frustration with teaching and his awareness of the low standard:

> and now back to the business of hammering square nails into round holes several sizes too small.[22]

His teaching gave him practical knowledge of possible new approaches to teaching. He commented on a school concert in Bathurst:

> The Friday night's amusement was of a less exciting kind, consisting of various pieces, part songs, solos &c by different girls at the school. Three things I noticed particularly; 1. almost absolute mechanical accuracy 2. utter want of expressive playing or singing 3. in the part songs, great preponderance of the lower parts, amounting sometimes almost to extinction of the

soprano. But none of the girls seemed to have the slightest idea of meaning of anything that they played — I should say, because they were set to play pieces which they didn't understand. I have no high opinion of the average colonial girl's intellect, though her gamey and sporting proclivities are admirable.[23]

He was involved in the revision of Conway's *English Grammar, Composition and Precis Writing*, a standard text book. Exasperated tones are detectable in his letters recounting arguments with Conway over points of grammar. The author had insisted on retaining incorrect grammatical rules simply because they had become a tradition in the Education Department. Eventually Conway acknowledged "the hopelessly confused present practice of the D. P. I.", and wrote the book in line with authoritative texts.[24]

Jose was dissatisfied with student teachers. He refers to a concerted effort he and Professor Scott were making which seemed to involve a new scheme of examination or inspection. In 1893-4, he became Public School Teachers' examiner. In his correspondence there is evidence that he was also involved with Professors Scott, Wood and MacCallum in the formation of the Teachers' Guild, the teachers' association of independent schools.[25]

Jose was an examiner with Wood of "Junior" and "Senior". In his eyes the standard of first-year university students was not high enough. In giving guidelines to an examiner he made some revealing comments:

The difference between a B & a C isn't very great, but it's a step toward cutting out the dull schoolboy element which at present makes our first year lectures a mere duplicate of fifth form school work. What's the use of paying Butler £900 a year to teach the same elementary Latin prose & translation that the schools teach. We really want our boys a year longer at school and a year later at the Univ.[26]

The standard of history teaching preoccupied Professor Wood, of whom R.M. Crawford wrote:

One task to which he gave much time was the reform of the teaching of history in the schools. His work as examiner of the "Junior" and "Senior" public examinations soon oppressed him with the evidence of bad teaching — the deadness, the 'exhibitions of the brute power of memory', the lack of ideas, the absence of any understanding why history would be taught at all ... He tried to shake the teachers out of a dull routine by talking to them, and by putting into his reports of the

> examinations ... the principles and methods which he believed would turn the dullest of subjects into the most interesting and valuable of all — 'not a burden on the memory but an illumination of the soul'.[27]

For his part, Jose recognised that more suitable text books might contribute to remedying the situation. He embarked on the writing of two history textbooks, *The Growth of the Empire* (1897) and *A Short History of Australasia* (1899).

The immediate aim of *The Growth of the Empire*, as we have seen, was to provide a new approach to the teaching of history. Jose thought textbooks should possess a clarity and vitality which interested the student, but also a wealth of detail to inspire the teacher. It is also apparent from his Preface that he hoped the book would reach a wider audience:

> For my own work I make bold to hope this fate at least — that it may interest the busy man, stimulate the indifferent man, and whet the appetite of the student (p.vii)

The same hopes for Australia's future, which he entertained as he watched Australian literature develop, inspired him to write his histories to promote the growth of an imperial-national consciousness. The two histories can be seen as an expression of imperial nationalism.

Jose's desire was that students be taught Imperial history with more emphasis on the colonies:

> Also will you let me know from what books people teach the "History of the British Empire and Constitution"? I can't get any out here that deal with things in that way — it's all British and no Empire in our textbooks.[28]

The spirit of new imperialism had received an impetus from Chamberlain's policies and was to find expression in Jebb's *Studies in Colonial Nationalism* (1905) and in Deakin's and Jose's hopes for an Imperial Secretariat to replace the Colonial Office.

In Jose's eyes, Australia could assume an importance hitherto undreamt of. It was partly a question of her natural riches, and partly that Darwinian belief expressed by Francis Adams that the Australian of the outback represented a new type whom Jose hoped would revitalise the Empire. Federation also offered the possibility of social and political innovations which could show a new path to the rest of the world.

The reviews of *The Growth of the Empire* had not all been published when Jose embarked on *A Short History of Australasia*. It is difficult now to appreciate the originality and foresight Jose showed in writing it. It was the first school textbook of Australian history, and was unrivalled until Ernest Scott's *A Short History of Australia* (1916) was published. Like *The Growth of the Empire* it was written to fill a vacuum. The main aim of the book was to show Australians the magnitude of their achievement in settling the country — the hardships and vicissitudes they had overcome, the obstacles and difficulties of exploration.

Jose's history blended instinct with a patriotism characteristic of his age. It might well have been that, in fostering among school children an appreciation of Australia's past, his book was fundamental in generating the new growth of interest in Australian history which developed towards the beginning of World War I. Among those he affected in the rising generation was the Anzac historian Charles Bean, whom he had taught at All Saints'.[29]

The idea of his histories grew out of Jose's work with the University Extension Movement. In his account of the Movement in *The Romantic Nineties*, Jose wrote that the University authorities recognised the intellectual curiosity of those in the country areas, and sought to remedy the situation. Jose referred to their lack of knowledge and, by implication from the context, to their deprivation; he quoted the opinion of a friend of long experience in the bush:

> Australians probably know less to start with than men of the same class in England; but they're infinitely more eager for knowledge and more capable of absorbing it. (*RN*, p.60)

In 1893 Jose was appointed Organizing Secretary of the Extension Scheme: in 1894 and 1895 enrolments in the lectures peaked at 934 and 727.[30] This position involved wide travelling throughout N.S.W. to decide where centres might feasibly be established.

One of Jose's hopes for the Scheme was that it would interest men of varying educational levels. It is significant that Edwin Bean described Jose's style as "both popular and refined". Jose's comments on the composition of the audience of his first lecture are worth noting:

> All sorts were there — Catholic priests, Baptist, Wesleyan, Presbyterian, Congregational, Anglican clergymen, two doctors, plenty of ladies, Mr. Bean, several old A.S.C. boys *and* (most important for the success of the lectures) a plumber, a working bricklayer, and other artisans and tradesmen.[31]

In *The Romantic Nineties,* he referred to miners, sheepmen, railwaymen, bank managers, school teachers, editors, school children. Jose hoped that the University Extension Scheme would supplement existing educational opportunities in rural areas. The courses would provide a breadth, a context and a tradition for aspiring writers, students and the general public. Jose lectured on a variety of topics, notably on English Literature and British History.[32] To gain some idea of the standard of the courses and students we can turn to Crawford's account of Wood's opinion of the scheme:

> The lectures he gave to extensions classes did not differ from those he gave in the University, and he used many of them in his university courses ... his extension classes contained some people as intelligent as the best of his university students. Certainly, he took them seriously, introducing them to solid reading and offering them expositions based on continued study.[33]

Towards the end of the decade, Jose found he could not establish any more centres, and that the numbers enrolling were dropping. At this stage he entertained the idea that the more substantial country centres might offer the first year of university courses to intending students. While the University of Queensland did grow out of one centre, the proposal was not realised. The University Extension Scheme died.

In examining *The Romantic Nineties,* we should consider the circumstances in which it was written, the way Jose himself regarded the book, and the picture it presents of the decade. The work is a compilation of a series of articles Jose was invited to write on the Nineties for the *Brisbane Courier* in 1932 shortly after his return from England. There was a sense that those with first-hand knowledge of the decade were aging: "all the grandpapas of Australian literature" commented A. G. Stephens, "are falling into the yellow leaf".[34] Within about a year, Christopher Brennan (1932), John Le Gay Brereton (1933), A. G. Stephens (1933) and George Robertson (1933) had died. Similarly it was felt that there was ignorance about the important figures of the Nineties. Jose's *Australia, Human and Economic* (1932) elicited the comment from Nettie Palmer:

> Mr. Jose's considered emphasis on the important figure of J. F. Archibald is particularly welcome when we notice how such a man, writing no books of his own, and living in country (sic) where few records are made, can be forgotten. Lately in two different Melbourne groups of well-read and artistic people, old and young, I have mentioned Archibald's name, only to meet with entire ignorance of it. Can anything give us a little more consecutive existence as a society? Archibald himself did much to bring about some such depth of perspective.[35]

And Jose in *The Romantic Nineties* wrote of the reclusive Brennan:

> and men high nowadays in the educational world (this may be hard to believe, but I vouch for it) last year asked me on what authority I had described him as a great Greek scholar — Brennan, the one Australian whom even Wilamowitz-Moellendorff recognized as worth serious attention (pp.30-1).

One of the unstated aims of *The Romantic Nineties* was, it is apparent, to construct a memorial to men who might otherwise be forgotten. A noticeable feature is the emphasis on the social aspect of literary activities: Jose is peopling the literary and artistic world of the 1890s.

More importantly, he emphasises in his Preface that the book is a personal account (p. v), distinguishing it sharply from his histories. Since it is a collection of reminiscences, we become aware of the imprecision of memory (as distinct from documentary sources) and the unknown personal factors which shape it. *The Romantic Nineties* is more surprising for what it omits than for what it includes. The author refers only in passing to his work as publisher's reader and reviser, and not at all to his *A Short*

History of Australasia, yet these had more far-reaching effects than his other activities during the decade. It is likely that he considered that his work with Robertson and the flourishing publishing firm was the substance behind the romance of the Nineties.

Jose's picture of the last decade of the nineteenth century vacillates between romanticism and detachment. The romanticism reveals itself in exaggeration, and in a tendency to gloss over the forgotten causes of crucial events. We can see an indulgent recreation of the camaraderie among writers and artists in Sydney, and people in the bush, and an idealization of the University Extension audience. For example, in his description of the discovery of the bank manager absorbed in Diderot, there is an implication that such intellectual zeal was common. In his account of the collapse of the University Extension Movement he fails to mention a declining interest in the scheme; retrospectively, he has exaggerated the scheme's success. At the same time he was aware of some of the audiences' limitations. He recounts anecdotes which reveal this: a local mayor who told him circuses were more to the townsfolk's taste; a headmaster who snored all the way through his lecture, and so on.

If Jose thought Australian literature of the Nineties had become a "lost tradition" and had failed to flourish, he did not look for the reasons. By the 1930s he half believed Australia had become an intellectual backwater, and had come to think that in the Nineties things were better. He did not probe the depths of the decade, or look again at all the faults he clearly saw at the time. In writing of Lawson, and perhaps thinking of Brennan, he merely commented:

> It seems to be the curse of Australia that she somehow misuses — or at least wastes — the best brains put at her disposal. (RN, pp.16-17.)

Notes to the Text

Introduction

1. John Docker, "The Feminist Legend: A New Historicism?", in Susan Magarey, Sue Rowley, and Susan Sheridan (eds.), *Debutante Nation: Feminism Contests the 1890s*. Sydney: Allen and Unwin, 1993, p.17.

2. Bernard O'Dowd, "*Such is Life* and the Liver Thereof". Paper presented before the Institute of Arts and Literature, Melbourne, 7 September, 1922. Reprinted in part in *Southerly*, Vol.14, No.2, 1953. See p.130.

3. Figures given in this paragraph are based on a count of titles listed in E. Morris Miller and Frederick T. Macartney, *Australian Literature, A Bibliography to 1938, Extended to 1950*, Sydney: Angus and Robertson, 1956.

4. See Cecil Hadgraft (ed.), *The Australian Short Story Before Lawson*, Melbourne, Oxford University Press, 1986, pp.1-56.

5. See Ken Stewart, discussion of Hadgraft's *The Australian Short Story Before Lawson*, *Australian Literary Studies*, Vol.12, No.4, October 1986, pp.538-542.

6. G. A. Wilkes, "The 1890s" in *Australian Literary Criticism* (ed. G. Johnston), Melbourne: Oxford University Press, 1962. Wilkes' article first published 1958.

7. See, e.g., A. A. Phillips, Vance Palmer, Geoffrey Serle, Russel Ward.

8. See, e.g., G. A. Wilkes. By "new criticism" in this context a combination of subjective evaluative methodology with formalist emphases in close textual analysis is implied.

9. See, e.g., H. P. Heseltine. By "Leavisism" a strong personal emphasis influenced by F. R. Leavis is implied, in conjunction with formalist emphases and close textual analysis.

10. See, e.g., Humphrey McQueen.

11. See, e.g., Graeme Davison and Leigh Astbury.

12. See, e.g. Marilyn Lake, Kay Schaffer, Susan Magarey, Sue Rowley and Susan Sheridan.

13. G. Davison, "Sydney and the Bush: An Urban Context for the Australian Legend", in J. Carroll (ed.), *Intruders in the Bush*, Melbourne: Oxford University Press, 1986, p.129. (First pub. 1978)

14. See Cliff Hanna, "The Ballads: Eighteenth Century to the Present" in L. Hergenhan (ed.), *The Penguin New Literary History of Australia*, Ringwood: Penguin Books, 1988, pp.194-209; and P. Butterss and E. Webby (eds.), *The Penguin Book of Australian Ballads*, Ringwood: Penguin Books, 1993 (introduction).

15. Susan Magarey, Sue Rowley, Susan Sheridan (eds.), *Debutante Nation*, p.xix.

16. Marilyn Lake, "The Poetics of Respectability. Identifying the Masculinist Context", *Historical Studies*, Vol.22, No.86 (1986), 116-131.

17. John Docker, "The Feminist Legend: A New Historicism", cited in footnote 1.
18. "The Feminist Legend", p.17.
19. John Docker, *The Nervous Nineties*, Melbourne: Oxford University Press, 1991.
20. John Barnes, *The Order of Things: A Life of Joseph Furphy*, Melbourne: Oxford University Press, 1990. For a feminised reading of Furphy see Julian Croft, "Who is She? The Image of Woman in the Novels of Joseph Furphy", in *Who is She?* (ed. S. Walker), St. Lucia: University of Queensland Press, 1983, pp.1-11.
21. Henry Lawson, "Some Popular Australian Mistakes", *Bulletin*, 18 November, 1893.
22. Quoted by Cecil Mann (editor), *The Stories of Henry Lawson*, Second Series, Sydney: Angus and Robertson, 1964, pp.81-2.
23. Thea Astley, "The Teeth Father Naked at Last: The Short Stories of Barbara Baynton", in her *Three Australian Writers*, Townsville: Foundation for Australian Literary Studies, 1979, pp.12-22.
24. Penne Hackforth-Jones, *Barbara Baynton*. Ringwood, Vic.: Penguin, 1989.
25. *Ibid.*
26. "Squeaker's Mate", in S. Krimner and A. Lawson (eds.), *Barbara Baynton*, St. Lucia: University of Queensland Press, 1988, p.25.
27. *Ibid.*, p.25
28. *Ibid.*, p.22
29. *Ibid.*, p.88
30. *Ibid.*, p.15
31. *Ibid.*, p.18
32. *Ibid.*, p.xii

Victorian Writers in the Nineties

1. Quoted by J. Holroyd, *George Robertson of Melbourne* (Melbourne: Robertson & Mullens, 1968, p.56.
2. Surely Tennyson also - at least Alexander Sutherland wrote a memorial poem for the *Age* (12 October 1892).
3. *Thirty Years in Australia* (London: Methuen & Co., 1903), pp.302-03.
4. *Australian Dictionary of Biography (ADB)* 5, p.310.
5. For whom, and nearly everyone mentioned in this article, see *ADB*.
6. Consider, e.g., the criticism by the Topp brothers, *Melbourne Review*, 1876, p.202, 1979, pp.108-10.
7. R. H. Croll, *I Recall* (Melbourne: Robertson & Mullens, 1939), p.17; Ada Cambridge, *Thirty Years*, p.302.
8. I shall not give references for the many following biographical sketches which are based on *ADB*, Green, Miller and Macartney, the *Oxford Companion* and other basic sources, except for quotations and to draw attention to recent illuminating work.

9. Blair to J. H. Hingston, 17 February 1895, 7 September 1896, Blair Papers, La Trobe Collection, State Library of Victoria (La Trobe Library).
10. H. Love, *James Edward Neild: Victorian Virtuoso* (Melbourne: Melbourne University Press, 1989); K. Stewart, "The Support of Literature in Colonial Australia", *Australian Literary Studies* 9 (1979-80): 479-81.
11. *Table Talk*, 6 January 1888.
12. *Age*, 15 August 1903; *Notes & Furphies*, April 1988, pp.1, 3; and see Lurline Stuart, *James Smith* (Sydney: Allen & Unwin, 1989).
13. I have closely followed Iain McCalman's entry, *ADB* 6.
14. H. McCrae, "My Father and my Father's Friends", *Story-book Only* (Sydney: Angus and Robertson, 1948), p.11.
15. *Ibid.*, pp.4, 10.
16. Has anyone ever tried to trace Caffyn papers in England?
17. Furphy to W. Cathels, 5 January 1893, Furphy Papers, Mitchell Library; C. Wallace-Crabbe, *Melbourne or the Bush* (Sydney: Angus and Robertson, 1974), pp.14-23; J. Barnes, ed., *The Portable Furphy* (St. Lucia: University of Queensland Press, 1981); Lois Hoffman, "Joseph Furphy: an Annotated Checklist of Items in Periodicals", *Australian Literary Studies* 11 (1983-84): 409-16.
18. Ada Cambridge, *Unspoken Thoughts*, ed. with commentary by Patricia Barton (Campbell: English Department, University College, Australian Defence Force Academy, 1988).
19. I. F. McLaren, *Mary Gaunt, a Cosmopolitan Australian: an Annotated Bibliography* (Melbourne: University of Melbourne Library, 1986); Patricia Clarke, *Pen Portraits. Women Writers and Journalists in Nineteenth Century Australia* (Sydney: Allen & Unwin, 1988), pp.189-93.
20. O'Hara to James Smith, 19 November 1895, Smith Papers, Mitchell Library; *Austral Light*, February 1896.
21. V. Palmer, *Intimate Portraits* (Melbourne: Cheshire, 1968), pp.103-07; R. McMullin, *Will Dyson* (Sydney: Angus & Robertson, 1984), pp.8-12; *Bulletin*, 21 November 1912.
22. M. M. Knowles, "Biographical Notes", La Trobe Library MSS 5705-07.
23. Clarke, *Pen Portraits*, pp.198-9.
24. M. E. Fullerton, "Memoirs", Moir Collection, La Trobe Library.
25. C. Hanna, "The Public Image of John Shaw Neilson", *Australian Literary Studies* 12 (1985-86): 397-400.
26. McCrae, *Story-book Only*, pp.68, 70, and "My Life and my Books", *Southerly* 33 (1973): 222-29.
27. K. S. Prichard, *Child of the Hurricane*, (Sydney: Angus & Robertson, 1963), p.52.
28. G. Serle, *From Deserts the Prophets Come* (Melbourne: William Heinemann, 1973), p.58.
29. P.7.
30. L. J. Blake, *The Land of the Lowan* (Nhill: Nhill & District Historical Society, 1976); H. Anderson and Blake, *John Shaw Neilson* (Adelaide: Rigby, 1972).
31. "The Solitary Shapers", *Melbourne or the Bush*, pp.3-12.

32. *The Yorick Club. Its Origin and Development* (Melbourne: Yorick Club, 1911); W. R. Grimwade, ed., *The Bohemians Melbourne* (Melbourne: The Bohemians, 1931); D. M. Dow, *Melbourne Savages* (Melbourne: Savage Club, 1947).
33. O'Dowd-Whitman correspondence, La Trobe Library; V. Kennedy and N. Palmer, *Bernard O'Dowd* (Melbourne: Melbourne University Press, 1954), pp.78-99; J. Jones, *Radical Cousins* (St. Lucia: University of Queensland Press, 1976).
34. *Proceedings, Royal Society of Victoria*, 1889-.
35. A. A. Wheeler, "Women's Clubs", *Centenary Gift Book*, ed. F. Fraser and N. Palmer (Melbourne: 1934); Clarke, *Pen Portraits*, passim; J. Gillison, *A History of the Lyceum Club* (Melbourne) (Melbourne: 1975), pp.19-23; *Punch*, 7 August 1890; *Bulletin*, 8 March 1890; *Table Talk*, 17 March 1893.
36. Fasoli's restaurant has gained more than its share of glory: there were other popular Continental restaurants - the Maison Doree, the Cafe Continental, the Savoy, as well as Italian wine-shops, etc. (A. S. Kenyon, *The Story of Melbourne* (Melbourne: Lothian, 1934), p.120)
37. E. Dyson Papers, La Trobe Library; Sarah Stephen, "Women, Wine and Song", *Royal Historical Society of Victoria, Journal* 55 (September 1984): 31, 33-4; *Bulletin*, 3 June 1893.
38. Australian Literature Society records, La Trobe Library; *Book Lover*, December 1900, March 1905.
39. Cited in G. Dutton, ed., *The Literature of Australia* (Ringwood: Penguin, 1964), p.278.
40. B. Nesbitt and S. Hadfield, *Australian Literary Pseudonyms* (Adelaide: Libraries Board of SA, 1972), p.5.
41. J. Barnes, ed., *The Writer in Australia. A Collection of Literary Documents* (Melbourne: Oxford University Press, 1969), p.66.
42. "Sydney and the Bush: an Urban Context for the Australian Legend", *Historical Studies* 18 (October 1978): 192. Cf. K. Stewart, *Australian Literary Studies* 13 (October 1988): 178. "The overwhelming majority of recognised colonial authors and journalists between 1860 and 1900 either were brought up in rural areas or spent a significant part of their working careers there."
Although there is ambiguity about what is the Bush, Davison's implication that those many born and brought up on the goldfields or in gold-towns had urban rather than rural backgrounds is decidedly dubious. His assertion, also, that many of the *Bulletin*'s second rank arrived in Australia as "adolescents or young adults" is not true of three of the ten he names: Astley, Broomfield and Will Lawson were small-child migrants.
43. Jephcott to O'Dowd, 13 December 1897, O'Dowd Papers, La Trobe Library; Kennedy and Palmer, *Bernard O'Dowd*, pp.121-3.
44. Quoted by C. H. Winter, *Bulletin*, Red Page, 16 January 1935).
45. *The Development of Australian Literature* (London: Longmans, Green, 1898), p.vii; A. D. Hope, "The Provincial Muse 1880-1900", *Australian Literary Studies* 8 (May 1977): 21.
46. Turner Papers, La Trobe Library.

47. "The Colonial Literati in Sydney and Melbourne", *Nellie Melba, Ginger Meggs and Friends*, ed. S. Darmody et al (Malmsbury: Kibble Books, 1982), pp.183, 188-9.
48. J. A. La Nauze and E. Nurser, eds., *Walter Murdoch and Alfred Deakin on Books and Men* (Melbourne: Melbourne University Press, 1974), pp.93-4.
49. All this correspondence is in the Deakin Papers, National Library of Australia.
50. "Alfred Deakin on Australian Literature", *Meanjin* 16 (Summer 1957): 428.
51. "Reflections after a Wandering Life in Australasia", *Atlantic Monthly* 63 (1889): 681
52. *Thirty Years*, p.303.
53. *Table Talk*, 5 June 1891; N. Palmer, ed., *Memoirs of Alice Henry* (Melbourne: 1944), pp.13-14; Knowles, "Some Causes of Discouragement to Aspiring Australian Writers", La Trobe Library MS 5668; Gaunt to W. P. Hurst, 24 July 1932, Hurst Papers, La Trobe Library MS 6107.
54. H. M. Green, *A History of Australian Literature* (Sydney: Angus & Robertson, 1961), I, pp.288-9; D. J. Mulvaney and J. H. Calaby, *"So Much that is New". Baldwin Spencer, 1860-1929* (Melbourne: Melbourne University Press, 1985), p.114.
    Here and in the following pages I am much indebted to Lurline Stuart, *Nineteenth Century Australian Periodicals. An Annotated Bibliography* (Sydney: Hale & Iremonger, 1979).
55. "The Characteristics of Australian Literature" in the November 1890 issue was probably by Morris. Academically authoritative though it seems, it illustrates his limitations. Morris's greatest contribution was to be his *Austral English* (1898).
56. R. G. Campbell, *The First Ninety Years* (Melbourne: Massina, 1949), especially p.134.
57. *History of Australian Literature*, I, p.735.
58. V. Lindesay, *The Way We Were. Australian Popular Magazines 1856-1969* (Melbourne: Oxford University Press, 1983), pp.51-7.
59. L. M. Henderson, *The Goldstein Story* (Melbourne: 1973), chs. 10, 12.
60. *Bulletin*, 23 July 1892.
61. *Ibid*, 7 October 1892; cf. H. H. Campion, *Book Lover*, 1899, p.62.
62. *Table Talk*, 28 June 1889, 29 January 1892.
63. K. Stewart, "The Support of Literature in Colonial Australia", p.485
64. Holroyd, *George Robertson of Melbourne*.
65. *Bohemia*, 21 May 1891.
66. G. B. Barton of Sydney (*Centennial Magazine*, 1889-90, pp.89-92) indignantly and emotionally complained about the state of colonial publishing and called for a Society of Authors. Cf. K. Stewart, *The Penguin New Literary History of Australia*, L. Hergenhan ed., (Ringwood: Penguin Books, 1988), pp.181-3.
67. Stewart, *ibid*, p.180.
68. Davison, "Sydney and the Bush", p.193.
69. A. W. Barker, ed., *Dear Robertson* (Sydney: Angus & Robertson, 1982), p.134.

70. *The Romantic Nineties* (Sydney: Angus & Robertson, 1933), pp.40-44.
71. L. Cantrell, ed., *The 1890s. Stories, Verse, and Essays* (St. Lucia: University of Queensland Press, 1977).

Vision Splendid or Sandy Blight? The Paterson-Lawson Debate

1. A. B. Paterson, "'Banjo' Paterson Tells His Own Story", *Sydney Morning Herald*, 11 February 1939, p.21.
2. Sylvia Lawson, *The Archibald Paradox*, Allen Lane & Penguin, Ringwood, 1983, p.125.
3. Paterson, *op. cit.*, p. 21.
4. A. B. Paterson, 'Australia for the Australians' (Sydney: Gordon & Gotch, 1889), in R. Campbell & P. Harvie, eds, A. B. 'Banjo' Paterson, *Complete Works Vol. 1, 1885-1900, Singer of the Bush*, (Sydney: Lansdowne, 1983), p.80.
5. Henry Lawson, 'The Mistakes of Other Colonies' (from the *Albany Observer*, n.d.), in Leonard Cronin, ed., Henry Lawson, *Complete Works, Vol. 1, 1885-1900, A Camp-fire Yarn*, (Sydney: Lansdowne, 1984, p.105.
6. Henry Lawson, 'The City and the Bush' (from *The Worker*, n.d.), in Cronin, p.402.
7. Henry Lawson, 'Letter to Aunt Emma', in Brian Kiernan, ed., *Henry Lawson* (St Lucia: U.Q.P., 1976), p.119.
8. Colin Roderick, ed., *Henry Lawson: Letters 1890-1922*, (Sydney: Angus & Robertson, 1970), p.49.
9. A. G. Stephens, *The Bulletin* 9 December 1899, Red Page.

Looking for Mr Backbone: The Politics of Gender in the Work of Henry Lawson

1. Marilyn Lake, "The Politics of Respectability: Identifying the Masculinist Context", *Historical Studies* 22 (1986), p.116.
2. Lake, 117.
3. For a discussion of the representation of woman in the *Dawn* see Susan Sheridan. *Along the Faultlines: Sex, Race and Nation in Australian Women's writing 1880s-1930*. St. Leonardo: Allen & Unwin, 1995. 71-80; Brian Matthews. *LOUISA*. Ringwood: Penguin, 1987. 167-85; and Chris Lee. 'Louisa Lawson: Feminism, Nationalism and the *Dawn*'. *LOUISA LAWSON: Poems with Selectef Critical Commentaries*. L. Rutherford and M. Roughley, eds. Armidale: CALLS, 1996.
4. Henry Lawson, *Henry Lawson: Prose Writings*. Vol.1 Collected Prose. Ed. Colin Roderick. Sydney: Angus and Robertson, 1984, p.413.
5. Henry Lawson, p.413.
6. Colin Roderick. *Henry Lawson: The Master Story-Teller: Commentaries on his Prose Writing*. Sydney: Angus and Robertson, 1985, p.215.

7. Carroll, John (ed.), *Intruders in the Bush*. Melbourne: Oxford University Press, 1982, p.109.
8. Henry Lawson, pp.411-12.
9. Henry Lawson, p.569. My emphasis.
10. Henry Lawson, p.569.
11. See Frederick Carpenter Shey, Hysteria: Remote Causes of Diseases in General Treatment by Toxic Agency. 2nd ed. London: Longmans, Green, Reader and Dyer, 1867, pp.54-55; James Hendrie Lloyd, "Hysteria" in Franco Xavier Denum (ed.), *Textbook on Nervous Diseases by American Authors*, Edinburgh: Pentland, 1895, p.93; J. G. Porter Phillips, "Involutional Conditions", in Frederick W. Mott (ed.) *Early Mental Disease*, London: Wakeley, 1912, p.90; Joseph Arderne Ormorod, "Hysteria", *System of Medicine* 9 (1898), p.690.
12. Porter Phillips, p.90.
13. Lloyd, pp.98-99.
14. Henry Lawson, p.373. My emphasis.
15. Henry Lawson, pp.571-572.
16. Henry Lawson, p.572.
17. Henry Lawson, p.52.
18. Frederick Norton Manning, "The Causation and Prevention of Insanity" *Journal and Proceedings of the Royal Society of New South Wales* 14 (1880), p.342.
19. Manning, p.342.
20. Stephens, A. G. "Henry Lawson", *Art in Australia*, November 1922; in John Barnes (ed.), *The Writer in Australia*, Melbourne: Oxford University Press, 1969, p.99.

Female and Juvenile Meanings in Late Nineteenth-century Australian Popular Theatre

1. Pamela Heckenberg and Philip Parsons, "The Struggle for an Australian Theatre (1910-1950) and the Decline of the Chains", in Harold Love, ed., *The Australian Stage: A Documentary History*. (Kensington: New South Wales University Press, 1984), p.125.
2. Harold Love, "Stock Companies, Travelling Stars and the Birth of 'The Firm' (1854-1900)", in Love, ed., *The Australian Stage*, p.57.
3. Love, ed., p.105. It seems odd that Boucicault should object to the popularity of his own Irish drama *The Shaughraun*.
4. Even such works as Richard White's *Inventing Australia: Images and Identity 1688-1980* (Sydney: Allen & Unwin, 1981), and Graeme Turner's *National Fictions: Literature, Film and the Construction of Australian Narrative* (Sydney: Allen & Unwin, 1986) mention theatre only fleetingly. Sylvia Lawson's *The Archibald Paradox: A Strange Case of Authorship* (Ringwood: Allen Lane, 1983) does not include the *Bulletin's* usually flippant construction of live theatre in her study of its discourses; a large field which requires examination. An exception is John Docker, who in his *In a Critical Condition: Reading Australian Literature* (Ringwood: Penguin, 1984) incorporates theatre, both art and popular, in his analyses of

the formation of critical canons, and has examined the continuity between the colonial stage and contemporary electronic media in his articles "Antipodean Literature: A World Upside Down?" in *Overland* 103 (July 1986), 48-56, and "In Defence of Melodrama: Towards a Libertarian Aesthetic" in *Australasian Drama Studies* 9 (October 1986), 63-81. In the field of theatre history, Margaret Williams in her *Australia on the Popular Stage 1829-1929: An Entertainment in Six Acts* (Melbourne: Oxford University Press, 1983) traces the bush nationalist impulse in local writing. Katherine Brisbane, ed., *Entertaining Australia: An Illustrated History* (Sydney: Currency, 1991) is a digest of more detailed information contained in the various forthcoming Currency Companions to theatre, music, film, television and radio, and is the most comprehensive overview to date of the range of the performing arts in Australia 1788 to present. Among literary histories, Terry Sturm's chapter on "Drama" in Leonie Kramer, ed., *The Oxford History of Australian Literature* (Melbourne: Oxford Press, 1981) remains the best overview of the colonial and modern periods. The role of colonial theatre's generic and industrial connections with its contemporary culture receives some welcome attention in essays by Ken Stewart, ("Journalism and the World of the Writer: The Production of Australian Literature (1855-1915)", and Elizabeth Webby "Melodrama and the Melodramatic Imagination" in Laurie Hergenhan, ed., *The Penguin New Literary History of Australia* (Ringwood: Penguin, 1988), 174-193; 210-222. The research of Eric Irvin, particularly his *Australian Melodrama: Eighty Years of Popular Theatre* (Sydney: Hale & Iremonger, 1981) and *Dictionary of the Australian Theatre 1788-1914* (Sydney: Hale & Iremonger, 1984) provide accessible data to the non-specialist, as do the essays and documents in Love, ed., *The Australian Stage*. Love's *The Golden Age of Australian Opera: W. S. Lyster and his Opera Companies 1861-1880* (Sydney: Currency, 1981) has had some dissemination beyond the theatre-history community. After the theatre-historical output of the 1980s, there is no reason to believe that basic information is unavailable, but it is only slowly finding its way into generalist cultural studies. Richard Waterhouse's *From Minstrel Show to Vaudeville: The Australian Popular Stage 1788-1914* (Sydney: University of New South Wales Press, 1990) traces the international influences on Australian popular and elitist performance culture. An important interdisciplinary study of the discursive and industrial connections between the sporting and theatrical industries, adducing original material on the construction of the dichotomies masculine/feminine, elitist/popular and English/Australian, is Richard Fotheringham, *Sport in Australian Drama* (Cambridge: Cambridge University Press, 1992).

5.   Kay Schaffer, *Women and the Bush: Forces of Desire in the Australian Cultural Tradition* (Cambridge: Cambridge University Press, 1988), p.21.

6. Susan Sheridan, "'Temper, Romantic; Bias, Offensively Feminine': Australian Women Writers and Literary Nationalism", *Kunapipi* 7, Nos. 2-3 (1985), 50-51.

7. Fredric Jameson, *The Political Unconscious* (Ithaca, N.Y.: Cornell University Press, 1981), pp.77, 142.

8. See Shirley Fitzgerald, *Rising Damp: Sydney 1870-1890* (Melbourne: Melbourne University Press, 1987) for details of urban conditions. In 1890, while Sydney had 86 miles of sewers, Melbourne had none. Infant mortality actually rose in Sydney during the 1870s and 1880s, with a rate of 194 per 1000 in 1875 (p.82). In 1870-90 the overall death rate for the white population was higher in the metropolis than the colonial average (pp.96-97).

9. See Joan Newman, "Reader-response to Transcribed Oral Narrative: *A Fortunate Life* and *My Place*" *Southerly*, 4 (1988), 376-389. Newman points out the strong oral and folk motifs in Facey's story and demonstrates their interaction with received cultural codes.

10. Michael Booth *et al.*, ed., *The Revels History of English Drama*, 6 (London: Methuen, 1975), p.265.

11. Fitzgerald, pp.76-88; 192-196.

12. "Early Settlers Gave Low Priority to Child Health", *University News* (University of Queensland), 252 (12 March 1986), pp.8-9.

13. Bryan Gandevia, *Tears Often Shed: Child Health and Welfare in Australia from 1788* (Sydney: Pergamon Press, 1978), pp.80, 92.

14. Comic or not, Little Willie was a coveted part for the juvenile (usually female) actor. In *Theatre in Australia* (Stanmore: Cassell Australia, 1978) John West reports that the young Gladys Moncrieff allegedly played the role in Dan Barry's company on its Queensland tours at the run of the century (p.87).

15. Thomas Keneally, *The Playmaker* (London: Sceptre, 1987), pp.359-60.

16. In his *Next Week - "East Lynne" Domestic Drama in Performance 1820-1874* (Lewisburg: Bucknell University Press, 1977) Gilbert Cross relegates the appeal of the domestic play to "sentimentality" and "self-pity". He does point out that "Death scenes had grim relevance when half the population died in childhood", and reclaims sentimentality as a "hopeful sign". "It was a deliberate overvaluing of the humble and the domestic in opposition to the undervaluing of them that a capitalistic economy encouraged" (p.91).

17. See Veronica Kelly, "Introduction" to Garnet Walch, *Australia Felix, or Harlequin Laughing Jackass and the Magic Bat* (St. Lucia: University of Queensland Press, 1988) pp.1-45.

18. Richard Fotheringham, "Introduction" to Alfred Dampier and Garnet Walch, *Robbery Under Arms* (Sydney: Currency/ADS, 1985), pp.xxvii-xxix.

19. Nina Auerbach, *Woman and the Demon: The Life of a Victorian Myth* (Cambridge: Harvard University Press, 1982).

20. Schaffer, p.63.

21. Schaffer, p.22.

22. Dorothy Dinnerstein, *The Mermaid and the Minotaur: Sexual Arrangements and Human Malaise* (New York: Harpur & Row, 1976) p.234.
23. Dinnerstein, pp.235-236.
24. Janet Achurch and Charles Charrington's Australian tour of *A Doll's House* (1889) is one of the turning points of colonial theatre history. The American Nance O'Neil premiered *Hedda Gabler* in Melbourne in 1900.
25. Though Dampier wrote an *East Lynne* in 1990, most texts performed here appear to be various of the innumerable English or American dramatisations. See Katherine Newey and Veronica Kelly, ed. and intro., *Ellen Wood's 'East Lynne' Dramatised by T. A. Palmer* (Brisbane: Australian Drama Studies Association, 1994).
26 . H. Chance Newton, *Cues and Curtain Calls: Being the Theatrical Reminiscences of H. Chance Newton* (London: John Lane, 1927), p.177. According to this, Wilson Barratt demanded a particular kind of play of his dramatists Henry Arthur Jones and Henry Herman: "... The play I want, and the play I mean to have from somebody or other, is a kind of *East Lynne* turned around. That is to say, instead of a fugitive wife and mother coming back disguised and being prevented from seeing or succouring her own children, I want a man (falsely accused, of course) put in the same position in the most poignant and most pathetic manner that I can get it."
27. Frank Rahill, *The World of Melodrama* (University Park: Pennsylvania State University Press, 1967), p.93.
28. Rahill, pp.203-204.
29. Some versions allowed a short-lived glimmer of recognition to the dying Willie, which is not in Wood's novel. See the 1862 New York version printed in J. O. Bailey, *British Plays of the Nineteenth Century: An Anthology to Illustrate the Evolution of the Drama* (New York: Odyssey Press, 1966), p.324.
30. See Julian Croft, "'Who is She?' The Image of Woman in the Novels of Joseph Furphy" in Shirley Walker, ed., *Who Is She?* (St Lucia: University of Queensland Press, 1983), pp.1-11, who shows that there is a romance world of 'metaphor, myth, coincidence and what could be called grace' with women at its centre, co-existing with the narrator's own "sternly determined world" but unrecognised by him (p.10).
31. Sally Mitchell, "Introduction" to *East Lynne* (New Brunswick: Rutgers University Press, 1984), p.xv.
32. For an example of a collision between the late colonial stage and the government, see Veronica Kelly, "The Banning of Marcus Clarke's *The Happy Land*: Stage, Press and Parliament", *Australasian Drama Studies*, 2 No. 1 (October 1983), 71-111.
33. "Resignation is a Crime", *The Dawn* (January 1902), quoted in Elaine Zinkhan, "Louisa Albury Lawson: Feminist and Patriot", in Debra Adelaide, ed., *A Bright and Fiery Troop: Australian Woman Writers of the Nineteenth Century* (Ringwood: Penguin, 1988), p.221.
34. In *East Lynne* Isabel is divorced by her husband; a plot device made technically possible by the 1857 English law which made female adultery the only possible grounds for divorce (see

Mitchell, p.xvii). This law and its condition passed into the various colonial legislatures from 1858 to 1873. Later amendments gave wives the power of petition, but they had to prove adultery as well as drunkenness, cruelty or desertion. Finally in Victoria (1890) and New South Wales (1892) the divorce laws allowed women to gain dissolution of the marriage on the grounds of cruelty alone. See Ruth Teale, ed., *Colonial Eve: Sources on Women in Australia* (Melbourne: Oxford University Press, 1978), pp.166-171. On the other hand paternal desertion of families was common, particularly in the Depression; enforcement of maintenance difficult; and domestic violence and alcoholism prevalent (Teale, pp.171-178).

35 . Harry Julius and Claude Mackay, *Theatrical Caricatures* (Sydney: 1912), cited in Love, p.156.

36. Cited in Toby Cole, ed., *Playwrights on Playwriting: The Meaning and Making of Modern Drama from Ibsen to Ionesco* (New York: Hill & Wang, 1961), p.165.

37. Schaffer, p.163.

38. It occurs in plays by Louis Nowra, particularly *Inside the Island* (1980) and *The Golden Age* (1985); and in Michael Gow's *The Kid* and *Away* (1986).

39. Patrocinio P. Schweikart, 'Reading Ourselves: Towards a Feminist Theory of Reading', in E. A. Flynn and P. P. Schweikart, ed., *Gender and Reading: Texts and Contexts* (Baltimore: Johns Hopkins Press, 1986) pp.42-43.

40. Janice Radway, *Reading the Romance: Women, Patriarchy and Popular Literature* (Chapel Hill: University of North Carolina Press, 1984), pp.608, 221.

41. See Deborah Campbell, "*A Doll's House:* The Colonial Response" in Susan Dermody, John Docker and Drusilla Modjeska, eds., *Nellie Melba, Ginger Meggs and Friends: Essays in Australian Cultural History* (Malmesbury: Kibble Books, 1982), pp.192-210.

42. Cited in Love, ed., p.107. See also J. E. Neild's review of the Melbourne season, pp.107-108.

43. Dinnerstein, p.236.

44. Patrice Pavis, *Languages of the Stage: Essays in the Semiology of Theatre* (New York: Performing Arts Journal Publications, 1986), p.86, quoted in Marie Maclean, *Narrative as Performance: The Baudelairean Experiment* (London: Routledge, 1988), p.35.

45 . Maclean, p.41.

46 . Irvin, *Dictionary of the Australian Theatre 1789-1914*, pp.254-55.

47. Fiona Giles, 'Romance: An Embarrassing Subject', in Laurie Hergenhan, ed., *The Penguin New Literary History of Australia*, pp.227, 233.

Postmodernism, Cultural History, and the Feminist Legend of the Nineties: *Robbery Under Arms*, the Novel, the Play

1.   See Andreas Huyssen, *After the Great Divide. Modernism, Mass Culture and Postmodernism* (London: Macmillan, 1988),

and John Docker, *Postmodernism and Popular Culture: A Cultural History* (Melbourne: Cambridge University Press, 1994).

2. Susan Sheridan, "Ada Cambridge and the Female Literary Tradition", in Susan Dermody, John Docker, Drusilla Modjeska, eds., *Nellie Melba, Ginger Meggs, and Friends* (Malmsbury: Kibble, 1982). For multicultural perspectives, see John Docker, *Dilemmas of Identity: The Desire for the other in Colonial and Post Colonial Cultural History*, Sir Robert Menzies Centre for Australian Studies, University of London, 1992.

3. Georg Stauth and Bryan S. Turner, "Nostalgia, Postmodernism and the Critique of Mass Culture", *Theory Culture and Society* V.5 ns. 2-3, 1988.

4. Tania Modleski, *Loving with a Vengeance* (New York: Methuen, 1984); Andrea Huyssen, "Mass Culture as Woman: Modernism's Other", in Tania Modleski ed. *Studies in Entertainment* (Indiana University Press, Bloomington, 1986); John Docker, "In Defence of Melodrama: towards a libertarian aesthetic, *Australasian Drama Studies* 9, 1986 and "In Defence of Popular TV: Carnivalesque V. Left Pessimism", *Continuum*, V.l, n.2, 1988.

5. Meaghan Morris, "Panorama, The Live, The Dead and The Living", in Paul Foss, ed. *Island in the Stream* (Sydney: Pluto, 1988).

6. Peter Brooks, *The Melodramatic Imagination* (New Haven: Yale University Press, 1976).

7. Marilyn Lake, "The Politics of Respectability: Identifying the Masculinist Context", *Historical Studies*, V.11, n.86, 1986, and "Socialism and Manhood: The Case of William Lane", *Labour History* 50, 1986. See also Susan Sheridan, "'Temper, Romantic; Bias, Offensively Feminine': Australian Women Writers and Literary Nationalism", in Kirsten Holst Petersen and Anna Rutherford ed.s *A Double Colonization. Colonial and Post-Colonial Women's Writing* (Denmark: Dangaroo, 1986), Judith Allen, "'Mundane' Men: Historians, Masculinity and Masculinism", *Historical Studies*, V.22, 1987, and the essays on feminism and the Nineties by Susan Sheridan, Kerry M. White and Judith Allen in *Australian Feminist Studies* 7 and 8, 1988. See also Kay Schaffer, *Women and the Bush* (Cambridge: Cambridge University Press, 1988). For essays interrogating or supporting the Feminist Legend, see Susan Magarey, Sue Rowley, Susan Sheridan, eds., *Debutante Nation: Feminism Contests the 1890s* (Sydney: Allen & Unwin, 1993).

8. Brian Matthews, "Eve Exonerated: Henry Lawson's Unfinished Love Stories", and Julian Croft, "Who is She?" The Image of Woman in the Novels of Joseph Furphy", in Shirley Walker, ed. *Who is She? Images of Woman in Australian Fiction* (St. Lucia: University of Queensland Press, 1983). See also Nina Knight, "Furphy and Romance: *Such is Life* Reconsidered", *Southerly*, n.4, 1969.

9. Mikhail Bakhtin, *The Dialogic Imagination* (Austin: University of Texas, 1981), pp.45-6.

10. Martha Vicinus, *The Industrial Muse* (London: Croom Helm, 1974), pp.10-11.
11. J. S. Bratton, *The Victorian Popular Ballad* (London: Macmillan, 1975), pp.97-8.
12. Rolf Boldrewood, *Robbery Under Arms* (Ringwood: Penguin, 1985), pp.216, 412, 98, 226 (in order of quotation).
13. *Ibid.*, pp.186, 123, 359, 24, 444, 27, 445, 483.
14. *Ibid.*, pp.364, 366, 137.
15. *Ibid.*, pp.226, 365, 276.
16. *Ibid.*, pp.78, 55, 227.
17. *Ibid.*, pp.384, 248-9, 259, 257.
18. *Ibid.*, pp.248-9, 439.
19. *Ibid.*, pp.91, 117, 364.
20. *Ibid.*, p.270.
21. Alfred Dampier and Garnet Walch, *Robbery Under Arms*, Richard Fotheringham (Sydney: Currency, 1985).
22. Boldrewood, *Robbery Under Arms*, pp.139-145.
23. Pamela Heckenberg and Philip Parsons, "Summary of theatrical events", in Peter Love ed. *The Australian Stage* (Sydney: New South Wales University Press, 1984), p.123.
24. Enid Welsford, *The Fool. His Social and Literary History* (New York: Anchor, 1961), p.306.
25. Peter Stallybrass, "'Drunk with the cup of liberty': Robin Hood, the carnivalesque, and the rhetoric of violence in early modern England", *Semiotica*, V.54, Ns.1-2, 1985; Natalie Davis, *Society and Culture in Early Modern France* (Stanford: Stanford University Press, 1975), ch.5.
26. Margaret Williams, *Australia on the Popular Stage 1829-1929* (Melbourne: O.U.P., 1983), pp.30, 160, 269-70.
27. Paul Richardson, "Theatrical treatment of local realities", in Love ed. *The Australian Stage*, p.73.
28. John Docker, "Antipodean Literature: A World Upside Down?", *Overland* 103, 1986. See also Susan Gardner, "*My Brilliant Career*: Portrait of the Artist as a Wild Colonial Girl", in Carole Ferrier ed. *Gender, Politics and Fiction: Twentieth-Century Australian Women's Novels* (St. Lucia: University of Queensland Press, 1985).
29. Williams, *Australia on the Popular Stage*, pp.10, 200, 223, 236-7, 244, 267.

"The same Itch ...": Poetry by Women in the 1890s

1. See for instance: Susan Sheridan, "Ada Cambridge and the Female Literary Tradition" in Dermody, John Docker & Drusita Modjeska, eds., *Nellie Melba, Ginger Meggs & Friends: Essays in Australian Cultural History.* (Malmsbury, Kibble Books, 1982.)
Marilyn Lake, "The Politics of Respectability: Identifying the Masculinist Context", *Historical Studies*, 22, 86 (1986), 116-131.
Magarey, S., Rowley, S. & Sheridan, S., eds. *Debutant Nation: Feminism Contests the 1890s.* (St Leonards, Allan & Unwin,

1993.) This volume reprints Lake's article and a response by John Docker: "The Feminist Legend: A new historicism?".

2. "Australian Literature I" in Leon Cantrell, ed., *A.G. Stephens: Selected Writings* Sydney: Angus & Robertson, 1978, esp. pp.86-88.

3. It remained common practise for Australian poets to self-publish until the 1970s. I have reluctantly excluded poetry published in periodicals from this discussion because it would be a project of a much larger scale, and the social and cultural assumptions surrounding the more ephemeral medium warrant separate treatment. Even so there are hints in the books which saw publication and in the very few newspapers which have been indexed of some of the riches which await the researcher.

4. See Efi Hatzimanolis, "Timing differences and investing in futures in multicultural (women's) writing" in Gunew, S. & Yeatman, A., eds. *Feminism and the Politics of Difference.* (St Leonards, NSW: Allen & Unwin, 1993.)

5. Margaret Jolly, "Colonizing women: The maternal body and Empire" in Gunew & Yeatman, *ibid.*

6. Susan. Sheridan, "'Temper, romantic; bias, offensively feminine': Australian Women Writers and Literary Nationalism" in K. H. Petersen, & A. Rutherford, eds. *A Double Colonization: Colonial and Post-Colonial Womens Writing.* (Denmark: Dangaroo, 1986.)

7. For an articulate discussion of the diverse views surrounding the labour debates and working women see Desley Deacon, "Reorganizing the Masculinist Context: Conflicting Masculinisms in the New South Wales Public Service Bill Debates of 1895" in Magarey et al (1993) *op cit.* This is a neat demonstration of the way in which the complexity of a specific issue may be lost through an "innocent/interested" ahistoricism.

8. Elizabeth Webby, "'Born to Blush Unseen': Some Nineteenth-Century Women Poets" in Adelaide, ed. *A Bright & Fiery Troop: Australian Women Writers of the Nineteenth Century.* Ringwood, Vic: Penguin, 1988, p.52. Many of the observations made in this discussion are applicable to the broader range of nineteenth century women's poetry but I am confining discussion to the 1890s because the period has been accepted as "seminal" to the development of an Australian literary identity.

9. For a further illuminating discussion of women creating 'a place of their own' in Australia see Helen Thomson, "Gardening in the Never-Never: Women Writers & the Bush" in Kay Ferres ed. *The Time to Write: Australian Women Writers 1890-1930.* (Ringwood, Vic: Penguin 1993.)

10. See Michael Ackland, *That Shining Band: A Study of Australian Colonial Verse Tradition.* (St Lucia: UQP, 1994), p.89.

11. Kay Ferres, "Introduction" in Ferres (1993) *op cit.*

12. See Bruce Scates, "'Knocking Out A Living': Survival Strategies and Popular Protest in the 1890s Depression" in Magarey et al (1993) *op cit.*, for a discussion of the pressing need for urban women to seek paid work to support themselves and their children when their male 'providers' left to pursue agricultural labouring jobs - or to escape.

13. Joy Hooton, "Mary Fullerton: Pioneering Feminism", Ferres (1993) *op cit.*
14. Barbara, Holloway, "'Woman' in Federation Poetry" in Magarey et al (1993) *op cit.*
15. Anna Yeatman, "Voice and representation in the politics of difference" in Gunew & Yeatman (1993) *op cit.*
16. Leon Cantrell, ed. "A G Stephens's *Bulletin* Diary" in B. Bennett, ed. *Cross Currents: Magazines & Newspapers in Australian Literature.* Melbourne: Longman, Cheshire, 1981, p.37. In his personal diary Stephens attributed Louise Mack's success to her 'considerable sexual passions' and the 'blood in her brain'.
17. Sue Rowley, "Things a bushwoman cannot do" in Magarey et al (1993) *op cit.*

Under Two Flags: Ada Cambridge and A Marked Man

1. Desmond Byrne, *Australian Writers* (London: Richard Bentley and Son, 1896) pp.134-5.
2. Ada Cambridge, *A Marked Man: Some Episodes in his Life.* introd. Debra Adelaide (1891; rpt. London: Pandora Press, 1987), p.4. Subsequent page references to the novel will be to this edition and will be incorporated parenthetically in the text.
3. Dunstanborough is clearly based on Hunstanton in Norfolk, where Cambridge spent her summers as a child; see her *Thirty Years in Australia* (London: Methuen, 1903), pp.273-4 and *The Retrospect* (London: Stanley Paul, n.d.), pp.206-8.
4. Cambridge, *The Retrospect*, p.154.
5. Cambridge, *Thirty Years in Australia*, p.251; ibid.; Cambridge, *Fidelis: A Novel* (New York: D. Appleton and Co., 1895), p.154.
6. For the camp's model, see Louise Wakeling, "The Historical Source for Ada Cambridge's 'The Camp'", *Australian Literary Studies* 14 (1989): 113-17.
7. Byrne, *Australian Writers*, pp.140-2, discusses perceptively the effect of Richard's challengingly honest response to his wife's death. Similar instances occur elsewhere in Cambridge's fiction. Polly, the unselfcritically autobiographical heroine of *Materfamilias* (London: Ward Lock, n.d.), for example, almost swoons with joy when she learns of her first husband's death (p.33), while Rachel, in *A Mere Chance* (3 vols.; London: Richard Bentley, 1882), enters upon her second marriage "with unexpected, if not unbecoming, rapidity" by Melbourne standards (III, 184).
8. Quotations from Fiona Giles, "Romance: An Embarrassing Subject", in *The Penguin New Literary History of Australia*, ed. Laurie Hergenhan (Ringwood, Vic.: Penguin Books, 1988), pp.223-37. I am indebted to this stimulating chapter and to Gillian Beer, *The Romance* (London: Methuen, 1970) for their valuable discussions of romantic convention.
9. It would be possible to argue that the foregrounding of English concerns and the romantic attenuation of Australian

experience reflect in some measure Cambridge's sense that the intellectual climate of late nineteenth-century Australia was inimical to new ideas in general and to new ideas from and about women in particular. On this, see Jill Roe, "'The Scope of Women's Thought is Necessarily Less': The Case of Ada Cambridge", *Australian Literary Studies* 5 (1972): 388-403.

10. An especially clear example of this occurs in Chapter 22, in which Richard reads aloud, in his Darling Point mansion, from J. S. Mill's *Principles of Political Economy* (pp.152-4). The section he chooses, "On the Probable Futurity of the Labouring Classes" (IV.vii), is centrally concerned with the ways in which change in the economic infrastructure will inevitably precipitate radical changes elsewhere - most importantly, perhaps, in the area of sexual politics. But the transformation Mill is outlining - from "the theory of dependence and protection" to "the theory of self-dependence" - is meaningless for Australia as Cambridge depicts it, and the passage can only have been included in the novel as a retrospective critique of English paternalism.

11. When it was first published as a serial in the Melbourne *Age* (1888-9), the novel was called "A Black Sheep". I would guess that the change to *A Marked Man* became necessary for the book's first English appearance (1890) because the earlier title had already been used by Edmund Yates for a relatively well-known novel of 1867.

12. Cambridge's novels contain a number of sympathetic honest doubters, though none of them is portrayed in such careful detail as Richard Delavel. Mr. Yelverton gently, and a little vaguely, introduces Elizabeth King to the higher criticism (*The Three Miss Kings* (1891; rpt. London: Virago Books, 1987), p.187) and Adam Drewe in *Fidelis* refuses, as a child, to be confirmed ("in a small way it was the ordeal of Richard Delavel over again" (p.82)), while Innes McGregor in *A Platonic Friendship* (London: George Bell, n.d.) argues that "we are responsible for ourselves" and that "disease is the root and substance of evil" (p.113). Apart from Richard, however, the most interesting of Cambridge's unbelievers (and one of her most rewarding creations) is the disfigured poet Hilda Penrose in *A Marriage Ceremony* (2 vols; London: Hutchinson, 1894) who finally takes her own life and one of whose poems, "a lament for the dead, who, as it seems assumed, were really dead, to live no more" (I, 59), bears a close resemblance to some of the pieces collected in *Unspoken Thoughts* (1887).

13. This is a puzzling reference. None of Arnold's contributions to the *Fortnightly Review* seems to fit the context, though it is just possible that Cambridge has in mind the essay "Count Leo Tolstoi" which appeared in that journal in December 1887 and which discusses Tolstoi's religious opinions at some length.

14. Mrs. Humphry Ward, *Robert Elsmere* (1888; London: Thomas Nelson, 1952) p.574. There is some slight resemblance between Robert Elsmere's marriage to Catherine and that of Yelverton to Elizabeth in *The Three Miss Kings*; in the latter novel, however, "the problems ... are very incidentally disposed of" (Henry Gyles Turner and Alexander Sutherland, *The*

Development of Australian Literature (Melbourne: George Robertson and Co., 1898), p.89). For a differently nuanced treatment of *A Marked Man*'s exploration of religious doubt and other contemporary issues, see Louise Wakeling, '"Rattling the Orthodoxies': A View of Ada Cambridge's *A Marked Man*", *Southerly* 49 (1989): 609-23.

15.   See Beer, *The Romance*, pp.59-77 and Kenneth Graham, *English Criticism of the Novel 1865-1900* (Oxford: Clarendon Press, 1965), pp.49-70. Cambridge's enthusiasm for Meredith implies a sophisticated awareness of contemporary experiment in fiction (see *Thirty Years in Australia*, p.187).

Catherine Helen Spence: Suffragist At Last

1.   R. B. Walker, "Catherine Helen Spence and South Australian Politics", *The Australian Journal of Politics and History*, Vol. XV, No. 1, (April 1969): 38.
2.   Kay Daniels, "Catherine Spence", *Women and History*, 1975 conference papers, published by the History Teachers' Association of N.S.W.
3.   Catherine Spence, *Autobiography*, (Adelaide: Libraries Board of South Australia, 1975), p.67.
4.   Leon Cantrell, Introduction to *The 1890s*, Portable Australian Authors (St. Lucia, University of Queensland Press, 1977), p. xx.
5.   Spence, *Autobiography*, p.97
6.   Marilyn Lake, "The Politics of Respectability: Identifying the Masculinist Context", *Historical Studies*, Vol. 22, No. 86 (April, 1986): 116.
7.   Lesley Durrell Ljungdahl ed., *A Week in the Future*: Catherine Helen Spence's 1888 Forecast of Life in 1988 (Sydney: Hale and Iremonger, 1988).
8.   Sylvia Lawson, *The Archibald Paradox: A Strange Case of Authorship* (Ringwood: Penguin Books, 1987), p.82.
9.   "Approaching Elections - Plain Words to Women Electors", S.A., 1896, 324, Mitchell Library.
10.   Susan Sheridan, "Louisa Lawson, Miles Franklin and Feminist Writing, 1888-1901", *Australian Feminist Studies*, Nos. 7 & 8, (Summer 1988): 40.
11.   Walker, p.42.
12.   Walker, p.36.
13.   Walker, p.38.
14.   Letter to Catherine Helen Spence from John Stuart Mill in the Franklin papers, MLMSS.364.Vol.63, in the Mitchell Library. I am grateful to Lesley Ljungdahl for drawing my attention to this letter.
15.   Jeanne F. Young, *Catherine Helen Spence: A Study and an Appreciation* (Melbourne and Sydney: The Lothian Publishing Co., 1937).
16.   *Autobiography*, p.81.
17.   *Autobiography*, p.86.

Tom Collins and Work

1. Throughout I have used *SiL* to indicate *Such is Life*, *RR Rigby's Romance*, and *BBB The Buln-Buln and the Brolga*. In all references to *SiL* the first number refers to the 1903 edition and its various facsimiles, the second to the 1944 edition. *RR*. Adelaide: Rigby, 1971. *BBB*. Adelaide: Rigby, 1971.

2. See Laurence Gronlund, *The Cooperative Commonwealth*, Cambridge, Mass.: The Belknap Press, 1965, 134-6, originally published in Boston in 1884 and cited with approval by Jefferson Rigby in *Rigby's Romance*.

3. D. L. Clark, "Single Tax, Free Trade and Land Values Taxation; Henry George and the Sydney Single Tax League" in *Papers Presented in Commemoration of the Publication of "Progress and Poverty" by Henry George*, Sydney: The Australian School of Social Science, 1979, 20.

4. Tom tells us that Barefoot Bob Bruce is on the shearers' side during their strike in in 1891. This gives us the earliest possible date for Tom's memoirs. *BBB*, 102.

5. I have made the case for this interpretation in my "Between Hay and Booligal: Tom Collins' Land and Joseph Furphy's Landscape". In *Mapped But Not Known: The Australian Landscape of the Imagination*, eds. P. R. Eaden and F. H. Mares, pp.154-70. Adelaide: Wakefield Press, 1986.

6. J. A. B. Fry, "Forty Years in the Civil Service" Fry Family Papers, Mitchell Library, ML MS 1159/2. Quoted extensively in Shirley FitzGerald, *Rising Damp: Sydney 1870-90*, Melbourne: OUP, 1987, 164-6. For an entertaining discussion of the appalling corruption and indolence in the NSW Lands Department during the same period see Cyril Pearl, *Wild Men of Sydney* (Sydney: Angus and Robertson, 1977) Chapter Twelve, 176-91.

7. Miles Franklin (in association with Kate Baker), *Joseph Furphy: The Legend of the a Man and his Book*, Sydney: Angus and Robertson, 1944, 39.

8. Julian Croft, "'Who is She?' The Image of Woman in the Novels of Joseph Furphy". In *Who is She?*, ed. Shirley Walker, pp.1-11. St Lucia: University of Queensland Press, 1983. "A 'Federation' Dedicated to Australia". In *The Federal and National Impulse in Australian Literature, 1890-1958*, Julian Croft, pp.5-20. Townsville: Foundation for Australian Literary Studies, 1989.

9. *Sartor Resartus* is the most obvious. Writing to his Scottish friend Cathels (12 January 1894), Furphy reviewed the contribution to literature and progressive thought by the Scots: "... what a rotten world it was before Paine preached and Burns sang and Byron scoffed and Carlyle snarled." Miles Franklin, 48. And in a letter to Kate Baker in 1897 he calls Carlyle 'the most readable of metaphysical writers; and Sartor Resartus his most met&c. *(sic)* book." MSS 2022/5/3, Kate Baker Papers, National Library of Australia.

10. Although there would seem to be great difference between Carlyle and Calvin, on the idea of labour and work there are

interesting correspondences. See Eloise Behnken, *Thomas Carlyle: "Calvinist Without the Theology"* Columbia, Miss.: University of Missouri Press, 1978, "The Significance of Labour", 10-40.

11. In a letter to A. G. Stephens (no date), Furphy tries to define his intellectual and spiritual position: "I am double damned, in the most literal sense. The church-goer stigmatises me as an infidel and a blasphemer, whilst the Bookfellow [Stephens] calls me a sanctimonious nameless and a canting, blanky hypocrite. Pour on; I will endure. But I will n o t (*sic*, spacing for emphasis) swim with the stream. Partly because Pessimism and Scepticism are the correct capers just now, I am an Optimist and a Christian - just as I am a Biological Agnostic because Darwinism is unduly boomed." MSS 2022/5/76, Kate Baker Papers, National Library of Australia.

12. Thomas Carlyle, *Sartor Resartus* (London: Chapman Hall, n.d.), Book II, Chapter IX, p.136.

13. Glover, in particular, is the best example in Furphy's fiction of the wage-slave, the manual worker who has to exist on the subsistence level of wages which Malthusian economics predict. Moriarty's unsympathetic view of a sick and dying worker is also in the Malthusian tradition: "'When a fellow comes to his state, he ought to be turned out for the summer in a swamp paddock, with the leeches on his legs; then you ought to sell him to Cobb and Co., to get the last kick out of him. Or else poll-axe the beggar.'" (*SiL* 363-4)

14. Letter to William Cathels, no date. MSS 2022/5/71, Kate Baker Papers, NLA.

15. MSS 2022/5/36, Kate Baker Papers, NLA.

16. MSS 2022/5/257, Kate Baker Papers, NLA.

17. MSS 2022/5/331, Kate Baker Papers, NLA.

18. Letter to William Cathels, no date. MSS 2022/5/11, Kate Baker Papers, NLA.

19. *Such is Life* 1898 typescript, p.168, MSS 364/65, Miles Franklin Papers, Mitchell Library.

20. Furphy's first piece of serious writing, for which he won first prize, was a poem for a competition celebrating the memory of Lincoln.

"The Yellow Peril": Invasion Scare Novels and Australian Political Culture

1. Vance Palmer's *The Legend of the Nineties* (Melbourne: Melbourne University Press, 1954) remains the classical analysis of the legend. In many ways it was a damning critique of the legend as a basis for Australian political culture. Yet while recognising its illusions and limitations he nevertheless at the end of the appraisal identified with this national vision. There was no quibbling about Australian fears of alien evils, especially Asian ones, but he explained this xenophobia in terms of the utopian myth itself. The European settler "wanted to think of Australia as a new world, having as few links as

2. For example, "A Hero of Babylon" by C.A. Jeffries, *Lone Hand*, Vol. 1 (May, 1907), pp.61-5.

3. For example, Randolph Bedford's "White Australia", which was first staged in Melbourne in 1909.

4. For example, Raymond Longford's "Australia Calls", which was written by C.A. Jeffries and John Barr and shown for the first time on 19 July 1913 at Spencer's Lyceum Theatre in Sydney.

5. In earlier studies I had concluded that C. H. Kirmess was probably a pseudonym for Frank Fox, who was at the time of the publication of "The Commonwealth Crisis" editor of the *Lone Hand* (see *Search for Security in the Pacific, 1901-1914*, Sydney, Sydney University Press, 1976, pp.159-161 and *Australia and the World*, Melbourne: Longman Cheshire, 1985, pp.176-180).

The evidence for such a view was quite substantial, even if circumstantial. On the one hand the only record that someone called C.H. Kirmess had existed was this one novel. Extensive research failed to uncover any other publications by Kirmess. Not one letter to or from Kirmess could be located in the manuscript collections of the National Library and the Mitchell Library, and his name did not appear on the New South Wales electoral rolls for 1908-1910 or in the *Sands Sydney and New South Wales Directory* for 1908. On the other hand Fox shared Kirmess's apprehensions and pursued an editorial policy aimed at alerting the Australian public to the Japanese menace. He had made contributions to the *Lone Hand*, both fictional and analytical, which in a more limited way, aired the same alarmist issues. Moreover Fox specifically used the "Commonwealth Crisis" to buttress his arguments about Australia's strategic vulnerability to the menace of Japan in *Problems of the Pacific* (London: Williams and Norgate, 1912, pp.251-57). The summary of the plot came trippingly off the pen and it was the only literary source which he referred to in the whole work. Furthermore Fox in 1923 published under his own name a novel, *Beneath an Ardent Sun*, which had a theme and style very similar to that of *The Australian Crisis*. Finally the adoption of a pseudonym seemed reasonable. Writers of invasion novels quite often hid behind nom de plumes. Fox himself had already employed a pseudonym, "Frank Renar", for his first book *Bushman and Buccaneer*. I had even wondered whether Fox might have taken a pseudonym for *The Australian Crisis* from the memoirs of J. F. Archibald which appeared in the first issue of the *Lone Hand*. In his autobiography Archibald, who was Fox's mentor and patron, had reported that he was taught at the Warrnambool grammar school by a fine old scholar, "Mr Henry Kemmiss". Both "Kemmiss" and "Kirmess" were unusual names in 19th century colonial Australia. As a result, however, of information received from Noel McLachlan of Melbourne University and Stuart Sayers, the historian of Lothian publishers (*The Company of Books: A Short History of the Lothian Book Companies, 1888-1988*,

Melbourne: Lothian, 1988, p.39), I am now convinced that someone who called himself Charles H. Kirmess was the author of *The Australian Crisis*. Kirmess had entered into a contract with John H. Lothian and Son of Melbourne to publish the book, and in the Lothian papers in the Victorian State Library (Ms. 6026), there is a collection of letters between C. H. Kirmess and Lothian publishers (including 21 letters from Kirmess, 19 of which are in his own hand) covering the period 22 August 1908 to 23 April 1910. The handwriting is certainly not that of Fox, and the content and character of the letters attest to their authenticity. The letters reveal that Thomas Lothian met Kirmess in Sydney and established a good working relationship with him, that Kirmess had business dealings with Fox and Arthur Henry Adams, who succeeded Fox as editor of the *Lone Hand*. Kirmess even spoke of having collaborated regularly with "several well-known Sydney University men", though to what end remains obscure.

Kirmess gave his address as 168 Cathedral Avenue, Sydney. This was the residence of a Mrs. Charlotte Emma Brown who it appears kept a boarding house. One James Allen, a miner, was along with Charlotte, David and James Brown, recorded on the N.S.W. electoral rolls as living at this address. Why Kirmess was not on the electoral roll is unclear. He was certainly interested in the politics of the time. John Holroyd, a Melbourne bibliophile, has stated that about 1970 Thomas Lothian told him that Kirmess was of German nationality and that he returned to his homeland just before the outbreak of the First World War (Kirmess in his last letter to Lothian, dated 23 April 1910, said that he was returning "to" Europe the following month). If Kirmess had German nationality then this would explain his absence from the electoral rolls. On the other hand Kirmess wrote fluent, idiomatic English and was very much at home in an English-speaking culture.

McLachlan has even speculated that Kirmess might have been attached to the German Consulate in Sydney and that *The Australian Crisis* might have been intended to stir up Australian distrust of the Mother Country. It is difficult to comment on such suggestions, but it should be pointed out that suspicions that Britain would not help Australia at a time of a crisis with an Asian power had a long history among Anglo-Australians. Kirmess' contribution to this fear was merely to apply it in the most thoroughgoing manner to the prospect of a Japanese invasion. From the novel and the letters, there is every reason to believe that Kirmess seriously believed in the "White Race" and wished both Britain and Australia to build up its naval and military defence to meet the "Yellow Peril" in the Pacific.

6. I.F. Clarke, *Voices Prophesying War, 1763-1984* (London: 1966), pp.44-9.

7. Neville Meaney, *Search for Security in the Pacific, 1901-1914* (Sydney: Sydney University Press, 1976); Myra Willard, *History of the White Australia Policy to 1920* (Melbourne: Melbourne University Press, 1923), chapters 2-6; A.T.

Yarwood and M.J. Knowling, *Race Relations in Australia: A History* (Melbourne: Methuen, 1982), chapters 8 and 10.
8. Clarke, p.57.
9. Palmer, pp.158-9.
10. Michael Wilding, introduction to "John Miller" (William Lane), *The Workingman's Paradise* (Sydney: Sydney University Press, 1980), pp.29-32, 35.
11. Kathryn Cronin, "The Yellow Agony", in Raymond Evans, Kay Saunders, Kathryn Cronin, *Exclusion, Exploitation and Extermination: Race Relations in Colonial Queensland* (Sydney: 1975), p.290.
12. Brisbane *Courier*, 7 March 1888.
13. Andrew Markus, *Fear and Hatred: Purifying Australia and California, 1850-1901* (Sydney: Hale and Iremonger, 1979), pp. 133-8.
14. Brisbane *Courier;* 7 May 1888.
15. Wilding, p.35.
16. William Lane, writing under the pseudonym "Tohunga" (Maori for prophet) in New Zealand *Herald;* 8 August 1914.
17. Willard, pp.71-5; Markus, pp.136-142.
18. N.S.W. *Parliamentary Debates, Vol. XXX, pp.3788-9, 5 April 1888.*
19. *Official Report of the National Australasian Convention Debates, 2 March to 9 April, 1891* (Sydney: 1891), p.3160, 13 March 1891.
20. N.S.W. *Parliamentary Debates,* Legislative Assembly; 13 October 1896, p.3963.
21. *Sunday Times;* 26 December 1897.
22. *Sunday Times,* 26 December 1897; *Daily Telegraph,* 29 December 1897; *The Catholic Press,* 1 January 1898.
23. p.212; both Stibbins and McLoskie were probably based on Sir Thomas McIlwraith.
24. p.350.
25. p.37.
26. p.157.
27. pp.112-3.
28. p.845.
29. p.351.
30. p.378.
31. p.344.
32. p.114.
33. N.S.W. *Parliamentary Debates,* Legislative Assembly, 13 October 1896, p.3963.
34. *SMH*, 11 December 1897.
35. *The Herald* (Melbourne), 12 and 13 June 1905.
36. *CPD*, 1905 session, XXIX, 5346, 22 November 1905.
37. Letter, Cook to Governor-General, Lord Denman, enclosed in despatch, Lord Denman to Lewis Harcourt, British Colonial Secretary, 3 March 1914, PRO, C.O. 532/66.
38. p.6.
39. *The Call* (May, 1907).

40. *Age,* 10 July 1909; *Bulletin,* 17 June 1909; *The Leader,* 5 June 1909; *Star,* 12 July 1909; *Sydney Mail,* 14 July 1909; *Sydney Morning Herald,* 29 May 1909.
41. Letter, Kirmess to Lothian, 12 October 1909, V.S.L., Ms. 6026.
42. For example see *CPD,* 1909 session, Vol. LI, pp.3613-19, 21 September 1909.
43. "Secret Report on the Naval Defence of Australia" by Commander W.H. Thring, 5 July 1913, AA MP 1049/13, file 15/854; "Secret Memorandum by the Chief of the general Staff on the Northern Territory of Australia, and its Effects on local, Naval and Military Preparations by Brigadier General J.M. Gordon, 16 June 1913, AA B197, file 1855/1/6.
44. p.71.
45. pp.87-88.
46. p.144.
47. pp.334-6.
48. pp.93-7.
49. pp.312-3.
50. See A.W.M., Kenneth Mackay papers, PR 87/207.
51. *The Lone Hand* (June, 1907), p.179; (August, 1908), p.352; (November, 1908), p.97; (February, 1909), p.470; (March, 1909), p.589.
52. Letter, Kirmess to Lothian, 2 June 1909, V.S.L. Ms. 6026.
53. *Problems of the Pacific* (London: Williams and Norgate, 1912), pp.107-119, 252-257.
54. *Beneath an Ardent Sun,* pp.119-24.
55. *Ibid.* p.166.
56. *Ibid.* pp. 285-6.
57. London: Stanley, Paul & Co, 1928. Especially Chapters III and VII.
58. *Kangaroo* (London: 1923), pp.218-9, 341-54.

"Useful Practice - Blooding the Pups": Australian Literature and the Boer War

1. The *Advertiser,* 29 April 1988, p.1.
2. L. M. Field, *The Forgotten War: Australian Involvement in the South African Conflict of 1899-1902* (Melbourne: Melbourne University Press, 1979.
3. Letter to the Editor, *Advertiser,* 14 May 1988, p.14.
4. *Advertiser,* 14 May 1988, p.26.
5. *Advertiser,* 8 June 1988, p.18.
6. C. N. Connolly, "Class, birthplace, loyalty: Australian attitudes to the Boer War", *Historical Studies,* 71 (1978), p.214.
7. Rayne Kruger, *Good-bye Dolly Gray: The Story of the Boer War* (London: Cassell, 1959), p.59.
8. Kruger, p.55
9. Kruger, p.6.
10. Kruger, p.26.
11. Charles Carrington, *Rudyard Kipling: His Life and Work* (London: Macmillan, 1955). Edition used is the Penguin reprint, pp.361-362.

12. Robin Gerster, *Big-noting: The Heroic Theme in Australian War Writing* (Melbourne: Melbourne University Press, 1987), p.17.
13. Kruger, p.54.
14. The *Bulletin*, 3 March 1900, p.18.
15. Stuart Macintyre The *Oxford History of Australia, Volume 4, 1901-1942: The Succeeding Age* (Melbourne: Oxford University Press, 1986, p.130.
16. Macintyre, p.122
17. Macintyre, p.123. W. K. Hancock still found the phrase useful in the 1930s.
18. *Bulletin*, 25 August 1900, p.22.
19. Quoted in Macintyre, p.130.
20. Field, p.124.
21. See Garnet Walch, "The Lion's Cubs: Patriotic Song and Chorus", in William T. Pyke, *The Coo-ee Reciter: by Australian, British and American Authors* (Melbourne: E. W. Cole, 1904), p.59.
22. Morgan Hawkes *Lays and Lyrics* (Adelaide: W. K. Thomas & Co., 1900), from "The Answer of the Colonies", p.90.
23. "The style of the British in their imperial mood was enormously potent, and was copied and envied everywhere. Lampooned though it would often be in the disillusioned aftermath of empire, we can recognize it now as one of history's great transforming energies." Jan Morris *The Spectacle of Empire: Style, Effect and the Pax Britannica* (London: Faber and Faber, 1982), p.13.
24. John M. Mackenzie, *Propaganda and Empire: The Manipulation of British Public Opinion 1880-1960* (Manchester: Manchester University Press, 1984), p.35.
25. *Bulletin*, 27 January 1900, p.24.
26. Lord Birkenhead, *Rudyard Kipling* (London: Wedenfeld & Nicolson, 1978), p.205.
27. Carrington, p.365.
28. Mackenzie, p.20. (p.253).
29. See Kruger, opposite p.212. See opposite pp.213 and 436, for, respectively, stills from genuine and faked propaganda film shot by the new-fangled cinematograph.
30.. Morris, p.15.
31 A. P. Haydon, "South Australia's First War", *Historical Studies* 42 (1964): pp.222-233.
32. Macintyre, p.130.
33. Quoted by Field, p.26.
34. George Essex Evans, *The Secret Key and Other Verses* (London: Angus & Robertson, 1906. Quoted in Frank Crowley *A Documentary History of Australia, Volume 3 Colonial Australia 1875-1900* (Melbourne: Nelson, 1980, pp.586-587. Crowley claims that the song was first published in the *New York Times*, of all places, 4 February 1900.
35. John M. Mackenzie, *Propaganda and Empire: The Manipulation of British Public Opinion, 1880-1960* (Manchester: Manchester University Press, 1984), p.254. See also White, Chapter Five, "The National Type", pp.63-84.
36. Mackenzie, p.2.

37. Mackenzie, p.203. Mackenzie's reminder about the popularity of Empire with children should be stressed. One of the most popular expressions of late-Victorian imperial sentiment was actually written by a first-generation Australian, the Reverend William Henry Fitchett ("Vedette"). On Christmas Day, 1899, the Little Boy at Manly might have found, in his Christmas stocking, the "India and Colonies" edition from George Bell and Sons, London, of *Deeds That Won the Empire: Historic Battle Scenes* (London: George Bell & Sons, 1898), "probably the most-read war book written by an Australian" (Gerster, p.15). Fitchett, "a passionate son of the British Empire" (Bede Nairn and Geoffrey Searle, eds., *Australian Dictionary of Biography Volume 8, 1891-1939* (Melbourne: Melbourne University Press, 1981), p.513, and, interestingly, a Wesleyan minister had published a series of sketches in the *Argus* Saturday feature celebrating glorious martial moments in British history, and found them enormously popular. They were "pirated in India, republished in a London weekly, published in shilling form in Australia... The book was placed by the Admiralty in all warships' libraries, adopted as a holiday-task book in some great English public schools... 100,000 copies of the sixpenny edition were sold" (*Australian Dictionary of Biography, Volume 8*, p.512). The Little Empire, for the Australian pups were still to be blooded. Or bloodied, for that matter. He would have found stories about Wellington, Wolfe and Nelson, about Waterloo and Trafalgar, Badajos [sic] and the Basque Roads, and there is little doubt he read the work with great pride in British military achievement. But he would have wondered how Australians would perform shoulder to shoulder with members of the great British regiments. By the Christmas of 1900, he would have known.
38. Mackenzie, p.6.
39. John Sandes (Oriel"), p.9.
40. Quoted by Gavin Souter, *Lion and Kangaroo: Australia 1901-1919: The Rise of a Nation* (Sydney: Collins, 1976), pp.61-62.
41. *Bulletin*, 31 March 1900, p.18, and 7 April 1900, p.13.
42. George Essex Evans, p.11. No wonder generations of Australians have found it difficult to work out the precise nature of the family relationship with England!
43. George Essex Evans, pp.79-80.
44. See Leon Cantrell (ed), *The 1890s: Stories, Verse, and Essays* (St. Lucia, Queensland: University of Queensland Press, 1977), p.108. The poem can also be found in William Thomas Pyke (ed.), *The Coo-ee Reciter: by Australian, British and American Authors* (Melbourne: E. W. Cole, 1904), p.49.
45. White, p.82.
46. Kruger, p.510.
47. John Sandes ("Oriel"), p.17.
48. John Sandes ("Oriel"), p.25.
49. Morgan Hawkes *Lays and Lyrics* (Adelaide: W. K. Thomas & Co., 1900), p.94.
50. See Connolly, p.211. John Rickard, in his *Class and Politics: New South Wales, Victoria and the Early Commonwealth, 1890-*

1910 (Canberra: Australian National University Press, 1976), notes that

> The importance of imperialist sentiment in cementing middle-class feeling cannot be overestimated. It is no accident that the period which sees the emergence of relatively stable classes in Australia is the period in which loyalty has been noted, may often serve as the prime expression of lower middle-class consciousness, and in Australia's case there is the added dimension that the adoption of an imperialist-oriented nationalism involved the rejection of a radical nationalist tradition more attuned to working-class values. Imperialist sentiment, of course, seeped through to the labour movement as well, but there it was to be a source of tension... rather than a source of unity. (p.302).

51. See Jane Ross, *The Myth of the Digger: The Australian Soldier in Two World Wars* (Sydney: Hale & Iremonger, 1985), which has little or nothing to say about the Boer War, and its role in the creation of the legend.
52. From "How I Wrote *Robbery Under Arms*", in Alan Brissenden, ed., *Rolf Boldrewood* (St Lucia, Queensland: University of Queensland Press, 1979), p.494.
53. George Essex Evans, p.83. Conan Doyle wrote "when the ballad makers of Australia seek for a subject, let them turn to Elands River, for there was no finer fighting in the war." (Quoted by Souter, p.55).
54. Humphrey McQueen, *A New Britannia: An argument concerning the social origins of Australian radicalism and nationalism* (Ringwood, Victoria: Penguin Books Australia, 1975), p.89. Lawson wrote as many poems about "the war to come" and about the Russo-Japanese War as he did about the Boer War.
55. Colin Roderick, e.d., *Henry Lawson Collected Verse: Volume One 1885-1900*, p.366.
56. Lawson, "The Blessings of War", in Roderick, pp.370-371.
57. *Bulletin*, 21 October 1899, p.8.
58. Collected by G. A. Wood, and quoted in R. M. Crawford, *'A Bit of a Rebel': The Life and Work of George Arnold Wood* (Sydney: Sydney University Press, 1975), p.170.
59. Bede Nairn and Geoffrey Searle, ed., *Australian Dictionary of Biography: Volume 9: 1891-1939* (Melbourne: Melbourne University Press, 1983), p.159.
60. Hales, pp.45-46.
61. Hales, pp.135-136.
62. Hales, pp.147.
63. *Bulletin*, 13 January 1900, p.10
64. See R. M. Crawford, *'A Bit of a Rebel': The Life and Work of George Arnold Wood* (Sydney: Sydney University Press, 1975), Chapters X-XIII in particular.
65. See Walker, pp.213-216. Walker claims that Brennan would not publish his poems, fearing the same fate that seemed likely to befall Wood.

66. Joseph Furphy "The Fly in the Ointment", in Marjorie Pizer, (ed.), *Freedom on the Wallaby: Poems of the Australian People* (Sydney: The Pinchgut Press, 1954), p.95.
67. *Bulletin*, 23 December 1899, p.7.
68. J. K. McDougall "The White Man's Burden", in Philip Neilson (ed.), *The Penguin Book of Australian Satirical Verse* (Ringwood, Vic,: Penguin, 1986), p.126. The *Bulletin* too did much to pour scorn on the militarist parsons, the "long line of dancing dervishes demanding that Blood should trickle". See, for example, 11 November, 1899, p.10.
69. *Bulletin*, 4 November 1899, p.6.
70. M. Grover "I Killed a Man at Graspan", included in *The Coo-ee Reciter*, p.8, the first poem in the anthology.
71. Patsy Adam Smith *Australian Women at War* (Melbourne: Thomas Nelson, 1984), p.14.
72. See Souter, pp.57-58.
73. *Bulletin*, 25 August 1900, p.12.
74. J. H. M. Abbott *Tommy Cornstalk: Being Some Account of the Less Notable Features of the South African War from the Point of View of the Australian Ranks* (London: Longmans, Green and Co., 1902).
75. Rosamund Campbell and Philippa Harvie *Singer of the Bush A. B. "Banjo" Paterson Complete Works 1885-1900* (Sydney: Lansdowne, 1983), pp.451-698.

Formation and Creation: Norman Lindsay's 1890s

1. Norman Lindsay, *My Mask* (Sydney: Angus & Robertson, 1970), p.156.
2. Norman Lindsay, *Bohemians of the Bulletin* (Sydney: Angus & Robertson, 1965), p.5.
3. *Bohemians of the Bulletin*, pp.14-15.
4. *Bulletin*, 1 February 1950.
5. *Bohemians of the Bulletin*, p.17.
6. Bernard Smith, *Place, Taste and Tradition*, 2nd edition (Melbourne: O.U.P., 1979), p.174.
7. P. R. Stephensen, *Kookaburras and Satyrs* (Cremorne: Talkarra Press, 1954), p.22.
8. Familial autobiographies which are relevant include Darryl Lindsay, *The Leafy Tree* (Melbourne: Cheshire, 1965); Lionel Lindsay, *Comedy of Life* (Sydney: Angus & Robertson, 1967); Rose Lindsay, *Model Wife* (Sydney: Ure Smith, 1967); Jane Lindsay, *Portrait of Pa* (Sydney: Angus & Robertson, 1973); and Philip Lindsay, *I'd Live the Same Life Over* (London: Hutchison, 1941). Jack Lindsay has written most extensively about his father's life, both in his autobiographical trilogy, *Life Rarely Tells, The Roaring Twenties* and *Fanfrolica and After* (London: Bodley Head, 1958, 1960, 1962) and in a series of articles: "Vision of the Twenties", *Southerly* 13 (1952): 62-71; "Aids to Vision", *Southerly* 14 (1953): 204-5; "Norman Lindsay: Problems of his Life and Work", *Meanjin* 29 (1970): 39-48; "The Life and Art of Norman Lindsay", *Meanjin* 33 (1974): 27-41; "Norman Lindsay as Novelist", *Bards,*

Bohemians and Bookmen, ed. Leon Cantrell (St Lucia: U.Q.P., 1976), pp.251-65; and "Norman", *The World of Norman Lindsay*, ed. Lin Bloomfield (Melbourne: Macmillan, 1979), pp.112-36. Norman Lindsay's autobiographies include the factual *My Mask* and *Bohemians of the Bulletin* and the series of novels, *Saturdee* (Sydney: Endeavour Press, 1933); *Redheap* (London: Faber, 1930) and *Halfway to Anywhere* (Sydney: Angus & Robertson, 1947), although most of his fictional output is autobiographical as argued above. *Southerly's* Norman Lindsay number (No.1 1959) also contains some autobiographical material. Lindsay's letters, ed. R. G. Howarth & A. W. Barker (Sydney: Angus & Robertson, 1979) are a particularly valuable source of biographical data. John Hetherington's biography, *Norman Lindsay. The Embattled Olympian* (Melbourne: O.U.P., 1973) is a competent, intelligent treatment of material made available by Lindsay and interviews with him. In addition, there is a vast amount of reminiscence and biography on the part of friends, disciples and even enemies. Significant studies of this nature include Douglas Stewart's personal memoir (Melbourne: Nelson, 1975), Kenneth Slessor, *Bread and Wine* (Sydney: Angus & Robertson, 1970) and Hugh McCrae, *Story-Book Only* (Sydney: Angus & Robertson, 1948). *The World of Norman Lindsay*, ed. Lin Bloomfield, includes reminiscences by Lindsay's friends and members of his family.

9. "Norman Lindsay as Novelist", p.261.
10. *Norman Lindsay. The Embattled Olympian*, pp.76-94.
11. In 1901 the *Bulletin's* offer of employment saved the recently married Lindsay from penury and in 1932 it offered similar relief during his period of creative sterility from 1929-34.
12. *My Mask* , pp.225-6.
13. *Letters*, p.145.
14. "The Life and Art of Norman Lindsay", pp. 32-3; "Norman Lindsay: Problems of his Life and Work", pp.41-3.
15. *My Mask*, p.34. Lindsay frequently described the world as a madhouse or a Bedlam.
16. *Letters*, pp. 152, 168; John Hetherington, *Norman Lindsay*, Australian Writers and their Work series 3rd edition (Melbourne: O.U.P., 1969), p.43; *Norman Lindsay. The Embattled Olympian*, p.13; *My Mask*, p.240; *Creative Effort*, first published 1920 (London: Cecil Palmer, 1924), p.114; *Bohemians of the Bulletin*, p.53. Such misanthropic, anti-life statements are common. Jane Lindsay reports, for instance, his cheerful response to the deaths of his brother Percy and his sons Phil and Ray, describing them as "lucky to be out of it". *Portrait of Pa*, p.171. In *My Mask* Lindsay declares that he never regretted the death of a friend: "nor will I pump up an air of portentousness over the procedure of stowing a corpse away underground, except to commend the profession of undertaker." (p.192). In the same book he regrets the fact that his own near-drowning in youth was averted. (p.42).
17. *Letters*, p.72.
18. *My Mask*, p.159.
19. *Bohemians of the Bulletin*, p.121.

20. *Letters,* p.115.
21. *Norman Lindsay* (1979), p.42.
22. *Saturdee,* p.190.
23. "Portrait of the Artist as a Young Australian", *Southerly* 41 (1981): 132. Lionel Lindsay responds in much the same terms to *Redheap*: "The texture of the book is coarse and ... none of the average decencies or aspirations of life finds a voice in it, with the exception of Mr Bandparts. A perpetual row seems ever in progress and little sordid egotisms clash and fester. The one saving grace is humour, but humour always at the expense of a victim." *Comedy of Life,* p.134.
24. *Norman Lindsay. The Embattled Olympians,* p.67. Lionel Lindsay reports his practice of taking a group of youngsters on picnics so that he could observe their scuffling, boasting and chanting, "the tribal antics of the eternal small boy, which set vibrating chords of memory." *Comedy of Life,* p.133.
25. *Redheap,* pp.53-4. My italics.
26. *My Mask,* p.33. My italics.
27. In *My Mask* Lindsay describes half-enviously Dr Lindsay's "aplomb", that is his ability to stroll out of difficult situations unruffled (p.1). Hetherington compares the old man's easy acquisition of popularity in London, with Norman's difficulty in getting a footing. *Norman Lindsay. The Embattled Olympian,* p.88.
28. *Bohemians of the Bulletin,* p.ix.
29. *Bohemians of the Bulletin,* p.144.
30. *Bohemians of the Bulletin,* p.106.
31. He discusses the poem in the *Bulletin* (20 June 1945), in *My Mask,* pp.231-2 and in a letter to Douglas Stewart, *Letters,* pp.372-3.
32. "The Life and Art of Norman Lindsay", p.40.
33. *Norman Lindsay. The Embattled Olympian,* p.1. Lindsay himself characteristically explained the illness as the working of his "daemon", enforcing habits of industry and observation. *My Mask,* p.37.
34. This seems to be the real cause of the breakdown of the relationship between Lionel and Norman. Lionel was clearly appalled by his brother's use of the diary, consigning most of it to the flames after it was returned to him. What disturbed him most was the crude interpretation Norman placed on his activities: "When I view the figure of Robert in Norman's novel *Redheap* ... I am scarcely convinced that this is the lad who had read the English poets, consorted with the post-master, the hospital doctor, and his schoolteacher, and had read everything on astronomy he could lay hands on, constructed a stellar map and become a pupil-assistant at the Melbourne Observatory in his fifteenth year." *Comedy of Life.,* p.132. Not only did he feel used as the letters between the two brothers at the time show (*Letters,* p. 143), but he was obviously shocked to see himself through his younger brother's eyes. In *My Mask* Norman comments on Lionel's characteristic ignorance of his impact on other people (pp. 32-3), and clearly the elder brother had regarded their relationship in another, more ideal light. Although the break was not finally made until 1922 and

ostensibly on the grounds of Lionel's objections to *Creative Effort* and Norman's dabbling in spiritualism, there is no doubt that after *Redheap*, which was read in unpublished form by Lionel in 1918, the friendship could never be renewed on the same terms.

35. *Comedy of Life*, p.132.
36. *Letters*, p.112.
37. *My Mask*, pp.62-3.
38. Lindsay's description of ship-modelling as a refuge is included in Warwick Hood's essay "Ship Models", *The World of Norman Lindsay*, ed. Bloomfield. Virtually every account of Lindsay makes reference to this passion. Lindsay's commitment to the solitary life of the imagination after 1911 was, I suggest, a retreat to the safe childhood world. His private haven was to suffer two major invasions, one caused by the war of 1914-18, which destroyed his popular brother Reg and confronted him with the certainty and horror of death, incidentally shattering his previous conviction that war was a great stimulus to artistic creation and that courage in battle was the supreme expression of human nobility. The other was the furore in 1931 caused by the Norman Lindsay number of *Art in Australia* in December 1930. Lindsay temporarily fled to America and England on that occasion, but he was by then well-insulated by his regime of elitist self-sufficiency and was far less vulnerable to the judgements of others than on his first visit to Europe.
39. "Norman Lindsay: Problems of his Life and Work", p.46.
40. In *My Mask* he comments that it was beyond him "to practice the Dionysic love for life that [he] sought to put into [his] work" (p.26). To Leon Gellert he confessed that he "never had any capacity for debauch in actuality". *Letters*, p.127.
41. Beverley Nichols, *Twenty-five*, (London: Cape, 1926) p.220. Jane Lindsay also discusses his dislike of alcohol in *Portrait of Pa.*
42. *My Mask*, p.126
43. *Redheap* p.310.
44. *Creative Effort*, pp. 4, 118.
45. Thus Arthur Adams in one of Lindsay's letters is dismissed as a feminist and sentimentalist (*Letters*, p.110), whereas Archibald's interest in the female form provokes the comment: "No man is worth a damn unless the spectacle of femininity has an eternal interest for him." *Bohemians of the Bulletin*, p.15.
46. *My Mask*, pp. 38, 126; *Halfway to Anywhere*, pp.8, 50-51; *My Mask*, pp.58-9; *Creative Effort*, p.50.
47. Douglas Stewart, *The Flesh and the Spirit*, (Sydney: Angus & Robertson, 1948), p.278. Robert Hughes is less impressed by their mystery: "Lindsay's melon-breasted, ham-thighed Playmates are wholesome and dated. Their eroticism is depersonalised and cow-like; the easy embodiment of adolescent sexual fantasy ... they smirk and pout and wiggle their elephantine buttocks." *The Art of Australia* Revised edn. (Ringwood, Vic.: Penguin Books, 1970), p.84.
48. Simone de Beauvoir, *The Second Sex* , transl. & ed. H. M. Parshley (Harmondsworth: Penguin Books, 1972), p.187.

49. *Redheap*, pp. 112, 95.
50. Dorothy Dinnerstein, *The Rocking of the Cradle and the Ruling of the World*, first published in 1976 titled *The Mermaid and the Minotaur* (London: The Women's Press,1987), p.93.
51. "The Life and Art of Norman Lindsay", p.40.
52. In *My Mask* he describes himself as having something of his grandfather in his make up (p.19) and both Lionel and Jane Lindsay perceive the affinity. *Comedy of Life*, p.73, *Portrait of Pa*, p.5.
53. "Lindsay the Sculptor", in *The World of Norman Lindsay*, p.72.
54. *My Mask*, pp.131, 244.
55. *Letters*, p.112.

A. W. Jose and the Nineties: Living, Remembering, Constructing a Decade

1. William H. Wilde, Joy Hooton, Barry Andrews, eds, *The Oxford Companion to Australian Literature*, (Melbourne: OUP, 1985), p.521.
2. Incomplete letter, n.d., Jose Papers in private hands.
3. *ibid.*
4. E. J. Hobsbawm, *The Age of Empire 1875-1914* (London: Weidenfeld & Nicholson, 1987), p.223.
5. Lawson, Dyson and Daley were particularly concerned that their work would receive acclaim in England.
6. Vivian Smith, "Poetry", in *The Oxford History of Australian Literature*, ed. Leonie Kramer (Melbourne: OUP, 1981), pp.272-3.
7. E. A. Badham, "An Australian School of Literature" quoted by Kramer in the Introduction, *ibid.*, p.14.
8. Arthur Jose, *The Romantic Nineties* (Sydney: Angus & Robertson, 1933), p.13, "It is hard to express to this generation our feelings about Daley the poet. We watched for his acceptance by the London critics with complete assurance, and their neglect of him staggered us ..."
9. Leonie Kramer, *Oxford History*, p.15.
10. Jose's "Notes for Dyson", 314/28 in the A&R Papers, Mitchell Library, Sydney.
11. *ibid.*
12. London *Athenaeum*, 4 January 1902, quoted in Colin Roderick, ed., *Henry Lawson Criticism 1894-1971* (Sydney: Angus & Robertson, 1972), pp 120-1.
13. Colin Roderick, *Henry Lawson: Commentaries on his Prose Writing* (Sydney: Angus & Robertson, 1985), p.4.
14. Proofs of *While the Billy Boils*, A1867 "Across the Straits" p.1, A & R Papers, Mitchell Library, Sydney.
15. *ibid.*, "The Drover's Wife", p.8
16. *ibid.*, "Remailed" p.1.
17. *ibid.*, p.2.
18. *ibid.*, "The Man Who Forgot", p.1.
19. See Colin Roderick, ed., *Henry Lawson Criticism 1894-1971* (Sydney: A & R, 1972), pp.104-5; 117-20.

20. A. W. Jose - May Jose, n.d., [1898] in the Jose Papers
21. A. W. Jose - Robertson, 9 August 1920, 314/18, A & R Papers, Mitchell Library. Reader's Report on Major Thomas Cherry's *Broken Pieces from the Holy Land:* "This is a remarkable book ... The publication of this book might not be profitable in cash but it would be greatly to the credit of the company". Robertson would not risk the financial loss but suggested to Cherry that he send the book to England where he thought it would be published. Another illustration of the difference between Australian and English audiences can be seen by examining the sales figures for Jose's *The Growth of the Empire;* it sold in Australia only when it was a prescribed text; on the other hand, in England, it enjoyed low but steady sales. For further details, see Teresa Pagliaro, "The Publishing Fortunes" of *The Growth of the Empire:"* in the *Bibliographical Society of Australia and New Zealand's Bulletin,* Vol. 7, No.1, (1983): pp. 1-14.
22. A. W. Jose - May Jose, 20 October 1885, Jose Papers.
23. A. W. Jose - W. W. Jose, 21 April 1885, Jose Papers.
24. Incomplete letter, n.d., [1899], Jose Papers.
25. Incomplete letter, n.d., [1893]; A. W. Jose - May Jose, 20 January 1894 in Jose Papers.
26. Incomplete letter, n.d. [1898] in Jose Papers.
27. R. M. Crawford, *'A Bit of a Rebel', the Life and Work of George Arnold Wood* (Sydney: Sydney University Press, 1975), p.118.
28. A. W. Jose - May Jose, 24 February 1895 in Jose Papers.
29. Dudley McCarthy, *From Gallipoli to the Somme: The Story of C.E.W. Bean* (Sydney: John Ferguson, 1983), p.25.
30. H. E. Barff, *A Short Historical Account of the University of Sydney* (Sydney: Angus & Robertson, 1902), p.111.
31. A. W. Jose - May Jose, 21 March 1888 in Jose Papers.
32. For details of the titles of Jose's lectures, 1888-1899 see the Minutes of the Senate and those of the University Extension Board in the University of Sydney Archives.
33. R. M. Crawford, *"A Bit of a Rebel',* p.250.
34. A. G. Stephens' Diary, 30 December 1931, p.119, 2/2835 in the Fryer Library, University of Queensland.
35. Nettie Palmer, "A Reader's Notebook", *All About Books,* 15 March 1933, pp.38-9.

Select Bibliography

The list below is of general studies only, and makes no attempt to be comprehensive. A more thorough compilation containing details of works on individual authors, notes on writers who flourished in the 1890s, and chronologically arranged listings, has been prepared for publication by the New South Wales Centre for Australian Studies (University of Western Sydney Macarthur).

Ken Stewart

Adelaide, Debra, ed. *A Bright and Fiery Troop: Australian Women Writers of the Nineteenth Century*. Ringwood: Penguin, 1988.

Allen, H. C. *Bush and Backwoods: A comparison of the Frontier in Australia and the United States*. [East Lansing]: Michigan State University Press, 1959.

Allen, Judith. 'Rose Scott's Vision: Feminism and Masculinity 1880-1925" in *Crossing Boundaries*, eds. B. Caine, E. A. Grossz, M. de Lepervanche. Sydney: Allen and Unwin, 1988.

Alomes, Stephen. *A Nation at Last? The Changing Character of Australian Nationalism 1880-1988*. North Ryde: Angus and Robertson, 1988.

Astbury, Leigh. *City Bushmen: The Heidelberg School and the Rural Mythology*. Melbourne: Oxford University Press, 1985.

Astley, Thea. *Three American Writers*. Townsville: Foundation for Australian Literary Studies, 1979. See esp. pp. 12-22 on Baynton.

Barnes, John, ed. *The Writer in Australia: A Collection of Literary Documents 1856-1964*. Melbourne: Oxford University Press, 1969.

Burgmann, Verity. *"In Our Time". Socialism and the Rise of Labor, 1885-1905*. Sydney: Allen and Unwin, 1985.

Byrne, Desmond. *Australian Writers*. London: Richard Bentley and Son, 1986.

Cantrell, Leon, ed. *A. G. Stephens: Selected Writings*. London: Angus and Robertson, 1978.

—. ed. *The 1890s: Stories, Verse and Essays*. St. Lucia: University of Queensland Press, 1978.

Carroll, John, ed. *Intruders in the Bush: The Australian Quest for Identity*. Melbourne: Oxford University Press, 1982.

Clark, Axel. *Christopher Brennan: A Critical Biography*. Carlton: Melbourne University Press, 1980.

Clunies Ross, Bruce. "Scrutinising Australian Nationalism and Myths". *Australian Literary Studies*, 14, no.4 (October 1990), pp.499-504.

Davison, Graeme. "Sydney and the Bush: An Urban Context for the Australian Legend". *Historical Studies*, 18, no. 7 (October 1978).

Dixon, Robert. *Writing the Colonial Adventure: Race, Gender and Nation in Anglo-Australian Popular Fiction, 1875-1914*. Cambridge, New York and Melbourne: Cambridge University Press, 1995.

Dixson, Miriam, *The Real Matilda: Women and Identity in Australia, 1788 to the Present*. Harmondsworth: Penguin, 1976. (Revised eds., Ringwood: Penguin, 1984, 1994).

Docker, John. "The Feminist Legend: A New Historicism?" In *Debutante Nation*, eds. S. Magarey, S. Rowley, and S. Sheridan, Sydney: Allen and Unwin, 1993, pp.16-20.

—. *The Nervous Nineties*. Melbourne: Oxford University Press, 1991.

—. "The Politics of Criticism: Leon Cantrell and the Gloom Thesis". *New Literature Review*, no. 6 (1979), pp.256-266.

Evans, Richard J. *The Feminists: Women's Emancipation Movements in Europe, America and Australasia 1840-1920*. London: Croom Helm, 1977.

Giles, Fiona. "Romance: An Embarrassing Subject". In *The Penguin New Literary History of Australia*, ed. Laurie Hergenhan, Ringwood: Penguin, 1988, pp.223-237.

Grimshaw, Patricia. "The Equals and Comrades of Men? *Tocsin* and 'The Woman Question'". In *Debutante Nation*, eds. S. Magarey, S. Rowley, and S. Sheridan, Sydney: Allen and Unwin, 1993, pp.100-114.

Grimshaw, Patricia, and Marilyn Lake, Ann McGrath, Marian Quartly. *Creating a Nation*. Ringwood: McPhee Gribble, 1994.

Hanna, Cliff. "The Ballads". In *The Penguin New Literary History of Australia*, ed. Laurie Hergenhan. Ringwood: Penguin, 1988, pp.194-209.

Hergenhan, Laurie, ed. *The Penguin New Literary History of Australia*. Ringwood: Penguin, 1988.

Heseltine, Harry. "Saint Henry Our Apostle of Mateship". *Quadrant*, 5, no.1 (1960-61), pp.5-11.

Hodge, Bob and Vijay Mishra. *Dark Side of the Dream: Australian Literature and the Postcolonial Mind.* Sydney: Allen and Unwin, 1991.

Holloway, Barbara. "Women in Federation Poetry". In *Debutante Nation*, eds. S. Magarey, S. Rowley and S. Sheridan. Sydney: Allen and Unwin, 1993, pp.150-163.

Hooton, Joy. "Australian Literary History and Some Colonial Women Novelists". *Southerly*, 50, no.3 (1990), pp.310-323.

—. *Stories of Herself When Young: Autobiographies of Childhood by Australian Women.* Melbourne: Oxford University Press, 1990.

Ikin, Van, ed. *Australian Science Fiction.* St. Lucia: University of Queensland Press, 1982.

Irvin, Eric. *Australian Melodrama.* Sydney. Hale and Iremonger, 1981.

Jarvis, Douglas. "The Development of an Egalitarian Poetics in the *Bulletin*, 1880-1890". *Australian Literary Studies*, 10, no.1 (1981), pp.22-34.

Jose, A. W. *The Romantic Nineties.* Sydney: Angus and Robertson, 1933.

Lake, Marilyn. "The Politics of Respectability: Identifying the Masculinist Context". *Historical Studies*, 22, no.86 (1986), pp.116-131.

Lawson, Olive, ed. *The First Voice of Australian Feminism: Excerpts from Louisa Lawson's The Dawn, 1886-1895.* Sydney: Simon and Schuster/New Endeavour Press, 1990.

Lawson, Sylvia. *The Archibald Paradox.* Melbourne: Allen Lane, 1983.

Levis, Ken. "The Role of the *Bulletin* in Indigenous Short-Story Writing during the Eighties and Nineties". *Southerly*, 11, no.4 (1950), pp.220-228.

Lindsay, Norman. *Bohemians of the Bulletin.* Sydney: Angus and Robertson, 1965.

Love, Harold, ed. *The Australian Stage: A Documentary History.* Sydney: University of New South Wales Press, 1984.

Magarey, Susan, Sue Rowley, and Susan Sheridan, eds. *Debutante Nation: Feminism Contests the 1890s.* Sydney: Allen and Unwin, 1993.

Maidment, W. M. "Australian Literary Criticism". *Southerly*, 24 (1964), pp.20-41.

Matthews, Brian. *Romantics and Mavericks: The Australian Short Story.* Townsville: Foundation for Australian Literary Studies, 1987.

McLachlan, Noel. *Waiting for the Revolution: A History of Australian Nationalism.* Ringwood: Penguin, 1989.

McLaren, John. "Colonial Mythmakers: The Development of the Realist Tradition in Australian Literature". *Westerly*, 25, no.2 (1980), pp.43-50.

McQueen, Humphrey. *A New Britannia: An Argument Concerning the Social Origins of Australian Radicalism and Nationalism.* Harmondsworth: Penguin, 1970.

Morgan, Patrick. "Realism and Documentary. Lowering One's Sights". In *The Penguin New Literary History of Australia*, ed. Laurie Hergenhan, Ringwood: Penguin, 1988, pp.238-252.

Morrison, Elizabeth. "Reading Victoria's Newspapers 1838-1901", *Australian Cultural History II* (1992), pp.128-140.

Nesbitt, Bruce. "Literary Nationalism and the 1890s". *Australian Literary Studies*, 5, no.1 (1971), pp.3-17.

Palmer, Vance. *The Legend of the Nineties.* Melbourne: Melbourne University Press, 1954.

Phillips, A. A. *The Australian Tradition: Studies in a Colonial Culture.* Melbourne: Cheshire, 1958 (revised edn. 1966).

Roderick, Colin, ed. *Henry Lawson Criticism, 1894-1971.* Sydney: Angus and Robertson, 1972.

Rolfe, Patricia. *The Journalistic Javelin: An Illustrated History of the Bulletin.* Sydney: Wildcat, 1979.

Schaffer, Kay. *Women and the Bush: Forces of Desire in the Australian Cultural Tradition.* Cambridge: Cambridge University Press, 1988.

Sheridan, Susan. "Ada Cambridge and the Female Literary Tradition". In *Nellie Melba, Ginger Meggs and Friends*, eds. S., Dermody, J. Docker and D. Modjeska. Malmsbury: Kibble Books, 1982.

Souter, G. A. *A Peculiar People: The Australians in Paraguay.* Sydney: Sydney University Press, 1981.

Stephens, A. G. *The Red Pagan.* Sydney: Bulletin, 1904.

Stewart, Ken. "The Colonial Literati in Sydney an Melbourne: in S. Dermody, J. Docker and D. Modjeska, eds., *Nellie Melba, Ginger Meggs and Friends: Essays in Australian Cultural History.* Malmsbury, Vic.: Kibble Books, 1982.

—. "Journalism and the World of the Writer, 1855-1915". In *The Penguin New Literary History of Australia,* ed. Laurie Hergenhan. Ringwood: Penguin, 1988, pp.174-193.

Stuart, Lurline. *Nineteenth Century Australian Periodicals: An Annotated Bibliography.* Sydney: Hale and Iremonger, 1979.

Tucker, T. G. *The Cultivation of Literature in Australia.* Melbourne: Echo, 1902.

Turner, Henry Gyles, and Alexander Sutherland. *The Development of Australian Literature.* Melbourne: George Robertson, 1898.

Walker, Shirley. "The Boer War: Patterson, Abbott, Brennan, Miles Franklin and Morant". *Australian Literary Studies,* 12, no.2 (1985), pp.207-222.

—. "Perceptions of Australia, 1855-1915". In *The Penguin New Library History of Australia,* ed. Laurie Hergenhan. Ringwood: Penguin, 1988, pp.157-173.

—. ed. *Who is She? Images of Women in Australian Fiction.* St. Lucia: University of Queensland Press, 1983.

Wallace-Crabbe, Chris, ed. *The Australian Nationalists: Modern Critical Essays.* Melbourne: Oxford University Press, 1971.

Ward, Russel. *The Australian Legend.* Melbourne: Oxford University Press, 1958.

—. 'The Australian Legend Re-Visited". *Historical Studies,* 18, no.71 (1978), pp.171-190.

White, Richard. *Inventing Australia: Images and Identity 1688-1980.* Sydney: George Allen and Unwin, 1981.

Whitlock, Gillian. "A. G. Stephens: An Internationalist Critic". *Australian Literary Studies,* 8, no.1 (1977), pp.82-91.

Wilkes, G. A. *The Stockyard and the Croquet Lawn: Literary Evidence for Australian Cultural Development.* Port Melbourne: Edward Arnold, 1981.

—. "The 1890s". *Arts,* I (1958), pp.17-26.

Woodward, Judith M. "Urban Influence on Australian Literature in the Late Nineteenth Century". *Australian Literary Studies,* 7, no.2 (1975), pp.115-129.

Index

202, 203, 206, 208, 209,
215, 225, 229, 256, 258,
260
Radway, Janice 125
Rambler 59
Ranter-Leveller tradition 232
realism 7, 66, 68, 86, 89, 91,
92, 116, 129, 154, 161,
188, 190, 191, 193, 199,
226, 315
Register 196, 202
Register (Adelaide) 197
Reid, George 176
religion 4, 5, 22, 168, 170, 172,
175
Reporters' Association 60
republicanism 4, 67, 201, 238,
239, 249, 250
Review of Reviews 37
*Review of Reviews for
Australasia* 58
Richardson, Ethel ("Henry
Handel") 34
Richardson, Samuel 187
Roberts, Morley 33
Roberts, Tom 35, 57, 63, 64
Robertson, George 58, 59, 60,
314, 326, 358
Robin Hood 144, 145, 148
Roderick, Colin 98
romance 7, 8, 15, 21, 38, 41,
94, 126, 129, 130, 132,
137, 145, 148, 150, 152,
153, 156, 159, 161, 162,
163, 164, 181, 188, 190,
191, 193, 199, 200, 226,
313, 337
romance fiction 161, 164
romanticism 68, 81, 85, 88,
156, 216, 315, 327
Ross, Howlett J. 51, 57
Rowley, Sue 342
Royal Society of Victoria 49
Royce, Josiah 56
Rusden, G. W. 33, 36
Russia 241, 242, 243, 244,
245, 253
Rutherford, A. 341
Ryan, J. T. 58

Sandes, John 9, 277
Ballads of Battle 274
Sandys, George 291

satire 154, 155, 164, 176
Savage Club, the 48
Scates, Bruce 341
Schaffer, Kay 13, 22, 111, 119,
124
Women and the Bush 10,
17, 110
Schreiner, Olive
*The Story of an African
Farm* 148
science fiction 229
Scott, Ernest 322
*A Short History of
Australia* 324
Scott, G. Firth 153
Scott, Rose 50, 209
Scott, Sir Walter 150, 153
secret ballot 205, 207
self-help 4, 8
serials 56, 58, 133
Serle, Geoffrey 32
*From Deserts the Prophets
Come* 46
Serle, Percival 45
Shakespeare Society 32, 45
Shakespeare, William 9, 36,
37, 218, 291
Hamlet 223
Macbeth 223
Othello 223
Shann, Edward 47
Shann, Frank 47
Shann, Frank (jnr.) 47
Sharkey, Michael 66
Shaw, G. B. 121
Shelley, Percy Bysse 43
Sheridan, Susan 8, 111, 340,
341
Shillinglaw, J. J. 33, 35, 48
shipwreck 112, 113
short stories 8, 18, 20, 41, 91,
160, 172, 269
"Sketcher" 228, 229, 239
Sladen, Douglas 9, 33
Slessor, Kenneth 129
"William Street" 84
Smiles, Samuel 212
Smith, C. 58
Smith, J. H. 58
Smith, James 9, 34, 57, 126
Social Darwinism 200, 229,
273, 274, 284

UQP STUDIES IN AUSTRALIAN LITERATURE

Black Words, White Page
Aboriginal Literature 1929-1988
Adam Shoemaker

This is the first comprehensive study of Black Australian literature in English. Combining historical and literary analysis, it attempts to come to terms with the diversity and difference of this new, exciting literature that has been gaining strength since 1929 when David Unaipon became the first published Aboriginal writer. **Winner: 1990 Walter McRae Russell Award.**

Poetry and Gender
Statements and Essays in Australian Women's Poetry and Poetics
edited by David Brooks and Brenda Walker

The exciting diversity of Australian women's poetry and poetics is explored through essays on the work of writers of the twenties and thirties, Aborigines, migrant women and other contemporary poets.

The Folly of Spring
A Study of John Shaw Neilson's Poetry
Cliff Hanna

This is the first comprehensive study of John Shaw Neilson's verse and the first chronological approach to his work. Using all of the available manuscript material, the study focuses on Neilson's lifelong battle with his Presbyterian "thunder-blue God", which eventually pushed him beyond Christianity into pagan myth. **Winner: 1991 Walter McRae Russell Award.**

Strange Country
A Study of Randolph Stow
Anthony J. Hassall

Strange Country explores the themes of alienation and the failure of love in the novels, poetry and stories of internationally acclaimed Australian writer, Randolph Stow. This new edition has an up-to-date chronology and a revised bibliography.

Imagined Lives
A Study of David Malouf
Philip Neilsen (new edition)

This first book-length study of David Malouf focuses primarily on a literary analysis of his six novels, from *Johnno* (1975) to *Remembering Babylon* (1993). It also deals with his key poems, especially as they relate to the fiction.

Parnassus Mad Ward
Michael Dransfield and the New Australian Poetry
Livio Dobrez

Avant-garde Australian poetry from the sixties to the eighties is explored here with flair and originality. This is the first book to place in perspective the New Australian Poetry, product of the extraordinary generation of '68. Dobrez discusses diverse poets against the broader background of cultural developments in Australia and abroad.

Flame and Shadow
A Study of Judith Wright's Poetry
Shirley Walker (new edition)

This book provides an accessible and indispensable complete analysis of the poetry of Judith Wright, from *The Moving Image* (1946) to *Phantom Dreaming* (1985). Shirley Walker places the poetry of one of Australia's most celebrated poets in social and aesthetic perspective, and against a background of twentieth century philosophical theories.

Boundary Conditions
The Poetry of Gwen Harwood
Jennifer Strauss (new edition)

This critical study of the work and career of Gwen Harwood explores the intellectual influences of music, philosophy and theology on the poetry, and looks also at the politics of gender in publishing. The interlocked themes of her writing are traced from Harwood's early poems through to *Present Tense*.

Fabricating the Self
The Fictions of Jessica Anderson
Elaine Barry (new edition)

Jessica Anderson is a writer who resists any easy labelling. Her technical virtuosity, range of narrative experimentation, and recurring themes are here discussed, through examination of all of her works, from *An Ordinary Lunacy* to *One of the Wattle Birds*.

The ALS Guide to Australian Writers
A Bibliography 1963-1990
Edited by Martin Duwell and Laurie Hergenhan
Associate Editors: Marianne Ehrhardt and Carol Hetherington

This is the most comprehensive published guide to recent commentary about Australian literature, ranging over critical, biographical and historical articles, reviews and interviews. It draws on, integrates and updates thirty years of the *Australian Literary Studies* Annual Bibliographies.

Dancing on Hot Macadam
Peter Carey's Fiction
Anthony J. Hassall (new edition)

This is the first comprehensive study of one of the world's most gifted and exciting writers. Alert to recent critical debates, it provides a lucid account of Peter Carey's fiction, its international literary context and critical reception.

That Shining Band
A Study of Australian Colonial Verse Tradition
Michael Ackland

This study illuminates a vital and forgotten part of Australia's cultural heritage by exploring the tradition of colonial verse that preceded the balladists of the 1890s. Neglected talents are rediscovered, particularly among women.

Helplessly Tangled in Female Arms and Legs
Elizabeth Jolley's Fictions
Paul Salzman

Elizabeth Jolley has been hailed as a major Australian writer since the publication of her two story collections, *Five Acre Virgin* and *The Travelling Entertainer* and her first novel, *Palomino*. This provocative study explores the critical reception of Jolley's fiction, and the varied interpretations it attracts.

Atomic Fiction
The Novels of David Ireland
Ken Gelder

This study discusses the fiction of one of Australia's most controversial writers, from *The Chantic Bird* to *A Woman of the Future*, exploring its "atomic" structure.

Australian Melodramas
Thomas Keneally's Fictions
Peter Pierce

Thomas Keneally is the writer most attuned to the melodramatic temper and genius of Australian literary culture. This first comprehensive critical study covers his plays and nonfiction as well as his novels.

The 1890s
Australian Literature and Literary Culture
Ken Stewart (ed.)

Fifteen lively essays by historians and literary critics re-evaluate the 1890s from the perspective of the 1990s. Contributors include Ken Stewart, Geoffrey Serle, Christopher Lee, Michael Sharkey, Mark Horgan, Julian Croft, Teresa Pagliano, Peter Pierce, John Docker, Veronica Kelly, Patricia Barton, Rick Hosking, Robert Dingley, Neville Meaney and Joy Hooton.

Kenneth Slessor
Critical Essays
Philip Mead (ed.)

This comprehensive collection of critical readings includes an authoritative introduction by Philip Mead, "classic" essays by Jack Lindsay, Vincent Buckley, Adrian Mitchell, Judith Wright, A.K. Thomson, John Docker and Andrew Taylor, and new essays by Greg Badcock, Peter Kirkpatrick, Julian Croft, Dennis Haskell, Leigh Dale and Kate Lilley, with a select bibliography and illustrations from newspapers and manuscripts.